The
TAYLOR RULE

and the Transformation of Monetary Policy

The Hoover Institution gratefully acknowledges the following individuals and foundations for their significant support of the WORKING GROUP ON ECONOMIC POLICY

Lynde and Harry Bradley Foundation

Preston and Carolyn Butcher

Stephen and Sarah Page Herrick

William E. Simon Foundation

The
TAYLOR RULE

and the Transformation
of Monetary Policy

Edited by

Evan F. Koenig
Robert Leeson
George A. Kahn

HOOVER INSTITUTION PRESS

Stanford University | *Stanford, California*

www.hoover.org

Hoover Institution Press Publication No. 615

Hoover Institution at Leland Stanford Junior University,
    Stanford, California, 94305-6010

First printing 2012
17 16 15 14 13 12   9 8 7 6 5 4 3 2

Manufactured in the United States of America

♾ The paper used in this publication meets the minimum Requirements of
the American National Standard for Information Sciences—Permanence of
Paper for Printed Library Materials, ANSI/NISO Z39.48-1992.

Library of Congress Cataloging-in-Publication Data

The Taylor rule and the transformation of monetary policy /
Evan F. Koenig, Robert Leeson, and George A. Kahn (Editors).
        pages   cm. — (Hoover Institution Press publication ; No. 615)
Includes bibliographical references and index.
ISBN 978-0-8179-1404-2 (cloth : alk. paper) —
ISBN 978-0-8179-1406-6 (e-book)
1. Taylor's rule. 2. Monetary policy—Mathematical models. 3. Monetary
policy—United States—History. 4. Taylor, John B.—Influence. I. Koenig,
Evan F., editor of compilation. II. Leeson, Robert, editor of
compilation. III. Kahn, George A. (George Arnett), 1956– editor of
compilation. IV. Series: Hoover Institution Press publication ; 615.
HG230.3.T393   2012
339.5′3015195—dc23   2012001953

CONTENTS

Preface   vii
Richard W. Fisher

Introduction   ix
Evan F. Koenig, Robert Leeson, and George A. Kahn

I. TAYLOR'S APPROACH TO MONETARY THEORY AND POLICY   1

1. Monetary Policy Rules: From Adam Smith to John Taylor   3
Pier Francesco Asso, Robert Leeson

2. The Taylor Rule and the Practice of Central Banking   63
George A. Kahn

3. A Comparison with Milton Friedman   103
Edward Nelson

4. Two Basic Principles   139
Robert E. Lucas

II. FROM THE GREAT MODERATION TO THE GREAT DEVIATION   143

5. The Great Moderation   145
Ben S. Bernanke

6. The Great Deviation   163
John B. Taylor

7. It's Not So Simple   173
Donald L. Kohn

III. NEW CHALLENGES IN THE DECADE AHEAD   183

8. Forecast Targeting as a Monetary Policy Strategy:
Policy Rules in Practice   185
Michael Woodford

9. The Dual Nature of Forecast Targeting and
Instrument Rules   235
John B. Taylor

10. Evaluating Monetary Policy   245
Lars E. O. Svensson

IV. TAYLOR'S INFLUENCE ON POLICYMAKING: FIRSTHAND ACCOUNTS   275

11. Overview   277
Ben S. Bernanke

12. The View from Inside the Fed   281
Janet Yellen

13. The View from Inside the European Central Bank   289
Otmar Issing

14. The View from Central Banks in Emerging Markets   293
Guillermo Ortiz

15. A View from the Financial Markets   301
John P. Lipsky

APPENDIX
The Pursuit of Policy Rules:
A Conversation between Robert Leeson and John B. Taylor   309

About the Contributing Authors   325

About the Hoover Institution's
Working Group on Economic Policy   331

Index   333

PREFACE

Richard W. Fisher

Back in the late 1970s and early 1980s, John Taylor and a few others embraced the notion that households and firms are forward-looking in their decision-making and intelligent in forming their expectations, but rejected the view that wages and prices adjust instantaneously to their market-clearing levels. It is these nominal frictions that give policy short-run leverage to influence the real economy. This approach to macroeconomics has grown in popularity to the point that it has become dominant inside and outside the Federal Reserve System. It has also stimulated interest in the nuts and bolts of how labor and product markets work.

Combine rational expectations with forward-looking, maximizing households and firms, and suddenly the private sector's behavior depends on the entire expected future path of policy. Taylor was a pioneer in thinking about monetary policy in this new, rich, and complicated setting. This book will explore some of the literature that Taylor inspired and will help us understand how the new ways of thinking that he pioneered have influenced actual policy here and abroad.

* * *

Taylor has divided his career between academia and government service, and both spheres owe him a debt of gratitude for having done so. Fundamentally, Taylor has demonstrated that it is possible to do serious

Richard W. Fisher is president and CEO of the Federal Reserve Bank of Dallas. The views expressed in this preface are those of the author and should not be attributed to the Federal Reserve.

economic research that takes monetary policy's role in the economy seriously. His efforts in this direction did much to restore a community of interests between academic and Federal Reserve economists at a time when the theoretical foundations underlying traditional monetary policy analysis were crumbling.

I am especially grateful to John Taylor for chairing the advisory board of the Dallas Fed's newly launched Globalization and Monetary Policy Institute, if only selfishly because it provides me and my colleagues with a vehicle for continuing to learn from him and work with him.

INTRODUCTION

Twenty years ago, John Taylor proposed a simple idea to guide monetary policy. Quickly the idea spread, not only through academia, but also to the trading floors of Wall Street and the Federal Reserve's board room in Washington, D.C. Financial analysts soon started writing newsletters to their clients about it. Policymakers started talking about it as they debated what to do next. Central bankers in other countries began to apply it. Academics began to modify it. People started calling it the Taylor rule. And before the 1990s were over, economists were able to show convincingly that policy decisions were remarkably close to it during periods of good economic performance, such as the Great Moderation of the 1980s and 1990s, and not so close to it during periods of poor economic performance like the Great Inflation of the 1970s.

Now, two decades later, the Taylor rule remains a focal point for discussion of monetary policy around the world. Some have used the rule to argue that the Federal Reserve held interest rates too low for too long in the years before the recent financial crisis and thus contributed to the boom which led to the crisis. Others use the Taylor rule to determine how long the interest rate should be held at zero once the rate hits the lower bound, or to determine whether or not unconventional monetary policies, such as quantitative easing, are appropriate. The Taylor rule also factors into doctrinal disputes, including the debate over whether the recent crisis means that economic theory has failed. The July 16, 2009, cover of *The Economist* pictured a book titled "Modern Economic Theory" melting into a useless blob to illustrate the story "What Went Wrong with Economics." Yet if a deviation from

The views expressed in this publication are those of the authors and should not be attributed to the Federal Reserve.

the Taylor rule was responsible for the crisis, then there is nothing fundamentally wrong with economics.

Of course the Taylor rule did not just pop out of thin air. It was derived from a dynamic approach to monetary theory and policy that Taylor and others began developing in the 1970s. According to this approach people are forward-looking and responsive to incentives, but take time to adjust their behavior because of certain real-world rigidities such as staggered wage and price setting. The approach is decidedly quantitative with empirical performance benchmarks such as an inflation-output variability trade-off, called the Taylor curve, and estimated models used for policy simulations.

This book explains and provides perspectives on Taylor's role in these revolutions in macro theory and policy. Included, also, are contributions to the debate on monetary policy's responsibility for the Great Moderation and Great Recession and a discussion of the pluses and minuses of the new "forecast targeting" approach to conducting and communicating policy. Many of the papers were presented at a conference honoring Taylor that was hosted at the Federal Reserve Bank of Dallas in October 2007. [Additional conference papers appear in Volume 55, Supplement 1 of the *Journal of Monetary Economics,* published in October 2008.] The list of authors is a "who's who" of the academic and policy communities and a testimony both to the influence of Taylor's work and to the high regard in which Taylor himself is held. Not surprisingly, there is greater agreement about the importance and value of Taylor's past contributions than there is about the implications of those contributions for current policy, or about where the theory and practice of monetary policy are headed.

This volume begins with a review of the history of policy rules in applied macroeconomic theory. Authors Francesco Asso and Robert Leeson argue that the rules-versus-discretion debate goes back at least to the 1840s and disputes between the British Currency and Banking Schools. The former stressed the importance of tying the money supply tightly to gold reserves as a way to limit currency issue and inflation in the face of political pressure to monetize government debt and accommodate aggregate-demand shocks. The latter favored a more flexible money supply: one that would expand and contract in line with the "needs of trade." The tension between the desire to prevent abuse of the printing press and the desire to allow short-term flexibility in the availability of money and credit in response to shifts in the demand for liquidity surfaces repeatedly in monetary history.

Early policy rules were generally passive, or "set it and forget it." The supply of money was to bear a fixed relation to gold reserves (the Currency School), or the price level was to be held constant (Irving Fisher), or the money supply was to grow at a specified rate (Milton Friedman). A. W. H. Phillips conceived of monetary policy rules in broader terms, as response functions embedded in a dynamic economic system. Taylor embraced Phillips' approach and applied it to economic systems incorporating rational expectations. As part of this effort, Taylor showed how overlapping labor contracts of realistic length can generate the sort of sluggishness in aggregate wage and price adjustment documented by Phillips and incorporated into Phillips' policy analysis.

Taylor helped bridge the gap between monetary theory and applied monetary policy when he showed that the set of activist feedback rules consistent with a well-behaved equilibrium includes certain interest-rate rules. The chief requirement is that the interest rate respond more than one-for-one to changes in inflation—a condition that is now commonly known as the Taylor principle. The Taylor rule—which has the monetary authority adjust the real overnight interest rate in response to economic slack and deviations of inflation from target inflation—is an example. The need to compare the performance of different policy rules led Taylor to develop the Taylor curve, which shows efficient combinations of output and inflation variability.

George Kahn picks up where Asso and Leeson leave off, noting that—thanks in large part to Taylor's efforts—monetary policy is now universally viewed as a systematic response to economic activity and inflation rather than as the solution to a period-by-period optimization problem. Kahn goes on to examine the background setting for the introduction of the Taylor rule and to discuss the rule's impact on central-bank practice. He notes that the monetary aggregates had already been de-emphasized in U.S. Federal Open Market Committee (FOMC) discussions at the time Taylor proposed his rule, due to a breakdown in historical money-demand relationships. Partly for that reason, policymakers were receptive to the idea of an interest-rate rule. The Taylor rule appealed, too, because of the way in which it anchors inflation over the long term, yet allows partial accommodation of supply shocks in the near term; because it is so obviously consistent with the Federal Reserve's mandate to seek both price stability and full employment; and because it complemented a broader move toward increased monetary-policy transparency and predictability. Additionally, the rule seemed to do a good job of explaining FOMC decisions over a period during which those decisions were generally agreed to have yielded satisfactory outcomes. Within a few years of Taylor's seminal idea, first presented in Pittsburgh in 1992, his rule was being used by FOMC participants to gauge whether policy was on approximately the right track. The staff of the Federal Reserve's Board of Governors began incorporating Taylor-type rules into its forecasting models and started providing the prescriptions from such rules to the FOMC.

As interest in the Taylor rule increased, various practical issues arose. There was debate over which inflation and output-gap measures to use in the Taylor rule and concern about the implications of a time-varying equilibrium real interest rate, the zero lower bound on the policy rate, and the difficulty of obtaining accurate real-time estimates of inflation and slack. Various refinements were suggested. Perhaps policy ought to be made contingent on forecasted inflation rather than actual inflation, ought to be adjusted gradually, or ought to respond differently to positive inflation deviations than to negative inflation deviations. These choices matter. In the wake of the 2001 and 2008–2009 recessions, for example, estimated forward-looking versions of the Taylor rule generally prescribed lower values for the overnight lending rate than did the Taylor rule as originally formulated. This sensitivity to implementation details helps explain the debate between those who blame the recent economic boom and bust on a departure from policy best practice and those who look to other causes—a debate that is discussed further below.

Central banks outside the United States commonly use the Taylor rule (or some variant thereof) in much the same way as the Federal Reserve—as a rough standard against which to compare current policy and as a baseline policy-response assumption when preparing forecasts. No bank mechanically follows a Taylor-style rule, though, and several prefer to think about and communicate policy in forecast-targeting terms. (See the chapter by Michael Woodford in this volume, discussed below.)

With Edmund Phelps and Stanley Fischer, Taylor formalized the argument for a purely temporary trade-off between real activity and inflation by adding temporary price and wage rigidities to models in which people have rational expectations. To make this approach operational, Taylor then developed a model of staggered wage- and price-setting. The informal argument for a vertical long-run Phillips curve had been presented by Friedman a decade earlier, in a famously prescient address to the American Economic Association. Despite strong similarities in their views on the operation of the macro economy, on the proper objectives for monetary policy, and on the importance of a rule-based nominal anchor, Friedman and Taylor were at odds on how policy ought actually to be conducted: Friedman preferred constant money growth to a Taylor-style feedback rule for the overnight interest rate, while Taylor argued that a Friedman-style constant-money-growth policy has "extremely undesirable" dynamic properties. Edward Nelson explores and explains this paradox in chapter 3 of this volume.

Nelson notes that Friedman's aversion to activist interest-rate rules was based primarily on experience-informed judgment. In Friedman's view, inflation's long response lag makes it unsuitable and potentially dangerous as a target for policy. On the other hand, targeting *expected* inflation would place too much reliance on imperfect structural forecasting models. Conditioning policy on slack is acceptable in principle, but measuring slack is difficult in practice, so a slack-contingent policy rule might easily go astray. Moreover, given that the natural tendency in the face of uncertainty and disagreement is to do nothing, an activist interest-rate rule might easily degenerate into a destabilizing, de facto interest-rate peg. Maintaining steady anticipated money growth, while perhaps not ideal as a policy rule, is safe and reliable. It protects the economy from major policy blunders.

Taylor, while leery of relying too heavily on any one model or narrow class of models as a guide to policy, has always been much less skeptical of structural modeling than Friedman; a series of modeling exercises convinced Taylor that simple activist interest-rate rules like the Taylor rule are robust to specification error and generally possess stabilization properties superior to those of constant-money-growth rules. Taylor's findings were all the more compelling because his modeling assumptions were generally ones with which Friedman was sympathetic. Indeed, they often formalized Friedman's own ideas. Most of the younger generation of economists was convinced, and even Friedman himself relented somewhat in response to the large money-demand shifts of the 1990s.

Ultimately, then, the different policy preferences of Friedman and Taylor were the outgrowth of a methodological difference: Taylor's preferences were much more shaped by formal modeling experiments than were Friedman's. In chapter 4 of this volume, Robert Lucas points to Taylor's ability to draw important practical policy lessons from carefully crafted, sometimes highly technical economic models as a rare and important talent that has allowed him to move easily between the academic and policy realms. Taylor's success also owes much to two key principles or ideas that have consistently characterized his analyses: first, the realization that policy must be incorporated into rational-expectations models as a rule; and second, the realization that any useful monetary model must include nominal rigidities.

Federal Reserve Chairman Ben Bernanke kicks off a discussion of the causes of the "Great Moderation" and subsequent "Great Recession" in chapter 5. He argues that while structural changes (such as improved inventory management, financial innovation, and globalization) and good luck (smaller and less frequent shocks) may well help explain the reduced volatility of output growth and inflation observed in the United States after 1984, improvements in the conduct of monetary policy likely played an important role, too. In terms of the Taylor curve trade-off between inflation volatility and output volatility, Bernanke's contention is that the economy moved closer to the efficient frontier during the Fed chairmanship of Paul Volcker.

During the 1960s and 1970s, Bernanke notes, monetary policymakers systematically overestimated the amount of slack in the economy and tended to attribute upward movements in inflation to "cost-push" shocks rather than to policymakers' own attempts to achieve and maintain artificially low rates of unemployment. As a result, longer-term inflation expectations were poorly anchored, and commodity and exchange-rate shocks that should have had only a small and transitory inflation impact instead had effects that were both large and persistent. In econometric studies that ignore the effects of expected future policy on inflation behavior, it has appeared that the shocks hitting the economy during the pre-Volcker period were unusually large. Essentially, these studies mistakenly attribute the effects of bad policy to the shock process itself. The flip side is that some of the salutary effects of the better policy that was pursued beginning in the 1980s have been mistakenly attributed to good luck.

According to John Taylor (chapter 6), Federal Reserve policy went off course after the 2001 recession in response to unwarranted fears of a Japanese-style deflation. As evidence that policy was inappropriate, Taylor points to unusually large and persistent shortfalls in the federal funds rate relative to the Taylor-rule prescription. Consequences included higher-than-desired headline inflation and over-investment in housing. Similar shortfalls relative to the Taylor-rule prescription were observed in other countries. Generally, the larger the shortfall in rates, the larger was the associated housing boom. Factors beside easy monetary policy may have played a role in the real estate boom and bust, but these other factors—the spread of complex mortgage-backed securities and government policies encouraging subprime mortgage lending—were of distinctly secondary importance. Subprime and adjustable-rate mortgages would not have caught on to nearly the extent they did had home prices not been inflated by artificially low interest rates.

Donald Kohn in chapter 7 argues that "It's Not So Simple." Instrument rules for monetary policy of the sort favored by Taylor can provide useful guidance to policymakers but they also have important limitations. The FOMC had good reasons to keep short-term interest rates as low as it did after the 2001 recession.

Kohn acknowledges that simple instrument rules, like the Taylor rule, have several valuable attributes. They often perform better across a wider range of model specifications than do optimal-control policies. They also provide a convenient framework for thinking about and communicating policy and they convey the important message that future policy settings are contingent on economic developments. In practical application, however, the Taylor rule is subject to ambiguities and limitations. It is not obvious, for example, which inflation measure ought to drive policy. Nor is it obvious that it is past inflation that ought to enter the rule, rather than forecasted inflation. The equilibrium real interest rate and the level of potential output—key Taylor-rule ingredients—vary over time and are not directly observable. Finally, the rule makes no allowance for skewed risks or asymmetric costs, such as may exist when inflation is low and prospective real growth is weak. All of these considerations came into play following the 2001 recession. Core inflation measures gave lower Taylor-rule funds rate prescriptions than those based on headline consumer inflation; the unemployment rate was signaling more slack than were (subsequently revised) Congressional Budget Office output-gap estimates; credit spreads suggested that the equilibrium real interest rate was low; and there was a real danger of coming up against the zero-interest-rate bound in the event of a negative shock. Under the circumstances, the FOMC's policy decisions were prudent.

Is there an alternative way to think about and communicate policy that avoids or minimizes the limitations of Taylor-style instrument rules? In chapter 8, Michael Woodford makes the case for a "forecast targeting" approach to monetary policy. Forecast targeting specifies a relationship or criterion that certain economic projections must satisfy if policy is to be optimal. The burden is then on policymakers to explain how it is that current and planned future instrument settings are consistent with the forecast-target criterion. Commitment to a properly specified criterion, like commitment to a properly specified instrument rule, provides a nominal anchor for the economy and protects it from short-sighted, discretionary policymaking. However, Woodford argues that optimal forecast-target criteria are often simpler and more robust to shifting economic circumstances, to model misspecification, and to private-sector learning than are instrument rules, and more reliably result in convergence to a desirable rational expectations equilibrium. It is satisfaction of the forecast-target criterion—and not the particular instrument settings required to implement it—that matters to private decision-makers.

The Norges Bank is an example of a real-world forecast-targeting central bank. Its target criterion takes the form

$$E_t[(\pi - \pi^*)_{t+h} + \phi(y - y^*)_{t+h}] = 0$$

for all t and all $h > 0$, where $\phi > 0$ is a fixed parameter, π and π^* are actual and target inflation, respectively, and y and y^* are actual and potential output. The interest-rate path required to satisfy this criterion depends on the structural details and current state of the Norwegian economy—things about which reasonable people may disagree. It is these issues that are discussed at the bank's policy meetings.

In a fairly standard sticky-price model, the optimal interest-rate rule is similar to a forward-looking Taylor rule: it depends on expected future inflation, expected future output gaps, and current and expected future natural rates of interest. It obeys the Taylor principle. Because expected future stimulus can substitute for current stimulus, however, today's optimal interest rate also depends on expected future *market* interest rates. Moreover, it is *private-sector* expectations of inflation, output gaps, and interest rates that enter the rule—not necessarily model-consistent expectations. Traditional Taylor rules ignore private-sector expectations: they implicitly assume that these expectations will be well-behaved. In contrast to the complexity of the optimal interest-rate rule, the optimal forecast-target criterion is a straightforward variation on that used by the Norges Bank: policy should try to keep the expected value of a weighted average of the inflation gap and the *change* in the output gap equal to zero.

John Taylor, in chapter 9, notes that Woodford's forecast-target criterion is a first-order condition for optimal policy within a given macroeconomic model. Actually implementing the optimal policy requires that this first-order condition be solved for an instrument rule. In practice, it's often possible to find a simple, intuitive approximation to the optimal instrument rule that performs well across a wide variety of models. Such approximately optimal instrument rules have a strong track record as policy guides. Since a central bank's performance is ultimately determined by how it adjusts its policy instrument, research on forecast-targeting criteria is ultimately useful only insofar as it helps us uncover better instrument rules.

In chapter 10, Lars Svensson seeks practical criteria for assessing central bank performance. The criteria are based on a modification of the Taylor curve that Svensson calls the "forecast Taylor curve," which he uses to calculate an empirical trade-off between the conditional variability of inflation and output forecasts. Svensson's discussion takes it for granted that the bank has an announced inflation objective. He argues, however, that in the near term policymakers are legitimately also concerned with stabilizing output relative to potential output. Partly for this reason and partly because realized inflation is subject to shocks that policy cannot fully offset, in assessing policy performance it is not correct simply to look at whether inflation stays near target. Instead, one must look at inflation and GDP *forecasts*. The forecasted path of inflation should converge fairly quickly to the inflation target, and ideally inflation will be forecasted to be above target only when output is forecasted to be below potential. The implicit weight that the central bank puts on keeping forecasted inflation close to target, as compared with keeping forecasted output close to potential, should be consistent over time.

Because the central bank must weigh alternative policy paths, its forecasts must be based on a structural model of the economy. Wise policy choices depend on the bank having a good model, and a good model ought to produce accurate forecasts.

If policy choices are consistent and the policy process is transparent, then the private sector should be able to predict how policy choices will change in response to new information. Consistency and transparency are important because the behavior of the economy depends as much on expectations about the future conduct of policy as it does on current policy settings. If the policy process and central-bank forecasting models are credible, then private-sector forecasts of policy and other important economic variables ought to conform to those of the central bank.

The focus of this volume next shifts to senior policy officials' perspectives on Taylor and his work. Federal Reserve Chairman Ben Bernanke starts off, noting the important contributions that Taylor has made to macroeconomic theory and policy as reflected in the Taylor-curve tradeoff between the volatilities of inflation and unemployment; the

Taylor-rule state-contingent interest-rate prescription; and the Taylor principle that the policy interest rate must respond more than one-for-one to changes in inflation if the economy is to have a well-behaved equilibrium.

Janet Yellen—vice-chair of the Fed's Board of Governors—elaborates. She points to three areas in which Taylor has made important contributions: (1) incorporating nominal rigidities into rational-expectations macroeconomic models, (2) developing and estimating large-scale macroeconometric models with rational expectations, and (3) formulating practical principles to guide monetary policy. In the area of nominal rigidities, Taylor was among the first to point out that pricing rigidities can give central banks an output stabilization role even in economies where expectations are rational. In the area of modeling, Taylor worked with Ray Fair on path-breaking methods for simulating large-scale rational-expectations macroeconometric models. In the area of monetary policy, Taylor has promulgated four basic principles: (1) monetary policy ought to be systematic and predictable—that is, it ought to follow a rule; (2) the nominal interest rate ought to move more than one-for-one with inflation; (3) the policy rule ought to offset shocks to aggregate demand but allow some short-term variation in inflation in response to supply-side shocks; and (4) the policy rule ought to perform well across a wide range of models and types of shocks.

Former European Central Bank chief economist Otmar Issing emphasizes Taylor's key role in making the theoretical case for the existence of a short-run trade-off between output and inflation and in teaching us that monetary policy should not be thought of as a sequence of independent, period-by-period optimizations. Rather, it is the expected *pattern* of policy actions that matters for private-sector behavior. Issing writes, "[M]onetary policy is about commitment and strategic design. Present-day monetary theory and best central banking practice are founded on this bedrock principle, which Taylor . . . has made straightforward and tangible."

Guillermo Ortiz reviews the tremendous changes to the practice of monetary policy in Mexico since the early 1990s, when the Banco de México first gained independence. These changes have included the move to a flexible exchange rate, the adoption of inflation targeting, and a switch to using an overnight interbank interest rate as the main policy instrument. During a supply-driven surge in inflation in 2007, policymakers were guided by the Taylor-rule prescription of partial accommodation. Taylor's overlapping wage-contract model, combining nominal rigidities with inflation inertia, has proven tremendously helpful for understanding the dynamics of the Mexican and other Latin American economies in the 1980s.

Finally, John Lipsky looks at Taylor's contributions from a financial-markets perspective, drawing on his experience as a Wall Street economist at Salomon Brothers and at JP Morgan Chase before he became first deputy managing director of the International Monetary Fund. He notes that the original Taylor-rule paper came out at a time when the relationship between the monetary aggregates and the economy was shifting and unreliable, but financial markets were very sensitive to inflation risks and the costs of high inflation. In this environment, the Taylor rule provided traders and investors with a much-needed guide to whether policy was on a track consistent with price stability.

Lipsky goes on to argue that, beginning in the early 1990s, the world economy benefited from rapid productivity gains made possible by the internationalization of trade and financial flows. These gains created an unusually favorable environment for monetary policy. The years ahead are likely to be considerably more challenging, requiring that policymakers give serious attention to exchange-rate and trade imbalances. Hopefully, Taylor and others in the academic community will provide new insights to help policymakers successfully meet these challenges.

—THE EDITORS

PART I

Taylor's Approach to Monetary Theory and Policy

ONE

MONETARY POLICY RULES: FROM ADAM SMITH TO JOHN TAYLOR

Pier Francesco Asso and Robert Leeson

1. Introduction

At the November 1992 Carnegie-Rochester Conference on Public Policy in Pittsburgh, John Taylor (1993a) suggested that the federal funds rate (r) should normatively (with qualifications) and could positively (at least in the previous five years) be explained by a simple equation:

$$r = p + 0.5y + 0.5(p - 2) + 2,$$

where y is the percent deviation of real GDP from trend and p is the rate of inflation over the previous four quarters.

Within a few months of the publication of the Carnegie-Rochester volume, members of the Federal Open Market Committee (FOMC)

This paper is based on a paper prepared for presentation at the Federal Reserve Bank of Dallas' conference on "John Taylor's Contribution to Monetary Theory and Policy." It has benefited from comments from Ray Fair, John Taylor, participants at the Dallas Fed conference, and seminar participants at the Federal Reserve Board of Governors and at the Federal Reserve Banks of Boston and New York. Pier Francesco Asso is Professor of History of Economics at the University of Palermo, Italy. Robert Leeson is a Visiting Professor of Economics at Stanford University and a Visiting Fellow at the Hoover Institution.

were using the formula to inform their monetary policy deliberations. Governor Janet Yellen indicated that she used the Taylor rule to provide her "a rough sense of whether or not the funds rate is at a reasonable level" (FOMC minutes January 31–February 1, 1995). Taylor visited the Fed board staff in early 1995 and was then asked to discuss the rule with the chairman and other members of the Board of Governors (December 5, 1995).

Athanasios Orphanides (2003) used the Taylor rule to examine the post-World War II history of U.S. monetary policy decisions. The purpose of the current paper is different: it is to shed light on the intellectual history of monetary policy rules, with special emphasis on the Taylor rule. Section 2 introduces the fundamental debate of rules versus discretion and output stabilization versus inflation stabilization. Sections 3–5 examine the early history of policy rules: from Adam Smith to the Great War (section 3), from the Great War to the Great Crash (section 4), plus gold and commodity standard rules (section 5). Sections 6–7 examine three influential rules-based advocates: Henry C. Simons (section 6) plus A. W. H. Phillips and Milton Friedman (section 7). Sections 8–9 examine the evolution of Taylor's thinking between 1976 and 1991, during his two spells at the Council of Economic Advisers (section 8), and in the months immediately preceding the Carnegie-Rochester conference (section 9). Section 10 examines the influence of the Taylor rule on macroeconomic research. Concluding remarks are provided in section 11.

2. Cutting the Gordian Knot

Taylor chose his timing well. In 1946, the year in which he was born, the two competing intellectual leaders of the rules versus discretion debate died. They were Henry Simons (the leader of the Chicago "rules party," who advocated stabilizing "p" using a price level rule) and John Maynard Keynes (whose followers emphasized the importance of stabilizing "y"). The year 1946 was also important for two economists who were to exert seminal influences over Taylor's intellectual development: A. W. H. Phillips enrolled at the London School of Economics and Milton Friedman returned to Chicago, where shortly afterward he rediscovered the quantity theory as a tool for challenging his Keynesian opponents and developed the k-percent money growth rule as an alternative to Simons' price-level rule. The Taylor rule (with r, not M, on the left-hand side) replaced the Friedman rule with a lag.

During the years between the Lucas critique and the Taylor rule (1976–1992), Taylor had a foot in academia and an almost equally sized foot in the policy apparatus (CEA 1976–77, Research Adviser at the Philadelphia Fed 1981–84, CEA 1989–91). By placing almost equal career coefficients on government service and academia, Taylor acquired an invaluable understanding of policy constraints and communication issues. The 1946 Employment Act created the CEA and initiated the *Economic Report of the President*. The act did not specify priorities about p and y: this dual mandate sought to "promote maximum employment, production, and purchasing power." But by the 1960s many economists saw an irreconcilable conflict between promoting maximum employment and production, on the one hand, and promoting stable prices (maximum purchasing power). Keynesians tended to favor a Phillips curve discretionary trade-off as an expression of the emphasis attached to y.

The Taylor rule synthesized (and provided a compromise between) competing schools of thought in a language devoid of rhetorical passion. The Great Depression created a constituency which tended to emphasize the importance of minimizing y (and hence tended to increase the weight attached to y). Inflation was accommodated as a necessary cost of keeping debt servicing low (pre-1951), tolerated, or "controlled away" by wage and price controls. The Great Inflation (circa 1965–79) and the costs associated with the Great Disinflation (post-1979) created a constituency that sought to minimize p (and hence tended to increase the weight attached to p).

Keynes intentionally divided economists into (obsolete) "classics" and (modern) Keynesians; Friedman divided the profession into (destabilizing) fiscalists and (stabilizing) monetarists. Taylor (1989a) heretically suggested that different schools of thought should be open to alternative perspectives; his *Evaluating Policy Regimes* commentary suggested that "some of the differences among models do not represent strong ideological differences" (1993b, 428). The Taylor rule with its equal weights has the advantage of offering a compromise solution between y-hawks and p-hawks.

The rules-versus-discretion debate has often been broadcast at high decibels. Part of the Keynesian-Monetarist econometric debate was described as the battle of the radio stations: FM (Friedman and [David] Meiselman) versus AM ([Albert] Ando and [Franco] Modigliani).

Around the time of Taylor's first publication (1968), the macro-economic conversation came to be dominated by what some regarded as the NPR "radio of the right" ("Natural" rate of unemployment, "Perfectly" flexible prices and wages or "Perfect" competition, and "Rational" expectations).

Robert Solow (1978, 203) detected in the rational expectations rev-olutionaries "a polemical vocabulary reminiscent of Spiro Agnew"; but the revolutionaries doubted that "softening our rhetoric will help mat-ters" (Lucas and Sargent 1978, 82, 60). In a review of Tom Sargent's *Macroeconomic Theory*, Taylor (1981a) commented on Sargent's "fre-quently rousing style" of adversely contrasting new classical macro with the "Keynesian-activist" view. The Taylor rule embraced "R" (and, in the background though it is not required, "N"), replaced "P" with contracts, and provided a policy framework minus the inflammatory rhetoric.

When new rational expectations methods led to real business cycle models without a stabilization role for monetary policy, Taylor (2007c) recalled that it was a tough time: the dark ages for monetary policy rules research. Academic interests appeared to become decoupled from the needs of policymakers. A small group of monetary economists saw themselves as "toiling in the vineyards" (McCallum 1999).

A revival (at least in policy circles) began in the later 1980s. In 1985, the Brookings Institution and the Center for Economic Policy Research (later in association with the International Monetary Fund) launched a research project to investigate international macroeconomic interac-tions and policy. At the December 1988 Macroeconomic Policies in an Interdependent World conference, several papers investigated policy rules. At this conference, Taylor (1989b, 125, 138) had the short-run interest rate as the primary operating instrument of monetary policy: "placing some weight on real output in the interest rate reaction func-tion is likely to be better than a pure price rule."

But the impressive body of rules-based academic literature appeared not to be leading to a consensus. In March 1990, Taylor (1993b, 426–9) noted that significant progress had been made, but "the results vary from model to model. No particular policy rule with particular param-eters emerges as optimal for any single country, let alone all countries. Because of the differences among the models and the methodology, I would have been surprised if a clear winner had presented itself." However, policy rules which focused "on the sum of real output and inflation" outperform other types: "a consensus is emerging about a functional form." Yet there was no consensus about the size of coefficients. Shortly afterward Taylor cut this Gordian knot with his simple but persuasive equation: a compromise between academic complexity and policy-influencing simplicity.[1]

3. From 1776 to the Great War

The problem of designing rational rules to preserve monetary stability or to achieve other policy objectives has long occupied the minds of monetary authorities and thinkers. Some historians have traced the early seeds of the modern "rules versus discretion" dichotomy as far back as the Roman Empire or the Middle Ages (Volckart 2007). However, it was in the age of David Ricardo, Henry Thornton, Lord Overstone, and Walter Bagehot that, for the first time, the importance of monetary policy being rule-guided acquired a great practical and institutional importance.

Major historical events provided economists with the ideal environment for writing and conceiving new rules of conduct in monetary policy. In fact, it was in coincidence with the rise of nation-states and with the general introduction of paper money and its progressive dematerialization that the economic implications of alternative money rules produced some first results both analytically and for practical action. The recurring crises which affected the British economy after the Napoleonic Wars also provided new rationales for discussion of the objectives and instruments of monetary policy. Furthermore, it was in the aftermath of World War I that economists began to reconsider monetary stability and monetary management as a crucial factor for promoting economic stability and growth.

Most of the nineteenth-century controversies on the functioning of alternative monetary systems or on the nature and importance of money in generating cyclical fluctuation can be read through the lenses of the "rules versus discretion" dichotomy. After the financial chaos generated by the Napoleonic Wars, the importance of rules of conduct in monetary affairs began to attract the attention of bankers, professional associations, and political parties. As payments technologies evolved and became more complex, an explicit commitment to abide by rules of conduct was conceived as part of an enforcing mechanism

---

1. A notable precursor to the Taylor rule is the research reported in Bryant, Hooper, and Mann (1993), which sought to identify interest rate policy rules that delivered satisfactory macroeconomic performance across a range of models. See also Orphanides (2007).

to avoid abuses, maintain or restore confidence in the value of money and in the legitimacy of the new financial instruments, and establish on firmer grounds the relationships between banks of issue and commercial banks.

Some early perceptions of our story can be found in Adam Smith's *The Wealth of Nations*. Despite the many financial crashes which had accompanied the introduction of paper money, Smith did not assume a dogmatic approach on behalf of metal standards. On the contrary, he clearly anticipated the possibility that metal shortages would check the prospects of growth and that economic systems would inevitably move beyond the adoption of commodity moneys. At that time, "a well-regulated paper-money" will substitute for metals "not only without any inconveniency, but, in some cases, with some advantages" (Smith 1776, b. iv, c. i). Among the latter, Smith suggested a greater degree of flexibility but also a possible increase in the overall stock of capital.

However, it was the British suspension of the gold standard in 1797 and the publication of the Bullion Report in 1810 which originated a wave of new reflections and writings. Economists and pamphleteers opened a profound discussion on the nature of money, the causes of wartime inflation, and the role of the banking system which went on until the passage of the 1844 Peel Act. The field was split between the adherents of the Currency School—who explained inflation in terms of the monetary abuses primarily caused by excessive government expenditure—and the Banking School, which gave a more complex interpretation of the reasons for monetary instability and liquidity creation. It could be argued that both the Currency School and the Banking School provided cases for subjecting the Bank of England to some preconceived rules of conduct.

Inspired by the writings of Ricardo and of Robert Torrens, the Currency School firmly stood in favor of legislated rules to govern the money supply and set the guidelines for the country's monetary policy. Rules of conduct were also required to enforce the capacity of the Bank of England to protect confidence in new payments technologies and as a consequence of the spread of new financial instruments.

The Banking School proposed a "softer" rule which the national banks of issue ought to follow in governing their issuing operations. This rule, which went under the name of "the real bills doctrine," had also received intellectual recognition in several passages of Smith's *Wealth of Nations*. Under the real bills doctrine, new liquidity could be created only for those invoices whose object was to finance real goods in the course of production and distribution. Following Smith, Thomas

Tooke, James Fullarton, John Stuart Mill, and other Banking School economists suggested that banks of issue should not be constrained by a rigid, quantitative rule: in fact, the optimum quantity of money would be forthcoming automatically if the banks themselves regulated their notes and other liabilities by responding to "the needs of trade." It followed that, so long as outright convertibility in commodity moneys persisted, over-issue was a very unlikely event. However, as has been suggested by David Laidler (2002), it was the ultimate fallacy of the real bills doctrine as a guiding principle of monetary policy and as a sound explanation of general price alterations that may help to explain the search for more specific, quantitatively determined price rules.

Another rationale for money rules rose from the need to enhance the autonomy and the independence of the national banks of issue and rescue them from the greed of the political powers. Full monetary autonomy was an essential prerequisite for achieving different policy objectives: the absorption of external shocks; the protection of confidence in a paper-money system; the smooth transition toward the restoration of full and automatic convertibility; and the indispensable "gradualism" in the adjustment process of external disequilibria. Here, the leading authority was Henry Thornton who, in his 1802 essay, clearly established a set of rules which the banks of issue ought to follow for an optimal regulation of the money supply. In the final pages of his book, Thornton elaborated a series of "restrictive principles of a practical order." The most relevant were: 1. "in no case, however, materially to diminish the sum in circulation, but to let it vibrate only within certain limits"; 2. "to afford a slow and cautious extension of it, as the general trade of the Kingdom enlarges itself"; 3. "to allow of some special, though temporary, encrease in the event of any extraordinary alarm or difficulty"; 4. "to lean to the side of diminution in the case of gold going abroad, and of the general exchanges continuing long unfavourable" (Thornton 1802, 295). According to Thornton, this was the "true policy" which the Bank of England ought to follow, without ever "suffering the solicitation of merchants, or the wishes of Government, to determine the measure of the bank issues."

The usefulness of money rules went beyond the necessity to halt inflation or avoid political abuses in the management of the money supply. In fact, as the market economy became more complex throughout the nineteenth century, economists began to realize the existence of dilemmas or conflicts among different policy objectives. This turned out to be a rather unpleasant discovery and it suggested that some external constraints should be placed upon the actions of policymakers.

In the age of Thornton and Ricardo, several economists noted that different varieties of economic and financial crisis tended to occur at the same time and seemed to require contrasting economic policy remedies. The most common experience took the shape of a sudden instability in the foreign exchange market which coincided with widespread episodes of depositors' runs. In these occurrences the dilemma took the shape of the alternative between financial stringency on one hand and the injection of more liquidity into the system on the other. Therefore, as Bagehot observed, sticking to a set of pre-announced or preconceived rules may become a good, second-best solution for these dilemmas. Also, the contrast between external and internal stability or the one between national autonomy and international coordination were often emphasized by political economists. Particularly after World War I, it was noted that money rules could become optimal instruments in this respect.

Moreover, as has often occurred in economic history, the growing complexity of the market economy did not correspond with a parallel evolution of norms and institutional settings which could help maintain confidence in the new payments technologies and protect purchasing power. Economists knew well that, in the past, many confidence crises had irredeemably swept away new financial innovations which—since the Middle Ages in both continental Europe and Asia—had been built around paper money and fiduciary credit instruments. This was just another reason why they believed that some prudential commitments on the part of banks of issue could become a helpful solution in times of institutional backwardness or fragilities in the management of monetary policy. In modern jargon, it could be said that rules could be conceived as a means to increase confidence under uncertainty and contractual incompleteness (Giannini 2004).

In the first half of the nineteenth century, another dilemma was often brought to the attention of policymakers. In fact many economists suggested the need for rules of conduct in the absence of central banks of issue, or for the reason that most central banks were private enterprises and often acted accordingly in the search for maximum profits on behalf of their shareholders. Many argued that the coexistence of two activities (issuing and banking) weakened the national banks' capacity to exert an effective control upon circulation. In fact the need for firmer rules stemmed from the often contradictory responsibilities which either the law or traditional working practices had attached to national banks of issue. The history of the Bank of England after the Napoleonic Wars well epitomizes these contradictions. Among its manifold functions, the Bank of England was the issuer of notes; had formal responsibilities for managing the public debt; operated as a private banking company; was custodian of the country's official gold reserves; and was from time to time required to intervene as the "lender of last resort," which it often did with a high degree of discretion. These contradictions at a micro level were often reinforced by further dilemmas which originated at a macro level, among them the existence of external versus internal conflicts with interest-rate ceilings which the usury laws often imposed on monetary policy.[2] Samuel Jones Loyd (later Lord Overstone) was among the most active supporters of this quest for less ambiguity and clearer rules of action on the part of the national monetary authorities. As he put it while discussing the Bank of England's multiple functions, "we fall into . . . confusion of ideas, and of course are led to many practical errors, when, seeing that the Bank is at once Manager of the Currency and Head of the banking operations of the country, we confound these distinct characters . . ." (quoted by Eltis 2001, 6).

Finally, as the economy and the payments systems became more complex, rules began to be thought of as useful methods for defending the reputation and guaranteeing the stability of the banking system (Goodhart 1988). With the move away from commodity moneys to legal moneys, economists realized that the production of confidence had become a crucial activity. In this regard, one useful step was to limit freedom of action on the strongest contractual part by restricting opportunities for increasing the money supply. Money rules were conceived in order to ensure the anti-inflationary credibility of monetary policy (Giannini 2004).

4. From the Great War to the Great Crash

World War I was another external shock that exerted a major influence on this debate and, more generally, played an important role in reshaping monetary policy in accord with some legislated commitment. Money rules were given pride of place in many stabilization plans upon which economists elaborated in the immediate post-war years as part of their efforts to find a remedy for wartime inflation and mitigate the

---

2. Thornton, Bagehot, and many other nineteenth-century economists wrote against the usury laws which established an artificial interest-rate ceiling, thus preventing the monetary authorities from obtaining foreign credits in times of gold shortages.

sharp cyclical fluctuations which occurred in foreign trade and real output. As we shall see in the following sections, it was in the interwar years that one can trace some possible antecedents of Taylor's rule.

It must be noted that in the post-war environment the conditions for the practical introduction of money rules seemed to be particularly favorable. In fact, economists began to realize that in order to be reliable, rules needed a greater availability of data and a greater statistical accuracy. Policy rules could thus become credible tools only after systematic empirical research was undertaken and introduced in macroeconomic models. Index numbers, construction of national accounting systems, and basic accessibility to quarterly disaggregated data were instrumental steps for rules design and other related financial innovations. Beginning in the early 1920s, the statistical bureaus of central banks were significantly reinforced (see, among others, Meltzer 2003, chap. 4). Moreover, upon the ashes of military destruction and imperial segregation, a network of new central banks was founded; in some instances, their statutory charters began to indicate a priority list of monetary policy objectives. With the writings of Ralph Hawtrey, John Maynard Keynes, Gustav Cassel, and Irving Fisher, the controversy between a managed monetary policy and the adoption of legislative rules became an element of alternative explanations of the business cycle as well as of the international debate on the restoration of the gold standard.

In the 1920s, the growing professional reputation of economists gave them a more prominent role in designing new policy instruments. Money rules were thus the outcome of a new season of international economic advocacy which was inaugurated by the economists' professional successes in the management of wartime real and financial requirements (Bernstein 2001). During the war, most particularly in the United States, economists earned respect for their technical capacities to fix the economic machine and rationally steer it toward optimal goals.

In the first three decades of the twentieth century, the rules-versus-discretion debate was characterized by a pervasive Fisherian influence. Perhaps the leading monetary theorist at the turn of the century, Irving Fisher had made first-rate contributions to the revivification of the quantity theory of money and important suggestions for the improvement of the classical gold standard (Fisher 1911). He also devoted many intellectual and financial resources to support legislation on price stability (Fisher 1920). As the stability of the international monetary system seemed jeopardized by political tensions and the debt overhang, Fisher fought hard to convince economists and the financial community at large that price stability should be included among the goals of the new Federal Reserve System. He also paid periodic visits to world political leaders urging them to sign a commitment on behalf of policy coordination and a new set of monetary rules (Asso 1994). Never before had one of the most promising young economic theorists virtually abandoned theoretical speculation to embrace a thirty-year crusade on behalf of "stable money," founding associations and pressure groups.

As we shall see below, Fisher himself was the father of many stabilization plans that entailed some form of money rule. It seems curious that Fisher's compensated dollar plan imposed a rather mechanical behavior on monetary authorities even though it completely disregarded the utility of the quantity theory of money he had helped to refine and reintroduce in economics with his 1911 treatise on the *Purchasing Power of Money* (Patinkin 1993). Until his very last days, Fisher tried to sell his plans to politicians, dictators, professional associations, and central bankers.

5. Golden Rules

The first golden rule in the history of economics is the "convertibility rule." According to this rule, the maintenance of convertibility of national moneys into gold at a fixed price is the dominant objective of monetary policy. Inspired by the influential Bullion Report, much of British monetary orthodoxy rested on the firm application of this rule. Through convertibility, it was believed that the domestic economy would be sheltered from external shocks, including governmental abuses in issuing paper money (Eltis 2001). Bullionists located the exclusive source of inflation in the central bank, which was also primarily responsible for the external drains of precious metals that led to the restriction of cash payments.

Thus, the "state of the exchanges" provided an automatic criterion with which to regulate the paper money supply. As Colonel Torrens put it, the one and only sound principle which should regulate the issue of banknotes was to let the money supply expand or contract according to the signs of the balance of payments. Issues could only be enlarged or contracted in response to gold inflows or outflows. Conversely, excessive issues not responding to this simple rule of conduct were the major cause of financial and banking crises.

In the age of the Bullion Report one can also find the first emergence of a concentrated and systematic application of the quantity theory as the standard conceptual framework for the analysis of monetary problems and the formulation of practical policy recommendations. Opinions differed sharply on the definition of what "money" really was. However, the Bullionists were the first to develop the idea that the stock of money or at least its currency component could be effectively regulated via the control of a more narrowly defined monetary base. As one historian has put it, the Bullionist debate is at the origins of the quantitative view that the control of a narrowly defined base of high-powered money implies the virtual control of the money supply (Humphrey 1974).

Classical economists generally expressed a strong commitment on behalf of a legislated rule which aimed to render a paper money economy very much alike to a pure metal economy. The ultimate objective was to maintain stability and, in the meantime, increase economic efficiency due to the development of money and credit markets. Smith (1776, b. ii, c. ii) believed that through the "judicious operations of banking" some real resources could be liberated and invested in productive sectors; the use of paper money instead of gold provided "a sort of wagon-way through the air" enabling a country "to convert a great part of this dead stock into active and productive stock . . . and to convert a great part of its highways into good pastures and cornfields." In his first published essay, Ricardo (1809, 505) wrote that stability of the standard was the one and only objective of monetary policy. Together with most classical economists he was quite optimistic that the imposition of the gold convertibility rule would render the monetary system less prone to financial instability (Laidler 2002). "Time" was also a crucial element in maintaining stability. In fact, the existence of a legal requirement on convertibility induced a prompt response on the part of monetary authorities which also implied that restrictive monetary policies would have a gradual and smooth nature. Risks of abuses, including abuses associated with imperfect information, could be avoided with the introduction of prudential rules. Ricardo and James Mill supported nationalization of the central bank to reduce margins of discretionality. In 1821 James Mill (1821, 113) wrote that the issue of notes was a business that governments must undertake, a business that could be reduced to a pure mechanism and to which a small number of clear and well-defined rules can be applied. For Thornton, practical rules were also a necessary means to assure a superintendence of general credit.

However, reality told a different story and the return to convertibility after the Napoleonic Wars was followed by a recurrent surge of economic and banking crises. Economists, bankers, and monetary writers began to argue that—contrary to the precepts of their Bullionist fathers—gold convertibility as such was an insufficient rule for maintaining price stability and avoiding excessive issue of banknotes. As would occur more than a hundred years later, the Banking School doctrine based upon the "legitimate requirements of trade" was blamed for the 1825 banking crisis. As a consequence, a new rule-guided doctrine began to be discussed by economists and bankers. The first who gave it a full articulation was a prudent banker, John Horsley Palmer, governor of the Bank of England from 1830–32.

The "Palmer rule" appeared on the scene for the first time when the governor testified before the Parliamentary Committee on the Bank of England Charter. Should the new doctrine be embodied in the country's monetary constitution—Palmer concluded his testimony—the monetary base would be passively and exclusively regulated "by the actions of foreign exchanges."

Actually, the so-called "Palmer rule" consisted of a set of rules. First, it established that the Bank's rate of rediscount performed as an interest rate ceiling. This provided the money market with a clear indication that the national bank of issue was no longer willing to act in open competition with other institutions; from this rule it also ensued that, in abnormal times of crisis, market rates would soon become higher than the Bank rate so that the Bank could increase its rediscounting facilities and sustain confidence. Second, Palmer announced that, under ordinary conditions, the Bank of England maintained a rigid quantitative ratio between assets and liabilities. More specifically, the Bank would back one-third of its short-term liabilities of currency notes plus short-term deposits with gold and silver bullion, while the remaining two-thirds would be covered with bonds and other interest-yielding assets. Again, on several occasions, Palmer put the emphasis on the fact that abnormal conditions may require a temporary waiving of this prudential rule. Third, in order to gain an effective control of the money market, the Bank should be granted full monopolistic powers in the issuing of notes, at the expense of the private issuing banks operating in the peripheral regions of the country. In particular, this last rule of conduct indicated that the latter would no longer be put in a position to offset the restrictive monetary policy of the former.

Optimism in the soundness of the Palmer rules proved to be misplaced and, in the making of the Peel Act, the Currency School preached for the introduction of a more restrictive set of rules. In fact, some economists objected that the Bank of England did not rigidly link its currency issue to its gold reserve; as gold flowed out in 1825, 1837, and 1839, the

Bank merely sold investments to sustain the two-thirds ratio, thus contributing to an expansion of its note issue (Eltis 2001).

Thus, between the Bullion Report (1810) and the Peel Act (1844), many writers belonging to the Currency School suggested that monetary policy responses to gold outflows and exchange rate movements had been destabilizing, perverse, or simply ineffective. Time was also an important variable in determining whether, in the end, money was a neutral factor for the country's long-term growth prospects. This was the reason why the Bank's intervention risked accentuating, rather than alleviating, economic disturbances. Since the Bank of England's reactions often arrived too late, her interventions did not protect reserves and ultimately weakened public confidence. Thus, what was needed was convertibility plus some strict regulation of the volume of bank notes. In the writings of members of the Currency School can be found a first manifestation of the belief that the only efficient rule was an outright, quantitative limitation of the stock of money.

The writings, speeches, and letters of Lord Overstone (1857) are particularly illuminating in this respect. There, one can find a clear statement that preservation of the convertibility rule could only be secured through another rule which concerned the backing of national banknotes and coinage with earmarked gold reserves. Unlike Bullionists, members of the Currency School argued that convertibility as such was inadequate to check over-issue for a number of reasons, including an unfavorable balance of payments and a weak foreign exchange rate (Humphrey 1974).

In fact, to effectively maintain stability in a paper-money economy, the simple convertibility rule required the existence of a class of spirited public servants who acted as wisely as disinterested mandarins. A very platonic world indeed—so it was clearly perceived by Ricardo and his followers—which needed further rules to increase its degree of resemblance to a world where corruption, selfishness, and the search for private interest dominated the behavior of the markets as well as of the sovereigns. As Lord Overstone (1857, as quoted by Eltis 2001) observed, ". . . if the banker, in addition to what may be properly called his ordinary and legitimate resources, is also entrusted with the power of issuing paper money *ad libitum*; is it not inevitable that he should abuse this power? . . . Will he, under such temptations, in no respect compromise his respective duties as a banker of issue and a banker of deposit and discount?"

More specifically, Currency School advocates sought rigid adherence to the principle of making the existing mixed gold-paper currency behave exactly as would a wholly metallic currency. As some historians have argued, under the decisive influence of Lord Overstone, the Issue Department of the Bank of England was transformed into a "quasi currency board" by requiring banknotes to expand and contract one-for-one with variations in gold reserves (Eltis 2001; Laidler 2002).

With the Peel Act, the Issue Department was completely separated from the Banking Department. In this manner, reinforcing the gold convertibility rule, the money supply came to be endogenously determined: the Act established that the Issue department would hold the bullion reserve and would be allowed to sustain a note circulation which exceeded this by £14 million. This figure itself indicated a very restrictive attitude since it was close to the lowest level to which the overall note issue had fallen between 1821 and 1844: ". . . hence Britain's monetary base of notes plus bullion would precisely track the Bank's gold and silver reserve upwards and downwards" (Eltis 2001). Thus, the fiduciary issue of £14 million could only be increased after a positive variation of gold reserve assets.

According to the Currency School, the expanded convertibility rule was meant to achieve three long-term policy objectives upon which the general doctrines of the classical school were built: external equilibrium, growth, and money neutrality. In fact, on the one hand, David Hume's argument on behalf of automatic adjustments of external disequilibria could be swiftly expanded to a paper-money economy. On the other, the money supply would become endogenously determined, growing in line with the "needs of trade" and setting the conditions for domestic price stability. Growth prospects ultimately depended on real factors.

In several passages of Overstone's (1857) writings we can find a detailed statement of this rule and of its stabilizing effects on market expectations: ". . . there can be no fixed and definite rule to determine the time and extent of the proper contraction of paper circulation, except correspondence with the bullion. Without such a rule, all must be left to the irregularity and uncertainty of individual discretion. The manager of the circulation must undertake to foresee and to anticipate events, instead of merely making his measures conform to a self-acting test. In the exercise of such a discretion, the manager of the circulation, be he whom he may, we may safely say will, in nine cases out of ten, fall into error; whilst the interests of the whole community, and the fate of all mercantile calculations, will be dependent upon the sound or unsound discretion of some individual or body; instead of depending upon their own prudence and judgement, exercised under the operation of a fixed and invariable law, the nature and provisions of which are equally known to every body."

In terms of other complementary rules, Overstone suggested that great consideration should be given to the "rule of transparency" on the part of the banks of issue. Enhancing the public's knowledge was a good thing for creating positive market sentiments. An essential feature of the new Banking Act was the regular publication of the state of the country's reserves since, as Overstone (1857) put it, "the public are thus furnished with accurate information from week to week . . . the public attention is now fixed upon the banking reserve."

As is quite well known, the 1844 Act closely followed the instructions of Lord Overstone and his fellows. In modern terms the Act established a marginal gold reserve requirement of 100 percent behind note issues (Humphrey 1974). New notes could be thus emitted only if the Bank had received an equivalent amount of gold. The principle that discretion in the management of the money supply was to be strictly limited by Parliament was later introduced in France (1848), the United States (1865), Italy (1874), Germany (1875), and Sweden (1897).

In the second half of the nineteenth century, Walter Bagehot was perhaps the economist most successful at reviving discussion of monetary policy. Bagehot addressed the issue of what rules of conduct central banks of issue should follow in order to safeguard financial stability. In his view, particularly whenever the emergency took the form of a short-term liquidity crisis, banks of issue should be actively involved in guaranteeing the stability of the banking system. It followed that the nation's central bank was required to act as a lender of last resort, support depositors' confidence, and defend the stability of the banking system, even though these actions might conflict with the profit motive. According to Bagehot, particularly in times of an international gold drain, the central bank should freely lend to domestic banks at higher interest rates.

The Bagehot rule implied that—contrary to the gold standard's "rules of the game"—central banks' foreign and domestic assets usually moved in opposite directions. In response to a sharp gold drain, Bagehot suggested that central banks inject liquidity into the system, thus sterilizing the impact of the gold losses on the money supply.[3] As Bagehot (1873, 27–8) put it: ". . . very large loans at very high interest rates are the best remedy for the worst malady of the money market

---

3. Sterilization policies were eased by central banks' cooperation and mutual lending policies. See the classic studies by Bloomfield (1959) and De Cecco (1984).

when a foreign drain is added to a domestic drain." The influential legacy of Bagehot's rule on the conduct of monetary policy up to 1914 was enduring and widespread; as Bloomfield's (1959, 48) seminal research has shown: "in the case of *every* central bank the year-to-year changes in international and domestic assets were more often in the opposite direction (60 percent of the time) than in the same direction (34 percent of the time)."

The intellectual commitment to the gold standard was weakened by World War I. Significant changes in the price level produced serious economic, political, and social repercussions. Economists were involved in studying how to restore "normalcy" and formulated a long series of stabilization plans which were discussed in academic journals but also at international conferences. Different plans had different attitudes toward the role of commodity moneys in the future monetary systems: some explicitly devised a dethronement of gold; others maintained some forms of anchorage to metals; others suggested that gold be merely relegated to finance international transactions and central banks' clearing operations.

However, common to most of these plans was the idea that domestic price stability was to be regarded as a more optimal preference when compared to foreign exchange stability.

While economists debated stabilization plans, in the post-war years national governments worked hard to reintroduce some commitment to the gold standard. In the first half of the 1920s, it could be argued that another sort of unwritten but rigorously applied rule dominated the scientific debate and, what was worse, the governments' agenda. This invisible rule took the name of the resumption rule and still paid tribute to the sacred and universal values represented by the classical gold standard.

Anyone who is familiar with the interwar debates on the reform of monetary policies and systems knows that the resumption rule introduced stringent commitments on general economic policies. The resumption rule indicated that if, after the occurrence of an exogenous shock (a war or a confidence crisis), gold convertibility was temporarily suspended, it had to be restored at traditional mint parity as soon as practicable—if necessary by deflating the domestic economy. Time of resumption was the only debatable option, but the possibility of "gradualism" did not have to weaken the long-run commitment to exchange stability and gold convertibility. The presumption that full gold convertibility would eventually be restored at the traditional pre-trouble parity was fiercely debated. Particularly in peripheral countries, economists argued that "gradualism" and "realism" ought to become the guiding principles in establishing the new grid of exchange rate parities.

The resumption rule de facto prevented governments from exerting a long-term influence on the level of domestic prices and was advocated with great force in the early 1920s. The reasons for this support can be identified in the contemporary evils of hyperinflation; in the defence of the prestige of London financial supremacy, i.e., the "City factor"; in the limited diffusion of bank moneys; and in the limited electoral powers of those who were most severely hit by the deflationary bent underlying the resumption rule (McKinnon 1993).

Despite the force of the resumption rule, interwar economists continued to conceive monetary policy in terms of legislated rules which ought to be gradually introduced in national constitutions and coordinated internationally through the concerted action of leading central banks. Keynes, Fisher, Cassel, Hawtrey, R. A. Lehfeldt, and other monetary theorists elaborated plans for monetary reforms which placed domestic price stability on top of the priorities of monetary policy. These reform plans considered the gold anchor as a "barbarous relic" (Keynes) or more politely relegated its functions to a minor role (Fisher and the compensated dollar plan).

In the 1920s critical essays on the actual working of the gold standard began to address the crucial question of how well it functioned according to some pre-established rules of the game. Keynes was not alone in viewing the gold standard not as an effective monetary rule that could automatically govern the monetary system but as a political institution that was managed by the discretion of central banks. It was a widespread perception that gold no longer provided a natural anchor for a rule-based monetary system. Most economists agreed that, in order to increase their effectiveness, money rules needed greater sophistication in the available data and in indexation schemes. World War I was also a key event in the development of the idea of a general price index. Many usable versions of measuring the purchasing power of money were formulated, thus increasing the potential for money rules.

Fisher offered a clear rule for stabilizing the domestic price level (Laidler 2002; Patinkin 1993). In his emphatic prose, Fisher (1920) wrote that the progress of modern capitalism is rooted on price stability: ". . . what is needed is to stabilize, or standardize, the dollar just as we have already standardized the yardstick, the pound weight, the pint cup . . . Once the yard was defined. . . as the girth of the chieftain of the tribe . . . could one imagine the modern American business man tolerating a dollar defined as the girth of the President of the United States?"

Unlike Keynes, the Yale economist believed that countries needed to maintain some connections with a commodity standard since history proved that full fiduciary systems had almost inevitably been "a curse" for the countries that adopted them. Well before the outbreak of World War I, Fisher thought that stability could be achieved through indexation schemes which automatically offset price variations by varying the gold content of the dollar. Hence he proposed the creation of a compensated dollar.

The essential property of the compensated dollar was to maintain gold convertibility but at a price that would be regularly adjusted to offset past fluctuations in gold's relative price in terms of goods. Such variations were measured by a suitable index number which would be regularly updated and published. Thus, Fisher advocated a price-level stability rule as an anchor for the monetary system and tried to get the U.S. Congress (and also other countries) to implement that rule in legislation. Fisher (1920, 81ff.) explained that if an index of the price level should increase by 1 percent, then the purchasing power of a dollar gold certificate would be restored by increasing the gold content of a dollar by 1 percent; if during the following quarter that should not succeed in restoring the original price level, the gold content would be further increased: "Let us correct gold instability, so that one dollar . . . buy[s] approximately that same composite basketful of goods . . . But how can we rectify the gold standard? By varying suitably the weight of the gold dollar . . . by adding new grains of gold to the dollar just fast enough to compensate for a loss in the purchasing power of each grain . . . What criterion is to guide the Government in making these changes in the dollar weight? Am I proposing that some Government official should be authorized to mark the dollar up or down according to his own caprice? Most certainly not . . . for every one per cent of deviation of the index number above or below par at any adjustment date, we would increase or decrease the dollar's weight by one per cent. In other words, to keep the price level of other things from rising or falling we make the price of gold fall or rise."

Here then, as Patinkin (1993) has argued, there was a rule in the modern sense of the term. The plan worked as an automatic device which, by simply changing one price in the economy, achieved the stabilization of the price level in general: "My aim was to make the whole plan of stabilization—both gold control and credit control—as automatic that is as free from discretion as possible" (Fisher 1920).

The Stable Money Association—founded and headed by Fisher—tried hard but unsuccessfully to impose a legal obligation upon the Fed to pursue price stability. Following Fisher's campaigns, Congressmen James A. Strong (R-KS) and T. Alan Goldsborough (D-MD) presented bills of amendment of the Federal Reserve Act with the aim of introducing price stability among the central bank's priorities. However, as Patinkin (1993) put it, "Fisher's persistent advocacy of his plan played a major role in placing the problem of stabilizing the price level on the agenda of U.S. monetary policy in the interwar period." Curiously, Fisher did not assign a primary role to the quantity of money. Despite his theoretical efforts to restore it at the center of monetary thinking, Fisher seemed to believe that the United States lacked an institutional framework that enabled offsetting changes in the quantity of money.

In Fisher's plan, the mechanical nature of gold-price adjustments did not exempt monetary authorities from practicing the virtuous policies of gradualism and fine-tuning: "So it is just like steering a bicycle or an automobile. If it deviates a little you turn the wheel slightly and if that is not enough you turn it some more, or if you turn too much you turn it back and keep the automobile in pretty nearly a straight line. Nobody can steer a machine with absolute straightness; but it is amazing how straight you can steer it if you only touch the wheel a little here and there; and that is exactly what we mean by these two bureaus, by trial and error every two months" (Fisher's testimony as quoted by Lawrence 1928, 86).

Another important contribution can be found in Fisher's more theoretical works. In agreement with the new Cambridge version of the quantity theory of money, Fisher wrote that monetary control could be achieved in a fractional reserve banking system via control of an exogenously determined stock of high-powered money. Here again we find the idea that the total stock of money and bank deposits would be a constant multiple of the monetary base, since banks desired to hold a fixed proportion of their deposits as reserves and since the public desired to maintain a constant ratio of cash holdings to demand deposits.

Although there were some interwar economists, such as Carl Snyder (1924) and Lionel D. Edie (1931), who explicitly advocated a constant-money rule, some historians have argued that it was the Swedish economist Knut Wicksell who, by the turn of the century, had outlined an approach to monetary policy which has the most striking similarities to the modern approach. The basic features of Wicksell's model include: the overriding objective of price stability; an interest rate instrument controlled by the rates of discount on settlement balances at the central bank; and a policy rule under which the instrument varies in response to deviations from the objective (Clinton 2006).

Unlike Fisher's rule, Wicksell's rule was divorced from any kind of commodity convertibility and was based on interest rate movements through bank discretion. As some have argued (Bernanke et al. 1999), it could be said that Wicksell's rule followed a constrained management principle based on the search for a neutral rate of interest, advocating a price stability norm rather than a price stability rule. In fact, as recent interpreters have argued (Clinton 2006), Wicksell's rule did not imply that central banks ought to be actively searching for a new "holy Grail," trying to ascertain what the natural rate actually was and how and why it was changing. More practically, central banks were required to analyze the current price level which provided a reliable test of the agreement or of the diversion between the two rates.

In fact, recent writers have argued that the Wicksell rule was designed to stabilize the inflation rate rather than the price level, being appropriate for inflation targeting but not with the objective of price stability. As Wicksell put it, ". . . we have acquired an objective basis for attempts to prevent such changes by rational methods . . . it is no easy task that lies before the combined forces of economic science and economic practice" (quoted by Clinton 2006, 20).

However, at least in the Anglo-Saxon world, in the interwar years the influence of Wicksell's early writings was virtually nonexistent and bound to remain so for a long time. When the Depression so severely hit the industrialized economies, the field of professional economists was sharply divided between those who favored full discretion and those who argued on behalf of a new, more rigid set of money rules.

Among the former, New Dealers such as Lauchlin Currie (1933, 356) wrote on behalf of discretion as a remedy against the structural weaknesses of the banking system. As he wrote in the midst of the Depression, in such a delicate and difficult task as the determination of proper central banking policy it would appear to be a safe generalization that automatic rules render more difficult the task of central bankers, while discretionary powers facilitate it.

6. Henry C. Simons

6.1. Rules versus discretion

In February 1936, Henry Simons ([1936] 1962) effectively created what Richard Selden (1962, 323) described as the Rules Party with his "Rules Versus Authorities in Monetary Policy." In the same month,

Keynes (1936, 164, 378, 220–1) explained that he had become "some-what skeptical of the success of a merely monetary policy directed to-wards influencing the rate of interest. I expect to see the State, which is in a position to calculate the marginal efficiency of capital-goods on long views and on the basis of the general social advantage, taking an even greater responsibility for directly organizing investment . . . I conceive, therefore, that a somewhat comprehensive socialization of investment will prove the only means of securing an approximation to full employment."

Alvin Hansen (the "American Keynes") favored a "dynamic ap-proach" which stood in contrast to the passive acceptance of "the play of 'natural' forces . . . many economists are coming to think that action along these traditional lines would by itself be wholly inadequate. It is increasingly understood that the essential foundation upon which the international security of the future must be built is an economic order so managed and controlled that it will be capable of sustaining full employment" (Hansen and Kindleberger 1942, 467).

In response, Simons (1939, 275) complained that Hansen's propos-als would generate "a continuing contest between the monetary au-thority seeking to raise employment and trade-unions seeking to raise wage rates." Simons also bemoaned that "the gods are surely on his side. What he proposes is exactly what many of us, in our most realistic and despairing moods, foresee ahead as the outcome of recent trends." If Hansen succeeded in establishing a monetary system "dictated by the *ad hoc* recommendations of economists like himself . . . the outlook is dark indeed."

For Simons ([1944] 1948, 1,213; 1943, 443–4), tariffs were part of the government sponsored "racketeering" which his rules were designed to thwart. Simons sought to defend Traditional Liberal Principles; his faith and hope for the post-war world rested on the construction of a "free-trade front." Simons (1936) believed that Keynes' *General Theory* could easily become "the economic bible of a fascist movement." Keynes had now embarked on a mission which Simons found repellent: an authen-tic genius "becoming the academic idol of our worst cranks and char-latans." According to Simons ([1945] 1948, 308), the New Deal had delegated arbitrary power to a series of agencies. This "high-road to dictatorship" was terrifying for "an old-fashioned liberal." Elevating the "government of men" over the "government of rules" was tantamount to "accepting or inviting fascism."

At the Chicago Harris Foundation lectures and seminars on "Un-employment as a World Problem," Keynes (1931, 94) advocated discretionary macroeconomic management to "keep the price index and the employment index steady." Hansen (1931, 94) asked whether it was not the case that "in our present state of knowledge we have no guide at all dependable, and consequently the system you propose is a purely Utopia one?" Keynes (1931, 94) responded that "statistics are becoming more adequate . . . I think we economists have given the practical business men very little real help in the past. If they were aided by more complete statistical data, then I think we should find central banks doing their best duty." When asked by Hansen (1931, 94) about the reliability of the judgment of the central bankers, Keynes (1931, 94) replied: "I think we already know enough to give them general suggestions . . . Painful experience works wonders. It is really the economists who are primarily at fault. We have never given any sort of scientific conclusions, such as you would expect. So long as the supposedly experts fail to agree among themselves, it seems to me reasonable for the practical business men to pay only moderate attention to them."

According to his disciples, Keynes "trusted to human intelligence. He hated enslavement by rules. He wanted governments to have discretion and he wanted economists to come to their assistance in the exercise of that discretion" (Cairncross 1978, 47–8).

6.2. Simons and the sticky-price tradition

The label attached to the combination of rules plus rational expectations and (sticky price) contracts is "New Keynesian." Yet rules, expectations, and sticky prices were also in the Simons tradition. Indeed, to counter one version of a money-demand Chicago oral tradition, Don Patinkin (1969) and his research assistant, Stanley Fischer, located a sticky-price Chicago oral tradition. Simons ([1944] 1948, 131–2) used sticky prices to build an expectations-augmented-insider-outsider model of the labor market. Where trade unions had power and labor turnover was costly to firms, insiders could "insulate themselves from the competition of new workers merely by making their costs excessive, that is, by establishing labor costs and *wage expectations* [emphasis added] which preclude expansion of production or employment in their field." Thus outsiders (new and displaced workers) would not typically migrate to such firms because jobs cannot be had. The privately optimal strategy for trade unions was to exclude lower-wage competitors.

This sticky-price tradition can be found in Simons' ([1934] 1948, 64–5) "Positive Proposal for Laissez Faire," in which he explains that it was important to consider "how different possible [monetary] policy rules would operate given the basic inflexibilities in the price structure . . . no monetary system, however perfectly conceived and administered, can make a free-enterprise system function effectively in the absence of reasonable flexibility in the price structure." It can also be found in Simons' (1933, 550–1) review of Charles Beard's *America Faces the Future*. It was, Simons stated, "perhaps an incontrovertible position that the excess of booms and depressions are attributable, on the one hand, to the system of commercial banking and, on the other, to an exceeding and increasing 'stickiness' in many parts of the price structure . . . many prices have become quite inflexible and especially resistant to downward pressure . . . Mr. Beard beseeches us to adopt measures which will make the 'sticky' prices as much stickier as possible. To adopt such measures, while neglecting the problem of money and credit, is to assure the next depression will make the present one seem altogether trivial."

7. Phillips and Friedman

Milton Friedman's *k* percent money growth rule (and its breakdown) exerted a profound influence on monetary economics; his various influences on Taylor (his Hoover colleague) are apparent. Less widely known, perhaps, is A. W. H. Phillips' influence on Taylor. Taylor's (1968) first publication ("Fiscal and Monetary Stabilization Policies in a Model of Endogenous Cyclical Growth") combined two strands of Phillips' (1954b, 134) theoretical evaluation of policy rules and models of cyclical growth (1961, 195). Taylor's (1968, 1) objective was to "describe the product and money markets as developed by Phillips, and derive the government policies which will regulate the model."

The money market had the interest rate as a function of the price level (P), actual income (Y_A) and the money supply (M):

$$r = f(P, Y_A, M).$$

The Phillips curve equation had the rate of inflation depending on the gap between actual and full capacity income and on capacity growth (a proxy for productivity):

$$p = b(x - 1) - Yg + d,$$

where p = inflation rate, x = ratio of actual output to full capacity output (Y_A/Y_F), Yg = the proportionate growth rate of full capacity output, and d = constant.

Taylor (1968, 5, n5) defined rules for both monetary and fiscal policy, noting that they were "modified versions of the types of fiscal policies first suggested by A. W. Phillips (1954)". In conducting monetary policy, the central bank would increase the money supply when actual output fell below full capacity output; that is, when x is less than one. "These [fiscal and monetary] polices are analogous to feedback methods of control which engineers have used in stabilizing electrical systems." It is not hard to imagine the clear similarities between these 1968 Taylor equations and the Taylor rule.

The Taylor rule can be seen as a method of compressing the swing of the business cycle—minimizing the deviations from the "optimal" spot on an inflation-anchored Phillips curve. The continuities between Taylor and Phillips and between Taylor in 1992 (age 45) and Taylor in 1968 (the 21-year-old undergraduate) will be outlined below.

Phillips made five distinct but inter-related contributions to the policy rules literature: the Phillips machine (Phillips 1950, 68); the adaptive inflationary expectations formula (1952, meeting with Milton Friedman); the theoretical Phillips curve, an apparatus that facilitated policy rule evaluation (Phillips 1954b, 134); empirical illustrations of the theoretical Phillips curve (Phillips 1958, 243; Phillips 1959, 269); and a Lucas-style critique (Phillips 1968, 468; Phillips 1972, 479). Given that the Taylor rule can be seen as operating on the low-inflation-expectations part of a Phillips curve, it is worth exploring the connections between Taylor and Phillips in this regard.

7.1. Phillips machine

As an undergraduate, Phillips constructed a large physical model with which to explore the macroeconomic policy options (one version is on permanent display at the Science Museum in South Kensington, London). Dennis Robertson "practically danced a jig" when he saw the Phillips Machine in operation. When the Chancellor of the Exchequer and the Governor of the Bank of England attended a dinner at the London School of Economics (LSE), they adjourned to the machine room where the chancellor was given control of the fiscal levers and the governor control of the monetary ones (Dorrance 2000). It continues to influence policy design (Leeson, forthcoming).

Phillips' (1950, 73, 76–7) exposition of the machine involved a brief discussion of the destabilizing influence of expectations about prices: "This simple model could be further developed, in particular by making a distinction between working and liquid stocks, introducing lags into the production and consumption functions, and linking the demand curve for liquid stocks to the rate of change of price through a co-efficient of expectations. Each of these developments would result in an oscillatory system. They will not be considered further here . . ."[4] The "simple model" assumed that prices were constant or that values were measured in "some kind of real units." Phillips demonstrated that it was possible to "introduce prices indirectly into the system," allowing real and nominal magnitudes to be considered (and graphed) separately. In the operational notes accompanying the machine, Phillips wrote, "With this number of relationships and assumptions concerning the effects of price changes there is not much chance of getting very precise numerical multiplier results on the machine. But since, under conditions of rising prices there is not much chance of getting them in reality either, this is not a very great disadvantage from the point of view of exposition either" (cited by Vines 2000, 62).

Phillips told his colleagues that the empirical curve was an extension of the unfinished research agenda of the machine (Yamey 2000). He (1954a, 187) criticized Michel Kalecki's *Theory of Economic Dynamics* (1954) for attaching "no causal significance . . . to price movements." The opening sentence of the theoretical Phillips curve (1954b, 134) stated that the method of "comparative statics . . . does not provide a very firm basis for policy recommendations [because] the time path of income, production and employment during the process of adjustment is not revealed. It is quite possible that certain types of policy may give rise to undesired fluctuations, or even cause a previously stable system to become unstable, although the final equilibrium position as shown by a static analysis appears to be quite satisfactory. Secondly, the effects

---

4. Phillips' (1950) source for this "co-efficient of expectation" is Lloyd Metzler's (1941) essay on "The Nature and Stability of Inventory Cycles." Metzler replaced the "artificial" assumption that business expectations about future sales depended solely on the past level of sales with the "natural" addition of the direction of change of such sales. Metzler's (1941, 119, 128–9) "co-efficient of expectation" was the ratio of the expected change of sales between periods t and $t-1$ and the observed change of sales between $t-1$ and $t-2$. Cyclical changes in the coefficient needed to be investigated, but its interaction with the accelerator inevitably generated instability. Indeed, the introduction of the coefficient "places very severe restrictions upon our stability conditions." It is possible to view Phillips' subsequent research as an attempt to address Metzler's imperative to investigate empirically and theoretically macroeconomic systems that included such features.

of variations in prices and interest rates cannot be dealt with adequately with the simple multiplier models which usually form the basis of the analysis." Thus Phillips' academic career was, from the start, associated with the attempt to explain the instabilities and discontinuities associated with rising prices. As David Vines (2000) put it in his discussion of the "Phillips tradition," there is "more in the Machine . . . than is allowed for in macroeconomic conventional wisdom."

Phillips' LSE colleagues turned to him for assistance with the analysis of inflationary expectations. Henry Phelps Brown, for example, acknowledged a specific debt to Phillips for "the form of the argument" about inflationary expectations and profit expectations—the situation where "the price level itself is taking the initiative, and moving under the influence of a preponderant expectation about the likelihood and feasibility of rises and falls in product prices, which has itself been built up by such factors as changes in . . . 'the market environment' . . . [which impart] a gentle but continuing motion to the price level" (Brown and Weber 1953, 279). In recognition of his contribution to macroeconomic analysis (including, presumably, the analysis of inflationary expectations), in 1955 Friedman wrote to offer Phillips a visiting position in Chicago.

7.2. *Phillips' adaptive inflationary expectations formula*

In formulating the k percent money growth rule, Friedman derived his missing equation from Phillips. In his famous methodological essay, Friedman concluded, "The weakest and least satisfactory part of current economic theory seems to me to be in the field of monetary dynamics, which is concerned with the process of adaptation of the economy as a whole to changes in conditions and so with short-period fluctuations in aggregate activity. In this field we do not even have a theory that can be appropriately called 'the' existing theory of monetary dynamics" (1953, 42; see also 1950, 467).

George Stigler (1941, 358–9) referred to expectations as "the promised land to some economists and a mirage to others. The reviewer must admit that he leans towards the latter view: much of the literature on expectations consists of obvious and uninformative generalizations of static analysis." With respect to "the revision of anticipations . . . progress depends much more on the accumulation of data (of a type almost impossible to collect!) than on an increase in the versatility of our technical apparatus." Friedman ([1946] 1953, 277–300) attacked Oskar Lange on similar grounds: "An example of a classification that has no direct empirical counterpart is Lange's classification of monetary changes . . . An explicit monetary policy aimed at achieving a neutral (or positive or negative) monetary effect would be exceedingly complicated, would involve action especially adapted to the particular disequilibrium to be corrected, and would involve knowledge about price expectations, that even in principle, let alone in practice, would be utterly unattainable."

In May 1952, Friedman (correspondence to Leeson, August 25, 1993) visited the LSE where he raised with Phillips the question of "how to approximate expectations about future inflation." Phillips then wrote down the adaptive inflationary expectations equation, which would later transform macroeconomics. At the time, economists were in no doubt about Phillips' implicit assumption about inflation: "*Implicitly* [emphasis added], Phillips wrote his article for a world in which everyone anticipated that nominal prices would be stable" (Friedman 1968a, 8). Friedman (correspondence to Leeson, August 25, 1993) explained that "the 'implicitly' is really needed . . . Phillips himself understood that his analysis depended on a particular state of expectations about inflation . . . Phillips' *Economic Journal* article (1954b) made a very real impression on me. However, his discussion of inflationary expectations in that article is very succinct."

Friedman returned from the LSE to Chicago, where he provided Phillip Cagan with the adaptive inflationary expectations formula. Cagan (1956), Marc Nerlove (1958, 231),[5] and Kenneth J. Arrow (1958, 299) used this formula to transform economic analysis. This formula is generally known as the Friedman-Phelps formula, but Cagan (2000) calls it Phillips' Adaptive Expectations Formula. It was this formula which Friedman (1956, 19–20) predicted would transform whole sections of economics: Cagan's "device for estimating expected rates of change of prices from actual rates of change, which works so well for his data, can be carried over to other variables as well and is likely to be important in fields other than money. I have already used it to estimate 'expected income' as a determinant of consumption (Friedman 1957) and Gary Becker has experimented with using this 'expected income' series in a demand function for money . . ."

Friedman (1958, 252) outlined the proposition that as inflationary expectations adjust to rising prices, the short-run advantages of inflation disappear: "If the advantages are to be obtained, the rate of price

---

5. "The history of the idea is unclear: A. W. Phillips may have suggested the idea to M. Friedman about 1950" (Nerlove et al. 1979, 296).

rise will have to be accelerated and there is no stopping place short of runaway inflation." In 1960, he outlined the natural rate model in full to Richard Lipsey during a visit to the LSE. Friedman (1962, 284) informed his Chicago students, "Considerations derived from price theory give no reason to expect any systematic long-term relation between the percentage of the labor force unemployed and the rate at which money wages rise."

Friedman (1966a) described the natural rate model during an exchange with Robert Solow at an April 1966 University of Chicago conference. In his *Newsweek* column (October 17, 1966b), Friedman made this prediction: "There will be an inflationary recession." In his address to the American Economic Association (AEA), Friedman (1968, 8, 4) added "one wrinkle" to the Phillips curve in the same way as Irving Fisher added "only one wrinkle to Wicksell." In so doing, Friedman predicted that the Phillips curve trade-off between inflation and unemployment existed temporarily, but not permanently. Friedman asserted that "Phillips' analysis . . . contains a basic defect—the failure to distinguish between *nominal* wages and *real* wages." In his Nobel Lecture, Friedman (1976, 217–9) asserted that "Phillips' analysis seems very persuasive and obvious. Yet it is utterly fallacious . . . It is fallacious because no economic theorist has ever asserted that the demand and supply of labor are functions of the *nominal* wage rate. Every economic theorist from Adam Smith to the present would have told you that the vertical axis should refer not to the *nominal* wage rate but to the *real* wage rate . . . . His argument was a very simple analysis—I hesitate to say simple minded, but so it has proved—in terms of *static* supply and demand conditions." (Emphases in text.)

Keynesians initially were not inclined to embrace this expectational constraint on macroeconomic discretion. Alvin Hansen (1964, 342–3, 288) discussed and dismissed "misguided expectations," preferring instead the "objective causes of the cycle." In academic year 1964–65, Paul Samuelson pondered before a blackboard, and dismissed as doubtful an early version of the natural rate model (Akerlof 1982, 337). James Tobin (1968, 53) argued that the coefficient on inflationary expectations was less than one: the worst outcome was that when inflationary expectations caught up with actual experience, unemployment would rise to its natural level. Solow (1968, 3), Harry Johnson (1970, 110–12), and Albert Rees (1970, 237–8) all continued to express faith in a moderate inflation-unemployment trade-off.

Shortly afterwards, Tobin (1972, 9) felt obliged to question the validity of the original Phillips curve which came to be described as "an empirical finding in search of a theory." Solow (1978, 205) concluded that in the 1960s and 1970s the profession experienced a "loss of virginity with respect to inflationary expectations."

7.3. Theoretical Phillips curve

In his PhD dissertation and a subsequent essay in the *Economic Journal*, Phillips (1954b) stated that flexible prices are integral-type forces; he demonstrated the alarming consequences of integral-type policies generating a "dynamically unstable [system] . . . In such a case the oscillations would increase in amplitude until limited by non-linearities in the system and would then persist within those limits so long as the policy was continued . . . There may, however, be a tendency for monetary authorities, when attempting to correct an 'error' in production, continuously to strengthen their correcting action the longer the error persists, in which case they would be applying an integral correction policy . . . It will be seen that even with a low value of the integral correction factor, cyclical fluctuations of considerable magnitude are caused by this type of policy, and also that the approach to the desired value of production is very slow. Moreover, any attempt to speed up the process by adopting a stronger policy is likely to do more harm than good by increasing the violence of the cyclical fluctuations . . ."

The final and most crucial sub-sections of Phillips' stabilization model (1954b, 153–7) were "Inherent Regulations of the System" and "Stabilization of the System," which began with: "Some examples will be given below to illustrate the stability of this system under different conditions of price flexibility *and with different expectations concerning future price changes*" (emphasis added). The theoretical Phillips curve was then tested against a variety of scenarios, inflationary expectations being a crucial factor in determining whether the system has satisfactory outcomes or not: "Demand is also likely to be influenced by the rate at which prices are changing, or have been changing in the recent past, as distinct from the amount by which they have changed, this influence on demand being greater, the greater the rate of change of prices . . . The direction of this change in demand will depend on expectations about future price changes. If changing prices induce expectations of further changes in the same direction, as will probably be the case after fairly rapid and prolonged movements, demand will change in the same direction as the changing prices . . . there will be a positive feedback tending to intensify the error, the response of demand to changing prices thus acting as a perverse or destabilizing mechanism of the proportional type."

Even if Phillips saw inflationary expectations as destabilizing aggregate demand alone, this by itself would destroy the possibility of a stable trade-off because the expectation of further inflation tends to introduce fluctuations: "The strength of the integral regulating mechanisms increases with the increasing degree of price flexibility, while the total strength of the proportional regulating mechanisms decreases as demand responds perversely to the more rapid rate of change of prices, and both these effects tend to introduce fluctuations when price flexibility is increased beyond a certain point. When price expectations operate in this way, therefore, the system . . . becomes unstable . . ." (1954b, 155).

Thereafter he worked on the "central theoretical problems" of the Ford Foundation-funded "Project on Dynamic Process Analysis" (May 1956–April 1963). The objective was to specify and estimate models for the control of economic systems. In this period, he presented some empirical illustrations of his stabilization proposals, while continuing to pursue the matter theoretically. The theoretical Phillips curve was published in June 1954; in the three years to June 1957, Phillips became familiar with the Nyquist stability criterion and experimented with electronic simulations of stabilization proposals using equipment at the National Physical Laboratory (NPL) and Short Brothers and Harland Ltd. From about 1952, Phillips interacted with Richard Tizard at the NPL; and, in 1956, Tizard resigned as head of the NPL Control Mechanisms and Electronics Division to take up a two-year fellowship at the LSE to work full-time with Phillips (Swade 2000). These collaborations led Phillips (1957, 169) to conclude that "the problem of stabilization is more complex than appeared to be the case." An empirical agenda was needed: ". . . improved methods should be developed for estimating quantitatively the magnitudes and time-forms of economic relationships in order that the range of permissible hypotheses may be restricted more closely than is at present possible." It seems likely that around June 1957 he began to work on the first empirical Phillips curve (1958).

7.4. Empirical Phillips curve

Having pioneered the destabilizing effects of inflationary expectations, Phillips provided very little discussion of this topic in his 1958 empirical curve. His second explanatory variable (the rate of change of unemployment) in Phillips' (1958, 243) model influenced wage changes through the expectation that the business cycle will continue moving upward (or downward).[6] Lipsey (1960, 20) labeled this "an expectation effect . . . the reaction of *expectations* [emphasis in text], and hence of competitive bidding, to changes in u." But there is no systematic analysis of inflationary expectations. It is possible that Phillips instructed Friedman, Phelps Brown, and others how to model adaptive inflationary expectations in their empirical work, but decided to ignore it in his own. An alternative explanation is that Phillips was primarily interested in the low inflation "compromise" zone where inflationary expectations are not a dominating force.

There is a distinct continuity between the 1954 theoretical Phillips curve; the 1958, 1959, and 1962, empirical Phillips curves; and his growth model. In "A Simple Model of Employment, Money and Prices in a Growing Economy," Phillips (1961, 201–2) described his inflation equation as being "in accordance with an obvious extension of the classical quantity theory of money, applied to the growth equilibrium path of a steadily expanding economy." His steady state rate of interest, r_s ("the real rate of interest in Fisher's sense, i.e., as the money rate of interest minus the expected rate of change of the price level"), was also "independent of the absolute quantity of money, again in accordance with classical theory." His interest rate function was "only suitable for a limited range of variation of Y_p/M." With exchange rate fixity the domestic money supply (and hence the inflation rate) become endogenously determined; the trade-off operates only within a narrow, low inflation band.

This was exactly how Phillips (1961, 201) described the limits of his model: he was only interested in ranges of values in which actual output (Y) fluctuates around capacity output (Y_n) by a maximum of 5 percent: "In order to reduce the model with money, interest and prices to linear differential equations in x [$=Y/Y_n$], y_n and p it is necessary to express log Y . . . in terms of log Y_n and x. For this purpose we shall use the approximation:

$$\log Y \cong \log Y_n + (Y - Y_n)/Y_n = \log Y_n + x - 1.$$

---

6. Phillips (1958, 243) wrote: ". . . employers will be bidding more vigorously for the services of labor than they would be in a year during which the average percentage unemployment was the same but the demand for labor was not increasing." In Phillips' model, when this "expectation effect" is removed, and demand held constant in the compromise zone, the rightward displacement of Phillips curve observations ceases.

The approximation is very good over the range of values of ($Y - Y_n$) / Y_n, say from −0.05 to 0.05, *in which we are interested* [emphasis added]." Since Phillips (1961, 196) stated that these output fluctuations were "five times as large as the corresponding fluctuations in the proportion of the labor force employed," this clearly indicates that Phillips limited his analysis to outcomes in the compromise zone of plus or minus 1 percentage point deviations of unemployment from normal. Phillips was restating the conclusion of his empirical work; normal capacity output (and approximately zero inflation) was consistent with an unemployment rate "a little under 2½ percent" (1958, 259).

Although Phillips drew an average curve representing the trajectory of the British economy as it swung from bust to boom and back again, at no stage did he suggest that *high* inflation would reduce unemployment for anything other than a temporary period. Yet Phillips' historical investigations had produced an average curve that encompassed 32 percent wage inflation and 22 percent unemployment (1958, 253, figure 25.9). Wage inflation in excess of 27 percent occurred in 1918 and this observation falls on Phillips curve. But Phillips' empirical analysis also reveals that 1918 was followed by two decades of extraordinarily high unemployment—hardly an augury of a stable high inflation trade-off. Phillips did not state or imply that any point on his average curve could be targeted for stabilization purposes.

But underpinning the original Phillips Curve was this argument: "One of the important policy problems of our time is that of maintaining a high level of economic activity and employment *while avoiding a continual rise in prices*" [emphasis added]. Phillips explained that there was "fairly general agreement" that the prevailing rate of 3.7 percent inflation was undesirable: "It has undoubtedly been a major cause of the general weakness of the balance of payments and the foreign reserves, and if continued it would almost certainly make the present rate of exchange untenable." His objective was, if possible, "to prevent continually rising prices of consumer goods while maintaining high levels of economic activity . . . the problem therefore reduces to whether it is possible to prevent the price of labor services, that is average money earnings per man-hour, from rising at more than about 2 percent per year . . . one of the main purposes of this analysis is to consider what levels of demand for labor the monetary and fiscal authorities should seek to maintain in their attempt to reconcile the two main policy objectives of high levels of activity and stable prices. I would question whether it is really in the interests of workers that the average level of hourly earnings should increase more rapidly than the average rate of productivity, say about 2 percent per year" (1959a, 261; 1959b, 269–80; 1962, 208; 1961, 201; 1962, 218; 1958, 259).

Like Phillips, Friedman (1968, 9–11) described the initial expansionary effects of a reduction in unemployment. But when inflation became high enough to influence expectational behavior, Friedman later argued that expansion "describes only the initial effects." Modern macroeconomics has several explanations for the existence of a temporary trade-off (involving monetary misperceptions and inter-temporal substitution). Friedman's version of the Phillips-Friedman-Phelps Critique suggested a temporary trade-off between unanticipated inflation and unemployment lasting two to five years, taking a couple of decades to return to the natural rate of unemployment. Friedman's mechanism involved real wage resistance in response to the initial "simultaneous fall *ex post* in real wages to employers and rise *ex ante* in real wages to employees." Thus real wage resistance plays an equilibrating role in Friedman's version.

Unlike Friedman, Phillips was highly skeptical about equilibrating forces. In a May 21, 1957, Robbins seminar paper on "Stability of 'Self-Correcting' Systems," Phillips examined a system in which the rate of change of prices was proportional to excess demand. Phillips concluded, "If the 'equilibrating forces' are too strong they will make the system unstable . . . The argument extends without difficulty to any system, in which there are 'equilibrating' or 'self-correcting' forces operating through time lags."[7]

Phillips' version of the Phillips-Friedman-Phelps Critique was a far more potent constraint on policymakers than Friedman's version: inflation had far more serious consequences for Phillips than for Friedman. For Friedman, the (purely internal) imbalance corrected itself through utility-maximizing labor supply adjustments, as inflation ceased to be incorrectly anticipated. Only a temporary boom would result, and it would soon be eroded by real wage resistance. But in Phillips' model, external imbalance (driven by only minor inflation differentials) could be addressed by exchange rate adjustment, leaving the internal imbalance in need of still greater attention. In addition, the role Friedman allocated to inflationary expectations was benign, whereas the role allocated to inflationary expectations by Phillips (1954) was far more destabilizing, denying the possibility of a stable target in the presence of such expectations.

---

7. Phillips papers, LSE.

Not only was there "fairly general agreement" (Phillips 1962, 207–8) that non-trivial (3.7 percent) inflation was intolerable, but the assumption of low (but unspecified) and stable inflation rates was commonly invoked by model builders in the pre-stagflation era. For example, the Robert Lucas and Leonard Rapping (1969, 748) model of "Real Wages, Employment and Inflation" was assumed to hold "only under reasonably stable rates of price increase. To define what is meant by reasonable stability, and to discover how expectations are revised when such stability ceases to obtain, seems to us to be a crucial, unresolved problem." Friedman (1968a, 6; 1968b, 21) also stated that the "price expectation effect is slow to develop and also slow to disappear. Fisher estimated that it took several decades for a full adjustment and recent work is consistent with his estimate." Friedman presented evidence about the time it took for "price anticipations" to influence behavior that was "wholly consistent with Fisher's." Phillips' opposition to inflation was axiomatic: an expression of one of the eternal truths that separate economists from monetary cranks. Nevertheless, he clearly stated the assumptions under which small amounts of inflation could be traded-off for small amounts of unemployment in the "compromise" zone. He did not suggest that a permanent trade-off existed outside the compromise zone.

Taylor's work was in this Phillips tradition: "Milton Friedman's (1968) AEA presidential address was given during the middle of my senior year. Since I had a Phillips curve in the model used in my thesis, I am sure I discussed the issue with my advisers. In the thesis I did not exploit the long-run trade-off implicit in the Phillips curve by increasing the money growth rate and the inflation rate permanently to get a permanently higher utilization rate. This could have reflected a judgment that one could not in practice exploit the curve this way, despite what the algebra said. More likely it was simply that I was interested in stabilization policy rules, and such rules, very sensibly, did not even consider such a possibility" (Taylor 2007a).

7.5. A Lucas-style critique

Robert Lucas' original handwritten "Econometric Policy Evaluation" paper was presented at least as early as April 1973 (Sargent 1996, 539, n3). Lucas (1976, 19, 22–3) used the Phillips curve to illustrate the proposition that one of the traditions in economics "is fundamentally in error." Lucas complained that econometricians were averse to inspecting data prior to 1947 and rarely used 1929–46 data as a check on post-war fits. Lucas refers to the "widespread acceptance of a Phillips 'trade-off' in the absence of *any* [emphasis in text] aggregative theoretical model embodying such a relationship." The reason for the urgency behind Lucas' reformulation was to undermine the Phillips curve: ". . . the case for sustained inflation, based entirely on econometric simulations, is attended now with a seriousness it has not commanded for many decades."

The Old Keynesian high inflation Phillips curve supposedly misled the Western world into the inflationary maelstrom of the 1970s (Lucas and Sargent 1978). The 1970s was the decade of "The Death of Keynesian Economics"—and the collapse of the Phillips curve trade-off, its failure to recognize the subtleties of both inflationary expectations and the Lucas Critique playing a major role in this "death rattle" (Sargent 1996, 543). As Lucas (1980, 18; 1981, 560; 1984, 56) put it: ". . . one cannot find good, under-forty economists who identified themselves or their work as Keynesian . . . I, along with many others, was in on the kill in an intellectual sense." According to Lucas, the quarry subjected to this "kill" was the proposition that "permanent inflation will . . . induce a permanent economic high . . . [the] shift of the 'trade-off' relationship to center stage in policy discussions appears primarily due to Phillips (1958) and Samuelson and Solow (1960)" . . . "We got the high-inflation decade, and with it as clear-cut an experimental discrimination as macroeconomics is ever likely to see, and Friedman and Phelps were right. It really is as simple as that" . . . "They went way out on a limb in the late '60s, saying that high inflation wasn't going to give us anything by way of lower unemployment."

Robin Court (2000) and Peter Phillips (2000) have highlighted A. W. H. Phillips' analysis of the relationship between policy control and model identification and the similarity between the equations used by Phillips and Lucas (1976) to derive their conclusions about econometric policy evaluation. Peter Phillips argues that the Phillips Critique implies "that even deep structural parameters may be unrecoverable when the reduced form coefficients are themselves unidentified. One can further speculate on the potential effects of unidentifiable reduced forms on the validity of econometric tests of the Lucas critique . . . [this] may yet have an influence on subsequent research, irrespective of the historical issue of his work on this topic predating that of Lucas (1976)."

Two decades before Lucas, Phillips (1956, 371) stressed, "There are, therefore, two questions to be asked when judging how effective a certain policy would be in attaining any given equilibrium objectives. First, what dynamic properties and cyclical tendencies will the system as a whole possess *when the policy relationships under consideration themselves form part of the system?* [Emphasis added.] Second, when the system has these dynamic properties, will the equilibrium objectives be attained, given the size of the probable disturbances and the permissible limits to movements in employment, foreign reserves, etc.? The answer to the first question is important, not only because the reduction of cyclical tendencies is itself a desirable objective, but also because the second question cannot be answered without knowing the answer to the first. And the first question cannot be answered without knowing the magnitudes and time-forms of the main relationships forming the system."

Phillips stressed the importance of dynamic analysis and taught a course at LSE called Dynamic Process Analysis.[8] The Final Report of the Dynamic Process Analysis Project stated, "It can be fairly claimed that the results obtained from [Phillips'] investigations, taken together, constitute a theoretical solution of the central problem which formed the basis of the project. It is believed that they can be applied directly to control problems arising in fields where fairly long time series are available from systems with stationary stochastic disturbances, for example in chemical manufacturing processes. It has to be admitted that direct applicability to control of an economy is limited by shortness of economic time series and the lack of stationarity of the system. However, the results obtained should provide the basis for valid work in this area." Four years later, these 1963 "admitted" doubts matured into the next stage of Phillips' critique of econometric policy evaluation.

Five months before Friedman's famous AEA Presidential Address, a conference was held in London in July 1967 on Mathematical Model Building in Economics and Industry (shortly before Phillips emigrated to Canberra). Richard Stone (1968) also delivered a paper to the conference. James Meade (2000) recalled that within months of arriving in Australia, Phillips wrote to him "asking whether there would be any chance of getting a position in Cambridge to work with Dick Stone and myself on dynamic macroeconomics again. It all came to nothing

---

8. In the first lecture (October 7, 1960), Phillips stated that he was concerned with "the study of processes which are changing" and the "study of time paths." Stochastic models of the economy were preferable to deterministic models which were ". . . not very adequate [although] better than comparative statics . . . Great simplification necessary to get quantitative dynamic model . . . We have no satisfactory way of checking and testing our models. Magnitude and timing must be estimated and this involves problems in statistical decision theory which are still unsolved." Phillips papers, LSE.

because very soon after he had his stroke ... Perhaps he had some very simple but immensely promising new thoughts on the subject. It is tragic that we will never know." It seems possible that Phillips had given some more thought to his policy evaluation critique, because the only paper that survives from this period (dated July 1972) is the handwritten paper that Court (2000) and Peter Phillips (2000) found to contain a contribution comparable to that later made by Lucas (1976).

Phillips (1968) concluded in his Model Building conference paper, "The possibility that operation of the control may prevent re-estimation of the system should lead us to ask whether the decision analysis we have been considering does not have some fundamental deficiency. And indeed it has. The basic defect is simply that in deriving the decision rules no account was taken of the fact that the parameters of the system are not known exactly, and no consideration was given to ways in which we can improve our knowledge of the system while we are controlling it. In my view it cannot be too strongly stated that in attempting to control economic fluctuations we do not have the two separate problems of estimating the system and of controlling it, we have a single problem of jointly controlling and learning about the system, that is, a problem of learning control or adaptive control."

Taylor (2007a) followed this "learning" path also: ". . . my PhD thesis was on policy rules. The problem was to find a good policy rule in a model where one does not know the parameters and therefore had to estimate them and control the dynamic system simultaneously. An unresolved issue was how much 'experimentation' should be built into the policy rule through which the instrument settings would move around in order to provide more information about the parameters, which would pay off in the future. I proved theorems and did simulations, which showed various convergence properties of the least squares or Bayesian learning rules. My main conclusion from that research, however, was that in many models simply following a rule without special experimentation features was a good approximation. That made future work much simpler of course because it eliminated a great deal of complexity."

8. Rational Expectations Plus Contracts:
the "General Theory" of Policy Rules

From the Lucas critique to the Taylor rule (1976–1992), Taylor had a foot in academia and an almost equally sized foot in the policy apparatus (CEA 1976–77, research adviser at the Philadelphia Fed 1981–84,

CEA 1989–91). These policy experiences led Taylor (1998; 1989b) to propose (in his Harry Johnson lecture) a "translational" theory of policy regime change, in contrast to Johnson-style emphasis on revolution and counter-revolution (Johnson 1971).

Shortly after leaving the CEA, Taylor—with Phelps (Phelps and Taylor 1977) and Fischer (1977)[9]—published a seminal article which rescued from the clutches of the Sargent and Wallace (1975) Policy Ineffectiveness Proposition the "old doctrine" that "systematic monetary policy matters for fluctuation of output and employment." Phelps and Taylor bottled the old wine, so to speak, in a rational expectations model in order to build a better model with which to evaluate monetary policy rules.

Taylor (2007a) was also persuaded by his first CEA experience to revise the Taylor curve paper (Taylor 1979, first draft 1976) to make it "more practical and more useful in practice." That paper had the first empirically realistic monetary policy rule that was calculated with new rational expectations methods. During his first CEA experience, Taylor (2007a) saw the need to "do a better job at explaining the persistence of inflation with rational expectations. That is where the staggered contract model came from." After leaving the CEA, Taylor (1977) wrote about the "incentive structure under which policy decisions are made" and "the fairly vigorous competition for ideas" and began to think systematically about the administrative dynamics of policymaking.

Taylor (2007a) recalled that "The Taylor Curve paper (Taylor 1979) was reviewed favorably at the time by people on both sides of the spectrum (the favorable review from Lucas was certainly a big boost for me), and because it showed that this approach to monetary policy could work in practice, it was a very big development on the road to the Taylor rule. The monetary policy rule in that paper had exactly the same variables on the right-hand side as the eventual Taylor rule. The rule had the objective of minimizing the weighted sum of the variance of output and variance of inflation; it also presented and estimated the first variance trade-off (Taylor Curve) with inflation and output and contained a simple staggered price setting model (laid out in an appendix and covered in much more detail in my 1980 JPE paper). The big difference from the future, of course, was that the money supply was on the left-hand side. The transition from the money supply to the interest rate on the left-hand side of the rule occurred a few years later."

---

9. For a connection between Fischer, Simons, rules, and sticky prices, see section 6.2 above.

Taylor (1999) saw the r-based rule as "complement[ing] the framework provided by the quantity equation of money so usefully employed by Friedman and Schwartz (1963) . . . this actually goes back to the inverted money demand equation in my 1968 paper. Such an inverted equation can generate interest rate behavior with similar characteristics to interest rate rules. When GDP rises, the interest rate also rises, for example. But the coefficients are not usually the same as interest rate rules like the Taylor rule" (Taylor 2007a).

At the Philadelphia Fed, Taylor (1981b, 145) assessed monetarist rules and nominal GNP targeting, concluding that monetarist rules were inefficient relative to a monetarist (no accommodation of inflation)/Keynesian (countercyclical) compromise: ". . . a classic countercyclical monetary policy combined with no accommodation of inflation is efficient." Taylor (2007) recalled: "This was a way for me to emphasize that monetary policy had to react more strongly to both real GDP and inflation. By providing no accommodation to inflation, by keeping money growth constant, in the face of inflation shocks, the central bank would create a larger increase in the interest rate. At the same time, they could also respond aggressively to reduction in real GDP."

With respect to nominal GNP targeting as a "new rule for monetary policy," Taylor (1985, 61, 81) detected merits (". . . the virtue of simplicity. Explaining how it works to policymakers seems easy . . .") and explanatory power (". . . during much of the postwar period, the Fed can be interpreted as having used a type of nominal GNP rule . . .") plus a fundamental flaw ("This rule, when combined with a simple price-adjustment equation, has contributed to the cycle by causing overshooting and 'boom-bust' behavior . . ."). As an alternative he proposed a "new policy rule . . . a modified nominal GNP rule that keeps constant the sum of the inflation rate and the proportional deviations of real output from trend . . . The rule can be generalized to permit less than, or more than, one-to-one reactions of real GNP to inflation, depending on the welfare significance of output fluctuations versus inflation fluctuations."

During his second CEA experience (1989–1991) Taylor co-wrote the February 1990 *Economic Report of the President*. This report (1990, 65, 84, 86, 64, 65, 107) noted that the "simple" (Friedman-style) monetary growth rule had become "unworkable"; it was "inappropriate" to follow "rigid monetary targeting." However, the Fed had "not regressed to an undisciplined, ad hoc approach to policy . . . a purely discretionary approach." Rather, it had "attempted to develop a more systematic, longer-run approach." Policies should be designed to "work well with a minimum of discretion . . . the alternative to discretionary policies might be called systematic policies . . . Unpredictable changes in economic and financial relationships imply that appropriate policy rules in some circumstances are rather general." The February 1990 *Economic Report of the President* was a "translational" play: an opportunity to move the ball toward the rules party goal line (Taylor 1998).

9. Immediate Prelude to the Taylor Rule

After leaving the CEA, Taylor (1993c, xv) returned to his almost-finished monograph on *Macroeconomic Policy in a World Economy: From Econometric Design to Practical Operation,* noting that "this book is considerably different from the book that would have been published three years ago." The Taylor rule must have been reflection-induced as the book was completed (1992): an equation in "Looking for a better monetary policy rule" almost described the Taylor rule (Taylor 1993c, 251).

It is likely that Taylor was influenced in his thinking by a March 1990 Brookings conference on "Evaluating Monetary Policy Regimes: New Research in Empirical Economics."[10] For the conference, participants prepared papers that compared the performance of various policy rules across a variety of models of the world economy—one of which was the multi-country model developed by Taylor and his colleagues at Stanford. While money supply and exchange rate rules were the primary rules considered, Dale Henderson and Warwick McKibbin asked the dozen or so modelers represented at the conference to evaluate interest rate rules. Initially, the interest rate rules that were proposed ran into problems of indeterminacy. Either they violated what came to be known as the Taylor principle—the idea that interest rates should be adjusted more than one-for-one with an increase in inflation—or the algorithms employed at the time may simply not have been adequate to solve the models.

As researchers become more familiar with algorithms for model solution, they found the interest rate rules to perform surprisingly well in a wide variety of models for various countries or regions (Minford, 2008, 333). Dale Henderson and Warwick McKibbin (1993a) described the results in a paper published in a Brookings conference volume

---

10. This paragraph and the next one draw heavily on Minford (2008). See Patrick Minford for further details.

edited by Ralph Bryant, Peter Hooper, and Catherine Mann (1993). Later, they presented another version of the paper at the Carnegie-Rochester conference where Taylor introduced his rule (Henderson and McKibbin 1993b).[11]

In the thirteen months prior to the Carnegie-Rochester conference, four other conferences also appeared to have influenced Taylor's progress toward the rule (the first two provocatively). At the October 25, 1991, Bank of Japan conference on "Price Stabilization in the 1990s," David Laidler (1993, 336, 353) argued that the apparent instability of money demand functions required discretionary offsetting shifts in money supply. Faith that a "legislated, quasi-constitutional" money growth rule would produce price stability now appeared "naïve . . . uncomfortably like those for perpetual motion or a squared circle." Laidler saw the optimal route to price stability through independent central banks: "We are left, then, with relying on discretionary power in order to maintain price stability." Taylor (1993a, 5) noted that "Michael Parkin's oral comments at the conference were consistent with that view, and I think that there was a considerable amount of general agreement at the conference."

In April 1992, Taylor commented on Ben Bernanke's and Frederic Mishkin's (1992) "Central Bank Behavior and the Strategy of Monetary Policy," taking particular exception to the proposition, "Monetary policy rules do not allow the monetary authorities to respond to unforeseen circumstances." Taylor (1992a, 235) argued that "if there is anything we have learned from modern macroeconomics it is that rules need not entail fixed settings as in constant money growth rules." Taylor appeared to be suggesting that Bernanke and Mishkin were leading monetary economics in the wrong direction: their paper "eschews models and technique, [and] endeavors to go directly to a policymaking perspective . . . My experience is that there are far too many policy papers in government that do not pay enough attention to economic models and theory."[12]

---

11. Earlier references in the literature to interest rate rules include Dewald and Johnson (1963), Christian (1968), Fair (1978), and McNees (1986, 1992). Koury (1990) provides a survey of these early rules from the post-war period. Thanks to Ray Fair for pointing out this earlier literature.

12. In September 1992 Ben Bernanke and Alan S. Blinder (1992, 910–912) published a paper with a section entitled "Federal Reserve's Reaction Function" in which they write, "If the Federal funds rate or some related variable is an indicator of the Federal Reserve's policy stance, and if the Fed is purposeful and reasonably consistent in its policymaking, then the funds rate should be systematically related to important macroeconomic target

At a meeting of the Federal Reserve System Committee on Financial Analysis at the St. Louis Fed in June 1992, Taylor (1992b) commented on an early draft of Jeffrey Fuhrer's and George Moore's (1995) "Inflation Persistence." (Fuhrer was senior economist at the Fed's Board of Governors, 1985–92.) Taylor noted that the authors had made "an important contribution to the methodology of monetary policy formulation . . . they look at the response of the economy to a policy rule which they write algebraically, arguing that the functional form comes close to what the Federal Reserve has been using in practice . . . Their results, taken literally, are quite striking. They find that a policy rule that is a fairly close representation of Fed policy for the last eight or ten years is nearly optimal. The rule entails changing the federal funds rate, according to whether the inflation rate is on a target and whether output is on a target. Their results are not very sensitive to the choice of a welfare function. Basically, as long as price stability and output stability are given some weight, movements too far away from this particular rule worsen performance. This is a remarkable result and deserves further research. What are the implications for policy? The literal implication is to keep following that rule . . . It is perhaps too abstract for policymakers to think in terms of a policy rule, but it seems to me that this is the only way to think of implementing or taking seriously the policy implications of the paper."

At the Reserve Bank of Australia conference on "Inflation, Disinflation and Monetary Policy" in July 1992, Taylor (1992c, 9, 13, 15, 26, 29) noted that the historical era of "great" inflation/disinflation was concluding. A repeat of this unfortunate history was unlikely, he said, adding that the intellectual justification for inflation (the Phillips curve trade-off) had been mistaken and based on faulty models. Taylor argued that "the most pressing task is to find good rules for monetary policy—probably with the interest rate as the instrument—that reflect such [short-term inflation-output] trade-offs . . . monetary policy should be designed in the future to keep price and output fluctuations low . . . the recent research on policy rules in this research is very

---

variables like unemployment and inflation." Bernanke and Blinder then present estimated policy reaction functions which "show this to be true . . . The results look like plausible reaction functions. Inflation shocks drive up the funds rate (or the funds rate spread), with the peak effect coming after 5–10 months and then decaying very slowly. Unemployment shocks push the funds rate in the opposite direction, but with somewhat longer lags and smaller magnitudes. To our surprise, these relationships did not break down in the post-1979 period. Reaction functions estimated in the same way for the 1979–1989 period looked qualitatively similar."

promising. There is a need to find ways to characterize good monetary policy as something besides pure discretion."

At the same conference, Charles Goodhart (1992, 326, 324) noted that "unspecified" 1946-era multiple goals had been replaced by a philosophy which was reflected in Article 2 of the Statute of the European System of Central Banks (1992): "The primary objective of the ESCB shall be to maintain price stability." Goodhart pondered about a "backbone brace" rule in which interest rates should rise by 1.5 percent for each 1 percent rise of inflation above zero with a requirement that any divergence from that rule should be formally accounted for by the monetary authorities. But this Goodhart rule was inflation-first-and-foremost-based and possibly "too mechanical."

10. Impact of the Taylor Rule: Macroeconomic Research

The Taylor rule had the side effect of fostering renewed interaction and communication between academic and central bank economists. In the late 1970s and early 1980s, the rational expectations/real business cycle revolution had led many academics to question the effectiveness of activist monetary policy. A communication gap emerged between academic economists studying the propagation of business cycles resulting from productivity shocks in flexible price models and economists at central banks who were still interested in designing stabilization policies in models where monetary policy had real effects.[13]

Two separate developments in economic thought helped close this gap in research agendas, and Taylor played an important role in both. First, models of sticky price and wage adjustment and, later, models of sticky information made activist feedback rules dominate rules without feedback. Taylor's work on long-term wage contracts was seminal in this area. Second, the Taylor rule expressed policy in terms of an interest rate instrument rather than a monetary growth rule. This simple idea helped translate monetary theory into more practical terms. Together, the two developments put academic and central bank economists back on the same research track. Today, economists and economic ideas move freely between academic and central bank research departments.

---

13. An exception to this communications gap was at the Minneapolis Fed, where research on rational expectations and real business cycles flourished during this period.

The literature on Taylor rules is vast and growing. Only a small part of it can be summarized here. The research has been both positive and normative, theoretical and empirical. A wide range of topics has been addressed, including the evaluation of historical monetary policy, the estimation of Taylor rule parameters, the development of more complex—and presumably better—versions of Taylor's rule, and the identification of "optimal" and robust specifications.

10.1. Historical analysis and uncertainty about the output gap

The simplicity of the Taylor rule was quick to be questioned. Bennett T. McCallum (1993) in his discussion of Taylor's 1993 paper pointed out that the rule was not strictly operational because the current quarter output gap could not be observed. Data on current quarter GDP are not released until well into the next quarter. Therefore, to implement the Taylor rule, a policymaker would need first to estimate current-quarter real GDP and the implicit price deflator. Ignoring the lag potentially leads to overstating the performance of a Taylor rule and can potentially generate instrument instability.

Researchers addressed this issue in one of two ways. First, lagged data on output and inflation were substituted for contemporaneous data. This had a limited effect on the fit of the Taylor rule because of the high degree of inertia in output and inflation. Second, researchers incorporated forecasts of output and inflation. This had the appeal of recognizing the forward-looking aspect of monetary policy (even though some have argued that the contemporaneous—or lagged—output gap term is a forward-looking indicator of inflation).

In addition to Taylor's use of his rule to describe monetary policy, a number of researchers have used the Taylor rule to understand monetary policy and macroeconomic performance before and after 1987. For example, John P. Judd and Glenn D. Rudebusch (1998) estimate a version of the Taylor rule over three periods delineated by the terms of three recent Fed chairmen. The authors estimate a version of the Taylor rule allowing for a gradual adjustment of the federal funds rate to their rule's policy prescription, including an additional lagged output gap term to test for possible speed effects and incorporating a structural estimate of potential GDP.

The authors found that movements in the funds rate during Fed Chairman Alan Greenspan's tenure were largely consistent with the

Taylor rule. However, the response of the funds rate to the output gap was more gradual than, but with roughly twice the response of, Taylor's 1993 specification. During the chairmanship of Paul Volcker at the Fed, the authors found their specification fit less precisely, but nevertheless affirmed a gradual movement of the funds rate to bring inflation down over time. In addition, they found policy responding more strongly to the growth rate of GDP as opposed to the level of the output gap. During the Arthur F. Burns chairmanship, the authors found a weak response to inflation. Instead, policy responded mainly to cyclical movements in output, perhaps due to an estimate of potential output that appeared too high.

Along the same lines, Richard Clarida, Jordi Galí, and Mark Gertler (2000) found that policy responded much more aggressively to inflation after the Volcker period than before. Their policy rule incorporated forecasts of output and inflation, a gradual adjustment of the funds rate to the funds rate target, and an estimate of the output gap from the Congressional Budget Office (CBO). They found that the funds rate responds less than one-for-one with expected inflation in the pre-Volcker period but far greater than one-for-one for the post-Volcker period. In addition, the funds rate was sensitive to the output gap in both periods but more so in the pre-Volcker period. The authors speculated that an overly optimistic estimate of potential output or a lack of understanding of inflation dynamics may have led policymakers to maintain the real funds rate at too low a level in the pre-Volcker period.[14]

Athanasios Orphanides (2001; 2003) examined the issue of real-time estimates of the output gap and found that, indeed, policymakers may have been misled by unreliable contemporaneous estimates of the output gap that were later revised. In addition, researchers using revised data for historical analysis may have mischaracterized the real-time policy actions of policymakers. For example, using real-time estimates of the output gap, Orphanides (2003, 984) found that the Taylor rule "serves as a particularly good description of policy . . . both when subsequent economic outcomes were exemplary as well as less than ideal."[15]

---

14. Taylor rules have also been used as the basis for historical monetary analysis in other countries. For example, Ed Nelson (2001) examines Taylor rules for different UK monetary policy regimes. Cecchetti, Hooper, Kasman, Schoenholtz, and Watson (2007) examine the historical fit of Taylor rules in Germany, the United Kingdom, Japan, and the United States.

15. Taylor (2000), in commenting on a paper by Orphanides at the American Economic Association meetings, questioned the view that policymakers based decisions on faulty offi-

The implication of Orphanides' research was that the Taylor rule was useful for historical analysis if the researcher was careful to use only information available at the time policy was made. Moreover, policymakers who followed the Taylor rule were not guaranteed good macroeconomic performance. Because of uncertainty about real-time estimates of the output gap, policymakers should down-weight the output gap as a factor in adjusting the funds rate or adopt a first-difference version of the Taylor rule. Assuming potential GDP grows at a fairly constant rate, first-differencing the Taylor rule would eliminate the need to estimate the output gap.[16]

Robert Hall (2005, 138) went even further. He rejected the idea that the business cycle could be separated from longer-run trend movements in the economy. "Only an elaborate, realistic version of the [real business cycle] model can deliver values of [potential output] and [the equilibrium real rate] that take proper account of the movements of productivity and exogenous spending. Even that model does not know how to deal with movements of unemployment." Thus, he suggested a first-difference policy rule in which policymakers would raise the nominal rate from its earlier value only when inflation threatened to exceed its target—without regard to the tenuous and difficult-to-estimate concepts of equilibrium real rates or output gaps.

10.2. "Optimal" policy rules

Taylor (1993a, 202) chose a specification for the Taylor rule that reflected "the general properties of the rules that have emerged from recent research," picking round numbers for the rule's coefficients that make for easy discussion. Other researchers have computed policy rules that are optimal with respect to a particular macroeconomic model and loss function. The loss function describes the objectives of the central

---

cial estimates of the output gap. Taylor argued that there was no record of a potential series produced at the Fed in the 1960s and 1970s, so it is not clear what measure of the output gap influenced Fed policymakers at the time. Moreover, "potential GDP and its growth rate became politicized as early as the late 1960s" and "serious economic analysts—like Burns and Greenspan—paid no attention to it." Economists at the time were skeptical about data series that indicated "a GDP gap of 15 percent in the mid-1970s—comparable to the Great Depression!" and knew that "the revision in 1977 was still too small." Finally, Taylor noted that the historical "concept of potential GDP was a max not a mean."

16. Taylor (2000) also cautioned against reacting to only real GDP growth and not its level. Focusing only on real GDP growth could lead to overshooting, where "policy is too easy when [the] economy is way above capacity and growing at [the] potential growth rate," or undershooting, where "policy is too tight when [the] economy is below capacity and growing at [the] potential growth rate."

bank, typically penalizing volatility in output, inflation, and sometimes the policy interest rate. Still other researchers have computed rules that maximize a representative agent's welfare in a typically small dynamic stochastic general equilibrium model.

The papers published in the 1999 conference volume edited by Taylor provide examples of both strategies for estimating optimal rules in the context of an economic model or models. As summarized by Christopher Sims (2001, 562), the papers reach the following general conclusions: Taylor rules that fit the post-1982 data perform well in most of the models. However, the variability of output and inflation can be reduced further by increasing the size of the coefficients on inflation and the output gap in the Taylor rule.[17] An optimized policy rule with a delay of one quarter in the response of policy to inflation and the output gap is almost as good as a rule with no delay. Simple rules perform almost as well as more complicated rules. And rules in which the change in the interest rate—as opposed to its level—is related to inflation and the output gap perform better than the original Taylor specification. Sims criticizes the papers for their lack of attention to statistical fit, their unquestioned assumption that policy has improved over the postwar period, the reliance on sticky-price models derived from optimizing monopolistic competition to justify price equations, and the focus on policy "as a 'rule' analogous to the decision rules of dynamic optimization" (p. 563).

10.3. Robustness

Another important area of research in the Taylor rule literature is the search for policy rules that are robust across a variety of structural macroeconomic models. Given uncertainty about the true structure of the economy, a key test of a policy rule is that it delivers favorable macroeconomic outcomes in a wide variety of models. Again, the papers in the 1999 Taylor conference volume provide evidence on this issue. Five different interest rate rules were evaluated across nine different models drawn from the papers in the conference volume. The rules varied the weights placed on the response of the policy rate to inflation, the output gap, and the lagged policy rate.

---

17. An exception is the rule recommended in the paper by Rotemberg and Woodford. This rule, which maximizes the welfare of the representative agent, puts a small weight on output and a very high weight on the lagged interest rate.

The comparison of policy rules across models yielded several findings. First, the result that a higher weight on the output gap improved macroeconomic performance was not robust across all models. While a higher weight on output led to less output variance in all models, it was associated with greater inflation variance in six of the nine models and greater interest rate variability in seven of eight models that reported interest rate variances. Second, rules with lagged interest rates did not dominate rules without a lagged interest rate. And third, lagged interest rate rules worked best in models with forward-looking behavior and rational expectations. Rules with lagged interest rates sometimes exhibited instability or extraordinarily high variances of output and inflation in backward-looking models.

Another, more recent, study (Andrew Levin and John Williams, 2003) examined the robustness of policy rules across non-nested models with varying assumptions about expectations formation and differing degrees of persistence of aggregate spending and inflation. The authors find that robust rules obtain only when the objective function places substantial weight on both output and inflation stabilization. A robust rule does not exist if the policymaker places no weight on output stabilization.

10.4. Taylor rules in small open economies

While most research on the Taylor rule has focused on closed economies, some researchers have looked at its applicability to small open economies. For example, recognizing the exchange rate as both an instrument and a channel of monetary policy, Laurence Ball (1999) modified the Taylor rule in two ways. First, he defined the policy variable—a monetary conditions index (MCI)—as a linear combination of the exchange rate and interest rate. And second, his measure of inflation was modified to filter out the direct effects of exchange rate fluctuations. Ball found that the weight on the exchange rate in the MCI in his version of the Taylor rule should be equal to or slightly greater than the exchange rate's relative effect on spending.

In contrast, Douglas Laxton and Paolo Pesenti (2003), using the IMF's Global Economic Model, found that there is only a very small role—if any—for the exchange rate to play in open economies "even when there are significant adjustment costs to export prices and short-run pass-through is relatively low. It may even be counterproductive for monetary policy to react strongly to movements in the exchange rate, the information content of which is already captured by either current or expected CPI inflation." Instead, policy should follow a simple rule that responds strongly to the forecast of inflation (pp. 1142–43).

10.5. Other issues

In the last five years, research on the Taylor rule has continued to flourish. A partial list of topics includes: conditions under which Taylor rules lead to a unique stable equilibrium, conditions under which it may be necessary or desirable to deviate from rule-like behavior, the use of forecast-based rules versus backward-looking rules, the generalization of Taylor rules to allow for regime switching or time variation in the rule's coefficients, the desirability of instrument rules versus target rules in central bank decision-making and communications, the variability of equilibrium real rates and their impact on the Taylor rule, and the role of asset prices in policy rules.

11. Concluding remarks

This paper has described an important component of the transformation that swept through the monetary policy landscape in a remarkably few years following the abandonment of monetary targeting. The Taylor rule became an operational framework for central banks just as time-consistency (credibility), transparency, and independence replaced a culture of discretion, "mystique," and "democracy" (i.e., politically driven or influenced monetary policy). The dynamics of macroeconomic policy formation are as important as conventional macroeconomic dynamics. This paper has attempted to illuminate aspects of that dynamic process.

REFERENCES

Akerlof, George A. 1982. "A Personal Tribute and a Few Reflections." In Feiwel 1982.

Arrow, Kenneth J., and Marc Nerlove. 1958. "A Note on Expectations and Stability." *Econometrica* 26:297–305.

Asso, Pier Francesco. 1994. "The Economist as Preacher: The Correspondence between Irving Fisher and Benito Mussolini and Other Letters on the Fisher Plan." In *Research in the History of Economic Thought and Methodology*, ed. Warren J. Samuels. Greenwich, CT: JAI Press.

Bagehot, Walter. 1873. *Lombard Street. A Description of the Money Market.* London: Henry S. King.

Ball, Laurence. 1999. "Policy Rules for Open Economies." In *Monetary Policy Rules*, ed. John Taylor, 127–56. Chicago: University of Chicago Press.

Bernanke, Ben S., and Alan S. Blinder. 1992. "The Federal Funds Rate and the Channels of Monetary Transmission." *American Economic Review*, September: 901–22.

Bernanke, Ben S., Thomas Laubach, Frederic Mishkin, and Adam S. Posen. 1999. *Inflation Targeting: Lessons from the International Experience.* Princeton, NJ: Princeton University Press.

Bernanke, Ben S., and Frederic Mishkin. 1992. "Central Bank Behavior and the Strategy of Monetary Policy: Observations from Six Industrialized Countries." *NBER Macroeconomics Annual.* Cambridge, MA: MIT Press.

Bernstein, Michael A. 2001. *A Perilous Progress: Economists and Public Purpose in Twentieth-Century America.* Princeton, NJ: Princeton University Press.

Bloomfield, Arthur I. 1959. *Monetary Policy Under the International Gold Standard: 1880–1914.* New York: Federal Reserve Bank of New York.

Blundell-Wignall, Adrian, ed. 1992. *Inflation, Disinflation and Monetary Policy.* Proceedings of a Conference, Reserve Bank of Australia, Sydney.

Brown, Henry Phelps, and Bernard Weber. 1953. "Accumulation, Productivity and Distribution in the British Economy 1870–1938." *Economic Journal,* June: 263–88.

Brunner, Karl, and Allan H. Meltzer, eds. 1976. *The Phillips Curve and Labour Markets*, Carnegie-Rochester Conference Series on Public Policy, vol. 1. Amsterdam: North-Holland Publishing Co.

Bryant, Ralph C., Peter Hooper, and Catherine L. Mann., eds. 1993. *Evaluating Policy Regimes: New Research in Empirical Macroeconomics.* Washington, DC: Brookings Institution Press.

Cairncross, Alexander. 1978. "Keynes and the Planned Economy." In Thirlwall 1978.

Cagan, Phillip. 1956. "The Monetary Dynamics of Hyperinflation." In Friedman 1956.

———. "Phillips' Adaptive Inflationary Expectations Formula." In Leeson 2000, 22.

Clinton, Kevin. 2006. "Wicksell at the Bank of Canada." Queen's Economics Department, Working Paper no. 1087, n. 6.

Cecchetti, Steven F., Peter Hooper, Bruce Kasman, Kermit Schoenholtz, and Mark W. Watson. 2007. *Understanding the Evolving Inflation Process.* Report presented to the U.S. Monetary Policy Forum, July.

Christian, James W. 1968. "A Further Analysis of the Objectives of American Monetary Policy." *Journal of Finance* 23:465–77.

Clarida, Richard, Jordi Galí, and Mark Gertler. 2000. "Monetary Policy Rules and Macroeconomic Stability: Evidence and Some Theory." *Quarterly Journal of Economics* 115 (February): 147–80.

Court, Robin. 2000. "The Lucas Critique: Did Phillips Make a Comparable Contribution?" In Leeson 2000, 460.

Croome, David R., and Harry G. Johnson, eds. 1970. *Money in Britain 1959–1969.* London: Oxford University Press.

Currie, Lauchlin. 1933. "Member Bank Reserves and Bank Debits." *Quarterly Journal of Economics* 47 (February): 349–356.

De Cecco, Marcello. 1984. *The International Gold Standard: Money and Empire.* Oxford: Frances Pinter.

Dewald, William G., and Harry G. Johnson. 1963. "An Objective Analysis of the Objectives of American Monetary Policy, 1952–61." In *Banking and Monetary Studies,* ed. Deane Carson, 171–89. Homewood, IL: Richard D. Irwin.

Dorrance, Graeme. 2000. "Early Reactions to Mark I and II." In Leeson 2000, 115.

Economic Report of the President. 1990. Washington, DC: U.S. Government Printing Office.

Edie, Lionel D. 1931. *The Banks and Prosperity.* New York: Harper and Bros.

Eltis, Walter. 2001. "Lord Overstone and the Establishment of British Nineteenth-Century Monetary Orthodoxy." University of Oxford, Discussion Papers in Economic and Social History, no. 42, December.

Fair, Ray. 1978. "The Sensitivity of Fiscal Policy Effects to Assumptions about the Behavior of the Federal Reserve." *Econometrica* 46:1165–79.

Federal Open Market Committee. 1995—2001. Transcripts of FOMC meetings, various issues, http://www.federalreserve.gov/fomc/transcripts.

Feiwel, George R., ed. 1982. *Samuelson and Neoclassical Economics.* Boston: Kluwer.

Fischer, Stanley. 1977. "Long-Term Contracts, Rational Expectations and the Optimal Money Supply Rule." *Journal of Political Economy,* February, 191–206. Reprinted in *Rational Expectations and Econometric Practice,* eds. Robert E. Lucas and Thomas Sargent. Minneapolis: University of Minnesota Press, 1981.

Fisher, Irving. 1911. *The Purchasing Power of Money.* New York: MacMillan.

———. 1920. *Stabilizing the Dollar.* New York: MacMillan.

Friedman, Milton. 1946. "Lange on Price Flexibility and Employment: A Methodological Criticism." *American Economic Review* 36. Repr. in *Essays in Positive Economics.* Chicago: University of Chicago Press, 1953: 277–300.

————.1950. "Wesley C. Mitchell as an Economic Theorist." *Journal of Political Economy* 58:6 (December): 465–493.

————.ed. 1956. *Studies in the Quantity Theory of Money.* Chicago: University of Chicago Press.

————. 1957. *A Theory of the Consumption Function.* Princeton, NJ: Princeton University Press.

————. 1958. "The Supply of Money and Changes in Prices and Output." In Lehman 1958.

————. 1962. *Price Theory: A Provisional Text.* Chicago: Aldine.

————. 1966a. "What Price Guideposts?" In Shultz and Aliber 1966.

————. 1966b. "An Inflationary Recession." *Newsweek,* October 17.

————. 1968. "The Role of Monetary Policy." *American Economic Review* 58:1–17.

————. 1976. *Price Theory.* Chicago: Aldine.

————. 1977. "Inflation and Unemployment: Nobel Lecture." *Journal of Political Economy* 85(3):451–472.

————. and Schwartz, Anna J. 1963. *A Monetary History of the United States, 1867–1960.* Princeton, NJ: Princeton University Press.

Fuhrer, Jeffrey, and George Moore. 1995. "Inflation Persistence." *Quarterly Journal of Economics* 110(1) (February): 127–159.

Giannini, Curzio. 2004. *L'età delle banche centrali.* Bologna: Il Mulino.

Goodhart, Charles A. E. 1988. *The Evolution of Central Banks.* Cambridge, MA: MIT Press.

————. 1992. "The Objectives for, and Conduct of, Monetary Policy in the 1990s." In Blundell-Wignall 1992.

Hall, Robert. 2005. "Separating the Business Cycle from Other Economic Fluctuations." *The Greenspan Era: Lessons for the Future,* a symposium sponsored by the Federal Reserve Bank of Kansas City, Jackson Hole, Wyoming, August: 133–79.

Hansen, Alvin. 1931. "Discussion." In Wright 1932.

————. 1964. *Business Cycles and National Income.* New York: W.W. Norton & Company.

————, and Charles P. Kindleberger. 1942. The Economic Tasks of the Post-war World. *Foreign Affairs*: 466–476.

Henderson, Dale W., and Warwick McKibbin. 1993a. "An Assessment of Some Basic Monetary Policy Regime Pairs: Analytical and Simulation Results from Simple Multi-Region Macroeconomic Models." In Bryant, Hooper, and Mann, 1993: 45–218.

————. 1993b. "A Comparison of Some Basic Monetary Policy Regimes for Open Economies: Implications of Different Degrees of Instrument Adjustment and Wage Persistence." *Carnegie-Rochester Conference Series on Public Policy* 39 (December): 221–317.

Humphrey, Thomas M. 1974. "The Quantity Theory of Money: Its Historical Evolution and Role in Policy Debates." The Federal Reserve Bank of Richmond *Economic Review*, May/June.

Johnson, Harry G. 1970. "Recent Developments in Monetary Theory—A Commentary." In Croome and Johnson 1970.

Judd, John P., and Glenn D. Rudebusch. 1998. "Taylor's Rule and the Fed: 1970–1997." The Federal Reserve Bank of San Francisco *Economic Review* 3: 3–16.

Kalecki, Michel. 1954. *Theory of Economic Dynamics*. London: George Allen & Unwin.

Kendall, Maurice, ed. 1968. *Mathematical Model Building in Economics and Industry*. London: Charles Griffin.

Keynes, John Maynard. 1931. "An Economic Analysis of Unemployment." In Wright 1932.

———. 1936. *The General Theory of Employment, Interest, and Money*. London: Macmillan.

Khoury, Salwa S. 1990. "The Federal Reserve Reaction Function: A Specification Search." In *The Political Economy of American Monetary Policy*, ed. Thomas Mayer, 27–49. Cambridge: Cambridge University Press.

Klamer, Arjo. 1984. *Conversations with Economists*. New Jersey: Rowman & Allanheld.

Laidler, David. 1993. "Hawtrey, Harvard and the Origins of the Chicago Tradition." *Journal of Political Economy* 101 (December): 1068–1103.

———. 2002. "Rules, Discretion and Financial Crises, in Classical and Neoclassical Monetary Economics." *Economic Issues* 7(2):11–33.

Lawrence, Joseph S. 1928. *The Stabilization of Prices*. New York: Macmillan.

Laxton, Douglas, and Paolo Pesenti. 2003. "Monetary Rules for Small, Open, Emerging Economies." *Journal of Monetary Economics* 50(5) (July): 1109–46.

Leeson, Robert, ed. 2000. *A. W. H. Phillips: Collected Works in Contemporary Perspective*. Cambridge: Cambridge University Press.

———. Forthcoming. "The Insights of the Moniac: Innovation and Stabilization in the Phillips Machine Model of the Macroeconomy." *Economia Politica*.

Lehman, John, ed. 1958. *The Relationship of Prices to Economic Stability and Growth*. Papers Submitted before the Joint Economic Committee. Washington, DC: U.S. Government Printing Office.

Levin, Andrew T., and John C. Williams. 2003. "Robust Monetary Policy with Competing Reference Models." *Journal of Monetary Economics* 50(5) (July): 945–82.

Lipsey, Richard G. 1960. "The Relation Between Unemployment and the Rate of Change of Money Wage Rates in the United Kingdom 1862–1957: A Further Analysis." *Economica* 27 (February): 456–87.

Lucas, Robert E. 1976. "Econometric Policy Evaluation: A Critique." In Brunner and Meltzer 1976.

———. 1980. "The Death of Keynesian Economics." *Issues and Ideas,* Winter: 18–19.

———. 1981. "Tobin and Monetarism: A Review Article." *Journal of Economic Literature* 19 (June): 558–67.

———. 1984. "Robert E. Lucas, Jr." In Klamer 1984.

———, and Thomas Sargent. 1978. "After Keynesian Macroeconomics" and "Response to Friedman." In *After the Phillips Curve: Persistence of High Inflation and High Unemployment.* Boston: Federal Reserve Bank of Boston.

———, and Leonard A. Rapping. 1969. "Real Wages, Employment and Inflation." *Journal of Political Economy* 77 (5) (October): 721–54.

McCallum, Bennett T. 1993. "Discretion and Policy Rules in Practice: Two Critical Points." *Carnegie-Rochester Conference Series on Public Policy* 39 (Autumn): 215–20.

———. 1999. "Issues in the Design of Monetary Policy Rules." In *Handbook of Macroeconomics vol. 1c,* eds. John B. Taylor and Michael Woodford. Amsterdam: North-Holland.

McNees, Stephen K. 1986. "Modeling the Fed: A Forward-Looking Monetary Policy Reaction Function." *New England Economic Review,* November/December: 3–8.

———. 1992. "A Forward-Looking Monetary Policy Reaction Function: Continuity and Change." *New England Economic Review,* November/December: 3–13.

McKinnon, Ronald I. 1993. "The Rules of the Game: International Money in Historical Perspective." *Journal of Economic Literature,* March: 1–44.

Meade, James E. 2000. "The Versatile Genius." In Leeson 2000, 18.

Meltzer, Allan H. 2003. *A History of the Federal Reserve, vol. 1, 1913–1951.* Chicago: University of Chicago Press.

Metzler, Lloyd A. 1941. The Nature and Stability of Inventory Cycles. *Review of Economic Statistics:* 113–29.

Mill, John Stuart. 1821. *Elements of Political Economy.* London: Baldwin, Cradock & Joy.

Minford, Patrick. 2008. "Commentary." Federal Reserve Bank of St. Louis *Review,* 90(4) (July/August): 331–38.

Muth, John F. 1961. "Rational Expectations and the Theory of Price Movements." *Econometrica* 29:315–335.

Nelson, Edward. 2001. *UK Monetary Policy 1972–97: A Guide Using Taylor Rules.* Centre for Economic Policy Research, Discussion Paper Series, No. 2931, August.

Nerlove, Marc. 1958. "Adaptive Expectations and the Cobweb Phenomena." *Quarterly Journal of Economics* 72: 227–40.

————. David M. Grether, and José L. Caravalho. 1979. *Analysis of Economic Time Series: A Synthesis.* New York: Academic Press.

Orphanides, Athanasios. 2001. "Monetary Policy Rules Based on Real-Time Data." *American Economic Review* 91(4) (September): 964–85.

————. 2003. "Historical Monetary Policy Analysis and the Taylor Rule." *Journal of Monetary Economics* 50(5) (July): 983–1022.

————. 2007. "Taylor Rules." *Finance and Economics Discussion Series.* Board of Governors of the Federal Reserve, No. 2007–18, January.

Overstone, Lord. 1857. *Tracts and Other Publications on Metallic and Paper Currency.* Ed. J. R. McCulloch. London: Longman, Brown and Co.

Patinkin, Don. 1969. "The Chicago Tradition, The Quantity Theory, And Friedman." *Journal of Money, Credit and Banking* 1(1) (February): 46–70.

————. 1993. "Irving Fisher and his Compensated Dollar Plan." The Federal Reserve Bank of Richmond *Economic Quarterly* 79(3) (Summer).

Phelps, Edmund, and John B. Taylor. 1977. "Stabilizing Powers of Monetary Policy under Rational Expectations." *The Journal of Political Economy* 85(1) (February): 163–190.

Phillips, A. W. 1950. "Mechanical Models in Economic Dynamics." In Leeson 2000, 68.

————. 1954a. "Michel Kalecki's *Theory of Economic Dynamics: An Essay on Cyclical and Long-Run Changes in the Capitalist Economy*: a review." In Leeson 2000, 186.

————. 1954b. "Stabilisation Policy in a Closed Economy." In Leeson 2000, 134.

————. 1956. "Some notes on the estimation of time-forms of reactions in interdependent dynamic systems." In Leeson 2000, 370.

————. 1957. "Stabilisation policy and the time-forms of lagged responses." In Leeson 2000, 169.

————. 1958. "The Relation between Unemployment and the Rate of Change of Money Wage Rates in the United Kingdom, 1861–1957." In Leeson 2000, 243.

————. 1959a. "Discussion of Dicks-Mireaux and Dow's 'The Determinants of Wage Inflation: United Kingdom, 1946–1956.'" In Leeson 2000, 261.

————. 1959b. "Wage Changes and Unemployment in Australia, 1947–1958." In Leeson 2000, 269.

————. 1961. "A simple model of employment, money and prices in a growing economy." In Leeson 2000, 195.

————. 1962. "Employment, Inflation, and Growth." In Leeson 2000, 207.

————. 1968. "Models for the Control of Economic Fluctuations." In Leeson 2000, 468.

————. 1972. "The Last Paper: A Foreshadowing of the Lucas Critique?" In Leeson 2000, 479.

Phillips, Peter. 2000. "The Bill Phillips Legacy of Continuous Time Modelling and Econometric Model Design." In Leeson 2000, 342.

————. 1972. "The Last Paper: A Foreshadowing of the Lucas Critique?" In Leeson 2000, 479.

Phillips, Peter. 2000. "The Bill Phillips Legacy of Continuous Time Modelling and Econometric Model Design." In Leeson 2000, 342.

Rees, Albert. 1970. "The Phillips Curve as a Menu of Policy Choice." *Economica* August: 223–38.

Ricardo, David. 1809. "Three Letters on the Price of Gold Contributed to the Morning Chronicle in August-November 1809." In *The Works and Correspondence of David Ricardo*, 11 volumes, eds. Piero Sraffa and M.H. Dobb, 1951–73. Cambridge: Cambridge University Press.

Rousseas, Stephen W., ed. 1968. *Inflation: Its Causes, Consequences and Control*. Wilton, CT: Calvin K. Kazanjian Economics Foundation.

Rotemberg, Julio J., and Michael Woodford. 1999. "Interest Rate Rules in an Estimated Sticky Price Model." In *Monetary Policy Rules*, ed. John B. Taylor, 57–119. Chicago: University of Chicago Press.

Samuelson, Paul A., and Robert Solow. 1960. "Analytical Aspects of Anti-Inflation Policy." *American Economic Review* May: 177–204.

Sargent, Thomas. 1996. "Expectations and the Non-Neutrality of Lucas." *Journal of Monetary Economics* 37:553–548.

———— and Neil Wallace. 1975. "'Rational Expectations,' the Optimal Monetary Instrument and the Optimal Money Supply Rule." *Journal of Political Economy* 83(2) (April): 241–54.

Shultz, George P., and Robert Z. Aliber, eds. 1966. *Guidelines, Informal Controls, and the Market Place*. Chicago: University of Chicago Press.

Selden, Richard T. 1962. *The Postwar Rise in the Velocity of Money: A Sectoral Analysis*. Cambridge, MA: National Bureau of Economic Research.

Simons, Henry C. 1933. "Mercantilism as Liberalism. A Review Article on *America Faces the Future*, ed. Charles A. Beard." *Journal of Political Economy* 41(4) (August): 548–51.

————. 1934. *A Positive Program for Laissez Faire. Some Proposals for a Liberal Economic Policy*. Public Policy Pamphlet no. 15. Chicago: University of Chicago Press.

————. 1936. "Rules versus Authorities in Monetary Policy." *Journal of Political Economy* 44(1) (February): 1–30.

————. 1939. "Review of *Full Recovery or Stagnation?* by Alvin Harvey Hansen." *Journal of Political Economy* 47(2) (April): 272–276.

————. 1944. "The US Holds the Cards." *Fortune*, September: 156–159 and 196–200.

————. 1945. "The Beveridge Program: An Unsympathetic Interpretation." *Journal of Political Economy* 53(3) (September): 212–33.

Sims, Christopher. 2001. "A Review of Monetary Policy Rules." *Journal of Economic Literature* 39(2) (June): 562–66.

Smith, Adam. 1776. *An Inquiry into the Nature and Causes of the Wealth of Nations.* London: Methuen & Co.

Snyder, Carl. 1924. "New Measures in the Equation of Exchange." *American Economic Review* 14 (December): 699–713.

Solow, Robert. 1968. "Recent Controversy on the Theory of Inflation: An Eclectic View." In Rousseas 1968.

———. 1978. "Summary and Evaluation." In *After the Phillips Curve: Persistence of High Inflation and High Unemployment.* Conference series. Boston: Federal Reserve Bank of Boston.

Stevens, Glenn. 1992. "Inflation and Disinflation in Australia: 1950–1991." In Blundell-Wignall 1992.

Stigler, George. 1941. Review of *Anticipations, Uncertainty and Dynamic Planning* by Albert G. Hart.. *American Economic Review,* June: 358–9.

Stone, J. R. N. (Richard). 1968. "Economic and Social Modelling." In Kendall 1968.

Swade, Doron. 2000. "The Phillips Machine and the History of Computing." In Leeson 2000, 120.

Taylor, John B. 1968. *Fiscal and Monetary Stabilization Policies in a Model of Endogenous Cyclical Growth.* Princeton, NJ: Princeton Econometric Research Program Series, October.

———. 1977. "The Determinants of Economic Policy with Rational Expectations." *Proceedings of IEEE Conference on Decision and Control,* December.

———. 1979. "Estimation and Control of a Macroeconomic Model with Rational Expectations." *Econometrica* 47(5):1267–86.

———.1980. "Aggregate Dynamics and Staggered Contracts." *Journal of Political Economy* 88 (1) (February): 1–23.

———.1981a. Review of *Macroeconomic Theory* by Thomas J. Sargent. *Journal of Monetary Economics,* September: 139–142.

———. 1981b. "Stabilization, Accommodation, and Monetary Rules." *American Economic Review, Papers and Proceedings* 71(2) (May 1981): 145–49.

———. 1985. "What Would Nominal GNP Targeting Do to the Business Cycle?" *Carnegie-Rochester Conference Series on Public Policy* 22. Amsterdam: North-Holland.

———. 1989a. "The Evolution of Ideas in Macroeconomics." *The Economic Record* 65 (June): 185–89.

———. 1989b. "Policy Analysis with a Multicountry Model." In *Macroeconomics Policies in an Interdependent World,* eds. Ralph C. Bryant, David A. Currie, Jacob A. Frenkel, Paul R. Masson, and Richard Portes, 122–41. International Monetary Fund, 1989.

———. 1992a. Comment on "Central Bank Behavior and the Strategy of Monetary Policy: Observations from Six Industrialized Countries," by Ben Bernanke and Frederic Mishkin. *NBER Macroeconomics Annual*: 234–37. Cambridge, MA.: MIT Press.

———. 1992b. Comments on "Inflation Persistence" by Jeffrey Fuhrer and George Moore. Federal Reserve Bank of St. Louis, June.

———. 1992c. "The Great Inflation, the Great Disinflation, and Policies for Future Price Stability." In Blundell-Wignall 1992.

———. 1993a. "Discretion Versus Policy Rules in Practice." *Carnegie-Rochester Conference Series on Public Policy* 39 (December): 195–214.

———. 1993b. "Comments on *Evaluating Policy Regimes: New Research on Empirical Macroeconomics*." In Bryant, Hooper, and Mann 1993.

———. 1993c. *Macroeconomic Policy in a World Economy: From Econometric Design to Practical Operation*. New York: W.W. Norton & Company.

———. 1998. "Applying Academic Research on Monetary Policy Rules: An Exercise in Translational Economics." The Harry G. Johnson Lecture, *The Manchester School Supplement* 66, June 1998. Blackwell Publishers: 1–16.

———. 1999. "An Historical Analysis of Monetary Policy Rules." In *Monetary Policy Rules*, ed. John B. Taylor. Chicago: University of Chicago Press.

———. 2000. "Comments on Athanasios Orphanides' 'The Quest for Prosperity Without Inflation.'" PowerPoint presentation to the American Economic Association meetings, January. http://www.stanford.edu/~johntayl/PptLectures/CommentsOnAthanosiosOrphanides+(Jan+2000).ppt.

———. 2007a. Interview with Robert Leeson.

———. 2007b. "Housing and Monetary Policy." Paper presented at the Federal Reserve Bank of Kansas City's Symposium on "Housing, Housing Finance, and Monetary Policy," Jackson Hole, Wyoming, August.

———. 2007c. "Thirty-five Years of Model Building for Monetary Policy Evaluation: Breakthroughs, Dark Ages and a Renaissance." *Journal of Money, Credit and Banking* 39(1): 193–201.

Thirlwall, Anthony P. 1978. *Keynes and Laissez-faire*. London: Macmillan.

Thornton, Henry. 1802. *An Inquiry into the Nature and Effects of the Paper Credit of Great Britain*. London: Hatchard.

Tinbergen, Jan. 1956. *Economic Policy: Principles and Design*. Amsterdam: North-Holland.

Tobin, James. 1968. "Discussion." In Rousseas 1968.

———. 1972. "Inflation and Unemployment." *American Economic Review* 62(1) (March): 1–18.

Vines, David. 2000. "The Phillips Machine as a 'Progressive' Model." In Leeson 2000, 39.

Volckart, Oliver. 2007. "Rules, Discretion or Reputation? Monetary Policy and the Efficiency of Financial Markets in Germany, 14th to 16th Centuries." SBS 649, Discussion Papers, n. 007.

Wicksell, Knut. 1898. *Interest and Prices. A Study of the Causes Regulating the Value of Money*. English translation, London: Macmillan, 1936.

Wright, Quincy, ed. 1932. *Unemployment as a World-Problem*. Chicago: University of Chicago Press.

Yamey, Basil S. 2000. "The Famous Phillips Curve Article: A Note on its Publication." In Leeson 2000, 335.

TWO

THE TAYLOR RULE
AND THE PRACTICE OF
CENTRAL BANKING

George A. Kahn

I. Introduction

The Taylor rule has revolutionized the way many policymakers at central banks think about monetary policy. It has framed the conduct of policy as a systematic response to incoming information about economic conditions, as opposed to a period-by-period optimization problem. It has emphasized the importance of adjusting policy rates more than one-for-one in response to an increase in inflation. And various versions of the Taylor rule have been incorporated into macroeconomic

George A. Kahn is a vice president and economist at the Federal Reserve Bank of Kansas City. This paper draws in part on "The Taylor Rule and the Transformation of Monetary Policy," Federal Reserve Bank of Kansas City Research Working Paper No. 07–11, and "The Taylor Rule and the Practice of Central Banking," Federal Reserve Bank of Kansas City Working Paper No. 10–05, which in turn are based on a paper prepared for presentation at the Federal Reserve Bank of Dallas's conference on "John Taylor's Contribution to Monetary Theory and Policy." The author thanks Francesco Asso, Dale Henderson, Robert Leeson, John Taylor, participants at the Dallas Fed conference, and participants at the Egyptian Banking Institute/Bank of England conference on "Inflation Dynamics and Monetary Policy" and the seventh Norges Bank Monetary Policy Conference on "The Use of Simple Rules as Guides for Policy Decisions." Ethan Struby provided research assistance. The views expressed in this chapter are those of the author and not necessarily those of the Federal Reserve Bank of Kansas City or the Federal Reserve System.

models that are used at central banks to understand and forecast the economy.

As documented by Francesco Asso and Robert Leeson in the previous chapter, the Taylor rule evolved from a long intellectual history that debated the merits of rules versus discretion. But it was John Taylor who, at the November 1992 Carnegie-Rochester Conference on Public Policy (1993), articulated a rule that gave rise to a new way of thinking about monetary policy among policymakers at central banks. The rule recommended that policymakers set the nominal federal funds rate as a function of deviations of inflation from target and deviations of the level of real GDP from trend GDP. With Taylor's parameterization calling for an inflation target of 2 percent, an equilibrium real federal funds rate of 2 percent, and equal weights of .5 on inflation and output deviations, the rule took the following form:

$$ffr = 2 + p + .5(p - 2) + .5(y - y^*),$$

where ffr is the nominal federal funds rate, p is the inflation rate measured by the GDP deflator over the previous four quarters, and $(y - y^*)$ is the percent deviation of the level of real GDP (y) from its trend level (y^*). With inflation at its assumed target of 2 percent and real GDP growing on its trend path of roughly 2 percent per year (so that $y = y^*$), the real ex post interest rate $(ffr - p)$ would also equal 2.

According to Taylor, ". . . the Taylor rule was not meant to be descriptive. Rather it was very explicitly meant to be prescriptive. I derived it by experimenting with different types of rules in stochastic simulations of different monetary models, including my multi-country model at Stanford, and by studying the results of other people's simulations. This pinned down the left-hand side variable and the right-hand side variables, and led to simple functional forms and coefficients."[1]

Although intended as a normative guide to policy, the rule described the setting of U.S. Federal Reserve policy in the late 1980s and early 1990s—a period of relatively favorable macroeconomic performance. The idea that a rule could describe the actual conduct of policy over a period of macroeconomic stability further contributed to the influence of the rule on policymakers.

However, not everyone was convinced. Fed Chairman Alan Greenspan (1997) regarded a substantial degree of discretion as desirable

---

1. http://johnbtaylorsblog.blogspot.com/2011/03/misunderstanding-prescriptive-versus.html.

so as to respond to shocks that were "outside our previous experience . . . policy rules might not always be preferable." The Taylor rule, Greenspan argued, assumed that the future would be like the past: "Unfortunately, however, history is not an infallible guide to the future." Just prior to the Carnegie-Rochester conference, Ben Bernanke and Frederic Mishkin (1992) argued, "Monetary policy rules do not allow the monetary authorities to respond to unforeseen circumstances," a view from which Taylor (1992) dissented.

This paper examines how the Taylor rule is used as an input in monetary policy deliberations and decision-making at central banks. Speeches by policymakers and transcripts and minutes of policy meetings are examined to explore the practical uses of the Taylor rule by central bankers. The paper characterizes the policy environment at the time of the development of the Taylor rule and describes how and why the Taylor rule became integrated into policy discussions and, in some cases, the policy framework itself. While many issues remain unresolved and views still differ about how the Taylor rule can best be applied in practice, the paper shows that the rule has advanced the practice of central banking.

Section II describes the policy environment at central banks around the time of the birth of the Taylor rule and discusses the appeal of the Taylor rule for the practice of central banking. Section III describes the influence of the Taylor rule on the Federal Reserve's conduct of monetary policy. Section IV looks at its impact on other central banks, including the European Central Bank (ECB), the Bank of Japan, and the Bank of England. Section V concludes.

II. A New Policy Framework

Taylor-type rules have become the standard by which monetary policy is introduced in macroeconomic models both small and large. They have been used to explain how policy has been set in the past and how policy should be set in the future. Indeed, they serve as benchmarks for policymakers in assessing the current stance of monetary policy and in determining a future policy path.

II.1. The new policy environment

In the years leading up to Taylor's 1993 paper, various institutional and procedural transformations were creating a new policymaking environment and culture. In 1991, when Mervyn King (2000, 2) joined the Bank of England and asked former Fed chairman Paul Volcker for a word of advice, Volcker obliged with the word "mystique." Volcker (1990, 6) described the central bankers of the Bretton Woods system as "high priests, or perhaps stateless princes." Fed watchers sought to divine the *Secrets of the Temple* (Greider 1987) by closely monitoring the open market operations of the New York Fed and their impact on market interest rates. The process was further complicated by the fact that, from 1989 to 1992, most policy changes were made in conference calls between regularly scheduled meetings of the Federal Open Market Committee (FOMC) (Sellon 2008).

Yet important changes were taking place. In February 1987, the Fed announced that it would no longer set M1 targets, and in July 1993 Chairman Greenspan testified before Congress that the Fed would "downgrade" the use of M2 "as a reliable indicator of financial conditions in the economy." Having returned to an explicit federal funds rate operating target after a brief interlude from 1979 to 1982 in which the Fed targeted non-borrowed reserves, the Fed kept the funds rate constant at 3 percent from late 1992 to January 1994. When the Fed tightened policy in February 1994, the tightening was accompanied by a new policy procedure; it was announced rather than left for financial markets to infer.

More changes were to follow. In 1995, the FOMC began announcing how changes in policy would be reflected in the Fed's target for the federal funds rate. In May 1999, the FOMC began to publicly announce its policy decision regardless of whether its policy rate had been adjusted. Further transparency was injected into the system with "direction of bias" announcements (May 1999) replaced by a "balance of risks" announcement (February 2000). Transcripts of FOMC meetings are now released (with a five-year delay), and since January 2005 FOMC minutes are released expeditiously (three weeks after the announcement of the FOMC's policy decision at each regularly scheduled meeting).[2]

Similar changes were happening elsewhere. Central banks that were experiencing undesirably high inflation rates gained greater independence from governments and many began to introduce formal

---

2. Transcripts were made available beginning in 1994 for meetings held five or more years earlier. Transcripts for meetings prior to 1994 were produced from original raw transcripts in the FOMC Secretariat's files. Shortly after each meeting beginning in 1994, audio recordings were transcribed and, where necessary to facilitate the reader's understanding, lightly edited by the FOMC Secretariat; meeting participants were then given an opportunity within the next several weeks to review the transcript for accuracy.

inflation targets—starting in New Zealand. There, a new government which came into power in July 1984 introduced substantial economic reforms (Brash 1996). The reforms included assigning the Reserve Bank of New Zealand (RBNZ) the goal of reducing inflation and granting the central bank more independence in its actions. The Reserve Bank of New Zealand Act of 1989, which took effect in 1990, formalized the goal of lowering inflation and required that the primary function of the central bank be to achieve and maintain price stability.[3] The Act stipulated that the Minister of Finance and the Governor of the Reserve Bank of New Zealand establish an economic target for monetary policy through a formal *Policy Targets Agreement (PTA)*.[4]

Other central banks soon followed suit. For example, in February 1991 the Governor of the Bank of Canada and the Minister of Finance jointly announced a series of formal targets for reducing inflation. The goal was to lower inflation to the midpoint of an assigned range—between 1 and 3 percent—by the end of 1995 (Thiessen 1998).

In the United Kingdom, on September 16, 1992, British interest rates and foreign exchange reserves were used in a futile effort to retain membership in the European Exchange Rate Mechanism with adverse consequences for housing foreclosures and Conservative Party re-election chances. King (2000, 2) believes that this episode facilitated a central banking revolution in the United Kingdom: "there are moments when new ideas come into their own. This was one of them . . . We decided to adopt and formalize a . . . commitment to an explicit numerical inflation target." The new inflation target was followed by increased transparency in the form of quarterly *Inflation Reports* and operational independence in May 1997.

By 1994, at least nine central banks—including Sweden, Finland, Australia, Spain, Israel, and Chile, in addition to the ones mentioned above—had introduced formal inflation-targeting regimes (Kahn and Parrish 1998).

Although the Federal Reserve did not join the inflation targeting club, its efforts to increase the transparency and predictability of its policy naturally led to a heightened interest in policy rules. Thus, when

---

3. The Bundesbank and the Swiss National Bank had, for some time, already had price stability as their dominant goal. In fact, the Bundesbank Act of 1957 established an independent German central bank with the stated objective of "safeguarding the currency." Also, the 1991 Maastricht Treaty contained norms which ensured the independence of the forthcoming European Central Bank and set forth its primary objective of price stability.

4. Goodhart (2010) provides a detailed review of the discussions in New Zealand in advance of the passage of the Reserve Bank of New Zealand Act.

Taylor proposed his rule, Fed policymakers and Fed watchers quickly took notice. Salomon Brothers advised its clients that "a hypothetical policy rule, modeled on the policy behavior that produced the latest decline in inflation, also indicated that the Federal funds rate is now too low" (Lipsky 1993, 9, 6, n6). This advice was followed up with some more detail: the parameters of the Taylor rule "capture the stated intentions of virtually all Fed officials." The Taylor rule was used to predict future interest rate changes for the remainder of that year: "the Taylor rule is likely to prescribe some relaxation of policy, barring a sharp run-up in current inflation" (DiClemente and Burnham 1995, 6). The Taylor rule also figured in the *Financial Times* (Prowse 1995) and *Business Week* (Foust 1995).

Glenn Rudebusch attended the Carnegie-Rochester conference and began to apply the Taylor rule to monetary policy analysis as a member of the staff of the Board of Governors. In spring 1993, Donald Kohn (then staff director for monetary affairs at the Fed and secretary to the FOMC) discussed the Taylor rule with its author during a stint as visiting professor at Stanford. This interest rapidly reached the FOMC. Governor Janet Yellen was the first to mention the Taylor rule at an FOMC meeting. At the first meeting of the committee in 1995, she indicated that she used the Taylor rule to provide her "a rough sense of whether or not the funds rate is at a reasonable level" (FOMC transcripts, January 31–February 1, 1995). In August 1995, Kohn requested from Taylor an update on the rule. Taylor visited with Fed staff economists for three days in September 1995, and by November 1995 board staff began providing the FOMC with a chart summarizing various versions of the Taylor rule. On December 5, 1995, Taylor discussed the rule with Chairman Greenspan and other members of the Board of Governors.[5]

II.2. The appeal of the Taylor rule

The broad appeal of the Taylor rule comes from its simplicity, intuitiveness, and focus on short-term interest rates as the instrument of monetary policy. The rule is simple in that it relates the policy rate—the federal funds rate—directly to the goals of monetary policy, thus minimizing fluctuations in inflation relative to its objective and output relative to potential output (the output gap). In addition, as originally described, the rule requires knowledge of only the current inflation

---

5. This paragraph is based in part on conversations with Rudebusch and Taylor.

rate and output gap. Taylor provided his own parameters for the key unobservables in the rule.

The rule is intuitive because it calls for policymakers to move the funds rate to lean against the wind of aggregate demand shocks and take a balanced approach to aggregate supply shocks. In addition, the Taylor principle embedded in Taylor's rule requires that the real federal funds rate be increased when inflation is above the inflation objective. In other words, the nominal funds rate should rise more than one-for-one with an increase in inflation above objective. It emerges by reorganizing Taylor's equation as follows:

$$ffr = 1.5p + 0.5(y - y^*) + 1.$$

The principle is also intuitive as a device for ensuring inflation remains anchored over time at its objective.

The Taylor rule has gained widespread influence because it can be implemented in policy regimes with a dual mandate for price stability and economic growth as in the United States or in regimes where inflation is the primary target as in most inflation-targeting countries. The equal weight that the Taylor rule places on deviations of inflation from target and real output from potential output makes the Taylor rule consistent with a dual mandate. However, for several reasons, the Taylor rule can also be applied in inflation-targeting regimes. First, it incorporates an explicit target for inflation. Second, most inflation-targeting central banks are *flexible* inflation targeters, meaning they give some weight to real economic activity and do not attempt to achieve price stability on a period-by-period basis, but rather over the medium term. Finally, interpreting the output gap as a harbinger of future inflationary pressures leads to a single mandate focused on current and future inflation.

The Taylor rule also has broad appeal because it approximates the way policymakers think about the conduct of monetary policy. In much, but not all, of the academic literature leading up to 1993, monetary policy was represented by an exogenous autoregressive process on the money supply. Needless to say, this was not how policymakers viewed themselves as making policy. Except perhaps for the 1979–1983 period, the main instrument of Fed policy in the period following the 1951 Treasury-Federal Reserve Accord has been a short-term interest rate, with the federal funds rate gaining increasing importance through the 1960s (Meulendyke, 1998). And, by the time Taylor had articulated his rule, policymakers in the United States were well on their way to abandoning the specification of target ranges for the monetary aggregates.

Of course the appeal of a simple, intuitive, and realistic policy rule would be considerably diminished if it could not describe past policy or provide guidance about the future. The Taylor rule did both. As Taylor (1993) showed, his rule closely tracked the actual path of the federal funds rate from 1987 to 1992. And because this was a period of relative macroeconomic stability, the rule subsequently became viewed as a prescription for conducting monetary policy going forward.[6]

However, Taylor (1993, 197) did not advocate that policymakers follow a rule mechanically: ". . . There will be episodes where monetary policy will need to be adjusted to deal with special factors." Nevertheless, Taylor viewed systematic policy according to the principles of a rule as having major advantages over discretion in improving economic performance: "Hence, it is important to preserve the concept of a policy rule even in an environment where it is practically impossible to follow mechanically the algebraic formulas economists write down to describe their preferred policy rules."

Given its practical appeal, the Taylor rule quickly moved from the halls of academia to the boardrooms of central banks. The rule first took hold within the Federal Reserve System, then spread throughout the world of modern central banking.

III. Impact of the Taylor Rule on the FOMC

Taylor (1993, 202–03) argued that the FOMC appeared to have acted systematically and in accordance with his simple rule from 1987 to 1992: "What is perhaps surprising is that this rule fits the actual policy performance during the last few years remarkably well. . . . In this sense the Fed policy has been conducted as if the Fed had been following a policy rule much like the one called for by recent research on policy rules."

Taylor (1993, 208) suggested that a specific policy rule could be added to the list of factors—such as leading indicators, structural models, and financial market conditions—that the FOMC already monitored. "Each time the FOMC meets, the staff could be asked to include

---

6. Taylor (1993) emphasized the normative aspect of the rule and the desirability of systematic rule-like behavior on the part of policymakers. Taylor also discussed the use of discretion within the context of a policy rule and issues involved in the transition from pure discretion to a policy rule or from one policy rule to another. The close fit of the Taylor rule to data from 1987 to 1992 suggested the rule was a feasible prescription for policy.

in the briefing books information about how recent FOMC decisions compare with the policy rule. Forecasts for the next few quarters—a regular part of the staff briefing—could contain forecasts of the federal funds rate implied by the policy rule. There are many variants on this idea. For instance, there could be a range of entries corresponding to policy rules with different coefficients, or perhaps a policy rule where the growth rate of real GDP rather than its level appears. Bands for the federal funds rate could span these variants."

The FOMC was likely unaware before 1993 that its behavior could be described by a simple policy rule. But the Taylor rule very quickly became a part of the information set that the FOMC regularly reviewed. Taylor's description of how a rule could be used in practice proved prescient. By at least 1995, FOMC members were regularly consulting the Taylor rule for guidance in setting monetary policy. A review of transcripts of FOMC meetings from 1993 to 2003—the last year for which transcripts have been made publicly available—shows that the FOMC used the Taylor rule very much the way Taylor recommended in 1993. Not only did the staff prepare a range of estimates of the current stance of policy and the future policy path based on various policy rules, but members of the FOMC also regularly referred to rules in their deliberations.

III.1. A guide for policy

According to the transcripts, the first mention of the Taylor rule at an FOMC meeting occurred at the January 31–February 1, 1995 meeting. At that meeting, Janet Yellen described the rule and its close approximation to actual FOMC policy decisions since 1986 and suggested that the rule was currently calling for a funds rate of 5.1 percent—close to the current stance of monetary policy. In contrast, she noted, the financial markets were expecting an increase of 150 basis points "before we stop tightening," and the Greenbook (the document prepared for each FOMC meeting describing the staff's detailed forecast for economic activity and inflation) suggested the federal funds rate should be 7 percent. "I do not disagree with the Greenbook strategy. But the Taylor rule and other rules . . . call for a rate in the 5 percent range, which is where we already are. Therefore, I am not imagining another 150 basis points." As it turned out at the meeting, the federal funds rate target was raised 50 basis points to 6 percent, where it stayed until July 1995, when it was cut to 5¾ percent.

In subsequent meetings, Yellen pointed repeatedly to the Taylor rule as a guide to her views on the proper stance for monetary policy. Other committee members—especially Governors Laurence Meyer and Edward Gramlich and San Francisco Fed President Robert Parry—also relied heavily on the Taylor rule.[7] Each made a number of references. For example:

> **Governor Meyer:** [My] judgment is reinforced by the Taylor rule projections that, as Governor Yellen pointed out at the last meeting, suggest that monetary policy is appropriately positioned today in light of prevailing inflation and utilization rates. (FOMC September 1996, 37)

> **President Parry:** At our Bank, we consult two monetary policy rules as a starting point for thinking about the appropriate stance of policy: an estimated version of Taylor's rule and a nominal income growth rate rule. . . . [B]oth rules suggest that the funds rate should be left at about 5¼ percent at the present time, although when applied to our forecast they do suggest higher rates will be needed in the future" (FOMC December 1996, 36)

> **Governor Meyer:** We should build in that pro-cyclicality of interest rates that would occur normally, for example, under a monetary growth rule with a stable money demand function or under a Taylor rule. (FOMC February 1997, 109)

> **President Parry:** . . . the two monetary policy rules we consult at our Bank . . . both suggest the need for an increase in the funds rate this quarter. (FOMC February 1997, 108)

> **Governor Gramlich:** ". . . I want to refer to some calculations that the staff has done on the Taylor rule. As I understand at least the fitted version of that rule, it, too, suggests that the funds rate is a bit on the low side. (FOMC November 1997, 85)

> **Governor Gramlich:** If the real interest rate is about 3 percent, steady inflation is arguably about 2 percent, and both inflation and unemployment are reasonably close to their target values—this is my own mental version of the Taylor rule—policy is roughly about right at this point. (FOMC August 1998, 54)

---

7. As discussed later, Gramlich later expressed skepticism about use of the Taylor rule in the absence of reliable estimates of the output gap.

III.2. A framework for analyzing issues

From 1995 to 2003, the Taylor rule was also used to analyze a range of issues. Many of the discussions paralleled research being conducted by academic and Federal Reserve economists on policy rules. Although firm conclusions were not always reached, it is clear from the transcripts that the Taylor rule became over time a key input into the FOMC's policy process. Among the issues debated were the following:

III.2.1. The sensitivity of the rule to the inflation measure

At the May 1995 meeting, FOMC members discussed what measure of inflation should be used in determining the Taylor rule's prescription for policy. Chairman Greenspan asked what measure of inflation Taylor used and noted that, when the data on GDP were revised, the normative prescription from the rule would change. Donald Kohn indicated that using the implicit price deflator gave a policy prescription for the funds rate of 4¼ percent, while using the Consumer Price Index (CPI) gave a prescription of around 5¾ percent. Kohn noted, however, that a rule using CPI inflation would not track committee actions in earlier years as well as the Taylor rule, which relied on inflation as measured by the implicit GDP deflator. Alan Blinder, vice chairman of the Board of Governors, added that the parameters of the Taylor rule would likely change if the variables on the right-hand side were to be changed (FOMC May 1995, 30).

III.2.2. Staff concerns and caveats

By November 1995, board staff began providing the FOMC with a chart summarizing various versions of the Taylor rule. In discussing the new chart at the November 1995 FOMC meeting, board staff noted several caveats. First, the Taylor rule was not forward looking except in the sense that the inclusion of the output gap on the right-hand side provided an indicator of future inflationary pressure. It was noted that the performance of a rule-based monetary policy might be improved by incorporating forecasts of inflation and the output gap instead of their current levels.

Second, the equal weights on inflation and the output gap in the Taylor rule may not always be appropriate. While equal weights might be well suited for supply shocks, a greater weight on the output gap may be better suited for demand shocks. This would allow for a "prompt closing of the output gap" that would "forestall opening up a price gap" (FOMC November 1995, 1–5).

Third, it was again noted that the Taylor rule's prescribed funds rate target is highly sensitive to how output and inflation are measured. According to the Taylor rule, the current setting of the funds rate was high relative to the equilibrium level, suggesting policy was restrictive. However, the current funds rate appeared close to its equilibrium level when measures of inflation other than the implicit GDP deflator were used in determining the deviation of inflation from Taylor's 2 percent objective.

Fourth, an estimated version of the Taylor rule that allows gradual adjustment in the funds rate target to the rate prescribed by the rule suggests the FOMC placed a greater weight on closing the output gap and less weight on bringing inflation down than in the Taylor rule. To some extent, this result reflected "the influence of the credit crunch period when the funds rate for some time was below the value prescribed from Taylor's specification."

Fifth, Federal Reserve monetary policy from 1987 to 1993 was focused on bringing inflation down and, therefore, policy was generally restrictive. Policy remained slightly restrictive in November 1995 with an estimated real funds rate somewhat higher than the 2 percent equilibrium funds rate assumed in the Taylor rule. However, the board staff's forecast called for steady inflation at the current nominal and real federal funds rate. In other words, the staff forecast implicitly incorporated a higher equilibrium real funds rate than that assumed in the Taylor rule: "The real funds rate is only an index or proxy for a whole host of financial market conditions that influence spending and prices in complex ways. Among other difficulties, the relationship of the funds rate to these other, more important, variables may change over time." Thus, the Board staff viewed the equilibrium real funds rate as a concept that changed over time, making the Taylor rule as originally specified less reliable.

III.2.3. Deliberate versus opportunistic disinflation

At the same meeting, members briefly discussed the Taylor rule as a framework for deliberate, as opposed to opportunistic, disinflation. Gary Stern, president of the Minneapolis Fed, questioned whether policy should be tighter than indicated by the Taylor rule "to bend inflation down further from here." Governor Lawrence Lindsey responded that, with inflation above the assumed Taylor rule target of 2 percent, the prescription for policy from the rule itself was *deliberately* restrictive, placing steady downward pressure on inflation (FOMC November 1995, 49–50).

This topic was taken up again at the next two meetings. For example, in January 1996 President Parry suggested that an opportunistic disinflation strategy would involve a much more complicated description of policy than a Taylor rule. An opportunistic strategy is one in which monetary policy aims to hold inflation steady at its current level until an unanticipated shock pulls inflation down. At that point, policymakers "opportunistically" accept the lower inflation rate as the new target for policy and attempt to maintain the lower inflation rate until an unexpected shock again pulls inflation down. Parry questioned whether such an opportunistic approach wouldn't require "a complicated mathematical expression of our policy processes with lots of nonlinearities?" Parry's concern was that adopting an opportunistic approach to further disinflation would inevitably lead to a "loss of understanding" in financial markets about how the FOMC reacts to incoming information (FOMC January 1996, 51).

In Taylor's terminology, opportunistic disinflation involves a series of *transitions* from one policy rule to another as the target inflation rate is opportunistically lowered. Taylor (1993, 207) cautions that "in the period immediately after a new policy rule has been put in place, people are unlikely either to know about or understand the new policy or to believe that policymakers are serious about maintaining it. Simply assuming that people have rational expectations and know the policy rule is probably stretching things during this transition period. Instead, people may base their expectations partly on studying past policy in a Bayesian way, or by trying to anticipate the credibility of the new policy by studying the past records of policymakers, or by assessing whether the policy will work." Thus, Taylor appears to have anticipated Parry's concerns.[8]

III.2.4. Forward- versus backward-looking Taylor rules

In 1997, various alternative specifications for the Taylor rule began to be considered by FOMC members. Governor Meyer noted that, while the standard Taylor rule suggested policy should remain on hold at the present time, the staff's forecast suggested policy would need to be tightened

---

8. See Orphanides and Wilcox (1996) and Orphanides, Small, Weiland, and Wilcox (1997) for other interpretations of opportunistic disinflation.

in the future. He argued that if current values of inflation and the output gap were replaced in the Taylor rule with forecasts, the rule would be prescribing an immediate tightening of policy. Using a "maxi/min" analysis, he viewed the cost of not tightening when tightening turns out to be the appropriate action as greater than the cost of tightening when not tightening turns out to be appropriate. The policy prescription coming from a forward-looking Taylor rule and the implications of a maxi/min strategy were among the reasons Meyer cited in support of a tightening of monetary policy (FOMC March 1997, 54–57).

The issue came up again in 2003 as the committee considered whether and how to raise the funds rate as economic conditions improved from its then-low of 1 percent. Governor Bernanke noted that a backward-looking Taylor rule was then recommending a federal funds rate of 1½ percent, while "[t]he actual current value of 1 percent presumably reflects in part our insurance policy against deflation." Removing that insurance gradually and following the path prescribed by the backward-looking rule would result in a gradual increase in the funds rate to 3.5 percent by the end of 2005. This path, Bernanke noted, was very close to what the federal funds futures market was predicting. In contrast, a forward-looking Taylor rule—which puts a high weight on inflation expectations—implied a much slower tightening process. According to that specification of the rule, "the funds rate will reach only 1.5 percent by the end of 2004 rather than the 2.25 percent forecast by both the futures market and the backward-looking rule."

Bernanke indicated he preferred the forward-looking version for two reasons. First, "it's a true real-time rule—that is, it estimates reaction functions given actual forecasts available at the time the policy decision was taken." Second, "we're now in a period that is very unusual, and historical relationships may not work. So it's useful that the forward-looking rule can take into account explicitly how forecasts affect current policy decisions." The implication, Bernanke said, is that the committee's policy stance going forward will depend on what it expects inflation to do. If the committee expects inflation to remain low and stable, based on the estimated forward-looking rule, "our policy tightening should be slower and more gradual than suggested by historical relationships or by the funds rate futures markets" (FOMC October 2003, 71–73).[9]

---

9. Governor Kohn, in the December 2003 meeting, followed up on Bernanke's comments, saying, "A zero real funds rate may not be way out of line for a 2 percent output gap, but it would be unusual to keep the funds rate that low as the output gap is closing next

As it turned out, at the November 2004 meeting the FOMC raised the funds rate target from 1.75 percent to 2 percent—between the 2003 backward- and forward-looking rule prescriptions for the end of 2004, but closer to the backward-looking prescription.

III.2.5. The equilibrium real federal funds rate

In 1997, FOMC members began to question the constant 2 percent equilibrium real federal funds rate assumed in the Taylor rule. Governor Meyer said, "While I am a strong believer in some of the wisdom embedded in the Taylor rule, I have been concerned for a long time that we need to be more careful about how we set its level by coming up with a more reasonable estimate of the equilibrium funds rate" (FOMC August 1997, 66–67). Two key issues at the time were the dependence of estimates of the equilibrium real rate on the particular measure of inflation and the possibility that the equilibrium real rate varied over time.

Later, as evidence mounted that trend productivity growth had increased, the issue of the equilibrium real rate re-emerged. Members were concerned that maintaining Taylor's fixed 2 percent real rate would lead to an overly stimulative policy. Alfred Broaddus, president of the Richmond Fed, said ". . . an increase in trend productivity growth means that real short rates need to rise. . . . [T]he reason is that households and businesses would want to borrow against their perception of higher future income now in order to increase current consumption and investment before it's actually available. . . . The Taylor rule doesn't give any attention to that kind of real business cycle reason for a move in rates. It only allows reaction to inflation gaps and output gaps" (FOMC June 1999, 99–100).

The issue of the equilibrium real rate came up again in August 2002. President Parry asked why the Taylor rule recommendation differed from the recommendation from simulations of a perfect foresight model reported in the Bluebook.[10] Vincent Reinhart, director of the Board of Governors' Monetary Affairs Division and secretary and

---

year. We can see this in the various versions of the Taylor rule, which all point to higher rates next year. . . . Taylor rules are just rough benchmarks, and I would not argue that we ought to follow them in any mechanical way. But these results do underline the questions about how we position ourselves going forward" (FOMC December 2003, 67).

10. The Bluebook or, more formally, "Monetary Policy Alternatives" is a document prepared for the FOMC by board staff that provides background and context on monetary policy alternatives for the FOMC's consideration.

economist to the FOMC, responded that while the Taylor rule was consistent with what the FOMC had done in the past, it did not account for the shifts in the equilibrium real federal funds rate. In contrast, the perfect foresight simulations allowed for a downward shift in the rate (FOMC August 2002, 69).

III.2.6. The zero interest rate bound

In 1998, board staff briefed the FOMC on issues arising from the zero constraint on nominal interest rates. Again, a good part of the discussion was based on how the Taylor rule might be adjusted to address the issue. One alternative was to increase the coefficients on the inflation and output gaps in the Taylor rule when interest rates were near the zero bound. Another alternative was to act more aggressively only when inflation is already deemed low. Jerry Jordan, president of the Cleveland Fed, suggested that conducting monetary policy "through a monetary base arrangement of supply and demand for central bank money" might be an alternative to the Taylor framework when interest rates were approaching the zero bound. President Parry pointed out that policy would be more preemptive under either a more aggressive Taylor rule or a forecast-based Taylor rule (FOMC June/July 1998, 89–96).

The issue of the zero bound arose again in early 2002 when inflation indicators available at the time signaled considerable downward pressure on core inflation and the federal funds rate was 1¾ percent and headed downward. At the January 29–30 meeting, board staff members David Reifschneider and John Williams gave a presentation on the implications of the zero bound for monetary policy. They ran simulations of the board staff's principal macroeconomic model, FRB/US, with policy represented by a standard Taylor rule. They found that at a low target inflation rate, the zero lower bound was hit frequently and that economic performance deteriorated with an inflation target below roughly 2 percent.

They concluded that the FOMC might want to move policy more aggressively than suggested by the standard Taylor rule when the economy was in imminent danger of hitting the zero bound. For example, they suggested that when the standard Taylor rule prescribes an interest rate below 1 percent, the FOMC might consider dropping it immediately to zero.[11] They also noted that one drawback of such a policy

---

11. They also suggested that the committee respond to past deviations of inflation from target—for example, by targeting the price level or the average inflation rate.

might be that it would be less transparent. At the same meeting, Marvin Goodfriend of the Richmond Fed's staff proposed expanding the monetary base to stimulate the economy at the zero lower bound.

The discussion that followed among the FOMC members was wide-ranging but not tightly focused on policy rules. Greenspan, for example, questioned the robustness of the results across different models. He and others questioned how useful model simulations could be when they were based on a period in which the zero bound had never been hit. That view led to an extended discussion of Japan's experience at the zero bound and its relevance or lack of relevance for the United States (FOMC January 2002).

In retrospect, this episode of monetary policy ultimately resulted in a funds rate of 1 percent that was maintained for a "considerable period." But the discussion of the zero bound foreshadowed what was to come in the aftermath of the global financial crisis of 2008–09 when the funds rate target fell to 0–25 basis points and was maintained there for an "extended period."

III.2.7. Uncertainty about the output gap

In February 1999, Meyer pointed out that virtually all versions of the Taylor rule then tracked by board staff for the FOMC—whether based on the CPI or GDP deflator, whether backward- or forward-looking, whether with Taylor's coefficients or estimated coefficients—prescribed a funds rate that was higher than the current funds rate target. He attributed this divergence from the rule to a number of factors including the Asian financial crisis, the Russian debt default, forecasts that had been calling for a spontaneous slowdown, and, importantly, structural change suggested by the combination of declining inflation and declining unemployment.

Meyer proposed an asymmetric strategy for setting the funds rate target in such an environment where there was uncertainty about the level of the non-accelerating inflation rate of unemployment (NAIRU). He suggested determining the level of the NAIRU under the assumption that the current setting of the funds rate was the one prescribed by the Taylor rule. Then, he recommended following the Taylor rule if above-trend growth pushed the unemployment rate even lower. In contrast, if the unemployment rate rose modestly, Meyer recommended taking no immediate action to ease policy. Similarly, Meyer recommended policy respond to an increase in (core) inflation according to the Taylor rule, but respond passively to a decline in inflation (FOMC February 1999, 65–66).

Other members offered other approaches to dealing with uncertainty about the output gap. For example, Gramlich suggested a "speed limit rule." He argued that the FOMC "should target growth in aggregate demand at about 3 percent, or perhaps a bit less, and stay with that policy for as long as inflation does not accelerate" (FOMC March 1999, 44–45). At a later meeting, Gramlich offered two additional approaches. First, the committee could drop the output gap term from the Taylor rule and implement an inflation-targeting rule.[12] And second, the FOMC could adopt a "nominal GDP standard" (FOMC May 1999, 45). Meyer viewed a temporary down-weighting of the output gap as sensible but rejected ignoring output all together: "This is a difference between uncertainty and total ignorance" (FOMC June 1999, 93–94). Broaddus suggested finding another variable to substitute for the output gap that would serve as a forward-looking indicator of inflation expectations such as survey information or long-term interest rates (FOMC June 1999, 99–100).

III.2.8. Uncertainty about the inflation target

As inflation moderated, FOMC members, in addition to questioning the role of the output gap, began to question Taylor's assumed inflation objective of 2 percent as measured by the implicit GDP deflator. Gramlich complained that "we must have point estimates of our targets for both inflation and unemployment. At the very best I think we have bands; we do not have point estimates" (FOMC December 1998, 45). Meyer suggested it might be more reasonable for the FOMC to tell the staff what its inflation objective is as opposed to simply accepting Taylor's assumption (FOMC June 2000, 90). He later expressed frustration that "we start off from the inflation target that John Taylor set but do so without any communication from the committee to the staff about the inflation objectives committee members might have" (FOMC January 2001, 187–88).

III.2.9. Interest rate smoothing

In January 2003, the FOMC took up the issue of how quickly the stance of policy should be adjusted toward the committee's desired target for the federal funds rate. In most industrial countries, the policy rate

---

12. Gramlich actually discussed his approaches in terms of the associated unemployment gap.

tends to be adjusted in small steps in the same direction. Moreover, estimated versions of the Taylor rule suggest that including a lagged value of the policy rate on the right-hand side is highly statistically significant and greatly increases the explanatory power of the rule. In setting the stage for the committee's discussion, Fed staff presented simulations based on the FRB/US model.[13] Assuming the objective of policy was to minimize fluctuations in the output gap and in inflation around its long-run target, an "optimal" policy rule was derived. The resulting rule was considerably more responsive to current economic conditions than the inertia-prone rule estimated with historical data. In particular, the optimal rule incorporated higher coefficients on inflation and the output gap and a lower coefficient on the lagged federal funds rate than the estimated rule.

The issue was important in early 2003 because the optimal rule was recommending an immediate easing of the policy rate to zero percent followed by an aggressive unwinding in the second half of the year. In contrast, the estimated rule called for a much more muted response. The optimal rule, however, was based on a number of unrealistic assumptions. First, the private sector was assumed to continue to form expectations on the basis of the estimated rule. Second, the policymakers were assumed to know the structure of the economy with certainty. And third, policymakers were assumed to be able to observe the current state of the economy. Relaxing these assumptions moved the optimal policy reaction function in the direction of the estimated Taylor rule, but not all the way. With numerous additional caveats, the analysis suggested policy should be more responsive to current conditions than historically.

Glenn Rudebusch offered an alternative view—arguing "there is essentially no policy inertia at a quarterly frequency and that, in fact, the funds rate typically is adjusted fairly promptly to economic developments" (Rudebusch 2009, 18). In his view, the apparent inertia in estimated Taylor rules results from occasional, persistent, and deliberate deviations from a non-inertial Taylor rule in response to factors other than current output and inflation.

As evidence against policy inertia, he documented the unpredictability of quarterly changes in the funds rate several quarters ahead. If interest rates were smoothed, a regression of actual changes in the funds rate on predicted changes should have considerable explanatory

---

13. Brian Sack and Robert Tetlow from the Board of Governors staff and Dean Croushore from the Philadelphia Federal Reserve Bank made the presentations.

power. In fact, they do not. "For example, Eurodollar futures have essentially no ability to predict the quarterly change in the funds rate three quarters ahead. . . . An alternative explanation is that the Taylor rule is an incomplete description of Fed policymaking and that the Fed responds to other persistent variables besides current output and inflation" (pp. 19–20). Two examples of such behavior are the Fed's response to the persistent credit crunch of 1992–93 and to the global financial crisis following the Russian debt default in 1998–99. Rudebusch concludes that our models may not capture all of the important factors influencing policy and, therefore, policymakers should be cautious in concluding that policy responds too timidly to economic conditions.

A lengthy discussion followed the staff presentation. Some comments were technical, while others were philosophical. The discussion had the following flavor: Chairman Greenspan appeared to question the validity of the exercise, arguing that "the underlying structure of the economy with which we are dealing and to which we are endeavoring to fit our models is in a continuous state of change."[14] He seemed to suggest that the analysis should be carried out not just with real-time data, but also with real-time models of the economy. He also suggested that risk aversion and concern about fragility of financial markets to large and unexpected changes in the policy rate were reasons for policymakers to move slowly. Then-Governor Bernanke argued that greater predictability of policy could give the central bank more leverage over long-term interest rates. Therefore, there should be more inertia in rates than suggested by the "optimal" Taylor rule. St. Louis Fed President William Poole stressed the importance of inertia in helping the public learn and understand the nature of the policy rule.

Governor Kohn gave a historical perspective of past episodes suggesting that the Fed acted gradually, but not as gradually as in estimated Taylor rules. These rules do not account for changes in the Fed's inflation target from 1987 to the second half of the 1990s while the Fed was pursuing opportunistic disinflation. In addition, the Fed was forward-looking and responding more to shocks that were perceived to be long-lasting than those that were expected to be short-lived. In short, the committee was responding to a larger information set than just current output and inflation. Finally, he suggested, "It's better generally for policy to act too strongly than too weakly to developing

---

14. The changing structure of the U.S. economy and the difficulty of modeling it were common themes for Greenspan. See, for example, the FOMC transcripts from the June 25–26, 2002, meeting, p. 20.

situations. Serious policy errors have been made when policy doesn't react aggressively enough to a developing situation. Examples are the Federal Reserve in the 1970s or the Bank of Japan in the 1990s" (FOMC January 2003, 42–43).

III.3. The Taylor rule and Fed policy since 2003

While transcripts of FOMC meetings since 2003 have not yet been made public, it is clear that the Taylor rule—in all of its various forms and uses—has continued to inform committee discussions. One area, which will likely be debated for many years to come, is: when is it appropriate to deviate from rule-like behavior? For example, in the aftermath of the 1987 stock market collapse and the 1998 Russian debt default, policymakers eased policy relative to the Taylor rule prescription to limit the impact of financial market turbulence on the real economy. These two relatively brief deviations from rule-like behavior have been viewed largely as successful examples of discretionary policy, although concern has emerged about the associated moral hazard.

More recently, policy deviated from the classical Taylor rule from 2003 to 2006, when the funds rate was kept below the Taylor rule prescription for a prolonged period in an effort to offset incipient deflationary pressures. Taylor (2007) criticized this use of discretion as contributing to the surge in housing demand and house-price inflation. According to counterfactual simulations, Taylor concluded that, if policy had adhered more closely to the Taylor rule, much of the housing boom would have been avoided. Moreover, the reversal of the boom, with its resulting financial market turmoil, would not have been as sharp.

Another issue of current concern, echoing back to 2003, is the divergence in the prescriptions of backward-looking and forward-looking, estimated and non-estimated, Taylor rules in the Great Recession of 2008–09.[15] For example, estimated forward-looking rules suggest a funds rate in the vicinity of negative 5 percent. Since the funds rate

---

15. The debate largely comes down to the weight assigned in the Taylor rule to economic slack—in the form of either the output gap, as in the Taylor rule (Taylor 2009), or the difference between the actual and natural unemployment rate as in Rudebusch (2009) and Meyer (2009). Rudebusch and Meyer assign a much bigger weight to economic slack and, therefore, their rules prescribe a much lower federal funds rate than Taylor. Other rules place a lower weight than Taylor on economic slack. For example, Hall (2005) recommends a weight of zero on the output gap based on his view that the natural rate is an ill-defined concept. Hall's rule would recommend a funds rate *higher* than Taylor's.

cannot fall below zero, this prescription might be taken as suggesting the Fed should employ non-conventional means—such as credit market interventions and quantitative easing—to further stimulate the economy. In contrast, non-estimated and non-forward-looking Taylor rules—such as Taylor's original 1993 rule—suggest the funds rate should be much nearer to zero. This prescription suggests limited need for nonconventional policies. Taylor, applying current data to his rule, clearly sides with the view that the funds rate should be closer to zero—about where the Fed is currently.

Looking ahead, the issue of discretionary deviations from rule-like behavior and the specification of policy rules themselves will likely continue to be debated among FOMC members. But few would argue against the merits of systematic policy, at least during normal times. In addition to the Taylor principle, perhaps Taylor's biggest contribution to policy is that it is now viewed through the lens of the Taylor rule as a systematic response to incoming information about economic activity and inflation as opposed to a period-by-period optimization problem under pure discretion.

IV. Impact of the Taylor Rule at Other Central Banks

Just as the Taylor rule became a central part of policy analysis at the Federal Reserve, to varying degrees it also has become incorporated into policy analysis and decision-making at other central banks. Both academic and central bank researchers have used the Taylor rule framework to characterize, understand, and recommend monetary policy across a wide range of economies from the highly industrialized to emerging markets.[16]

This section examines the extent to which the Taylor rule is used in practice by policymakers at central banks beyond the Federal Reserve. However, without access to transcripts of policy meetings at central banks other than the Federal Reserve, the analysis relies on policymakers' speeches, minutes of policy meetings, and/or staff reports.

---

16. See, for example, Clarida, Galí, and Gertler (1998), who examined Germany, Japan, the United Kingdom, France, and Italy; Lubik and Schorfheide (2007), who examine Australia, Canada, New Zealand, and the United Kingdom; and Schmidt-Hebbel and Werner (2002), who examine Brazil, Chile, and Mexico. See also Aizenman, Hutchison, and Noy (2008) and references therein for more examples of studies of Taylor rules in emerging markets and Loayza and Schmidt-Hebbel (2002) for studies on Latin American countries (including Chile), the United Kingdom, Canada, Israel, and South Africa.

Because the level of the examination of these other central banks is less deep than that of the Federal Reserve, it is possible that the approach understates the importance of the Taylor rule in actual policy discussions at other central banks. For example, if the analysis of the Federal Reserve's use of the Taylor rule were based entirely on the minutes of FOMC meetings and speeches of FOMC members instead of complete transcripts of the meetings, it is likely that the Taylor rule would appear to have been less influential than it was in actual policy discussions. With this caveat, the analysis represents a diverse sample of central banks, relying on information that is publicly available and, to the extent possible, based on the stated views of policymakers.

In forecasting key macroeconomic variables, monetary policymakers must necessarily make assumptions about the future path of the policy rate they control. Forecasts can be based on assumptions ranging from a constant path set at the current level of the policy rate to a path based on the markets' expectation for the policy rate to a path that is consistent with the policymakers' own goals for the economy or a policy reaction function such as the Taylor rule.[17] According to a survey of central banks conducted by the Bank for International Settlements (BIS), roughly a third of the thirty-five banks surveyed base their assumptions on an interest rate reaction function. Two-fifths base their forecasts on "a neutral assumption such as unchanged rates," about two-fifths base their forecasts on the market's outlook for inflation, and "a number" of central banks provide forecasts based on several different assumptions (Nelson 2008, 7–8).

Clearly, policy reaction functions play a role in central bank forecasting, but the question remains: do they influence policy decisions? The remainder of this section examines practices at a sample of central banks to shed light on the influence of the Taylor rule in the decision-making process of policymakers.

IV.1. The ECB

The European Central Bank (ECB) views the usefulness of the Taylor rule with a degree of skepticism—at least based on official statements and publications. In part, this is due to the ECB's emphasis on price stability as its primary goal and the prominence of "monetary analysis"—analysis of monetary and credit conditions—in its policy assessment.

---

17. Kahn (2007) describes the approaches chosen by ten central banks and their pros and cons.

The primary objective of ECB monetary policy is to maintain price stability, defined as inflation rates "below, but close to, 2 percent over the medium term." The strategy of the ECB in meeting its objective is based on two pillars—monetary analysis and economic analysis. The two pillars are used in "organizing, evaluating, and cross-checking the information relevant for assessing the risks to price stability" (ECB 2010).

The monetary analysis pillar, which has no counterpart in the Federal Reserve, consists of a detailed analysis of the implications of money and credit developments for inflation and economic activity.[18] The analysis is contained in the *Quarterly Monetary Assessment* (QMA). This document analyzes developments in the monetary aggregates, not simply for their own sake but to understand their implications for inflation and monetary policy. The analysis focuses not on short-run fluctuations but on the implications of money growth for inflation dynamics over the medium to long run. Finally, the analysis incorporates information from a variety of sources in addition to the monetary aggregates, including a range of financial assets, prices, and yields.

The economic analysis pillar—where the Taylor rule potentially plays a role—takes the form of a broad-based economic assessment called the "macroeconomic projections exercise." In this exercise, the ECB's staff identifies and analyzes economic shocks and the cyclical dynamics of economic activity and inflation. The staff also produces forecasts of inflation and economic activity over the coming two to three years. The analysis is similar to the policy analysis conducted at the Federal Reserve and other central banks.

The ECB's area-wide model (AWM), used in assessing economic conditions, forecasting, and policy analysis in the euro area, incorporates a money demand equation and a yield curve.[19] Short-term interest rates are determined by a standard Taylor rule. However, "it is worth pointing out . . . that the plausibility or policy relevance of [this otherwise standard relationship] is not at stake as such. In fact, [this] supplementary [equation is] used primarily because [it is a] necessary [element] to close the model as a full system, which would otherwise not converge to some steady-state path" (Fagan, Henry, and Mestre 2001, 25).

The ambivalence suggested by the statement above can also be heard in the views expressed by members of the ECB governing council. For example, Otmar Issing has argued that a simple Taylor-type

---

18. The discussion of the use of monetary aggregates at the ECB draws heavily on Fischer, Lenza, Pill, and Reichlin (2006, 2–11) and Kahn and Benolkin (2007).

19. http://www.ecb.int/home/html/researcher_awm.en.html.

rule, had it been available during three past historical episodes, would not have been of help in preventing policy mistakes. Instead, he argues that a policy based on the quantity theory of money, using the money supply as a key indicator, "could have been instrumental in yielding a better macroeconomic outcome" (2002, 192–93). The three episodes include the Federal Reserve's conduct of policy in the 1920s and subsequent Great Depression, the Bank of Japan's experience in the second half of the 1980s in the face of an asset price bubble, and Europe's experience over the same period before the adoption of the euro. In each case, Issing argues, a measure of "excess" money growth would have provided policymakers a better signal than the prescription from a Taylor rule.[20]

More generally, the ECB has spelled out its concerns about the usefulness of Taylor rules in an article appearing in its *Monthly Bulletin* (2001). Many of the concerns echo those of Greenspan and others regarding the use of Taylor rules by the Federal Reserve.

First, it is argued that other policy strategies including ones based on money growth targeting, if successful in maintaining price stability over a long period, might be empirically indistinguishable from a policy based on the Taylor rule. Thus, a Taylor rule that fits the data well empirically may have little to say about what information policymakers actually responded to and how they reached policy decisions. Moreover, real-time data are required for any careful assessment of policy.

Second, more information—including data on such variables as money and credit growth, exchange rates, asset prices, fiscal indicators, commodity prices, and wages—may be needed in the conduct of policy. Decisions cannot be based solely on current inflation and the output gap. A simple Taylor rule would ignore insights gleaned from a wealth of additional information.

Third, different types of economic shocks require different policy responses. For example, do they arise from the demand side or the supply side, are they temporary or permanent? "In short, driving forces

---

20. Moreover, Jürgen Stark, member of the Executive Board of the ECB, has questioned whether a simple Taylor rule captures all the information that the ECB responds to in setting interest rates: "Central banks which are concerned with domestic price stability seek to offset potentially destabilising shocks. In a globalised world, though, different central banks naturally respond in part to similar global factors. And, as we know, a number of these factors are not well captured by a mechanical policy rule of the type which John Taylor takes as a benchmark for good monetary policymaking. Adequate policy reactions to global factors, and to the risks that they pose for domestic price stability, will thus show up—within the context of a simple rule—in the residual term. . . . However, often the residual is a measure of the lack of explanatory power of the simple policy rule itself" (Stark 2008, 2–3).

of different natures, possibly associated with the same inflation outturn or forecast, require offsetting actions of varying intensity and duration, as they set in motion quite different dynamics and are associated with possibly opposite tendencies in the evolution of real variables. Taylor rules, by unduly restricting the universe of information brought to bear upon policy decisions, are not a reliable guide for policy from this perspective" (European Central Bank 2001, 42).

Fourth, the Taylor rule as formulated is not strictly implementable since the output gap and the equilibrium real interest rate are not observable. Estimating these concepts in real time is a complicated task involving both empirical and theoretical considerations as well as questionable assumptions. The effort may lead to a range of estimates so large that the Taylor rule provides no clear policy prescriptions.

Fifth, a forecast-based Taylor rule would suggest a dual mandate for policy by making both inflation and the output gap distinct targets. This would be inconsistent with the ECB's mandate for price stability as its primary objective.

Finally, the ECB questions whether Taylor rules can truly be stabilizing. One reason Taylor rules may fail to stabilize the economy is that interest rates cannot fall below zero—even though the Taylor rule might on occasion prescribe such a remedy. Another reason is that, if the Taylor rule is forward looking, it "can exacerbate the tendency of economic systems to be excessively sensitive to arbitrary revisions of expectations" (European Central Bank 2001, 41–43).

After leaving the ECB, Issing's views on the Taylor rule appear somewhat more sympathetic. As he describes in chapter 13 of this volume, "The View from Inside the European Central Bank," "The Taylor rule has become a benchmark for monetary policy in many respects. At the ECB we were confronted with extreme uncertainty on data for the output gap and the equilibrium interest rate. Notwithstanding this difficulty it was important always to monitor estimates of the Taylor rule using a variety of data."

IV.2. The Bank of Japan

While the Federal Reserve and other central banks were incorporating the Taylor rule into their policy processes in the early to mid-1990s, the Bank of Japan was headed toward a zero interest rate policy—the result of a bursting of Japan's property price bubble, falling inflation and real GDP growth, and rising unemployment. Certainly, officials at the Bank of Japan were aware of the work on Taylor rules because Taylor was an honorary adviser to the Bank of Japan from 1994 to 2001. But, as the Japanese policy rate hit virtually zero in late 1995, the Taylor rule lost the practical relevance that it might earlier have had. Nevertheless, according to minutes of the Bank of Japan's policy meetings, the Taylor rule was cited in 1999 and 2000 by at least one member of the Bank's Policy Board in the debate over whether to engage in quantitative easing and, later, whether to end the Bank's zero interest rate policy.

In April 1999, according to the views of "many" members of the Bank's board expressed in the minutes, the Japanese economy appeared to have stopped deteriorating, but economic activity remained weak and the outlook for recovery was uncertain. Moreover "the current easy monetary policy" was supporting financial markets and "expected to spread gradually to economic activity." In these circumstances, a majority of board members favored continuing the Bank's existing policy by "maintaining the overnight call rate at zero percent until deflationary concern was dispelled." One member argued, however, that the Bank should shift to quantitative easing: "[A]n estimate using the Taylor rule . . . showed that the current monetary easing, which had realized 4–5 percent annual growth in the monetary base, was insufficient. Such a low growth rate of the monetary base might cause market expectations for monetary easing to dwindle" (Minutes of Policy Meeting, April 22, 1999).

As it turned out, quantitative easing did not begin until March 2001. In the meantime, the Taylor rule was used as justification for both a continuation of, and end to, the Bank's zero interest rate policy. For example, in April 2000 "many members" thought the economy was "approaching but had not yet reached a situation where it could be said that deflationary concern had been dispelled." A majority of members therefore favored continuing the zero interest rate policy. While one member advocated terminating the zero interest rate policy, another member called for "a certain amount of latitude." His analysis was based on a Taylor rule that had been prescribing an overnight call rate below zero and that only recently had recovered to around zero. "On this basis, the member and some other members said that they were not confident about whether the momentum of a self-sustained recovery in private demand could absorb the shocks from the expected reduction in stimulative measures from the fiscal side, and that there was almost no risk of inflation." The concern was that if the zero interest rate policy were terminated, the economy could stall and the zero interest rate policy would have to be reinstated (Minutes of Policy Meeting, April 10, 2000).

Later, in June 2000, board member Noboyuki Nakahara dissented against the majority's decision to maintain the zero interest rate policy. He argued in his dissent that it was necessary to further stimulate the economy, that economic conditions might deteriorate further because of increases in nonperforming loans and cautious lending by financial institutions, and that "some sort of explicit policy rule, such as the Taylor rule or the McCallum rule, should be employed to help enhance communication with the market" (Minutes of Policy Meeting, June 12, 2000).

In the following policy meeting, a member made reference to the interest rate prescription from an "optimal" Taylor rule—stating that it "might have risen close to zero percent depending on the assumption used for the calculation . . . Some might think it necessary to wait until the optimal interest rate had risen clearly above zero percent before it could be said that deflationary concern had been dispelled. It should be noted, however, that the optimal interest rate derived from the Taylor rule was merely one factor, among many, that helped in decision-making" (Minutes of Policy Meeting, June 28, 2000). A similar discussion occurred at the July meeting.

Finally, in August 2000, after considerable debate, the Bank moved away from its zero interest rate policy by moving the overnight call rate target to on average around 0.25 percent. One member who was not convinced that the economy had reached the point where deflationary concern had been dispelled "presented an analysis of the optimal interest rate derived from the Taylor rule, commenting that the level of the optimal interest rate should be evaluated with a certain amount of latitude. According to the calculations, the optimal interest rate in the current economic situation, where there was a large supply-demand gap, was in the range of slightly above to slightly below zero percent." As a result, ". . . the Bank should continue the zero interest rate policy until the optimal interest rate had more clearly risen above zero." In response, another member who supported an end to the zero interest rate policy argued that it was not just the size of the supply-demand imbalance at a point in time that mattered; ". . . the direction of changes in the gap was also a major factor that could affect price developments" (Minutes of Policy Meeting, August 11, 2000).

The Taylor rule has also been used on an ex post basis to evaluate Japanese monetary policy during the 1980s and 1990s. Numerous studies have been conducted by researchers within and outside the Bank of Japan.[21] They generally find evidence that, relative to a Taylor rule prescription, policy was held somewhat too tight in Japan from 1993 onward. However, commenting in 2002 on the economic environment in which the Bank of Japan was operating, Deputy Governor Hirohide Yamaguchi suggested that at the early stages of Japan's financial crisis ". . . there was a presumption that shocks would be contained within the financial sector and would not spread to the real side of the economy." Therefore, there was a belief that economic conditions would improve, making the case for additional stimulus less clear.

More recently, in a speech, Board member Miyako Suda (2007) discussed his view of the Taylor rule: "Needless to say, the structure of an economy is complex in reality, and central banks should not mechanistically apply a particular policy rule. In addition, since there are many versions of the Taylor rule, the central bank and the market may not necessarily share an identical one when they communicate with each other. Nevertheless, the Taylor rule is helpful, at least as one of the benchmarks for the conduct of monetary policy when we consider how a central bank should respond to various shocks, and therefore its communication with the market will improve and its accountability will be enhanced."

IV.3. Bank of England

The Bank of England is among a large group of central banks operating under a formal inflation targeting regime. As such, the Bank views itself as following a flexible "inflation targeting" rule as opposed to an instrument rule such as the Taylor rule. This does not suggest, however, that there is any inherent inconsistency in inflation targeting and the Taylor rule. Even in the extreme case, where a central bank placed no weight on output in its objective function, it may still include output in its instrument rule. For example, output may serve as an indicator of future inflation. Alternatively, in the case of a "flexible" inflation targeting regime, the central bank may still place a positive weight in its objective function on minimizing output fluctuations.

The key difference between an inflation forecast targeting rule and an instrument rule such as the Taylor rule relates primarily to the way

---

21. See, for example, Ahearne, Gagnon, Haltimaier, and Kamin (2002), Billi (2009), and Kuttner and Posen (2004) for the view from outside the Bank of Japan, or Mori, Shiratsuka, and Taguchi (2001), Okina and Shiratsuka (2001), or Fujiwara, Hara, Hirakata, Kimura, and Watanabe (2007) for the view from the Bank of Japan.

policymakers communicate with each other and the public. Inflation targeters tend to talk in terms of adjusting the policy rate as needed to bring a medium-term forecast of inflation into alignment with the inflation target, as opposed to adjusting the policy rate in response to a simple rule. One reason might be that they view themselves as relying on "optimal" policy rules that are inherently complicated, model-dependent, and difficult to communicate. Additionally, as discussed below, their forecast of inflation may be explicitly conditioned on an exogenously given future policy path as opposed to an endogenous rule.

The United Kingdom first established inflation targets in October 1992 after the suspension of sterling from the European Monetary Union (EMU) when the Chancellor of the Exchequer announced the initial inflation target. At the time the Bank of England had little independence from the Treasury. In May 1997, however, the Bank gained more autonomy when the Chancellor announced that the government was giving the Bank "operational responsibility for setting interest rates to meet the Government's inflation target." In addition, the Chancellor announced that the Bank's Monetary Policy Committee (MPC) was to make operational decisions (Bank of England 1997, 16).

Under the Bank's inflation targeting regime, the MPC bases policy decisions on its forecast of inflation over the medium term. This does not mean that the Bank ignores real economic activity in setting policy. While the 1998 Bank of England Act establishes the inflation target as the Bank's primary goal, it also requires the Bank to support the government's other goals. In practice, this requirement has meant the Bank considers how its actions will affect output volatility. As a result, the timeframe for bringing inflation back to target after an economic shock may vary depending on how the shock affects real output (Nikolov 2002).

The MPC's inflation forecast is based on the market's expectation of the future path of interest rates.[22] Thus, the forecasting model does not incorporate a Taylor rule or any policy reaction function that tries to characterize the systematic response of the MPC to economic indicators. In addition, there is no mechanical link between the forecast of inflation, the uncertainty around the forecast, and the ultimate policy decision. According to King (2001, as quoted in Nikolov 2002), ". . . if

---

22. The committee also considers alternative projections based on a constant interest rate path.

the deviation from the rule or target is too great then its use either as a means of discipline or a form of communication becomes low. But there is equally no mechanical link between any particular summary statistic of the inflation forecast and the choice of policy instrument. . . . There is always a judgment about what policy setting is appropriate given the outlook for inflation."

The Bank views its targeting rule as having a number of advantages over an instrument rule. For example, simple instrument rules such as Taylor's (that are easy to communicate to the public) are unlikely to be optimal, and optimal rules are unlikely to be simple (and therefore are likely to be difficult to communicate). In addition, they imply a mechanical link between a narrow set of economic conditions and policy decisions to which few policymakers would be willing to commit. In contrast, targeting a forecast of inflation allows policymakers to respond flexibly to a wide range of indicators and to exercise considerable judgment. Moreover, the inflation target is transparent, easily communicated, and focused on the goals of policy rather than the instruments.[23]

While Taylor rules are not prominent in the policy framework of the Bank of England, they do play a background role—as they do in most other central banks. MPC members and staff "review the prescriptions of a number of measures of the stance of policy and inflationary pressure as part of its 'suite of models' approach to policy briefing and forecasting." Prescriptions of various policy rules—including the Taylor rule—are compared with the current policy rate. "But because of the disadvantages of all of these simple rules, the MPC does not place a large weight on any individual measure" (Nikolov 2002, 8).

In the staff's version of the Taylor rule, the output and inflation gaps are lagged one period, the inflation target is 2.5 percent, the output gap is measured using a production function approach, the equilibrium real interest rate is derived from index-linked bonds, and the weight on the output gap is varied from 0.25 to 0.75. The staff analyzes and tries to explain differences between the Taylor rule prescriptions and the Bank's actual policy rates when they arise. In addition, the staff uses monetary policy rules "in both estimated and calibrated macroeconomic models to inform thinking about issues of monetary strategy" (Nikolov 2002, 8–10).

---

23. See Nikolov for more details. Mishkin (1999) and Svensson (1999) also argue in favor of targeting rules rather than instrument rules.

IV.4. Other central banks

Other inflation targeting central banks use Taylor rules in a similar fashion to the Bank of England. At the Reserve Bank of Australia, "Consideration of the current stance of policy . . . is supplemented by . . . the output of a suite of Taylor rule-type calculations . . . Staff research over the years has identified a couple of Taylor rule formulations which we think are worth checking periodically" (Stevens 2001).

In the model used for forecasting and policy analysis at the Reserve Bank of New Zealand (RBNZ)—the original inflation-targeting central bank—a specific reaction function characterizes the flexible inflation targeting regime. The policy rate is set equal to 1.4 times the sum of forecast deviations of inflation from target, six to eight quarters ahead (Black et al. 1997, as described in Huang et al. 2002, 6). Incidentally, the RBNZ claims to be the first central bank that "prepares *and* publishes economic projections based on endogenous interest rates—an approach we adopted in 1997" (Hampton 2002, 5).[24]

The Swiss National Bank draws on a variety of models in developing the Bank's inflation forecast. A Taylor rule is incorporated in both its medium-sized and small-sized macro models. Other models in use at the Bank include a VAR model and an M3 model (Jordan and Peytrignet 2002).

The use of Taylor rules at central banks in emerging market economies is complicated by the prominent role played by exchange rates in monetary policy in most of these countries. This prominence is due to the high degree of pass-through of the exchange rate to domestic inflation, the desire to maintain competitiveness in the tradable goods sector, and concern for financial stability (Mohanty and Klau 2004, 1). Nevertheless, Taylor (2000) argues that "for those emerging market economies that do not choose a policy of a 'permanently' fixed exchange rate (perhaps through a currency board or a common currency [dollarization]), then the only sound policy is one based on the *trinity of a flexible exchange rate, an inflation target, and a monetary policy rule*" (pp. 2–3, emphasis in the original).

Taylor acknowledged, however, that certain features of policy rules may need to be modified for application to emerging market economies. First, he suggested that policymakers in emerging markets might

---

24. Since 1997, other central banks—including the central banks of Norway and Sweden—have begun to condition forecasts on the bank's own expected future path of the policy rate (Kahn 2007).

want to give consideration to a rule using a monetary aggregate as the instrument instead of an interest rate. Second, it may be appropriate to have a target for the exchange rate—provided it is consistent with the inflation target over the long run. Third, without well-developed long-term capital markets, it may be necessary for central banks in emerging markets to move the policy instrument "more quickly and by a larger amount because short-term interest rates will have to do more of the work" (p. 14). Finally, based on a number of studies he concludes that a rule that focuses on minimizing inflation and output fluctuations and does not react too much to the exchange rate might work well in emerging market economies.[25]

Less clear is how emerging market central banks actually use policy rules in practice.[26] M. S. Mohanty and Marc Klau (2005) survey the objectives and instrument setting of central banks in a number of emerging market economies. All of the banks surveyed (from a sample of seven) sought to maintain stable inflation, reduce inflation, or hit an inflation target. Most of the banks, in addition, had goals for output as well as objectives for the exchange rate. Two banks had financial market conditions as an additional goal. Moreover, some central banks announce "guidelines" for setting interest rates. "These guidelines generally include how the central bank will react to a particular shock and under what circumstances it might choose to accommodate some of the shocks," Mohanty and Klau write.

"For example, the Central Bank of Chile (2000) provides a clear statement of action in the event of a price shock: only shocks that affect trend inflation are neutralized by interest rate changes, and the response is symmetric to positive and negative deviations." Another example is Korea, where the Bank of Korea follows a "look-at-everything approach. In situations of conflict of objectives—for instance, an economic slowdown or financial market uncertainty coinciding with overshooting of the inflation from the target—it follows an eclectic approach and relies heavily on judgment in setting the policy stance. Moreover, save in exceptional situations, the Bank adjusts its policy rate in small steps, usually a quarter percentage point, each time it considers a rate change" (Mohanty and Klau 2004, 3–4).

---

25. These studies include Ball (1999), Svensson (2000), and Batini, Harrison, and Millard (2001).

26. See Vašíček (2009) and Mohanty and Klau (2004) for estimated policy reaction functions for emerging market economies.

V. Concluding Remarks

The Taylor rule expressed in simple terms the view that monetary policy should be considered a systematic response to incoming information about economic conditions, as opposed to a period-by-period optimization problem. It also imbued policymakers with the concept of the Taylor principle—the idea that the policy rate should be adjusted more than one-for-one with an increase in inflation.

The idea of policy as a contingency plan, clearly spelling out how to adjust policy instruments to changing circumstances, spread quickly from academic papers, conferences, and publications to the boardrooms of central banks. At the Federal Reserve, various versions of the Taylor rule became integrated into macroeconomic models and policy analysis. FOMC members occasionally based policy positions on the recommendations of Taylor rules. Many economic developments and policy strategies were discussed in terms of policy rules. But some FOMC members, such as Alan Greenspan, remained skeptical.

While other central banks followed the Federal Reserve's lead, using Taylor rule recommendations in their models and as a cross-check to policy decisions, the Taylor rule arguably played a less central role. At the ECB, analysis of monetary and credit market conditions took greater prominence. At the Bank of Japan, persistent deflation and a zero interest rate policy limited the applicability of any interest rate rule. At the Bank of England, policy may be more accurately described as flexible inflation-forecast targeting rather than summarized by a simple instrument rule. And, in open and emerging market economies, the role of the exchange rate in practice is still hotly debated.

The Taylor rule can be seen as part of a broader movement in which commitment (and therefore credibility), transparency, and independence replaced a culture of discretion, "mystique," and occasional political influence. While many issues remain unresolved and views still differ about how the Taylor rule can best be applied in practice, the paper shows that the rule has advanced the practice of central banking.

References

Ahearne, Alan, Joseph Gagnon, Jane Haltimaier, and Steve Kamin. 2002. "Preventing Deflation: Lessons from Japan's Experience in the 1990s." Board of Governors of the Federal Reserve System. *International Finance Discussion Papers No. 729.*

Aizenman, Joshua, Michael M. Hutchison, and Ilan Noy. 2008. "Inflation Targeting and Real Exchange Rates in Emerging Markets." Manuscript.

Asso, Francesco, George A. Kahn, and Robert Leeson. 2007. "The Taylor Rule and the Transformation of Monetary Policy." Federal Reserve Bank of Kansas City Research Working Paper No. 07–11, December.

———. 2010. "The Taylor Rule and the Practice of Central Banking." Federal Reserve Bank of Kansas City Research Working Paper No. 10–05.

Asso, Francesco, and Robert Leeson. 2011. "Monetary Policy Rules: From Adam Smith to John Taylor." *John Taylor's Contribution to Monetary Theory and Policy*. Stanford: Hoover Institution Press.

Ball, Laurence. 1999. "Policy Rules for Open Economies." In Taylor 1999.

Bank of England. 1997. *Inflation Report*. May.

Bank of Japan. 1999–2000. "Minutes of Policy Meetings," various months.

Batini, Nicoletta, Richard Harrison, and Stephen Millard. 2001. "Monetary Policy Rules for an Open Economy." Bank of England Working Paper No. 149, December.

Bernanke, Ben S., and Frederic Mishkin. 1992. *Central Bank Behavior and the Strategy of Monetary Policy: Observations from Six Industrialized Countries*. National Bureau of Economic Research, Macroeconomics Annual. Cambridge, MA: MIT Press.

Billi, Roberto M. 2009. "Was Monetary Policy Optimal During Past Deflation Scares?" Federal Reserve Bank of Kansas City *Economic Review* 94(3) (3rd quarter): 67–98.

Black, Richard, Vincenzo Cassino, Aaron Drew, Eric Hansen, Benjamin Hunt, David Rose, and Alisdair Scott. 1997. "The Forecasting and Policy System: The Core Model." Reserve Bank of New Zealand, Research Working Paper No. 43, August.

Blundell-Wignall, Adrian, ed. 1992. *Inflation, Disinflation and Monetary Policy*. Proceedings of a Conference, Sydney: Reserve Bank of Australia.

Brash, Donald T. 1996. "New Zealand's Remarkable Reforms." Speech at the Institute of Economic Affairs, London, June.

Central Bank of Chile. 2000. *Monetary Policy of the Central Bank of Chile: Objectives and Transmission*.

Clarida, Richard, Jordi Galí, and Mark Gertler. 1998. "Monetary Policy Rules in Practice: Some International Evidence." *European Economic Review* 42: 1033–67.

DiClemente, Robert V., and Burnham. 1995. "Policy Rules Shed New Light on Fed Stance." *Economic and Market Analysis: Monetary Policy Update*. Salomon Brothers, June 26.

European Central Bank. 2001. "Issues Related to Monetary Policy Rules." *Monthly Bulletin*, October: 37–50.

———. 2010. http://www.ecb.int/mopo/strategy/html/index.en.html.

Fagan, Gabriel, Jerome Henry, and Ricardo Mestre. 2001. "An Area-Wide Model (AWM) for the Euro Area." European Central Bank Working Paper Series No. 42, January.

Federal Open Market Committee. 1995–2001. Transcripts of FOMC meetings, various issues, http://www.federalreserve.gov/monetarypolicy/fomc_histori cal.htm.

Fischer, Björn, Michele Lenza, Huw Pill, and Lucrezia Reichlin. 2006. "Money and Monetary Policy: The ECB Experience 1999–2006." Second draft of a paper prepared for the fourth ECB Central Banking Conference on *The Role of Money: Money and Monetary Policy in the Twenty-First Century*, Frankfurt, Germany, November.

Foust, Dean. 1995. "How Low Should Rates Be?" *Business Week,* October 9: 68–72.

Fujiwara, Ippei, Naoko Hara, Naokisa Hirakata, Takeshi Kimura, and Shinichiro Watanabe. 2007. "Japanese Monetary Policy during the Collapse of the Bubble Economy: A View of Policymaking under Uncertainty." Bank of Japan, *Monetary and Economic Studies* 25(2): 89–128.

Goodhart, Charles A. E. 1992. "The Objectives for, and Conduct of, Monetary Policy in the 1990s." In Blundell-Wignall 1992.

———. 2010. "The Political Economy of Inflation Targets: New Zealand and the UK." In *Canadian Policy Debates and Case Studies in Honour of David Laidler,* ed. Robert Leeson, 171–214. London: Palgrave Macmillan.

Greenspan, Alan. 1993. Testimony before the Committee on Banking, Finance, and Urban Affairs, U.S. House of Representatives, July 20.

———. 1997. Speech at Center for Economic Policy Research (CEPR), Stanford University, September 5.

Greider, William. 1987. *Secrets of the Temple: How the Federal Reserve Runs the Country.* New York: Simon and Schuster.

Hall, Robert. 2005. "Separating the Business Cycle from Other Economic Fluctuations." *The Greenspan Era: Lessons for the Future,* 133–80. Symposium sponsored by the Federal Reserve Bank of Kansas City.

Hampton, Tim. 2002. "The Role of the Reserve Bank's Macro-model in the Formulation of Interest Rate Projections." Reserve Bank of New Zealand *Bulletin* 65(2):5–11.

Huang, Angela, Dimitri Margaritis, and David Mayes. 2002. "Monetary Policy Rules in Practice: Evidence from New Zealand." Paper prepared for the workshop on *The Role of Policy Rates in the Conduct of Monetary Policy,* European Central Bank, Frankfurt, March 11–12.

Issing, Otmar. 2002. "Monetary Policy in a Changing Economic Environment." In *Rethinking Stablization Policy,* 183–205, Federal Reserve Bank of Kansas City.

———. 2007. "John Taylor and the Theory and Practice of Central Banking: Some Reflections," Federal Reserve Bank of Dallas Conference on "John Taylor's Contribution to Monetary Theory and Policy," October 12–13.

Jordan, Thomas, and Michel Peytrignet. 2002. "Forecasting Inflation at the Swiss National Bank." Paper prepared for the workshop on *The Role of Policy Rates in the Conduct of Monetary Policy,* European Central Bank, Frankfurt, March 11–12.

Kahn, George K. 2007. "Communicating a Policy Path: The Next Frontier in Central Bank Transparency?" Federal Reserve Bank of Kansas City *Economic Review* 92(1) (1st quarter): 25–51.

———, and Scott Benolkin. 2007. "The Role of Money in Monetary Policy: Why Do the Fed and ECB See it So Differently?" Federal Reserve Bank of Kansas City *Economic Review* 92(3) (3rd quarter): 5–36.

———, and Klara Parrish. 1998. "Conducting Monetary Policy with Inflation Targets." Federal Reserve Bank of Kansas City *Economic Review* 83(3) (3rd quarter): 5–32.

King, Mervyn. 2000. Speech to the joint luncheon of the American Economic Association and the American Finance Association, Boston. January 7.

———. 2001. "Comment on L. Svensson." *The Monetary Transmission Process: Recent Developments and Lessons for Europe.* Deutsche Bundesbank.

Kuttner, Kenneth N., and Adam S. Posen. 2004. "The Difficulty of Discerning What's Too Tight: Taylor Rules and Japanese Monetary Policy." *North American Journal of Economics and Finance* 15:53–74.

Lipsky, John P. 1993. "Keeping Inflation Low in the 1990s." *Economic and Market Analysis: Prospects for Financial Markets.* Salomon Brothers, December.

Loayza, Norman, and Klaus Schmidt-Hebbel, eds. 2002. *Monetary Policy: Rules and Transmission Mechanisms.* Santiago: Banco Central de Chile.

Lubik, Thomas A., and Frank Schorfheide. 2007. "Do Central Banks Respond to Exchange Rate Movements? A Structural Investigation." *Journal of Monetary Economics* 54(4) (May): 1069–87.

Meulendyke, Ann-Marie. 1998. *U.S. Monetary Policy and Financial Markets.* New York: Federal Reserve Bank of New York.

Meyer, Laurence. 2009. "Dueling Taylor Rules." *Monetary Policy Insights,* Macroeconomic Advisers, August 20.

Mishkin, Frederic. 1999. "International Experiences with Different Monetary Policy Regimes." *Journal of Monetary Economics* 43(3) (June): 579–606.

Mohanty, Madhu S., and Marc Klau. 2004. "Monetary Policy Rules in Emerging Market Economies: Issues and Evidence." BIS Working Papers, No. 149, March.

———. 2005. "Monetary Policy Rules in Emerging Market Economies: Issues and Evidence." In *Monetary Policy and Macroeconomic Stabilization in Latin Amer-*

ica, eds. Rolf J. Langhammer and Lúcio Vinhas de Souza, 177–97. Berlin: Springer-Verlag.

Mori, Naruki, Shigenori Shiratsuka, and Hiroo Taguchi. 2001. "Policy Responses to the Post-Bubble Adjustments in Japan: A Tentative Review." *Monetary and Economic Studies* 19 (S-1), Institute for Monetary and Economic Studies, Bank of Japan.

Nelson, William R. 2008. "Monetary Policy Decisions: Preparing the Inputs and Communicating the Outcomes." Bank for International Settlements, BIS Papers No. 37, February.

Nikolov, Kalin. 2002. "Monetary Policy Rules at the Bank of England." Paper prepared for the workshop on *The Role of Policy Rates in the Conduct of Monetary Policy,* European Central Bank, Frankfurt, March 11–12.

Okina, Kunio, and Shigenori Shiratsuka. 2002. "Asset Price Bubbles, Price Stability, and Monetary Policy: Japan's Experience." *Monetary and Economic Studies* 20(3), Institute for Monetary and Economic Studies, Bank of Japan.

Orphanides, Athanasios, and David Wilcox. 1996. "The Opportunistic Approach to Disinflation." Finance and Economics Discussion Series, 96–24, Board of Governors of the Federal Reserve System, May.

Orphanides, Athanasios, David Small, Volker Wieland, and David Wilcox. 1997. "A Quantitative Exploration of the Opportunistic Approach to Disinflation." Finance and Economics Discussion Series 97–36, Board of Governors of the Federal Reserve System, June.

Prowse, Michael. 1995. "Decision Time for Alan Greenspan." *Financial Times,* July 3.

Rudebusch, Glenn D. 2009. "The Fed's Monetary Policy Response to the Current Crisis." Federal Reserve Bank of San Francisco *Economic Letter,* no. 2009–17, May 22.

Schmidt-Hebbel, Klaus, and Alejandro Werner. 2002. "Inflation Targeting in Brazil, Chile, and Mexico: Performance, Credibility, and the Exchange Rate." *Economica,* Spring: 31–89.

Sellon, Gordon H. 2008. "Monetary Policy Transparency and Private Sector Forecasts: Evidence from Survey Data." Federal Reserve Bank of Kansas City *Economic Review* 93(3) (3rd quarter): 7–34.

Stark, Jürgen. 2008. "Implications for the Conduct of Monetary Policy." *International Symposium: Globalization, Inflation and Monetary Policy.* Paris: Banque de France.

Stevens, Glenn. 2001. "The Monetary Process at the RBA." Speech to the Economic Society of Australia (Victorian Branch) Forecasting Conference, Melbourne, October 10.

Suda, Miyako. 2007. "The Current Situation and the Outlook for Japan's Economy and the Conduct of Monetary Policy." Speech to a Meeting with Business Leaders in Mie, Japan, September 27.

Svensson, Lars E.O. 1999. "Inflation Targeting as a Monetary Policy Rule." *Journal of Monetary Economics* 43(3) (June): 607–54.

———. 2000. "Open-Economy Inflation Targeting." *Journal of International Economics* 50(1) (February): 155–83.

Taylor, John B. 1992. "Comment on B. Bernanke and F. Mishkin, 'Central Bank Behavior and the Strategy of Monetary Policy: Observations from Six Industrialized Countries'," 234–37. *NBER Macroeconomics Annual.* Cambridge, MA: MIT Press.

———. 1993. "Discretion Versus Policy Rules in Practice." *Carnegie-Rochester Conference Series on Public Policy* 39 (December): 195–214.

———, ed. 1999. *Monetary Policy Rules.* Chicago: University of Chicago Press.

———. 2000. "Using Monetary Policy Rules in Emerging Market Economies." Revised version of a paper presented at the Seventy-fifth Anniversary Conference, "Stabilization and Monetary Policy: The International Experience," Bank of Mexico, November 14–15.

———. 2007. "Housing and Monetary Policy." *Housing, Housing Finance, and Monetary Policy.* Kansas City: Federal Reserve Bank of Kansas City, August.

———. 2009. "The Need for a Clear and Credible Exit Strategy." In *The Road Ahead for the Fed,* eds. John Ciorciari and John Taylor. Stanford: Hoover Institution Press.

Thiessen, Gordon G. 1998. "The Canadian Experience with Targets for Inflation Control." The Gibson Lecture. Queen's University, Kingston, Ontario, October 15.

Vašíček, Bořek. 2009. "Monetary Policy Rules and Inflation Process in Open Emerging Economies: Evidence for 12 New EU Members." William Davidson Institute Working Paper No. 968, University of Michigan, September.

Volcker, Paul. 1990. "The Triumph of Central Banking." The 1990 Per Jacobsson Lecture, Per Jacobsson Foundation, Washington, D.C., September 23.

Yamaguchi, Yutaka. 2002. "Monetary Policy in a Changing Economic Environment." Federal Reserve Bank of Kansas City, *Jackson Hole Economic Symposium*: 241–51.

THREE

A COMPARISON WITH MILTON FRIEDMAN

Edward Nelson

1. Introduction

Thirty years ago, John Taylor observed, "Of course, you have to go back and try to interpret what early economists actually said. Because they were never quite as explicit as economists tend to be now, this is not easy."[1] Taylor probably did not have Milton Friedman in mind when he made those remarks. But, in retrospect, they fit Friedman very well, as Friedman's work rarely used models that were very explicit, especially by today's standards. Moreover, Friedman qualifies as a significant "early economist" for the research areas that Taylor has been most associated with: nominal rigidities; the role of expectations in price setting; welfare analysis and trade-offs for monetary policy; and monetary policy rules. In the discussion that follows, I attempt to provide a

Edward Nelson is chief of the Monetary Studies section in the Division of Monetary Affairs at the Federal Reserve Board.

The author is indebted to Otmar Issing, Benjamin Keen, Kevin Kliesen, Evan Koenig, and John Taylor for helpful comments on earlier versions of this paper. The author also acknowledges the skilled research assistance provided for this paper by the late Faith Weller. The views expressed in this paper are solely the responsibility of the author and should not be interpreted as reflecting the views of the Board of Governors of the Federal Reserve System or of any person associated with the Federal Reserve System.

1. November 1982 remarks, quoted in Klamer (1983, 173).

systematic comparison of Friedman's and Taylor's views on these issues and their implied modeling choices.

2. Objective Function

How do Friedman's and Taylor's views of policymaker objective functions compare? Taylor was more explicit on this issue, so I consider him first.

Taylor on policymaker objectives

As is well known, Taylor (1979) worked with a policymaker objective function that penalized deviations of inflation from a target and output from its natural level. The function consisted of the expected value of the sum across periods of the loss function,

$$\lambda(y_t - y_t^*)^2 + (1-\lambda)(\pi_t - \pi^*)^2, \ \lambda \in [0,1], \tag{1}$$

where $y_t - y_t^*$ is the output gap (i.e., the difference between the logs of output and the value that output would take if there were no nominal rigidities), π_t is inflation, and π^* is an inflation target. Taylor subsequently argued that this choice of objective function was an implication of rational expectations models that included nominal rigidities:

> [T]he objective of macroeconomic policy is to reduce the size (or the duration) of the fluctuations of output, employment, and inflation from normal or desired levels . . .
>
> [T]he rational expectations approach is fairly specific about what the objectives of policy should be. Changing the natural or normal levels of output and employment is not the direct objective of stabilization policy . . . As a first approximation, these normal levels are not influenced by macroeconomic policy . . . [I]t is important to choose a target [inflation] rate that maximizes economic welfare . . . [and] to minimize fluctuations around the target. . . . (Taylor 1986a, 159, 160)

On the other hand, Taylor (1986a, 153) conceded that rational expectations models with staggered nominal contracts "need some bolstering of their microeconomic foundations" and also (1987, 351) described the aforementioned stabilization goal as the "assumed goal," not necessarily the model-implied goal. In fact, staggered-contracts models with deeper micro-foundations and a model-consistent welfare function do largely support the loss function that Taylor used, as shown by Julio Rotemberg and Michael Woodford (1997).[2] There are, however, two major qualifications:

First, the setting of the output target at the natural output level is not automatically implied by these models. One case that delivers a zero-output-gap target is when the natural level of output corresponds to the efficient level of output. This is essentially what occurs in Rotemberg and Woodford (1997): though their model contains imperfect goods-market competition and so tends to deliver an inefficiently low long-run level of aggregate output, they assume that a fiscal subsidy raises steady-state output to the efficient level.

Alternatively, the natural level of output may be lower than the social optimum, but the monetary authority might explicitly disown attempts to push output above its natural value. Taylor has consistently advocated this stance, most explicitly in Taylor (1987), and it is also the position taken by Bennett T. McCallum (1995), Mervyn A. King (1997), and Lars E. O. Svensson (1997).[3] Specifically, Taylor has argued that monetary policy analysis should not concern itself with whether the natural level of output is efficient and should instead treat the natural level as the value around which output should be stabilized (Taylor 1987, 351; Robert E. Hall and Taylor 1997, 478).

The zero-output-gap target is natural to Taylor because it captures the message of the natural rate hypothesis. He has always endorsed this hypothesis in his writings, maintaining that models should reflect, and policymakers should take into account, the notion that "the economy tends to return to the natural rate of unemployment" irrespective of monetary policy rule; conformably, "no long-term relationship exists between inflation and the deviation of real GDP from potential GDP."[4] With no scope for policymakers to steer output away

---

2. The Rotemberg-Woodford objective function that sums the loss function across periods does differ from the one that Taylor proposed, since Taylor argues for no discounting (see Taylor 1979, 1276; 1986a, 159; and Hall and Taylor 1997, 474), whereas Rotemberg and Woodford recommend that the welfare function feature discounting (using the representative household's rate of discount).

3. As shown in Woodford (2003), a model with inefficient potential output and no subsidy usually does not admit a quadratic approximation for the welfare function. My conjecture is that in this environment the Taylor (1987) procedure amounts to the following: as far as is possible, rewrite the approximation of the welfare function so that terms in output appear as deviations from potential output; any leftover output terms are then ignored when the policymaker carries out optimization.

4. The quotations are from Taylor (1987, 351) and Taylor (1994, 38).

from the natural level in the long run, a loss function featuring a zero-output-gap objective better reflects the economic structure. Likewise, Taylor has not been in favor of economic analysis that postulates a policymaker desire to target a positive output gap, either in positive-economics or normative applications. This was a major reason why Taylor was one of the earliest to speak out against time-consistency explanations for the Great Inflation, which rely on policymakers having an output target in excess of the natural level of output (see, e.g., Taylor 1992, 14–15).

The second qualification is that the presence of wage stickiness means that price-inflation variability is generally not the only inflation term in the social welfare function; wage-inflation variability appears, too (Erceg, Henderson, and Levin 2000). I defer discussion of wage stickiness in Taylor's framework until section 4 below.

Friedman on policymaker objectives

A close reading of Friedman's work suggests that he favored a policy-maker objective function close to that advanced by Taylor, i.e., penalizing inflation deviations from target and output gap deviations from zero, with no other terms in the objective function. Moreover, he believed that by the early 1980s policymakers had moved to a strategy meant to pursue this objective.

To establish this, the first thing to note is that Friedman's advocacy of monetary targeting (discussed further below) did not amount to a denial of the position that the principal objective of monetary policy should be price stability. Though believing that real money holdings generate utility (see Friedman 1969), Friedman did not base his advocacy of monetary targeting on this component of utility; he did not list stability in real money balances as an ultimate objective.[5] Rather, the appropriate welfare function for monetary policy puts highest weight on price stability:

> With respect to ultimate objectives, it's easy to cite the holy trinity that has become standard: full employment, economic growth, and stable prices . . . What is the special role of monetary policy in contributing to these objectives? . . . [T]here is today a worldwide consensus, not

---

5. Friedman specifically disavowed the carrying out by monetary policy of the rule he derived in his 1969 paper, so he was not interested in bringing the level of real balances to the value that satiated households.

only among most academic economists but also among monetary practitioners, that the long-run objective of monetary policy must be price stability (Friedman 1982a, 100).

As would be expected from his work on the natural rate hypothesis (Friedman 1968), Friedman interpreted the full-employment objective as a stabilization objective, i.e., minimizing fluctuations in the output gap. Therefore, the goals of policy should be "a reasonably stable economy in the short run and a reasonably stable price level in the long run."[6]

Friedman acknowledged that the stabilization objective could in principle be pursued jointly with the price-stability objective, in which case one would be "pursuing the long-run policy in a manner that contributes to minimizing economic fluctuation."[7] He also indicated that he did not disagree with the weights in the objective function used in Keynesian work.[8] Acceptance of such an objective function would imply some allowance in setting policy for trade-offs between objectives to the extent that such trade-offs existed. Friedman granted this in principle, subscribing to the view that in public policy there should be "a sane balance among competing objectives."[9] Indeed, Friedman's belief in the existence of a short-run output gap/inflation trade-off, considered further below, was one reason for his preference, in a situation starting from high inflation, for a progressive step-down in money growth toward a constant money growth rule. He argued that such a program offered a superior way of managing the short-run trade-off to what had been pursued in practice during the Volcker disinflation. The Volcker disinflation, he argued, had brought inflation down too quickly and produced a deeper than necessary trough in output.[10] Further details of the arguments underlying Friedman's advocacy of constant money growth can be brought out by considering his and Taylor's positions on monetary policy rules.

---

6. In Joint Economic Committee (1959, 605).

7. Friedman (1982a,100).

8. "I doubt very much that there is any significant difference between [Modigliani] and me, for example, on the value judgments we attach to unemployment and inflation." (Friedman 1977a, 12.)

9. Friedman (1979a).

10. Friedman and Friedman (1984, 91–92).

3. Monetary Policy Rules

It is tempting to think of Friedman and Taylor as on opposite ends of the spectrum on the issue of monetary policy rules. That may seem a natural conclusion given the rules they came to advocate: Friedman, a constant money growth rule; Taylor, an activist interest-rate rule. And, yes, Taylor (1982) went on record with the view that Friedman's constant-money-growth rule was "extremely undesirable." But focusing on this statement by Taylor, or on a contrast between Taylor's (1993a) rule and Friedman's monetary rule, would lead one to overstate the differences between the two on the issue of policy rules. As we will see, Taylor has often emphasized the links between his recommendations and those of Friedman; in particular, the focus on a non-accommodative and rule-based policy. Taylor also downplayed the distinction between money-growth and interest-rate rules. Where Taylor and Friedman differ most is in their judgments about how much monetary policy should be based on assumptions about the structural behavior of the economy. This leads naturally to different judgments about the appropriate degree of activist stabilization policy and also about the connection of policy decisions to ultimate policy objectives.

Friedman's framework

Friedman's money growth rule separates the variables that he believed should appear in the policymaker objective function (inflation and the output gap) from the variable that policy should directly target (money or money growth). The focus on an intermediate variable and on a non-activist rule reflected his opposition, discussed below, to deploying optimal control methods; more generally, it reflected his doubts about the practical success of monetary policy rules that responded to final objectives or rested on structural economic models.

Friedman's opposition to responding to final objectives arose from distinct rationalizations for each of the two final objectives, inflation and the output gap.

Inflation. Friedman noted that monetary policy affected inflation with a lag; current inflation was therefore unsuitable as a target and inappropriate as a variable on which to feed back, since that "would produce a monetary policy that was always fighting the last war."[11] Targeting

---

11. Friedman (1982b). This argument foreshadowed Bernanke, Laubach, Mishkin, and Posen's (1999, 298) criticism of "policies that react to inflation only after it has become a

expected future inflation, on the other hand, would require too much reliance by policymakers on their estimates of structural relationships linking monetary policy actions and inflation (i.e., it would be sensitive to the specification of the IS, LM, and Phillips curve relationships), and policy actions could be destabilizing in practice. Hence Friedman's judgment that responding to prices or inflation implied "a bad rule although a good objective" and his conclusion, "A rule in terms of the quantity of money seems to me far superior, for both the short and the long run, than a rule in terms of price-level stabilization."[12]

Nevertheless, Friedman did not regard activist rules that responded to inflation, nominal income, or nominal income growth as non-monetarist. He noted that an implication of his own research was that "monetary policy is an appropriate and proper tool directed at achieving price stability or a desired rate of price change."[13] Though targeting nominal variables other than the money stock required too much fine-tuning for Friedman's liking, he saw them as monetarist rules because they shared "the quantity theory emphasis on nominal magnitudes."[14] This way of phrasing matters does not adequately reflect the relationship between the quantity theory and policy rules. A more precise way of putting things is that these rules reflect the quantity theory's emphasis on nominal magnitudes as *the variables ultimately determined by the monetary authorities*. Many expositions of the quantity theory, including some of Friedman's, do emphasize real variables, but as variables determined in the long run by factors other than monetary policy.

Output gap. Friedman's most important basis for excluding real variables from the list of targets was the natural rate hypothesis: real variables reverted to their natural values in the long run, irrespective of what monetary policy did. This position, however, was not a satisfactory basis for denying monetary policy a stabilization role. In principle, as Friedman (1968) acknowledged, the absence of a long-run influence still left real variables as candidate data on which policy might feed back, provided they appeared in gap form. Gaps would likely provide

---

problem," although Bernanke et alias' suggested solution, in contrast to Friedman's proposals, was to concentrate on expected future inflation. As it turns out, policy rules that respond to current inflation typically perform well—i.e., are stabilizing—in simulated New Keynesian models, largely because the forward-looking nature of price setting compensates for the delayed character of the policy response.

12. The quotations are from Friedman (1982b) and Friedman (1967, 4; 1969 reprint, 84).

13. Friedman (1977a, 13).

14. Friedman (1987, 18).

information about inflation; moreover, the stabilization of gaps was itself a desirable goal.

But Friedman came out against policy responses to unemployment or output even when these were expressed as deviations from natural values; instead, he argued, full employment should not be sought "directly" by monetary policy (Friedman 1982a, 100). First, the lack of knowledge required for fine-tuning again produced the danger of policy being destabilizing in practice. Second, targeting a gap variable required estimation of the unobserved natural rates of interest, output, or unemployment. This in principle was subject to bias since "it is almost impossible to define full employment in a way that is logically precise" and in practice had resulted in "unduly ambitious targets of full employment."[15] Stabilization policy intended to promote a zero output gap had thus led to unintended targeting of positive gaps, making inflation worse. Money growth targeting protected monetary policy from problems associated with responding to gaps.

There are clear links between these positions and the work of Athanasios Orphanides (2003) on the danger of relying on real-time measures of the output gap when formulating policy. Orphanides himself motivates his work with Friedman statements going back to the 1940s. Orphanides also notes that Friedman's money rule is in terms of growth rates and it is based on data that tend not to have the large serially correlated revisions associated with levels of series. Friedman's money growth rule was also insensitive to data revisions for a more subtle reason. While Friedman generally advocated an M2-type aggregate as the monetary target, he stressed as an important feature of the rule the arrangement that the open market operations used to hit the M2 target be announced ahead of time (see especially Friedman 1982a). That is, Friedman's M2 growth rule is less usefully thought of as a targeting rule (as in Svensson 2005) than as an operational instrument rule (as in McCallum and Nelson 2005). Accordingly, information obtained in subsequent periods would not lead to a different retrospective prescription from the rule, even if such information would have secured more precision in hitting the M2 target. Data revisions would fall into this category. Strictly speaking, therefore, Friedman's money growth rule prescription is not subject to a real-time/final data distinction.

Friedman (1960, 23, 98) freely acknowledged that a constant money growth rule did not correspond to optimal monetary policy. Rather, he

---

15. The quotations are from Friedman (1963; 1968 reprint, 40) and Friedman and Friedman (1980, 311).

offered it as a way of preventing both the policy mistakes that could result from activist monetary policy in the presence of imperfect knowledge and the repetition of historical policy mistakes that had been associated with large variations in the money stock. The latter consideration comes out in Friedman's statement, "the major argument for the rule has always seemed to me to be far less that it would moderate minor cyclical fluctuations than that it would render impossible the major mistakes in monetary policy that have from time to time had such devastating effects."[16]

Monetary policy rules in Taylor's framework

Taylor saw rational expectations as changing the monetary policy debate from being about rules versus discretion to being about the choice of monetary policy rule:

> [M]acroeconomic policy should be stipulated and evaluated as a rule, rather than as one-time changes in the policy instruments . . . There is a big distinction between "discretionary" and "activist" policies . . . Activist and constant-growth-rate policy rules have much more in common with each other than do activist policy rules and discretionary policy. (Taylor 1986a, 155, 157)

Taylor therefore was not inclined to see the constant money growth rule as in a different spirit from the feedback rules, nor did he always stress a contrast between interest-rate and money growth rules. He looked on arrangements that used money as the instrument as implying a particular form of the interest-rate rule and wrote favorably of aspects of a constant-money-growth rule in that light: fixed money growth implied "an automatic increase in the interest rate" when aggregate demand rises, and this was one of its "stabilizing properties" (Taylor 1999a, 64–65). Confirming these stabilizing properties of a constant money growth rule, Taylor (1979, 1,282) found in simulations that the rule produced a lower output gap variance than did the historical postwar U.S. policy rule.

But the fact is that Taylor was never a supporter of a constant money growth rule, coming up with an alternative rule in his published research in 1979 (Taylor 1979) and strongly rejecting constant money growth as a desirable policy option in a congressional submission in

---

16. Friedman (1966a; 1969 reprint, 154).

1982 (Taylor 1982). His own proposed activist rules have evolved from optimal-control-based rules in the 1970s to simple policy rules for money in the early and mid-1980s to his advocacy of interest-rate rules today. The constant theme has been rule-based policymaking with feedbacks but with lack of accommodation of inflation.

Optimal control

An initial source of disagreement between Friedman and Taylor in the 1970s was on the value of optimal control in monetary policy analysis. The disagreement is made apparent by simply juxtaposing the title of Taylor's (1979) paper, "Estimation and Control of a Macroeconomic Model with Rational Expectations," against Friedman's (1973a, 9) statement that "control theory . . . requires delicate fine-tuning for which the Fed has neither the knowledge nor the demonstrated capacity."

This did not become, however, the area of durable disagreement between Taylor and Friedman on rules. By the early 1980s, Taylor was de-emphasizing optimal control in favor of simple policy rules (see, for example, Taylor 1981a). He now stressed that optimal control was complex and model-specific (Taylor 1986a, 162). Instead, what he now emphasized was "a simpler rule," relying on few arguments, which might be a good approximation of optimal policy in Taylor's model but by implication was less model-sensitive.

Taylor's move to simple rules

These early rules had the money supply as the policy instrument. Taylor (2007, 195) has described the money supply rule inspired by his 1979 analysis as "effectively a 'Taylor rule,' though for the money supply." Experiments in Taylor (1981a) intended to determine the best simple-rule approximation to the optimal rule of 1979 actually reached a rule with somewhat different arguments from those in the Taylor rule. Instead of responding to inflation and the output gap, the simple rule for money growth had no inflation term, with responses to the output gap and the change in the output gap. But the absence of inflation from the money growth rule is not a source of material difference from the Taylor rule. A zero response of money growth to inflation implies policymaker non-acquiescence to the existing inflation rate, while anything short of a larger-than-unit-response of an interest-rate rule to inflation will (other things equal) tend to perpetuate the existing inflation rate, or worse. The simplified 1979 money rule therefore shares with the

Taylor rule the qualitative feature that it is non-accommodative, and both rules encapsulate Taylor's (1986a, 162) position that "monetary policy has a stabilization role but no accommodation role." The non-zero response to the change in the output gap (a speed-limit response) is a material difference between the simplified 1979 rule and the Taylor rule. But estimates of interest-rate rules inspired by the Taylor rule sometimes allow for a speed-limit response by including more than one lag of the output gap (or of de-trended output) as regressors (see, for example, Rotemberg and Woodford 1997).

Taylor was unequivocal on the point that his proposed feedback rules were preferable to Friedman's money growth rule: "[a] specific activist rule would work better than a monetarist rule" (Taylor 1986a, 162). He recognized, as many had not, that Friedman had never claimed that a money growth rule was optimal. The claim that the money growth rule could not be beaten was a product of the flexible-price rational expectations literature, not a contention of Friedman's. Indeed, Taylor offered one of Friedman's most clear-cut statements on the issue: "A believer in monetarist theory still can favor an activist monetary policy as a way to offset other changes in the economy."[17] Taylor understood that Friedman's case for a money growth rule rested instead on a model-uncertainty argument. But Taylor disagreed with Friedman on the quantitative importance of this issue and rejected model uncertainty as the basis for refraining from activist rules. Taylor's definitions of policy rules tended to presume an activist rule, as in his reference to policy rules as "the way the policymakers respond to events."[18]

In discussing Taylor's position on activism, I find it useful to separate the discussion into two issues: allowing the money supply to respond to money demand shocks; and then, more generally, systematic monetary policy responses to other economic shocks.

Money demand shocks. An area of direct disagreement between Friedman and Taylor was whether the monetary policy rule should attempt to accommodate money demand shocks. Friedman argued that there was too much uncertainty about money demand to make accommodation desirable:

---

17. Friedman (1984a, 3), quoted in Taylor (1986a, 153). Similarly, Friedman (1985, 15) stated, "A monetarist no less than a Keynesian interpretation of economic fluctuations can lead to a fine-tuning approach to economic policy."

18. Taylor (1986b, 2039).

> In principle, if we knew about autonomous changes in the real demand for money, it would be right to adjust the nominal supply to them. However, we don't know about them. (Friedman 1973b, 31).

> [W]hat you really have to demonstrate is that, over time, you will in fact know enough about such changes and will be able to identify them soon enough, so that you can make adjustments which, on the average, will do more good than harm. (Friedman 1977a, 26)

There is considerable substance to this reservation on Friedman's part. How much accommodation is needed to insulate the economy from money demand shocks is not a question that can be put on auto-pilot. For example, using changes in velocity to gauge the required amount of monetary accommodation is not without problems. Since velocity is defined residually as the ratio of nominal GDP to money, a velocity movement might reflect not a permanent money demand shift but instead a faster response of money than of nominal income to a shock that will ultimately move income by the same amount as money. Of course, holding the nominal interest rate constant in the face of a money demand shock will mean that the shock is accommodated one-for-one, but it will also mean that other shocks which create pressure on interest rates will be accommodated. Thus Friedman feared that a scheme other than constant money growth will provoke monetary responses to "all sorts of changes that . . . should not be accommodated" (Friedman 1977a, 18).

This criticism applies more fundamentally to interest-rate pegging than to an appropriately formulated, non-accommodative, interest-rate rule; it would not usually apply to the Taylor rule, for example. In fact, while Friedman was a notable critic of using the short-term nominal interest rate as a policy instrument, his two main objections were not generic criticisms of interest-rate rules. Instead, they highlighted two particularly weak types of rule: pure rate-pegging; and rules that did not take into account the nominal rate/real rate distinction. It is true that, in the 1960s and 1970s, examples of successful interest-rate rules were hard to find, so that one was more entitled to the presumption that movement to a base money rule was in practice necessary for delivering the requisite anti-inflationary movements of interest rates. When considering the choice between instrument rules that were more competitive with one another—i.e., money base instrument rules versus nominal interest-rate rules that incorporated vigorous responses to nominal variables—Friedman continued to be in favor of base rules, but admitted that it was a tactical, not a strategic, issue.

Taylor, by contrast, has been consistently more optimistic than Friedman on the scope for monetary policy to offset money demand shocks. Taylor (1982) observed:

> In my view, however, it is possible for the monetary authorities to discover shifts in money demand and to react to them with a relatively short lag. Such shifts should be accommodated by changing the supply of money.

Other shocks. Taylor (1992, 29) observed that "good policy is characterized by systematic responses to economic shocks." Identifying economic shocks such as disturbances to the Phillips curve, production function, and preferences, and determining the stabilizing policy reaction, are surely even more model-dependent exercises than in the case of money demand shocks. Accordingly, Taylor firmly associated himself with using structural models both in policy analysis and policy formulation. He judged that the appropriate response to the Lucas critique was to use models whose parameters (including parameters governing nominal rigidity) could be legitimately treated as structural and not as functions of the policy regime.[19] Monetary policy rules could then be coherently analyzed with these models. Moreover, structural models should be used in policymaking: "policy actions should be based on structural relationships" and "structural models . . . might be useful for formulating policy."[20]

The position that policymakers should use structural models is also implied by Taylor's advocacy of monetary policy rules that include a response to the output gap. Taylor (1999a, 63) acknowledged "a large degree of uncertainty about measuring potential GDP (and, thus, the output gap)." But he argued that the appropriate policy reaction to this uncertainty was to use a simple policy rule with a reduced, but still positive, response to the output gap (Taylor 1999a, 63–64). He has encountered this issue both in his policy and research work. While at the Council of Economic Advisers in 1976–77, Taylor was involved in a major downward revision of potential output published in the 1977 *Economic Report of the President.* Furthermore, after his early work

---

19. See Taylor (1986a, 156; 1986b, 2038).
20. The quotations are from Taylor (1981b, 81) and Taylor (1993b, 5).

used output gap estimates that implied an average postwar gap for the United States of minus 1.9 percent (Taylor 1979, 1282), Taylor utilized more economic structure when estimating the gap by imposing the natural-rate-hypothesis condition that the gap be zero on average in postwar data (see, for example, Taylor 1986c, 641).

Taylor also acknowledged that the Taylor rule requires an estimate (for the intercept term in the rule) of the steady-state equilibrium real interest rate, but has rejected this problem as a justification for turning to money growth rules. Instead, he has argued that the way to overcome policy errors that might result from a biased equilibrium-rate estimate is to increase the response to inflation in the interest-rate rule (Taylor 1994, 26).

Even in 1982 during the new-operating-procedures period, Taylor thought of the Fed as operating on interest rates.[21] So, while his early work used money growth rules, Taylor was probably more accustomed than most U.S. monetary economists at the time to viewing monetary policy in terms of an interest-rate rule. By 1992 he had concluded that the monetary policy literature would now focus on rules "probably with the interest rate as the instrument."[22] Since even his money-supply rule proposals involved accommodation of money demand shocks (and other sources of permanent velocity movement), Taylor did not see a dramatic normative contrast between money-stock and interest-rate rules and he emphasized the mapping between money-growth rules and interest-rate rules.[23] But a focus on interest-rate rules made it easier to compare proposed rules with reaction functions of the type used to describe historical monetary policy regimes.

Friedman's later views on rules

It would be inaccurate to say that Friedman ever stopped favoring fixed money growth as his first preference for a monetary policy rule. But his criticisms of alternative rules did diminish in the 1990s. He acknowledged that understanding of the economy had improved since the 1960s and that he had been surprised at the success with which

---

21. ". . . the Fed would have to contract demand by increasing interest rates" (Taylor 1982). Also, Taylor (1981b, 78) thought of stabilization policy in terms of policy influence on real interest rates on securities and noted the zero lower bound on nominal interest rates as an obstacle to achieving the required real interest-rate movement.

22. Taylor (1992, 15).

23. See, for example, Taylor (1998, 5–6; 1999b).

this knowledge had been translated into stabilization policy by policy-makers since the mid-1980s. Moreover, financial changes had unambiguously made money harder to define, reflected in the increased tendency for alternative monetary aggregates to give different signals; in that environment, money growth targeting did not imply stepping away from activism, given the increased difficulty of settling on the right concept of money and hitting the target. He still saw value in a money growth rule as a constraint on policymaker discretion. And Japan's experience in the 1990s served as Friedman's trump card in support of his older arguments, suggesting to him that a money growth rule might still be preferable to an interest-rate reaction function based on final objectives.

4. Sources of Nominal Rigidity

Nominal rigidity plays a central role in both Friedman's and Taylor's views of the transmission mechanism. They each contributed theoretical breakthroughs related to nominal rigidity: the natural rate hypothesis in Friedman's case; staggered contracts in Taylor's. As I discuss below, both of them emphasized simultaneous wage and price stickiness. At the same time, as argued below, I believe that their views of the transmission mechanism are actually better represented by a model in which there is little wage stickiness and that their views on the social welfare function are to some extent inconsistent with the existence of substantial wage stickiness.

Friedman on nominal rigidity

Turning to Friedman first, I have occasionally seen interpretations of his view of the transmission mechanism that take him as making an implicit assumption of both price and wage flexibility—so that the effect of monetary policy on output comes only from imperfect information.[24] But in fact such a vision is not implicit in his view of the economy; the explicit record of Friedman's writings shows repeated stress on the role of nominal rigidity. Taylor (1999c) recognized this by opening his article on nominal rigidities with a capsule Friedman quotation from

---

24. See the Nobel Committee (2006) for a recent discussion where this position is attributed to Friedman.

1982, "Prices are sticky."[25] Indeed, as early as 1967 Friedman described himself as "in full agreement" with the view that it "is the rigidity of prices that converts fluctuations in aggregate demand into fluctuations in output and employment."[26] He made specific reference to "wage and price contracts" in one of his earliest expositions of the vertical Phillips curve idea (Friedman 1966b).

Taking for granted therefore that Friedman had in mind a long-run vertical Phillips curve based on nominal rigidity, what is the most appropriate way of formalizing his views further? I find it useful to break the discussion of Friedman's price adjustment ideas into several considerations: whether the expectations term is formed rationally; whether prices are a "jump" or predetermined variable; and the date of the expectation in the Phillips curve (i.e., whether it refers to period-$t+1$ or t inflation, and whether this expectation is based on a period-t or period-$t-1$ information set). I defer until my discussion of Taylor the issue of whether nominal rigidity pertains to wages or prices in Friedman's framework.

Forward-looking behavior

Though he is often associated with adaptive expectations and with accelerationist versions of the natural rate hypothesis, Friedman does not appear to have been opposed to rational expectations in principle. He accepted that it could be an "enormous mistake of extrapolating present conditions to the indefinite future"[27] and, in particular, that it was "most unreasonable" to use adaptive expectations when this involves extrapolating from a different regime (Friedman and Schwartz 1982, 569). He suggested that rational expectations models were acceptable provided they got away from the implication of serially uncorrelated effects of monetary policy on output (Friedman 1977a, 14). He spoke out in favor of rational expectations models with long-term nominal

---

25. Friedman (1982c). In addition to opening Taylor's chapter (1999c), this quotation also appears in Hall and Taylor (1997, 235).

26. Friedman (1967, 2, 6; 1969 reprint, 82, 86). Friedman's statements in the 1940s and 1950s also endorsed the existence of nominal rigidity (e.g., in Friedman 1948, 254, and in Joint Economic Committee 1959, 628). The rigidity Friedman endorsed as relevant was temporary nominal rigidity, rather than the permanent nominal rigidity which he associated with early Keynesianism.

27. In Joint Economic Committee (1973, 139).

contracts and defended these models against critics of rational expectations (Friedman and Schwartz 1982, 415).

The above elements suggest that a forward-looking Phillips curve represents Friedman's views well. He did suggest (see Friedman 1974a) that commodity price shocks could stimulate inflationary expectations, a suggestion which might imply the presence of some price indexation and a lagged inflation term in the Phillips curve; likewise, Friedman (1984b) said that there was a tendency for inflation "to feed on itself." But there is strong evidence that Friedman did not believe in full indexation: the aforementioned effect of commodity price shocks on expectations was described as temporary and Friedman emphasized the need for reforms to make indexation more widespread and so reduce relative price distortions (see Friedman 1974b).[28]

Prices: jump or predetermined

Friedman (1979b) noted the existence of

> contractual arrangements that fix prices and wages in advance for some time. Even when prices and wages are not fixed explicitly, it is often undesirable to change them frequently. As a result, output and employment are generally more flexible over short periods than prices and wages, though less flexible over long periods.

While recognizing here the existence of long-term price contracts, Friedman nevertheless believed that a portion of the aggregate price index is a jump variable. It is clear from his expositions of the vertical-Phillips-curve idea (in, e.g., Friedman 1966b and 1968) that he saw some prices as able to increase immediately when nominal aggregate demand rises. Therefore, the price level is a jump variable notwithstanding the presence of a predetermined subset of prices. As Friedman (1974b, 30) put it: "Some prices . . . are fixed a long time in advance; others can be adjusted promptly."

The coexistence of some predetermined prices and some "jump" prices makes Friedman's framework compatible with a Guillermo A. Calvo (1983) or Taylor price contract scheme, but not with Rotemberg (1982) price setting.

---

28. In this respect Friedman anticipated the cost of inflation that is emphasized in the New Keynesian literature. See Nelson and Schwartz (2008) for further discussion.

Reference date for expectations

Does the expected-inflation term in Friedman's Phillips curve refer to period-t or period-$t+1$ inflation, and when are these expectations formed? Traditionally, the expected-inflation term in Friedman's Phillips curve is interpreted as being lagged expectations of current inflation, i.e., $E_{t-1}\pi_t$. Certainly the $t-1$ date on expectations formation is justified. Friedman (1974b, 30) said, "It will take still more time before expectations about inflation are revised"; that is, expectations of π are inertial relative to p itself.

In some of Friedman's discussions, it is implied that the inflationary expectations that matter for period-t inflation are forward looking, i.e., they pertain to expectations of policy beyond period t. For example, Friedman (1966b) said that prices are "set in the light of anticipations of inflation." Friedman (1972) argued that business decisions depend on confidence in future monetary policy and that a preannounced policy of steady money growth was more stabilizing than a discretionary policy that ex post delivered the same degree of steadiness in money growth.[29] Friedman (1984b) argued that inflation depends on "the public's perceptions about future inflation." Similarly, Friedman and Friedman (1980, 326) observed that inflation expectations depend on signals about future policy. So Friedman's framework is compatible with $E_{t-1}\pi_{t+1}$ rather than $E_{t-1}\pi_t$ in the Phillips curve.

Summing up, Friedman's Phillips curve views seem to be in line with the Christiano-Eichenbaum-Evans (2005) generalization of Calvo contracts, as expressed in output-gap space by Marc Giannoni and Woodford (2005):

$$(\pi_t - \gamma\pi_{t-1}) = (E_{t-1}\pi_{t+1} - \gamma\pi_t) + \alpha(y_t - y_t^*) + u_t, \alpha > 0. \tag{2}$$

Relative to Giannoni-Woodford, equation (2) has been modified by (*i*) imposing a vertical-Phillips-curve restriction (i.e., a unit weight on expected inflation), following John Roberts (1995); and (*ii*) allowing

---

29. Fischer (1990, 1169) points to Friedman's 1972 article as an indication of a forward-looking framework. Pre-1972 expositions by Friedman of the properties of his rule also alluded to forward-looking private sector behavior; for example, in Joint Economic Committee (1959, 628), Friedman said his rule would "provide a background of certainty in terms of which people can make their plans and in terms of which the system can operate, so you know what policy is going to be." Friedman (1978) argues that recognition of forward-looking behavior is implicit in his writings back to the 1950s.

some response by a portion of firms to current information by making the output gap appear in realized rather than expected form. In both cases, the modifications are designed to make the specification better reflect Friedman's views. For reasons discussed above, the indexation term g is likely nonzero, but low, in Friedman's framework. The cost-push shock term u_t, familiar from Clarida, Galí, and Gertler (1999) as an addition to the New Keynesian Phillips curve, is discussed later when I turn to sources of trade-offs.

Taylor on nominal rigidity

Taylor argued in 1982, "I do not think that you can accurately model macroeconomic behavior assuming that prices are perfectly flexible."[30] That view has underpinned Taylor's emphasis on contracting models. It is also implied by Taylor's emphasis, since the 1970s, on the output gap concept and on stabilization of the output gap as a goal to be pursued through monetary policy rules. This approach distinguished him from many earlier users of rational expectations models. In most of these early models, the flexible-wage/flexible-price assumption meant that the gap was identically zero or, at best, a white noise process incapable of being influenced by activist, predictable monetary policy actions.

Taylor has proposed a very specific Phillips curve based on staggered contracts. Neglecting shock terms for the moment, in the two-period-contract case this is built up from a "basic . . . contract determination equation" for the log contract, $z_t = 0.5 z_{t-1} + 0.5 E_t z_{t+1} + \xi [(y_t - y_t^*) + E_t(y_{t+1} - y_{t+1}^*)]$, $\xi > 0$, and an "aggregate price level" definition describing log prices, $p_t = 0.5 z_t + 0.5 z_{t-1}$—the latter definition presuming a constant markup.[31] After some further approximations (see Roberts 1995),[32] the result is a version of the New Keynesian Phillips curve:

$$\pi_t = E_t \pi_{t+1} + \alpha(y_t - y_t^*) + u_t. \tag{3}$$

---

30. In Klamer (1983, 174).

31. Taylor (1981b, 72).

32. These approximations involve suppressing some endogenous expectational errors that appear in the linearized Phillips curve. Because these endogenous terms are responsible for some of the effects of monetary policy in Taylor-contracts models, some authors have argued that the approximations are not innocuous—see, e.g., Westaway (1997) and Musy (2006)—and that the New Keynesian Phillips curve should not be used to represent Taylor staggered contracts.

Taylor contracts imply a mixed backward-looking/forward-looking price level and a strictly forward-looking inflation rate. The absence of an indexation term from equation (3) reflects Taylor's view that the dynamics of this equation should be relied upon to deliver inflation persistence (see Hall and Taylor 1997, 441), in preference to appealing to intrinsic inflation persistence as in Lawrence J. Christiano, Martin Eichenbaum, and Charles Evans (2005) or Jeffrey C. Fuhrer and George R. Moore (1995). The equation also reflects the fact that, in contrast to Friedman, Taylor believes that the expected-inflation term in the Phillips curve is formed using period-t information (see Taylor 1986a, 158).

Wage versus price stickiness

Despite the explicitness of Taylor's specification and its nominal-contracts motivation, there is an important ambiguity common to the discussion of nominal rigidity in both Taylor's and Friedman's work. They both tended to refer to both price and wage stickiness and to play down the distinction between the two. Occasionally, they would highlight wages as subject to contracts to a greater degree than were prices (see Friedman 1966b and Taylor 1982). But I will argue that the staggered-contracts specification that best describes their views about policy and economic structure refers to the gradual adjustment of prices, not wages.

Taylor (1986a, 153) was an early economist to accept the label of "New Keynesian."[33] In the 1980s New Keynesian economics was sometimes characterized as entailing a shift from sticky-wage models to sticky-price models (see, e.g., N. Gregory Mankiw 1987). There have been occasions on which Taylor has himself given the appearance of moving from a framework based on sticky wages to one based on sticky prices. For example, Taylor (1981b, 72) gave a price-contract interpretation of his work, explicitly replacing, in that application, an interpretation of the Phillips curve based on nominal wage contracts. Similarly, Taylor (1992, 22) said, "The structural interpretation I have favored involves a macroeconomic model with sticky prices and rational expectations . . ." More recently, Taylor (2000a, 1401) again explicitly reinterpreted his model as "referring directly to prices," taking firms as having staggered

---

33. Taylor (1981a, 146) noted, however, that his modeling choices and his emphasis on rules "a few years ago . . . [would] seem monetarist from the start," an observation which sheds light on the connections between New Keynesian economics and monetarism.

price contracts and abstracting from labor market frictions. And Hall and Taylor (1997, 432) cited sticky prices as important, noting that "firms . . . find it convenient to stay with existing prices."

But evidently these exercises did not signify a fundamental change in Taylor's position, for he has never disowned the importance of wage stickiness. His belief in the importance of wage stickiness resurfaced in his recent remark, "If I had to give a list of criticisms of the recent work, it would start with the frequent abstraction from wage rigidities."[34]

Nevertheless, the move between sticky-wage and sticky-price assumptions in Taylor's work, as well as his remark in Taylor (1981b, 72) that his setup was "general enough" for the nominal rigidity in the model to be interpreted as referring to either wages or prices, points to the aspect of nominal stickiness on which it seems Taylor placed most importance.

To elaborate, what these elements suggest is that Friedman and Taylor believed that wage stickiness was largely manifested in—or was a motivation for—price stickiness. Accordingly, in both Friedman's and Taylor's work, there was a single Phillips curve in which price inflation and the output gap were the only endogenous variables. Taylor (1980, 5–6), for example, moved from wages to prices via a constant markup and worked with a price-inflation Phillips curve. As users of dynamic general equilibrium models have shown, this Phillips curve can be rigorously derived from sticky-price models, not sticky-wage/flexible-price models (see, e.g., V. V. Chari, Patrick J. Kehoe, and Ellen R. McGrattan 2000 and Christopher J. Erceg, Dale W. Henderson, and Andrew T. Levin 2000).

Another reason why a sticky-price rather than sticky-wage assumption is closer to Taylor's framework is that, from the beginning, Taylor made goods-price inflation the variable that policymakers care about. Both Friedman and Taylor, as we have seen, treated the social welfare function as containing as arguments only price inflation variability and output gap variability. But nominal wage inflation variability becomes a third argument of the welfare function if wages are sticky (see Erceg, Henderson, and Levin 2000).[35] In fact, I do not think that either Friedman or Taylor failed to recognize that wage stickiness in principle

---

34. Taylor (2007, 198).

35. It may be, as Schmitt-Grohé and Uribe (2006) argue, that rules that respond only to price inflation still perform well when wage inflation variability matters for welfare; but the issue that concerns me here is instead how to rationalize Taylor's exclusion of wage inflation fluctuations from the policymaker objective function.

made wage stabilization a desirable objective. In discussing the views of Henry Simons, Friedman observed:

> [Simons believed] that the sticky and inflexible prices were factor prices, especially wages . . . [Aggregate] stability in these prices . . . would minimize the necessity for changes in the sticky prices. (Friedman 1967, fn. 11)

This passage is notable for showing Friedman's recognition of the idea that the location of nominal stickiness bears on what is the appropriate price index to target; if wages are sticky, the wage index should be stabilized. The fact that he and Taylor nevertheless focused on price inflation as a final objective could be taken as implying that goods-price stickiness is the economy's main nominal distortion.

It is true that Hall and Taylor (1997, 433–443) stress the empirical relevance of wage staggering. But they also place emphasis on the notion that wages in period t are set before the realization of the period-t price level. Predetermined wages, and in particular the idea that wage contracts are conditional on lagged expectation of the price level, are also an important element of Friedman's (1968, 1976) analysis. So I would suggest that while prices are sticky in both Friedman's and Taylor's frameworks, the only essential assumption about the labor market is that wages are predetermined, not that they are staggered. Wage behavior therefore might be adequately represented by one-period Fischer (1977) contracts rather than by a dynamic Phillips curve.

It is true that wage stickiness provides a rationale for a disturbance term like u_t in equation (2) or (3) (see Erceg, Henderson, and Levin 2000). It has therefore been argued that wage stickiness delivers a tradeoff between inflation variability and output-gap variability that is absent from the sticky-price baseline. But other rationalizations are available for the u_t term that do not rely on wage stickiness. Let us therefore consider the issue of the source of policy trade-offs in Friedman's and Taylor's analyses.

5. Source of Trade-Offs

Taylor (1986d, 673) observed,

> ". . . as I showed in a 1979 *Econometrica* paper [Taylor 1979], the shocks to the price adjustment equation are what cause the trade-off between

output and inflation variance: attempts to stabilize inflation sometimes require increased fluctuations in output, a factor . . . that I think is a major factor in the business cycle."

The Phillips curve or price adjustment equation in Taylor's framework therefore contained a shock term, for which Taylor (1981b, 79) offered the terminology "cost-push or supply shocks" or "contract shocks." Of these labels, "supply shocks" is less attractive because it has connotations of shocks to potential output; the shocks in question, however, are not potential GDP shocks but instead shocks to inflation that occur for a given path of the output gap (i.e., given the path of output relative to its flexible-price value).

As Taylor observes in the preceding quotation, the cost-push shock rationalizes an output-gap variance/inflation variance trade-off. It is this trade-off which Taylor has emphasized as the durable trade-off implied by Phillips curves that incorporate the natural rate hypothesis and so imply no long-run output gap/inflation level relationship. The cost-push shock therefore also underpins the Taylor curve, depicting the menu of output-gap variance/inflation variance combinations arising under optimal monetary policy for various weights in the policymaker objective function (see Taylor, 1979). But, as discussed below, the existence of cost-push shocks is also implicit in *Friedman*'s framework, though considerable digging is required to ascertain his views on the issue. Moreover, the treatment of cost-push shocks is symmetric across Taylor's and Friedman's writings. In both their frameworks, cost-push shocks are white noise and only monetary accommodation of these shocks can propagate them (as sources of inflation movement) beyond their initial impact effect. It is Taylor's contention that monetary authorities *have*, historically, accommodated these shocks in the course of trading off output-gap and inflation stabilization.

Friedman (1980) acknowledged the existence of cost-push shocks: there is a "basic inflation rate" from which actual inflation can deviate due to "transitory shocks." That such shocks included cost-push shocks, and not just transitory shocks to the components of the output gap, is implied by Friedman and Friedman's (1984, 84) observation that "a sudden upward jump in the price of a product that is widely used . . . may temporarily raise the level of inflation."

Cost-push shocks therefore exist in Friedman's framework, but are white noise. The transitory character of the shocks is why he classified them as "sources of temporary blips of inflation" (Friedman 1977b) or, equivalently, sources of once-and-for-all movements in the price level.

In an exposition of his monetary explanation for inflation, Friedman noted that "[m]any phenomena can produce temporary fluctuations in the rate of inflation" for given money growth (Friedman 1987, 17), thereby allowing for cost-push shocks, but emphasized that only monetary accommodation can make them relevant for ongoing inflation. The existence of cost-push shocks is also implied by Friedman's (1987, 18) recognition of "often conflicting objectives of policymakers"; an expectational Phillips curve does not in itself usually imply conflicting objectives, but does so in the presence of cost-push shocks. Similarly, Friedman (2006) acknowledged the existence in principle of an inflation variance/output-gap variance trade-off of the type that Taylor uses in his work.

Taylor (1993a, 196) himself observed that quarterly inflation movements can reflect "blips in the price level due to factors such as temporary changes in commodity prices."

He had earlier judged these blips as reflecting "changes in relative supplies and demands for commodities [which] can cause a price index to move erratically" (Taylor, 1982). These fluctuations rationalize a cost-push shock because not all the sources of the erratic price movements can be summarized by an index of the output gap; for example, increases in a national sales tax create a price shock (Hall and Taylor 1997, 497). The characterization of these shocks as erratic blips reflects Taylor's view of them as volatile but not persistent. Accordingly, Taylor (1981b, 79) suggested that the cost-push shocks have an "impulse effect" on inflation but that "monetary policy is crucial for the propagation effect." Taylor is therefore in agreement with Friedman that cost-push shocks are a white noise process with no automatic tendency to produce persistent movements in inflation. In line with this position, Hall and Taylor (1997, 231, 441) use the label "price shocks"—rather than inflation shocks—for cost-push shocks, and emphasize that it is the extent to which monetary policy is predicted to accommodate these shocks that determines whether "inflation may be expected in the future" in the wake of a price shock.[36]

The plausibility of the white-noise characterization of the shock depends, of course, on its precise rationalization. In the preceding

---

36. A white-noise interpretation of Phillips curve shocks is also consistent with Bernanke, Laubach, Mishkin, and Posen's (1999, 59) observation that "prior price-level rises" do not rule out the possibility that "inflation expectations remain contained." In a New Keynesian Phillips curve environment, the insensitivity of inflation expectations ($E_t \pi_{t+1}$) to price-level shocks that affect π_t is implied by those shocks being white noise (assuming no accommodation, and therefore unchanged expectations of the output gap).

discussion I took the potential output concept underlying the output gap definition as inclusive of inefficient variations in potential GDP, as in Friedman (1968) and Taylor (1987). Leaving them out of the output-gap definition would put them into the Phillips curve disturbance (see Giannoni and Woodford 2005). Also, if the shock is motivated as a shock to contracts (as in Taylor 1981b), rather than a shock to the aggregate price level equation, this tends to imply a moving-average Phillips curve shock due to staggering of contracts. In line with this alternative, the Phillips curve shock is treated as MA(1) in some of Taylor's work. But on the whole there is a strong presumption in Friedman's and Taylor's work that the Phillips curve shock will be close to white noise.

6. Sources of Shocks

Other than the white-noise Phillips curve shock, what other types of shock did Taylor and Friedman emphasize?

Taylor has relayed a complex but consistent picture of the U.S. business cycle which can be summarized as follows. (1) Monetary policy shocks—in the sense of exogenous, univariate shocks to the monetary policy rule—have not been an important source of U.S. business cycle fluctuations in the postwar period. (2) While, in addition to the Phillips curve shock discussed above, real shocks have been an important contributor to fluctuations, pre-1984 business cycle fluctuations did not reflect variations in potential output in response to real shocks; they instead reflected inefficient monetary policy interacting with price stickiness. (3) Potential output does not typically vary much in response to real shocks; so if prices were flexible and/or monetary policy were efficient, real shocks would not lead to large output fluctuations. (4) Smooth output in the era of the Great Moderation reflects efficient monetary policy, not a reduction in the variance of real shocks.

A denial of an important role for monetary policy shocks and a stress instead on the systematic component of the monetary policy rule as an important source of fluctuations were laid out by Taylor in 1982:

> [I]n the last 15 to 20 years in the United States . . . instability has originated in supply shocks, such as the OPEC price increases. Monetary policy has influenced how these supply shocks have affected the economy. . . . (Taylor, 1982)

He went on to argue that price stickiness magnified output fluctuations in the United States over 1952–83 (Taylor, 1986c), implying that output is more variable than potential output. Indeed, Taylor has frequently modeled potential output using a smooth trend, which suggests that he does not believe that real shocks would produce much output variability under price stickiness (see, for example, Taylor 1986c and 1994).[37] Rather, monetary policy reaction to the shocks in the postwar decades produced cycles in output and opened up the output gap, in turn leading to movements in inflation and to a later policy reaction. Taylor (1987, 355) went so far as to say this:

> "It is not much of an exaggeration to say that all the significant fluctuations in the macroeconomy during the last thirty years have been due to these relationships between output and inflation."

While this may seem an extreme statement, it is much the same conclusion as that stated by Ben S. Bernanke, Thomas Laubach, Frederic S. Mishkin, and Adam S. Posen (1999, 298). It also underlines the fact that attributing output instability to real shocks, as Taylor does, is not the same thing as endorsing a real business cycle account of cyclical fluctuations; on the contrary, Taylor's is a monetary view of the business cycle based on the scope for monetary policy (interacting with price stickiness) to magnify the effects of real shocks on output.

Monetary policy rules and the Great Moderation

Given his belief that nominal rigidities magnified U.S. output fluctuations in 1952–83, and in the existence of a cost-push shock in the Phillips curve, and assuming constant parameters in all relevant structural equations,[38] the source of the Great Moderation after 1983 is limited in Taylor's framework to:

---

37. Likewise, Hall and Taylor (1997, 408) *define* "business cycle fluctuations" as "the percentage deviation of real GDP from potential GDP."

38. Taylor (2005, 274) expresses doubt about the importance of structural change for understanding changes in U.S. business cycle behavior. Of course, the natural rate of unemployment has likely fallen in many countries, but this does not necessarily imply a structural change in aggregate output behavior. The relationship between production and employment (i.e., the Okun's Law relationship) might change at the same time that the natural unemployment rate changes, in a way that cancels out implications for potential output.

- Reduction in the variance of monetary policy shocks
- Reduction in the variance of the Phillips curve shocks
- Reduction in the variance of preference and production shocks
- More efficient monetary policy, reducing the upward effect of nominal rigidity on the variance of output.

The first three bulleted candidate explanations are not ones that Taylor favors. As noted above, Taylor (1982) ruled out monetary policy shocks as important in postwar data up to 1982, so any reduction in their variance cannot be important in explaining post-1982 economic stability. An explanation based on a reduction in Phillips curve shock variance is ruled out by his confidence in a reasonably stable inflation variance/output-gap variance trade-off (see Taylor 1994 and 1999a, 60). Taylor (2000b) casts doubt on the likelihood that the variances of real shocks have fallen, concluding that "on balance it seems hard to make the case that exogenous shocks have gotten smaller, less frequent, or more benign."[39]

Logically, therefore, we come to Taylor's explanation for the Great Moderation: monetary policy. Hall and Taylor (1997, 429) referred to "the stability of monetary policy in the United States and other major economies from 1982 to the present." Appealing to such stability, Taylor (1999a, 60) argues that changes since 1982 in observed inflation variance/output-gap variance combinations reflect a movement toward the efficient policy frontier. In particular, with stable inflation there are fewer recessions triggered by attempts to rein in inflation, so the "improvement in output stability . . . is an important consequence of the improvement in price stability." In terms of the Phillips curve equation (3), the variability of the expected-inflation term has been reduced by the change in monetary policy rule; the inflation/output gap cycle that Taylor (1987) argued was responsible for essentially all important GDP variation has been removed.

In Taylor's framework, this change in policy did not constitute a switch from "discretion" to "rules," but instead an improvement in the specification of the U.S. monetary policy rule. Taylor (e.g., 1979 and 1999c) found it useful to characterize U.S. monetary policy in

---

39. See also Taylor (1998, 5). Since, in Taylor's view, potential output varies little, lower real shock variance would not necessarily remove a major source of fundamental output variation. Rather, lower real shock variance would imply a lower variance for the inputs of the monetary policy reaction function, and so would reduce the destabilizing effects of an inefficient monetary policy.

the postwar decades[40] as following a "rule," even though that period was frequently associated with poor economic outcomes. By taking the form of a rule (a reaction function) rather than a series of one-time decisions, monetary policy responses in this regime were often quite predictable; nevertheless, this predictability did not contribute to reduced macroeconomic uncertainty. Both Taylor and Friedman shared the belief that the virtue of rules is that they can and should reduce uncertainty. This shared perspective is brought out by considering Friedman's (1983, 3) observation that the "policy implications that monetarists like myself have drawn . . . is that the primary task of the monetary authorities should be to avoid introducing uncertainty in the economy," alongside Taylor's (1993b, 6) statement: "Economic theory shows that things work better if there is more certainty about the conduct of monetary policy." But the monetary policy rule in the initial postwar decades did not make things work better, because it implied responses to the state of the economy that worsened inflation and output fluctuations.

Friedman's view of fluctuations

Friedman advanced positions that were in essential agreement with Taylor. Specifically, while real shocks have been a major source of economic fluctuations, this reflected monetary policy reaction to those shocks, whose effect has "merely [been] to make the economy less rather than more stable"[41] and to "produce inappropriate fluctuations in output."[42] Many real shocks are relevant for potential output but, were it not for monetary policy's role in magnifying their effect on *actual* output, the shocks would merely constitute "the myriad of factors making for minor fluctuations in economic activity."[43] Accordingly, Friedman regarded potential output as smooth: with the exception of events like the major OPEC actions, "[t]he real factors that determine

---

40. Specifically, 1953 Q1–1975 Q4 in Taylor (1979); 1960 Q1–1979 Q4 in Taylor (1999c).

41. In Joint Economic Committee (1959, 611). Woodford (1998) similarly interprets Friedman as implying that monetary policy actions in postwar decades destabilized the economy's adaptation to real shocks.

42. Friedman (2006).

43. In Joint Economic Committee (1959, 611).

the potential output of an economy . . . generally change slowly and gradually."[44] Friedman, like Taylor, accordingly attributed the Great Moderation to a more efficient monetary policy, which eliminated the destabilizing properties that monetary policy has exhibited historically (see Friedman's observations in Taylor 2001).

Friedman and Taylor therefore had similar views to one another on the sources of shocks. In common with the subsequent New Keynesian dynamic general equilibrium literature, they emphasized the importance of systematic monetary policy in determining output behavior. In contrast to most New Keynesian discussions, however, Friedman and Taylor treated potential output as smooth. Real shocks presumably can generate large variations in the natural rate of interest in their frameworks but, typically, not in potential output.

7. The Power and Duty of Monetary Policy

One way of thinking about John Taylor's work on nominal contracts is that it formalized the natural rate hypothesis, and in particular treated expectations formation and adjustment rigorously, while still preserving the emphasis on nominal rigidity (wage or price stickiness) that had been common to both Friedman's and A. W. Phillips' work. Earlier formalizations of the natural rate hypothesis, such as Robert E. Lucas Jr. (1972), had not featured nominal rigidity. Here I discuss another sense in which Taylor followed Friedman's Phillips-curve ideas and, in so doing, further departed from the original Phillips (1958) analysis.

To incorporate Friedman's Phillips-curve views, one needs three elements: expectations have to appear in the Phillips curve; their coefficient should be unity; and *they must be endogenous.* If you add expectations as an exogenous forcing process in the Phillips curve, you are introducing a variable that shifts the relation between the output gap and inflation, but you are not capturing the notion that monetary policy ultimately pins down inflation and inflation expectations alike.

And it seems to me that some of Phillips' work on inflation might be vulnerable to this criticism. Certainly Friedman thought so: he suggested (1976, 219) that the absence of expectations adjustment from

---

44. Friedman and Schwartz (1982, 414).

the original Phillips curve analysis followed from the Keynesian tradition that the "price level could be regarded as an institutional datum." The fundamental contribution of Phillips curve analysis relative to pre-Phillips curve Keynesianism was to make inflation an endogenous variable. But this contribution was not integrated completely into Phillips' own analysis, as he was willing to treat a large fraction of inflation variation as exogenous (an institutional datum, in Friedman's terminology). For example, Phillips (1958) related wage inflation to unemployment and made exogenous movements in inflation a curve-shifting variable—so, for example, he attributed deviations from the empirical Phillips curve to import price inflation and invoked this factor as an exogenous source of wage-price spirals.[45] This perspective is clearly different from that in Friedman's writings, in which monetary restraint is (via control of aggregate demand) a necessary and sufficient condition for inflation control. In Friedman's framework, as discussed above, there *is* an exogenous element to current inflation—the u_t term in equation (2)—but it is a transitory element that hardly matters for expected inflation; in fact, it does not matter for expectations at all if the lagged-coefficient term g in equation (2) is zero rather than merely low.

The Friedman framework rejects the notion that shocks to specific prices can in themselves be a source of ongoing inflation. If these shocks are associated with a change in the mean of inflation, it is because the monetary authority's reaction to the shock has had the effect of shifting the mean of inflation. This position on the power of monetary policy is also that adhered to by Taylor,[46] as discussed above, and shows up clearly also in policy discussions such as that of Mishkin (2007).

In Friedman's framework, therefore, inflation and expected inflation are endogenous variables ultimately pinned down by monetary policy; and the convergence of inflation and expected inflation means that the output gap is zero on average, irrespective of monetary policy. Phillips, on the other hand, attributed considerable inflation variation to exogenous factors, while also advancing an aggregate supply specification that implied that the output gap was generally nonzero in the long run.

---

45. See especially Phillips (1958, 284).

46. This is not to deny influences of Phillips' work on Taylor, which are stressed by Asso and Leeson (chap. 1, this volume). But I argue that these influences were mainly reflected in Taylor's early interest in optimal control analysis rather than in Taylor's ultimate views on what monetary policy could and should do.

8. Conclusions

The preceding discussion has emphasized that while the names of Taylor and Friedman are associated with different monetary policy rules, the difference between Taylor and Friedman on how the economy works is not great. Taylor and Friedman both emphasized Phillips curve specifications that impose temporary nominal price rigidity and the long-run natural-rate restriction; and there was basic agreement between them on policymaker objectives, the sources of shocks, and policy trade-offs. Where they differed was on the extent to which structural models should enter the monetary policy decision-making process. This difference helps account for the differences in their preferred monetary policy rules. Their rules do share an emphasis on nominal variables and reflect the agreement between them that it is both feasible and desirable for monetary policy to preclude deviations in inflation expectations from a constant, low rate. In this respect, Taylor and Friedman both put greater emphasis than Phillips did on the power and duty of monetary policy.

REFERENCES

Bernanke, Ben. S., Thomas Laubach, Frederic S. Mishkin, and Adam S. Posen. 1999. *Inflation Targeting: Lessons from the International Experience.* Princeton: Princeton University Press.

Calvo, Guillermo A. 1983. "Staggered Prices in a Utility-Maximizing Framework." *Journal of Monetary Economics* 12:383–98.

Chari, V. V., Patrick J. Kehoe, and Ellen R. McGrattan. 2000. "Sticky Price Models of the Business Cycle: Can the Contract Multiplier Solve the Persistence Problem?" *Econometrica* 68:1151–1179.

Christiano, Lawrence J., Martin Eichenbaum, and Charles Evans. 2005. "Nominal Rigidities and the Dynamic Effects of a Shock to Monetary Policy." *Journal of Political Economy* 113:1–45.

Clarida, Richard, Jordi Galí, and Mark Gertler. 1999. "The Science of Monetary Policy: A New Keynesian Perspective." *Journal of Economic Literature* 37: 1661–1707.

Erceg, Christopher J., Dale W. Henderson, and Andrew T. Levin. 2000. "Optimal Monetary Policy with Staggered Wage and Price Contracts." *Journal of Monetary Economics* 46:281–313.

Fischer, Stanley. 1977. "Long-Term Contracts, Rational Expectations, and the Optimal Money Supply Rule." *Journal of Political Economy* 85:191–206.

Fischer, Stanley. 1990. "Rules Versus Discretion in Monetary Policy." In *Handbook of Monetary Economics, vol. 2,* eds. B. M. Friedman and F. H. Hahn, 1155–1184. Amsterdam: North-Holland.

Friedman, Milton. 1948. "A Monetary and Fiscal Framework for Economic Stability." *American Economic Review* 38(3) (June): 245–64.

———. 1960. *A Program for Monetary Stability.* Fordham, NY: Fordham University Press.

———. 1963. *Inflation: Causes and Consequences.* New York: Asia Publishing House. Reprinted in *Dollars and Deficits: Living with America's Economic Problems,* Milton Friedman, 21–71. Englewood Cliffs, NJ: Prentice Hall, 1968.

———. 1966a. "Interest Rates and the Demand for Money." *Journal of Law and Economics* 9:71–85. Reprinted in *The Optimum Quantity of Money and Other Essays,* Milton Friedman, 141–156. Chicago: Aldine, 1969.

———. 1966b. "Inflationary Recession." *Newsweek,* October 17: 92.

———. 1967. "The Monetary Theory and Policy of Henry Simons." *Journal of Law and Economics* 10:1–13. Reprinted in *The Optimum Quantity of Money,* Milton Friedman, 81–96. Chicago: Aldine, 1969.

———. 1968. "The Role of Monetary Policy." *American Economic Review* 58:1–17.

———. 1969. "The Optimum Quantity of Money." In *The Optimum Quantity of Money,* Milton Friedman, 1–50. Chicago: Aldine, 1969.

———. 1972. "The Case for a Monetary Rule." *Newsweek,* February 7: 67.

———. 1973a. "How Much Monetary Growth?" *Morgan Guarantee Survey,* February: 5–10.

———. 1973b. *Money and Economic Development: The Horowitz Lectures of 1972.* New York: Praeger.

———. 1974a. "Inflation Prospects." *Newsweek,* November 4: 52.

———. 1974b. "Monetary Correction." IEA Occasional Paper No. 41. Reprinted in *Tax Limitation, Inflation and the Role of Government,* Milton Friedman, 22–51. Dallas: Fisher Institute, 1978.

———. 1976. *Price Theory,* 2nd ed. Chicago: Aldine.

———. 1977a. "Discussion of 'The Monetarist Controversy.'" Federal Reserve Bank of San Francisco *Economic Review,* Spring (supplement): 12–26.

———. 1977b. "Why Inflation Persists." *Newsweek,* October 3: 84.

———. 1978. "How Stands the Theory and Practice of Monetary Policy?" Paper presented at Mont Pelerin Society meeting, Hong Kong.

———. 1979a. "Iran and Energy Policy." *Newsweek,* December 31: 61.

———. 1979b. "Inflation and Jobs." *Newsweek,* November 12: 97.

———. 1980. "Carter's Anti-Inflation Plan." *Newsweek,* March 24: 40.

———, and Rose D. Friedman. 1980. *Free to Choose.* New York: Harcourt Brace Jovanovich.

————. 1982a. "Monetary Policy: Theory and Practice." *Journal of Money, Credit and Banking* 14:98–118.

————. 1982b. "Letter to Senator Roger W. Jepsen, Vice-Chairman, Joint Economic Committee." In *Monetarism and the Federal Reserve's Conduct of Monetary Policy: Compendium of Views Prepared for the Use of the Subcommittee on Monetary and Fiscal Policy*, 73–74. Joint Economic Committee, Washington, DC: Government Printing Office.

————. 1982c. "Defining 'Monetarism.'" *Newsweek*, July 12: 64.

————, and Anna J. Schwartz. 1982. *Monetary Trends in the United States and the United Kingdom: Their Relation to Income, Prices, and Interest Rates, 1867–1975*. Chicago: University of Chicago Press.

————. 1983. "Monetarism in Rhetoric and in Practice." *Bank of Japan Monetary and Economic Studies* 1:1–14.

————. 1984a. "Has Monetarism Failed?" *Manhattan Report* 4:3–4.

————. 1984b. "Inflation Isn't Beaten." *New York Times*, April 3: A31.

————, and Rose D. Friedman. 1984. *The Tyranny of the Status Quo*. New York: Harcourt Brace Jovanovich.

————. 1985. "Comment on Leland Yeager's Paper on the Keynesian Heritage." In *The Keynesian Heritage*, Center Symposia Series No. CS-16, 12–18. Center for Research in Government Policy and Business, University of Rochester Graduate School of Management.

————. 1987. "Quantity Theory of Money." In *The New Palgrave: A Dictionary of Economics, vol. 4, Q to Z*, eds. John Eatwell, Murray Milgate, and Peter Newman, 3–20. London: Macmillan.

————. 2006. "Tradeoffs in Monetary Policy." Manuscript, Stanford University.

Fuhrer, Jeffrey C., and George R. Moore. 1995. "Inflation Persistence." *Quarterly Journal of Economics* 110:127–159.

Giannoni, Marc P., and Michael Woodford. 2005. "Optimal Inflation-Targeting Rules." In *The Inflation-Targeting Debate*, eds. Ben S. Bernanke and Michael Woodford, 93–162. Chicago: University of Chicago Press.

Hall, Robert E., and John B. Taylor. 1997. *Macroeconomics*, 5th ed. New York: W.W. Norton & Company.

Joint Economic Committee. 1959. *Employment, Growth, and Price Levels, Hearings, Part 4*. Washington, DC: Government Printing Office. Friedman's opening testimony reprinted as Milton Friedman, "Monetary Theory and Policy." In *Inflation*, eds. R. J. Ball and Peter Doyle, 136–45. London: Penguin, 1969.

Joint Economic Committee. 1973. *How Well Are Fluctuating Exchange Rates Working? Hearings*. Washington, DC: Government Printing Office.

King, Mervyn A. 1997. "Changes in U.K. Monetary Policy: Rules and Discretion in Practice." *Journal of Monetary Economics* 39:81–97.

Klamer, Arjo. 1983. "Interview: John Taylor." In *Conversations with Economists,* Arjo Klamer, 170–76. Totowa, NJ: Rowman and Littlefield.

Lucas, Robert E., Jr. 1972. "Expectations and the Neutrality of Money." *Journal of Economic Theory* 4:103–124.

Mankiw, N. Gregory. 1987. "The New Keynesian Microfoundations." *NBER Macroeconomics Annual* 2:105–110.

McCallum, Bennett T. 1995. "Two Fallacies Concerning Central Bank Independence." *American Economic Review (Papers and Proceedings)* 85:207–211.

McCallum, Bennett T., and Edward Nelson. 2005. "Commentary on Lars E. O. Svensson, 'Targeting versus Instrument Rules for Monetary Policy: What is Wrong with McCallum and Nelson?'" Federal Reserve Bank of St. Louis *Review* 87(5):627–31.

Mishkin, Frederic S. 2007. "Globalization, Macroeconomic Performance, and Monetary Policy." Speech at "Conference on Domestic Prices in an Integrated World Economy," Washington, DC, September 27, http://www.federalreserve.gov/newsevents/speech/mishkin20070927a.htm

Musy, Olivier. 2006. "Inflation Persistence and the Real Costs of Disinflation in Staggered Prices and Partial Adjustment Models." *Economics Letters* 91:50–55.

Nelson, Edward, and Anna J. Schwartz. 2008. "The Impact of Milton Friedman on Modern Monetary Economics: Setting the Record Straight on Paul Krugman's 'Who Was Milton Friedman?'" *Journal of Monetary Economics,* forthcoming.

Nobel Committee. 2006. "Advanced Information: Edmund S. Phelps' Contribution to Macroeconomics," October 9.

Orphanides, Athanasios. 2003. "The Quest for Prosperity without Inflation." *Journal of Monetary Economics* 50:633–63.

Phelps, Edmund S. 1968. "Money-Wage Dynamics and Labor-Market Equilibrium." *Journal of Political Economy* 76:678–711.

Phillips, A. W. 1958. "The Relationship between Unemployment and the Rate of Change of Money Wage Rates in the United Kingdom, 1861–1957." *Economica* 25:283–299.

Roberts, John. 1995. "New Keynesian Economics and the Phillips Curve." *Journal of Money, Credit, and Banking* 27:975–984.

Rotemberg, Julio J. 1982. "Sticky Prices in the United States." *Journal of Political Economy* 90:1187–1211.

Rotemberg, Julio J., and Michael Woodford. 1997. "An Optimization-Based Econometric Framework for the Evaluation of Monetary Policy." *NBER Macroeconomics Annual* 12: 297–346.

Sargent, Thomas J. 1971. "A Note on the 'Accelerationist' Controversy." *Journal of Money, Credit, and Banking* 3:721–25.

Schmitt-Grohé, Stephanie, and Martin Uribe. 2006. "Comparing Two Variants of Calvo-Type Wage Stickiness." NBER Working Paper no. 12740.

Svensson, Lars E. O. 1997. "Inflation Forecast Targeting: Implementing and Monitoring Inflation Targets." *European Economic Review* 41:1111–46.

Svensson, Lars E. O. 2005. "Targeting versus Instrument Rules for Monetary Policy: What is Wrong with McCallum and Nelson?" Federal Reserve Bank of St. Louis *Review* 87(5):613–625.

Taylor, John B. 1979. "Estimation and Control of a Macroeconomic Model with Rational Expectations." *Econometrica* 47:1267–86.

———. 1980. "Aggregate Dynamics and Staggered Contracts." *Journal of Political Economy* 88:1–23.

———. 1981a. "Stabilization, Accommodation, and Monetary Rules." *American Economic Review (Papers and Proceedings)* 71:145–149.

———. 1981b. "On the Relation between the Variability of Inflation and the Average Inflation Rate." *Carnegie-Rochester Conference Series on Public Policy* 15:57–86.

———. 1982. "Letter to the Honorable Robert W. Jepsen, August 31, 1982." In *Monetarism and the Federal Reserve's Conduct of Monetary Policy: Compendium of Views Prepared for the Use of the Subcommittee on Monetary and Fiscal Policy,* Joint Economic Committee, 156–59. Washington, DC: Government Printing Office.

———. 1986a. "An Appeal for Rationality in the Policy Activism Debate." In *The Monetary Versus Fiscal Policy Debate: Lessons from Two Decades,* ed. R. W. Hafer, 151–63. Littlefield, NJ: Rowman and Allenheld.

———. 1986b. "New Econometric Approaches to Stabilization Policy in Stochastic Models of Macroeconomic Fluctuations." In *Handbook of Econometrics, vol. 3,* eds. Zvi Griliches and Michael Intriligator, 1998–2055. Amsterdam: Elsevier.

———. 1986c. "Improvements in Macroeconomic Stability: The Role of Wages and Prices." In *The American Business Cycle: Continuity and Change,* ed. R. J. Gordon, 639–59. Chicago: University of Chicago Press.

———. 1986d. "Reply." In *The American Business Cycle: Continuity and Change,* 672–77.

———. 1987. "Externalities Associated with Nominal Price and Wage Rigidities." In *New Approaches to Monetary Economics,* eds. William A. Barnett and Kenneth J. Singleton, 350–67. Cambridge: Cambridge University Press.

———. 1992. "The Great Inflation, the Great Disinflation, and Policies for Future Price Stability." In *Inflation, Disinflation and Monetary Policy,* ed. Adrian Blundell-Wignall, 9–31. Sydney: Ambassador Press.

———. 1993a. "Discretion Versus Policy Rules in Practice." *Carnegie-Rochester Series on Public Policy* 39:195–214.

———. 1993b. "Price Stabilization in the 1990s: An Overview." In *Price Stabilization in the 1990s: Domestic and International Policy Requirements,* eds. Kumiharu Shigehara and Yasushi Mieno, 1–6. London: Macmillan.

———. 1994. "The Inflation-Output Variability Tradeoff Revisited." In *Goals, Guidelines, and Constraints Facing Monetary Policymakers,* ed. Jeffrey C. Fuhrer, 23–28. Boston: Federal Reserve Bank of Boston.

———. 1998. "Monetary Policy and the Long Boom." Federal Reserve Bank of St. Louis *Review* 80:3–11.

———. 1999a. "Commentary: Challenges for Monetary Policy: New and Old." In *New Challenges for Monetary Policy,* 59–68. Kansas City: Federal Reserve Bank of Kansas City.

———. 1999b. "An Historical Analysis of Monetary Policy Rules." In *Monetary Policy Rules,* ed. John B. Taylor, 319–41. Chicago: University of Chicago Press.

———. 1999c. "Staggered Price and Wage Setting in Macroeconomics." In *Handbook of Macroeconomics, vol. 1B,* eds. John B. Taylor and Michael Woodford, 1009–50. Amsterdam: Elsevier.

———. 2000a. "Low Inflation, Pass-Through, and the Pricing Power of Firms." *European Economic Review* 44:1389–1408.

———. 2000b. "Remarks for the Panel Discussion on 'Recent Changes in Trend and Cycle.'" Presented at the Federal Reserve Bank of San Francisco/SIEPR conference "Structural Change and Monetary Policy," March 3–4.

———. 2001. "An Interview with Milton Friedman." *Macroeconomic Dynamics* 5: 101–131.

———. 2005. "The International Implications of October 1979: Toward a Long Boom on a Global Scale." Federal Reserve Bank of St. Louis *Review* 87:269–76.

———. 2007. "Thirty-Five Years of Model Building for Monetary Policy Evaluation: Breakthroughs, Dark Ages, and a Renaissance." *Journal of Money Credit and Banking* 39:193–201.

Westaway, Peter. 1997. "How Costly Is Inflation Reduction? An Investigation of Simple Interest-Rate Rules under Different Models of Nominal Inertia." Paper presented at Monetary Policy Workshop, Reserve Bank of New Zealand, October 20.

Woodford, Michael. 1998. "Comment on John Cochrane, 'A Frictionless View of U.S. Inflation.'" *NBER Macroeconomics Annual* 13:390–418.

Woodford, Michael. 2003. *Interest and Prices: Foundations of a Theory of Monetary Policy.* Princeton: Princeton University Press.

FOUR

TWO BASIC PRINCIPLES

Robert E. Lucas

One of the most important and welcome developments in government over the last fifty years or so has been what I would call the professionalization of economic policy. If I had to date the beginning of this development I would choose 1961, when the Kennedy administration was formed. I was just beginning graduate work then, and all of a sudden people on my reading lists—Walter Heller, James Tobin, Robert Solow, Kenneth Arrow, W. W. Rostow—were headed to Washington. Robert McNamara brought a group of economists to the Department of Defense to apply the cost-benefit analysis that Arnold Harberger was teaching us about in class.

The Vietnam years were a setback to this growth in the influence of economists, but only a temporary one. Increasingly, first-rate economists have been centrally involved in the formulation and execution of economic policy. This is obvious in the governance and staffing of the Federal Reserve System, where the chairman, most of the members of the Board of Governors, and now many of the bank presidents are economists with international research reputations. The Council of Economic Advisers (CEA) has generally maintained the high standards of the Kennedy years, and many of its members and staffers have gone on to important roles elsewhere in the executive branch.

Robert E. Lucas Jr., is the John Dewey Distinguished Service Professor of Economics at the University of Chicago.

This progress—and I mean progress for our society, not just for our profession—has been built on the research of several generations. But this tradition of research would not have been translated into concrete policy the way it has been in the last few decades without the contribution of a new generation, a generation of people who can move comfortably back and forth between the technical research frontier and policy roles at the highest level. For me, John Taylor's career is a leading example of this kind of intellectual flexibility and effectiveness. When I first met John he was a new assistant professor at Columbia, a student of T. W. Anderson's. He was on top of control theory and time-series methods back in those days before Christopher Sims and Thomas Sargent had made these topics part of the core curriculum. He and Ned Phelps were applying these methods to the then-novel rational expectations models of monetary economies. John was quick to see that policy discussion in such models would have to be conducted in terms of the properties of policy *rules*. He also insisted from the beginning that a useful monetary model would have to incorporate, in some form, the inflexibilities that can make bad monetary policy so dangerous. Since those years, John's modeling efforts and thinking on policy have evolved in many ways, but as far as I know he has never moved away from these two principles.

I could see then that John was a first-class technician, but I wondered how much economics he knew, and I was surprised when I learned that he had gone to work at the CEA. It did not seem a good match. But talking with him after he left the Council, I could see that he had thrived on the huge variety of different problems that had come across his desk there, and seemed to have something interesting and knowledgeable to say about every current problem in economic policy. You can see this same ability to switch from one problem to the next without missing a beat in his new book, *Global Financial Warriors*.

After his CEA days in the 1970s, John plunged back into the hard technical problems of econometric model-building, now incorporating international interactions. Over the years since then, he has moved back and forth between government and academia, thriving and contributing in both environments. I think that each of these two career paths has contributed to the astonishing success of the Taylor rule.

The academic origins of monetary rules can be traced back to Henry Simon's advocacy of 100 percent reserves, adopted by Milton Friedman (1948). Somehow, this idea of eliminating the banking industry never caught on with bankers, and Friedman moved on to a 4 percent growth rule for M1 or M2 in his writing in the 1950s. But why commit ourselves to a single number for all time; and even if we wanted to, how would we do it? Robert Gordon and Ben McCallum proposed more flexible but, I think, equally well-motivated and effective rules for targeting nominal income. For my taste, the McCallum rule is as good as it gets in the monetary rule business: it tells us when to put more reserves into the system and when to take them out, and if it doesn't work the first time we can keep doing it until we get it right. The problem is that everyone in the business and banking worlds wants to talk about monetary policy in terms of a short-term interest rate. John saw that the way the Fed was behaving in the Volcker and Greenspan years corresponded pretty well to what any decent rule for reserves, like McCallum's, would do in any given situation. By capturing this highly successful monetary policy behavior in a coherent and easily interpreted formula, he gave us a specific rule that can be imitated, even committed to, by future open market committees. This is real economic and political progress.

There is a passage in Lawrence Klein's Yrjo Jahnsson Lectures that has stayed in my mind. As I remember it, he is trying to explain to a non-technical audience why we value mathematically explicit macro-economic models. There have been brilliant policymakers in the past, he says, and there will be more in the future. They do not seem to need our models and yet we cannot deny their successes. But when they leave office, they do not leave behind knowledge that might enable others to replicate their successes. We have to start over, again and again. Our task as quantitative economists, he wrote, was to incorporate the main features of these successes into cumulative science so that future generations might repeat them. Except for the fact that Klein's Lectures were given in 1968, you might think he was writing with Paul Volcker, Alan Greenspan, and John Taylor in mind.

Reference

Friedman, Milton. 1948. "A Monetary and Fiscal Framework for Economic Stability." *American Economic Review* 38(3):245–264.

PART II

From the Great Moderation to the Great Deviation

FIVE

THE GREAT MODERATION

Ben S. Bernanke

One of the most striking features of the economic landscape over the past twenty years or so has been a substantial decline in macroeconomic volatility. In a recent article, Olivier Blanchard and John Simon (2001) documented that the variability of quarterly growth in real output (as measured by its standard deviation) has declined by half since the mid-1980s, while the variability of quarterly inflation has declined by about two-thirds.[1] Several writers on the topic have dubbed this remarkable decline in the variability of both output and inflation "the Great Moderation." Similar declines in the volatility of output and inflation occurred at about the same time in other major industrial countries, with the recent exception of Japan, a country that has faced a distinctive set of economic problems in the past decade.

Reduced macroeconomic volatility has numerous benefits. Lower volatility of inflation improves market functioning, makes economic planning easier, and reduces the resources devoted to hedging inflation risks. Lower volatility of output tends to imply more stable employment

---

Ben S. Bernanke is chairman of the Federal Reserve Board. This chapter is based on remarks he made at the meetings of the Eastern Economic Association, Washington, D.C., February 20, 2004.

1. Kim and Nelson (1999) and McConnell and Perez Quiros (2000) were among the first to note the reduction in the volatility of output. Kim, Nelson, and Piger (2003) show that the reduction in the volatility of output is quite broadly based, affecting many sectors and aspects of the economy. Warnock and Warnock (2000) find a parallel decline in the volatility of employment, especially in goods-producing sectors.

and a reduction in the extent of economic uncertainty confronting households and firms. The reduction in the volatility of output is also closely associated with the fact that recessions have become less frequent and less severe.[2]

Why has macroeconomic volatility declined? Three types of explanations have been suggested for this dramatic change; for brevity, I will refer to these classes of explanations as structural change, improved macroeconomic policies, and good luck. Explanations focusing on *structural change* suggest that changes in economic institutions, technology, business practices, or other structural features of the economy have improved the ability of the economy to absorb shocks. Some economists have argued, for example, that improved management of business inventories, made possible by advances in computation and communication, has reduced the amplitude of fluctuations in inventory stocks, which in earlier decades played an important role in cyclical fluctuations.[3] The increased depth and sophistication of financial markets, deregulation in many industries, the shift away from manufacturing toward services, and increased openness to trade and international capital flows are other examples of structural changes that may have increased macroeconomic flexibility and stability.

The second class of explanations focuses on the arguably *improved performance of macroeconomic policies*, particularly monetary policy. The historical pattern of changes in the volatilities of output growth and inflation gives some credence to the idea that better monetary policy may have been a major contributor to increased economic stability. As Blanchard and Simon (2001) show, output volatility and inflation volatility have had a strong tendency to move together, both in the United States and other industrial countries. In particular, output volatility in the United States, at a high level in the immediate postwar era, declined significantly between 1955 and 1970, a period in which inflation volatility was low. Both output volatility and inflation volatility rose

---

2. The United States has experienced only two relatively mild recessions since 1984, compared with four recessions—two of them quite deep—in the fifteen years before 1984. Indeed, according to the National Bureau of Economic Research's monthly business cycle chronology, which covers the period since the Civil War, the 120-month expansion of the 1990s was the longest recession-free period the United States has enjoyed, and the 92-month expansion of the 1980s was the third longest such period.

3. McConnell and Perez Quiros (2000) and Kahn, McConnell, and Perez Quiros (2002) make this argument. McCarthy and Zakrajsek (2003) provide an overview and evaluation of this literature; they conclude that better inventory management has reinforced the trend toward lower volatility but is not the ultimate cause. Willis (2003) discusses structural changes that may have contributed to reduced variability of inflation.

significantly in the 1970s and early 1980s and, as I have noted, both fell sharply after about 1984. Economists generally agree that the 1970s, the period of highest volatility in both output and inflation, was also a period in which monetary policy performed quite poorly, relative to both earlier and later periods (Romer and Romer 2002).[4] Few disagree that monetary policy has played a large part in stabilizing inflation, and so the fact that output volatility has declined in parallel with inflation volatility, both in the United States and abroad, suggests that monetary policy may have helped moderate the variability of output as well.

The third class of explanations suggests that the Great Moderation did not result primarily from changes in the structure of the economy or improvements in policymaking but occurred because the shocks hitting the economy became smaller and more infrequent. In other words, the reduction in macroeconomic volatility we have lately enjoyed is largely the result of *good luck,* not an intrinsically more stable economy or better policies. Several prominent studies using distinct empirical approaches have provided support for the good-luck hypothesis (Ahmed, Levin, and Wilson 2002; Stock and Watson 2003).

Explanations of complicated phenomena are rarely clear cut and simple, and each of the three classes of explanations I have described probably contains elements of truth. Nevertheless, sorting out the relative importance of these explanations is of more than purely historical interest. Notably, if the Great Moderation was largely the result of good luck rather than a more stable economy or better policies, then we have no particular reason to expect the relatively benign economic environment of the past twenty years to continue. Indeed, if the good-luck hypothesis is true, it is entirely possible that the variability of output growth and inflation in the United States may, at some point, return to the levels of the 1970s. If instead the Great Moderation was the result of structural change or improved policymaking, then the increase in stability should be more likely to persist, assuming of course that policymakers do not forget the lessons of history.

My view is that improvements in monetary policy, though certainly not the only factor, have probably been an important source of the Great Moderation. In particular, I am not convinced that the decline in macroeconomic volatility of the past two decades was *primarily* the result of good luck, as some have argued, though I am sure good luck had

---

4. Using more formal econometric methods, Kim, Nelson, and Piger (2003) also found that structural breaks in the volatility and persistence of inflation occurred about the same number of times as the changes in output volatility.

its part to play as well. In the remainder of my remarks, I will provide some support for the "improved-monetary-policy" explanation for the Great Moderation. I will not spend much time on the other two classes of explanations, not because they are uninteresting or unimportant, but because my time is limited and the structural change and good-luck hypotheses have been extensively discussed elsewhere.[5] Before proceeding, I should note that my views are not necessarily those of my colleagues on the Board of Governors or the Federal Open Market Committee.

The Taylor Curve and the Variability Trade-off

Let us begin by asking what economic theory has to say about the relationship of output volatility and inflation volatility. To keep matters simple, I will make the strong (but only temporary!) assumption that monetary policymakers have an accurate understanding of the economy and that they choose policies to promote the best economic performance possible, given their economic objectives. I also assume for the moment that the structure of the economy and the distribution of economic shocks are stable and unchanging. Under these baseline assumptions, macroeconomists have obtained an interesting and important result. Specifically, standard economic models imply that, in the long run, monetary policymakers can reduce the volatility of inflation *only* by allowing greater volatility in output growth, and vice versa. In other words, if monetary policies are chosen optimally and the economic structure is held constant, there exists a long-run trade-off between volatility in output and volatility in inflation.

The ultimate source of this long-run trade-off is the existence of shocks to aggregate supply. Consider the canonical example of an aggregate supply shock, a sharp rise in oil prices caused by disruptions to foreign sources of supply. According to conventional analysis, an increase in the price of oil raises the overall price level (a temporary burst in inflation) while depressing output and employment. Monetary policymakers are therefore faced with a difficult choice. If they choose to tighten policy (raise the short-term interest rate) in order to offset the effects of the oil price shock on the general price level, they may well succeed—but only at the cost of making the decline in output more severe. Likewise, if monetary policymakers choose to ease in order to

---

5. Stock and Watson (2003) provide a recent overview of the debate.

mitigate the effects of the oil price shock on output, their action will exacerbate the inflationary impact. Hence, in the standard framework, the periodic occurrence of shocks to aggregate supply (such as oil price shocks) forces policymakers to choose between stabilizing output and stabilizing inflation.[6] Note that shocks to aggregate demand do not create the same trade-off, as offsetting an aggregate demand shock stabilizes both output and inflation.

This apparent trade-off between output variability and inflation variability faced by policymakers gives rise to what has been dubbed the *Taylor curve*, reflecting early work by the Stanford economist and current [in 2004] Undersecretary of the Treasury John B. Taylor.[7] (Taylor also originated the eponymous Taylor rule, to which I will refer later.) Graphically, the Taylor curve depicts the menu of possible combinations of output volatility and inflation volatility from which monetary policymakers can choose in the long run. Figure 1 shows two examples of Taylor curves, marked *TC1* and *TC2*. In figure 1, volatility in output is measured on the vertical axis and volatility in inflation is measured on the horizontal axis. As shown in the figure, Taylor curves slope downward, reflecting the theoretical conclusion that an optimizing policymaker can choose less of one type of volatility in the long run only by accepting more of the other.[8] A direct implication of the Taylor curve framework is that a change in the preferences or objectives of the central bank alone—a decision to be tougher on inflation, for example—cannot explain the Great Moderation. Indeed, in this framework, a conscious attempt by policymakers to try to moderate the variability of inflation should lead to higher, not lower, variability of output.

How, then, can the Great Moderation be explained? Figure 1 suggests two possibilities. First, suppose it were the case, contrary to what we assumed in deriving the Taylor curve, that monetary policies during

---

6. Strictly speaking, according to standard models, policymakers face a trade-off between volatility of inflation and volatility of the output *gap*, the difference between potential output and actual output. If the economy's potential output grows relatively smoothly, variability in the output gap will be closely related to variability in actual output.

7. Chatterjee (2002) provides an overview of the Taylor curve and its implications. For an exposition by Taylor himself, see Taylor (1998).

8. The policy trade-off between the variability of inflation and the variability of output implied by the Taylor curve is reminiscent of an older proposition: that policymakers could achieve a permanently higher level of output (and thus a permanently lower level of unemployment) by accepting a permanently higher *level* of inflation. However, for both theoretical and empirical reasons, this older idea of a long-run trade-off between the levels of inflation and output has been largely discredited, and the Taylor curve trade-off is in some sense its natural successor.

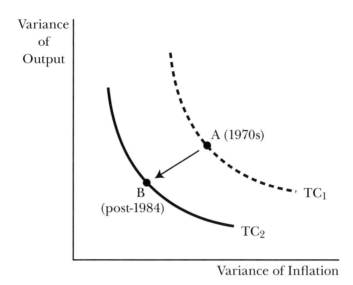

Variance of Inflation

Figure 1. Monetary Policy and the Variability of Output and Inflation

the period of high macroeconomic volatility were not optimal, perhaps because policymakers did not have an accurate understanding of the structure of the economy or of the impact of their policy actions. If monetary policies during the late 1960s and the 1970s were sufficiently far from optimal, the result could be a combination of output volatility and inflation volatility lying well above the efficient frontier defined by the Taylor curve. Graphically, suppose that the true Taylor curve is the solid curve shown in figure 1, labeled *TC2*. Then, in principle, sufficiently well-executed policies could achieve a combination of output volatility and inflation volatility such as that represented by point *B*, which lies on that curve. However, less effective policies could lead to the economic outcome represented by point *A* in figure 1, at which both output volatility and inflation volatility are higher than at point *B*. We can see now how improvements in monetary policy might account for the Great Moderation, even in the absence of any change in the structure of the economy or in the underlying shocks. Improvements in the policy framework, in policy implementation, or in the policymakers' understanding of the economy could allow the economy to move from the inefficient point *A* to the efficient point *B*, where the volatility of both inflation and output are more moderate.

Figure 1 can also be used to depict a second possible explanation for the Great Moderation, which is that, rather than monetary policy having improved, the underlying economic environment may have become more stable. Changes in the structure of the economy that increased its resilience to shocks or reductions in the variance of the shocks themselves would improve the volatility trade-off faced by policymakers. In figure 1, we can imagine now that the true Taylor curve in the 1970s is given by the dashed curve, *TC1,* and the actual economic outcome chosen by policymakers is point *A,* which lies on *TC1.* Improved economic stability in the 1980s and 1990s, whether arising from structural change or good luck, can be represented by a shift of the Taylor curve from *TC1* to *TC2,* and the new economic outcome as determined by policy is point *B.* Relative to *TC1,* the Taylor curve *TC2* represents economic outcomes with lower volatility in output for any given volatility of inflation, and vice versa. According to the "shifting Taylor curve" explanation, the Great Moderation resulted not from improved practice of monetary policy (which has always been as effective as possible, given the environment) but rather by favorable structural change or reduced variability of economic shocks. Of course, more complicated scenarios in which policy becomes more effective *and* the underlying economic environment becomes more stable are possible and indeed likely.

With this bit of theory as background, I will focus on two key points. First, without claiming that monetary policy during the 1950s or in the period since 1984 has been ideal by any means, I will try to support my view that the policies of the late 1960s and 1970s were particularly inefficient, for reasons that I think we now understand. Thus, as in the first scenario just discussed (represented in figure 1 as a movement from point *A* to point *B*), improvements in the execution of monetary policy can plausibly account for a significant part of the Great Moderation. Second, more subtly, I will argue that some of the benefits of improved monetary policy may easily be confused with changes in the underlying environment (that is, improvements in policy may be incorrectly identified as shifts in the Taylor curve), increasing the risk that standard statistical methods of analyzing this question could understate the contribution of monetary policy to the Great Moderation.

Reaching the Taylor Curve: Improvements in the Effectiveness of Monetary Policy

Monetary policymakers face difficult challenges in their efforts to stabilize the economy. We are uncertain about many aspects of the workings of the economy, including the channels by which the effects of monetary policy are transmitted. We are even uncertain about the current economic situation as economic data are received with a lag, are typically subject to multiple revisions, and in any case can only roughly and partially depict the underlying economic reality. Thus, in practice, monetary policy will never achieve as much reduction in macroeconomic volatility as would be possible if our understanding were more complete.

Nevertheless, a number of economists have argued that monetary policy during the late 1960s and the 1970s was unusually prone to creating volatility, relative to both earlier and later periods (DeLong 1997; Mayer 1998; Romer and Romer 2002). Economic historians have suggested that the relative inefficiency of policy during this period arose because monetary policymakers labored under some important misconceptions about policy and the economy. First, during this period, central bankers seemed to have been excessively optimistic about the ability of activist monetary policies to offset shocks to output and to deliver permanently low levels of unemployment. Second, monetary policymakers appeared to underestimate their own contributions to the inflationary problems of the time, believing instead that inflation was in large part the result of nonmonetary forces. One might say that, in terms of their ability to deliver good macroeconomic outcomes, policymakers suffered from excessive "output optimism" and "inflation pessimism."

The output optimism of the late 1960s and the 1970s had several aspects. First, at least during the early part of that period, many economists and policymakers held the view that policy could exploit a permanent trade-off between inflation and unemployment, as described by a simple Phillips curve relationship. The idea of a permanent trade-off opened up the beguiling possibility that, in return for accepting just a bit more inflation, policymakers could deliver a *permanently* low rate of unemployment. This view is now discredited, of course, on both theoretical and empirical grounds.[9] Second, estimates of the rate of unemployment that could be sustained without igniting inflation were typically unrealistically low, with a long-term unemployment rate of 4 percent or less often being characterized as a modest and easily

---

9. Friedman (1968) provided a major theoretical critique of the idea of a permanent trade-off. Scholars disagree about when and to what degree U.S. monetary policymakers absorbed the lessons of Friedman's article.

attainable objective.[10] Third, economists of the time may have been unduly optimistic about the ability of fiscal and monetary policymakers to eliminate short-term fluctuations in output and employment, that is, to "fine-tune" the economy.

What I have called inflation pessimism was the increasing conviction of policymakers in the 1960s and 1970s, as inflation rose and remained stubbornly high, that monetary policy was an ineffective tool for controlling inflation. As emphasized in recent work on the United States and the United Kingdom by Edward Nelson (2004), during this period policymakers became more and more inclined to blame inflation on so-called cost-push shocks rather than on monetary forces. Cost-push shocks, in the paradigm of the time, included diverse factors such as union wage pressures, price increases by oligopolistic firms, and increases in the prices of commodities such as oil and beef brought about by adverse changes in supply conditions. For the purpose of understanding the upward trend in inflation, however, the most salient attribute of cost-push shocks was that they were putatively out of the control of the monetary policymakers.

The combination of output optimism and inflation pessimism during the latter part of the 1960s and the 1970s was a recipe for high volatility in output and inflation—that is, a set of outcomes well away from the efficient frontier represented by the economy's Taylor curve. Notably, the belief in a long-run trade-off between output and inflation, together with an unrealistically low assessment of the sustainable rate of unemployment, resulted in high inflation but did not deliver the expected payoff in terms of higher output and employment. Moreover, the Fed's periodic attempts to rein in surging inflation led to a pattern of "go-stop" policies, in which swings in policy from ease to tightness contributed to a highly volatile real economy as well as a highly variable inflation rate. Wage-price controls, invoked in the belief that monetary policy was ineffective against cost-push forces, also ultimately proved destabilizing.

Monetary policymakers bemoaned the high rate of inflation in the 1970s but did not fully appreciate their own role in its creation.

---

10. Orphanides (2003) has emphasized the importance of poor estimates of potential output and the closely associated concept of the natural rate of unemployment for explaining the inflationary policies of the 1970s. He notes the difficulty that policymakers of the time faced in distinguishing the productivity slowdown of the period from a cyclical decline in output. Analytical support for the view that confusion between the cyclical and secular aspects of the 1970s' slowdown had inflationary consequences is provided by Lansing (2002) and Bullard and Eusepi (2003).

Ironically, their errors in estimating the natural rate and in ascribing inflation to nonmonetary forces were mutually reinforcing. On the one hand, because unemployment remained well above their over-optimistic estimates of the sustainable rate, they were inclined to attribute inflation to outside forces (such as the actions of firms and unions) rather than to an overheated economy (Romer and Romer 2002; Nelson 2004). On the other hand, the view of policymakers that exogenous forces largely drove inflation made it more difficult for them to recognize that their estimate of the sustainable rate of unemployment was too low. Several years passed before policymakers were finally persuaded by the evidence that sustained anti-inflationary monetary policies would actually work (Primiceri 2003). As you know, these policies were implemented successfully after 1979, beginning under Fed Chairman Volcker.

Better known than even the Taylor curve is John Taylor's famous Taylor rule, a simple equation that has proved remarkably useful as a rule-of-thumb description of monetary policy (Taylor 1993). In its basic form, the Taylor rule relates the Federal Reserve's policy instrument, the overnight federal funds interest rate, to the deviations of inflation and output from the central bank's desired levels for those variables. Estimates of the Taylor rule for the late 1960s and the 1970s reflect the output optimism and inflation pessimism of the period, in that researchers tend to find a weaker response of the policy rate to inflation and (in some studies) a relatively stronger response to the output gap than in more recent periods.[11] As I will shortly discuss further, an insufficiently strong response to inflation let inflation and inflation expectations get out of control and thus added volatility to the economy. At the same time, strong responses to what we understand in retrospect to have been over-optimistic estimates of the output gap created additional instability. As output optimism and inflation pessimism both waned under the force of the data, policy responses became more appropriate and the economy more stable. In this sense, improvements in

---

11. See, for example, Judd and Rudebusch (1998), Taylor (1999), Clarida, Galí, and Gertler (2000), Cogley and Sargent (2002), and Mehra (2002). Orphanides (2003) argues that if one takes account of policymakers' mis-estimates of the output gap in the 1970s, the same Taylor rule that describes policy after 1979 applies to the 1970s as well. The debate is an important one, but it may bear more on what policymakers actually thought they were doing—and thus on the history of ideas—than on the question of whether monetary policy was in fact inefficient or even destabilizing during the period. There seems to be little doubt that it was.

policymakers' understanding of the economy and the role of monetary policy allowed the economy to move closer to the Taylor curve (or, in terms of figure 1, to move from point *A* to point *B*).

Improved Monetary Policy or a Shifting Taylor Curve?

Improvements in monetary policy that moved the economy closer to the efficient frontier described by the Taylor curve can account for part of the Great Moderation. However, several empirical studies have questioned the quantitative importance of this effect and emphasized instead shifts in the Taylor curve, brought about by structural change or good luck. For example, in a paper presented at the Federal Reserve Bank of Kansas City's annual Jackson Hole conference, James Stock and Mark Watson (2003) use several alternative macroeconomic models to simulate how the economy would have performed after 1984 if monetary policy had followed its pre-1979 pattern. Although inflation performance after 1984 would clearly have been worse if pre-1979 monetary policies had been used, Stock and Watson find that output volatility would have been little different. They conclude that improved monetary policy does not account for much of the reduction in output volatility since the mid-1980s. Instead, noting that the variance of the economic shocks implied by their models for the 1970s was much higher than the variance of shocks in the more recent period, they embrace the good-luck explanation of the Great Moderation. Interesting research by Timothy Cogley and Thomas Sargent (2002) and by Shaghil Ahmed, Andrew Levin, and Beth Anne Wilson (2002) likewise finds a substantial reduction in the size and frequency of shocks in the more recent period, supporting the good-luck hypothesis.

Both the structural change and good-luck explanations of the Great Moderation are intriguing and (to reiterate) both are no doubt part of the story. However, an unsatisfying aspect of both explanations is the difficulty of identifying changes in the economic environment large enough and persistent enough to explain the Great Moderation, both in the United States and abroad. In particular, it is not obvious that economic shocks have become significantly smaller or more infrequent, as required by the good-luck hypothesis. Tensions in the Middle East, often blamed for the oil price shocks of the 1970s, have hardly declined in recent years, and important developments in technology and productivity have continued to buffet the economy (albeit in a more positive direction than in the 1970s). Nor has the international economic environment become obviously more placid, as a series of financial crises struck various regions of the world during the 1990s and the powerful forces of globalization have proceeded apace. In contrast, following the adverse experience of the 1970s, changes in the practice of monetary policy occurred around the world in similar ways and during approximately the same period.

Certainly, stability-enhancing changes in the economic environment have occurred in the past two decades. However, an intriguing possibility is that some of these changes, rather than being truly exogenous, may have been induced by improved monetary policies. That is, better monetary policies may have resulted in what appear to be (but only appear to be) favorable shifts in the economy's Taylor curve. Here are some examples of what I have in mind.

First, monetary policies that brought down and stabilized inflation may have led to stabilizing changes in the structure of the economy as well, in line with the prediction of the famous Lucas (1976) critique that economic structure depends on the policy regime. High and unstable inflation increases the variability of relative prices and real interest rates, for example, distorting decisions regarding consumption, capital investment, and inventory investment, among others. Likewise, the high level, variability, and unpredictability of inflation profoundly affected decisions regarding financial investments and money holdings. Theories of "rational inattention" (Sims 2003), according to which people vary the frequency with which they re-examine economic decisions according to the underlying economic environment, imply that the dynamic behavior of the economy would change—probably in the direction of greater stability and persistence—in a more stable pricing environment, in which people reconsider their economic decisions less frequently.

Second, changes in monetary policy could conceivably affect the size and frequency of shocks hitting the economy, at least as an econometrician would measure those shocks. This assertion seems odd at first, as we are used to thinking of shocks as exogenous events, arising from "outside the model," so to speak. However, econometricians typically do not measure shocks directly but instead infer them from movements in macroeconomic variables that they cannot otherwise explain. Shocks in this sense may certainly reflect the monetary regime. For example, consider the cost-push shocks that played such an important role in 1970s' thinking about inflation. Seemingly unexplained or autonomous movements in wages and prices during this period, which analysts would have interpreted as shocks to wage and price equations, may in fact have been the result of earlier monetary policy actions, or (more subtly) of monetary policy actions expected by wage- and price-setters to take place in the future. In an influential paper, Robert Barsky and Lutz Kilian (2001) analyze the oil price shocks of the 1970s in this spirit. Barsky and Kilian provide evidence that the extraordinary increases in nominal oil prices during the 1970s were made feasible primarily by earlier expansionary monetary policies rather than by truly exogenous political or economic events.

Third, monetary policy can also affect the distribution of measured shocks by changing the sensitivity of pricing and other economic decisions to exogenous outside events. For example, significant movements in the price of oil and other commodities continued to occur after 1984. However, in a low-inflation environment, with stable inflation expectations and a general perception that firms do not have pricing power, commodity price shocks are not passed into final goods prices to nearly the same degree as in a looser monetary environment. As a result, a change in commodity prices of a given size shows up as a smaller shock to output and consumer prices today than it would have in the earlier period. Likewise, there is evidence that fluctuations in exchange rates have smaller effects on domestic prices and economic activity when inflation is less volatile and inflation expectations are stabilized (Gagnon and Ihrig 2002; Devereux, Engel, and Storgaard 2003).

Fourth, changes in inflation expectations, which are ultimately the product of the monetary policy regime, can also be confused with truly exogenous shocks in conventional econometric analyses. Marvin Goodfriend (1993) has suggested, for example, that insufficiently anchored inflation expectations have led to periodic "inflation scares," in which inflation expectations have risen in an apparently autonomous manner. Increases in inflation expectations have the flavor of adverse aggregate supply shocks in that they tend to increase the volatility of both inflation and output, in a combination that depends on how strongly the monetary policymakers act to offset these changes in expectations.

Theoretical and empirical support for the idea that inflation expectations may become an independent source of instability has grown in recent years.[12] As I mentioned earlier, a number of researchers

---

12. See Bernanke (2003, 2004) for more extensive discussions.

have found that the reaction of monetary policymakers to inflation has strengthened, in that the estimated coefficient on inflation in the Taylor rule has risen from something less than 1 before 1979 to a value significantly greater than 1 in the more recent period. If the policy interest rate responds to increases in inflation by less than one-for-one (so that the real policy rate does not rise in the face of higher inflation), economic theory tells us that inflation expectations and the economy in general can become unstable. The problem arises from the fact that, if policymakers do not react sufficiently aggressively to increases in inflation, spontaneously arising expectations of increased inflation can ultimately be self-confirming and even self-reinforcing. Incidentally, the stability requirement that the policy rate respond to inflation by more than one-for-one is called the Taylor principle (Taylor 1993 and 1999)—the third concept named after John Taylor that has played a role in this talk. The finding that monetary policymakers violated the Taylor principle during the 1970s but satisfied the principle in the past two decades would be consistent with a reduced incidence of destabilizing expectational shocks.[13]

Support for the view that inflation expectations can be an independent source of economic volatility has also emerged from the extensive recent literature on learning and macroeconomics (Evans and Honkapohja 2001). For example, Athanasios Orphanides and John C. Williams (2003a and 2003b) have studied models in which the public must learn the central bank's underlying preferences regarding inflation by observing the actual inflation process.[14] With learning, inflation expectations take on a more adaptive character; in particular, high and unstable inflation will beget similar characteristics in the pattern of inflation expectations. As Orphanides and Williams show, when inflation expectations are poorly anchored, so that the public is highly uncertain about the long-run rate of inflation that the central bank hopes to achieve, they can become an additional source of volatility in the economy. An analysis that did not properly control for the expectational effects of changes in monetary policy might incorrectly conclude that the Taylor curve had shifted in an adverse direction.

---

13. In a similar spirit, Stefania Albanesi, V. V. Chari, and Lawrence Christiano (2003) have shown that when the central bank's commitment to fighting inflation is perceived to be weak, as may have been the case during the 1970s, self-confirming increases in expected inflation are possible and will tend to destabilize the economy.

14. See Bernanke (2004) for additional discussion.

Conclusion

The Great Moderation, the substantial decline in macroeconomic volatility over the past twenty years, is a striking economic development. Whether the dominant cause of the Great Moderation is structural change, improved monetary policy, or simply good luck is an important question about which no consensus has yet formed. I have argued today that improved monetary policy has likely made an important contribution not only to the reduced volatility of inflation (which is not particularly controversial) but to the reduced volatility of output as well. Moreover, because a change in the monetary policy regime has pervasive effects, I have suggested that some of the effects of improved monetary policies may have been misidentified as exogenous changes in economic structure or in the distribution of economic shocks. This conclusion on my part makes me optimistic for the future, because I am confident that monetary policymakers will not forget the lessons of the 1970s.

I have put my case for better monetary policy rather forcefully today, because I think it likely that the policy explanation for the Great Moderation deserves more credit than it has received in the literature. However, let me close by emphasizing that the debate remains very much open. Although I have focused on its strengths, the monetary policy hypothesis has potential deficiencies as well. For example, although I pointed out the difficulty that the structural change and good-luck explanations have in accounting for the rather sharp decline in volatility after 1984, one might also question whether the change in monetary policy regime was sufficiently sharp to have had the effects I have attributed to it.[15] The consistency of the monetary policy explanation with the experience of the 1950s, a period of stable inflation during which output volatility declined but was high in absolute terms, deserves further investigation. Moreover, several of the channels by which monetary policy may have affected volatility that I have mentioned today remain largely theoretical possibilities and have not received much in the way of rigorous empirical testing. One of my goals today was to stimulate further research on this question. Clearly, the sources of the Great Moderation will continue to be an area for fruitful analysis and debate.

---

15. Stock and Watson (2003) make this point. Supporting their argument, in Bernanke (2004) I present evidence that even today inflation expectations may not be anchored as well as we would like.

References

Ahmed, Shaghil, Andrew Levin, and Beth Anne Wilson. 2002. "Recent U.S. Macroeconomic Stability: Good Policies, Good Practices, or Good Luck?" Board of Governors of the Federal Reserve System, International Finance Discussion Paper 2002-730 (July).

Albanesi, Stefania, V. V. Chari, and Lawrence Christiano. 2003. "Expectation Traps and Monetary Policy." Federal Reserve Bank of Minneapolis, Research Department Staff Report 319 (August).

Barsky, Robert, and Lutz Kilian. 2001. "Do We Really Know That Oil Caused the Great Stagflation? A Monetary Alternative." In *NBER Macroeconomics Annual*, eds. Ben Bernanke and Kenneth Rogoff, 137–}82. Cambridge, MA: MIT Press for the National Bureau of Economic Research (NBER).

Bernanke, Ben. 2003. "'Constrained Discretion' and Monetary Policy." Remarks before the Money Marketeers of New York University, New York, February 3.

———. 2004. "Fedspeak." Remarks at the meetings of the American Economic Association, San Diego, California, January 3.

Blanchard, Olivier, and John Simon. 2001. "The Long and Large Decline in U.S. Output Volatility." *Brookings Papers on Economic Activity* 1: 135–64.

Bullard, James, and Stefano Eusepi. 2003. "Did the Great Inflation Occur Despite Policymaker Commitment to a Taylor Rule?" Federal Reserve Bank of Atlanta, working paper 2003–20 (October).

Chatterjee, Satyajit. 2002. "The Taylor Curve and the Unemployment-Inflation Tradeoff." Federal Reserve Bank of Philadelphia *Business Review* (3rd quarter): 26–33.

Clarida, Richard, Jordi Galí, and Mark Gertler. 2000. "Monetary Policy Rules and Macroeconomic Stability: Evidence and Some Theory." *Quarterly Journal of Economics* 115: 147–80.

Cogley, Timothy, and Thomas Sargent. 2002. "Drifts and Volatilities: Monetary Policies and Outcomes in the Post-WWII U.S." Working paper, Arizona State University and New York University (August).

DeLong, J. Bradford. 1997. "America's Peacetime Inflation: The 1970s." In *Reducing Inflation: Motivation and Strategy*, eds. Christina Romer and David Romer. Chicago: University of Chicago Press for NBER.

Devereux, Michael, Charles Engel, and Peter Storgaard. 2003. "Endogenous Exchange-Rate Pass-through when Nominal Prices Are Set in Advance." National Bureau of Economic Research working paper 9543 (March).

Evans, George, and Seppo Honkapohja. 2001. *Learning and Expectations in Macroeconomics*. Princeton, NJ: Princeton University Press.

Friedman, Milton. 1968. "The Role of Monetary Policy." *American Economic Review* 58 (March): 1–17.

Gagnon, Joseph, and Jane Ihrig. 2002. "Monetary Policy and Exchange-Rate Passthrough." Board of Governors of the Federal Reserve System, International Finance Discussion Paper 2001-704 (latest version March 2002).

Goodfriend, Marvin. 1993. "Interest Rate Policy and the Inflation Scare Problem, 1979–1992." Federal Reserve Bank of Richmond *Economic Quarterly* 1 (Winter): 1–23 (on the Federal Reserve Bank of Richmond Web site).

Judd, John, and Glenn Rudebusch. 1998. "Taylor's Rule and the Fed: 1970–1997." Federal Reserve Bank of San Francisco *Economic Review* 3:3–16.

Kahn, James, Margaret McConnell, and Gabriel Perez Quiros. 2002. "On the Causes of the Increased Stability of the U.S. Economy." Federal Reserve Bank of New York *Economic Policy Review* 8:183–202.

Kim, Chang-Jin, and Charles Nelson. 1999. "Has the U.S. Economy Become More Stable? A Bayesian Approach Based on a Markov-Switching Model of the Business Cycle." *Review of Economics and Statistics* 81:608–16.

Kim, Chang-Jin, Charles Nelson, and Jeremy Piger. 2003. "The Less Volatile U.S. Economy: A Bayesian Investigation of Timing, Breadth, and Potential Explanations." *Journal of Business and Economic Statistics,* forthcoming. [*JBES* 22(2004): 80–93.]

Lansing, Kevin. 2002. "Learning about a Shift in Trend Output: Implications for Monetary Policy and Inflation." Federal Reserve Bank of San Francisco, working paper (July).

Lucas, Robert, Jr. 1976. "Econometric Policy Evaluation: A Critique." *Carnegie-Rochester Conference Series on Public Policy* 1:19–46.

Mayer, Thomas. 1998. *Monetary Policy and the Great Inflation in the United States: The Federal Reserve and the Failure of Macroeconomic Policy, 1965–79.* Cheltenham, UK: Edward Elgar.

McCarthy, Jonathan, and Egon Zakrajsek. 2003. "Inventory Dynamics and Business Cycles: What Has Changed?" Federal Reserve Bank of New York and Board of Governors of the Federal Reserve System, working paper (June).

McConnell, Margaret, and Gabriel Perez Quiros. 2000. "Output Fluctuations in the United States: What Has Changed since the Early 1980s?" *American Economic Review* 90:1464–76.

Mehra, Yash. 2002. "The Taylor Principle, Interest Rate Smoothing, and Fed Policy in the 1970s and 1980s." Federal Reserve Bank of Richmond, working paper 02-3 (December).

Nelson, Edward. 2004. "The Great Inflation of the Seventies: What Really Happened?" Federal Reserve Bank of St. Louis, working paper (January).

Orphanides, Athanasios. 2003. "The Quest for Prosperity Without Inflation." *Journal of Monetary Economics* 50 (April): 633–63.

Orphanides, Athanasios, and John C. Williams. 2003a. "Imperfect Knowledge, Inflation Expectations, and Monetary Policy." In *Inflation Targeting,* eds. Ben

Bernanke and Michael Woodford. Chicago: University of Chicago Press for NBER, forthcoming. [*The Inflation Targeting Debate* (2005): 201–246.]

———. 2003b. "Inflation Scares and Forecast-Based Monetary Policy." Board of Governors of the Federal Reserve System, Finance and Economics Discussion Series 2003-41 (August).

Primiceri, Giorgio. (2003). "Why Inflation Rose and Fell: Policymakers' Beliefs and U.S. Postwar Stabilization Policy." Princeton University, working paper (November).

Romer, Christina, and David Romer. 2002. "The Evolution of Economic Understanding and Postwar Stabilization Policy." *Rethinking Stabilization Policy*, Federal Reserve Bank of Kansas City: 11–78.

Sims, Christopher. 2003. "Implications of Rational Inattention." *Journal of Monetary Economics* 50 (April): 665–90.

Stock, James, and Mark Watson. 2003. "Has the Business Cycle Changed? Evidence and Explanations." Prepared for the Federal Reserve Bank of Kansas City symposium, "Monetary Policy and Uncertainty," Jackson Hole, Wyoming, August 28–30.

Taylor, John B. 1993. "Discretion versus Policy Rules in Practice." *Carnegie-Rochester Conference Series on Public Policy* 39:195–214.

———. 1998. "Monetary Policy Guidelines for Employment and Inflation Stability." In *Inflation, Unemployment, and Monetary Policy,* eds. Benjamin Friedman and Robert Solow. Cambridge, MA: MIT Press.

———. 1999. "A Historical Analysis of Monetary Policy Rules." In *Monetary Policy Rules,* ed. John B. Taylor, 319–40. Chicago: University of Chicago Press for NBER.

Warnock, M. V. Cacdac, and Francis Warnock. 2000. "The Declining Volatility of U.S. Employment: Was Arthur Burns Right?" Board of Governors of the Federal Reserve System, International Finance Discussion Paper no. 677 (August).

Willis, Jonathan. 2003. "Implications of Structural Changes in the U.S. Economy for Pricing Behavior and Inflation Dynamics." Federal Reserve Bank of Kansas City *Economic Review* (1st quarter): 5–27.

SIX

THE GREAT DEVIATION

John B. Taylor

The classic explanation of financial crises, going back hundreds of years, is that they are caused by excesses—frequently monetary excesses—that lead to a boom and an inevitable bust. In the recent crisis we had a housing boom and bust, which in turn led to financial turmoil in the United States and other countries. I begin by showing that monetary excesses were the main cause of that boom and the resulting bust.

Loose-Fitting Monetary Policy

Figure 1 was published in *The Economist* magazine in October 2007 as a simple way to illustrate the story of monetary excesses. The figure is based on a paper[1] that I presented at the annual Jackson Hole conference where central bankers from around the world had assembled in August 2007. It examines Federal Reserve policy decisions—in terms of the federal funds interest rate—from 2000 to 2006.

The line that dips down to 1 percent in 2003, stays there into 2004, and then rises steadily until 2006 shows the actual interest rate decisions of the Federal Reserve. The other line shows what the interest

---

John B. Taylor is the George P. Shultz Senior Fellow in Economics at the Hoover Institution and the Mary and Robert Raymond Professor of Economics at Stanford University.

1. "Housing and Monetary Policy," in *Housing, Housing Finance, and Monetary Policy* (Kansas City: Federal Reserve Bank of Kansas City, 2007).

Loose fitting
Federal funds rate, actual and counterfactual, %

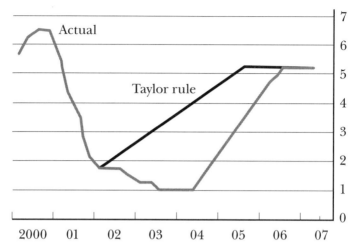

Figure 1. Chart from *The Economist*, October 18, 2007
Source: John Taylor, "Housing and Monetary Policy," Sept. 2007

rate would have been had the Fed followed the type of policy that it had followed fairly regularly during the previous twenty-year period of good economic performance. *The Economist* labels that line the Taylor rule because it is a smoothed version of the interest rate one gets by plugging actual inflation and gross domestic product (GDP) into the policy rule that I proposed in 1992. When he was president of the Federal Reserve Bank of St. Louis, William Poole presented a similar chart, covering a longer period and without the smoothing, in an essay called "Understanding the Fed," published in the Federal Reserve Bank of St. Louis *Review* in 2007. The important point is that this line shows what the interest rate would have been had the Fed followed the kind of policy that had worked well during the period of economic stability called the Great Moderation, which began in the early 1980s.

Figure 1 shows that the actual interest rate decisions fell well below what historical experience would suggest policy should be. It thus provides an empirical measure that monetary policy was too easy during this period, or too "loose fitting," as *The Economist* puts it. This was an unusually big deviation of monetary policy from the Taylor rule. No greater or more persistent deviation of actual Fed policy had been seen since the turbulent days of the 1970s. So there is clearly evidence that there were monetary excesses during the period leading up to the housing boom.

The unusually low interest rate decisions were, of course, made with careful consideration by monetary policymakers. One can interpret them as purposeful deviations from the "regular" interest rate settings based on the usual macroeconomic variables. The Fed used transparent language to describe the decisions, saying, for example, that interest rates would be low for "a considerable period" and that they would rise slowly at a "measured pace," ways of clarifying that the decisions were deviations from the rule in some sense. Those actions were thus essentially discretionary government interventions in that they deviated from the regular way of conducting policy in order to address a specific problem, in particular a fear of deflation, as had occurred in Japan in the 1990s.

The Counterfactual: No Boom, No Bust

In presenting this chart to the central bankers in Jackson Hole, Wyoming, in late summer 2007, I argued that this extra easy policy accelerated the housing boom and thereby ultimately led to the housing bust. Others had made similar arguments. *The Economist* wrote, in the issue then on the newsstands, "By slashing interest rates (by more than the Taylor rule prescribed) the Fed encouraged a house-price boom . . ."

To support the argument empirically I provided statistical evidence that the interest rate deviation in figure 1 could plausibly bring about a housing boom. I did this by using regression techniques to estimate a model of the empirical relationship between the interest rate and housing starts; I then simulated that model to see what would have happened in the counterfactual event that policy had followed the rule in figure 1. In this way I provided empirical proof that monetary policy was a key cause of the boom and hence the bust and the crisis.

Figure 2 summarizes the results of this empirical approach. It is a picture of housing starts in the United States during the same period as figure 1; it is drawn from that same 2007 Jackson Hole paper. The jagged line shows actual housing starts in thousands of units. Both the housing boom and the housing bust are very clear in this picture.

The line labeled "counterfactual" in figure 2 is what a statistically estimated model of housing starts suggests would have happened had interest rates followed along the rule in figure 1; clearly, there would

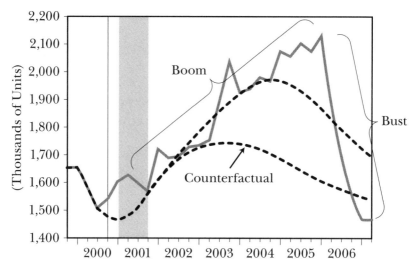

Figure 2. The Boom-Bust in Housing Starts
Compared with the Counterfactual

have not been such a big housing boom and bust. Hence, figure 2 provides empirical evidence that the unusually low interest rate policy was a factor in the housing boom. One can challenge this conclusion, of course, by challenging the model; but by using a model and an empirical counterfactual, one has a formal framework for debating the issue.

Not shown in figure 2 is the associated boom and bust in housing prices in the United States. The boom-bust was evident throughout most of the country but was worse in California, Florida, Arizona, and Nevada. The exceptions were in states such as Texas and Michigan, where local factors offset the monetary excess stressed here.

Although the housing boom was the most noticeable effect of the monetary excesses, they also could be seen in more gradually rising overall prices. Inflation based on the consumer price index (CPI), for example, averaged 3.2 percent annually during the past five years, well above the 2 percent target suggested by many policymakers and implicit in the policy rule in figure 1. It is always difficult to predict the exact initial impacts of monetary shocks, but housing was also a volatile part of GDP in the 1970s, another period of monetary instability before the onset of the Great Moderation. The more systematic monetary policy followed during the Great Moderation had the advantages of keeping both the overall economy stable and the inflation rate low.

Competing Explanations: A Global Saving Glut

Some argue that the low interest rates in 2002–04 were caused by global factors beyond the control of the monetary authorities. If so, then the interest rate decisions by the monetary authorities were not the major factor causing the boom. This explanation is appealing at first glance because long-term interest rates remained low for a while after the short-term federal funds rate started increasing. This alternative explanation focuses on global saving. It argues that there was an excess of world saving—a global saving glut—which pushed interest rates down in the United States and other countries.

The main problem with this explanation is that there is actually no evidence of a global saving glut. On the contrary, as figure 3 shows in very simple terms, there seems to be a saving shortage. This figure, produced by staff at the International Monetary Fund in 2005, shows that the global saving rate—world saving as a fraction of world GDP—was very low in the 2002–04 period, especially when compared with the 1970s and 1980s. Thus, this alternative explanation does not stand up to empirical testing using data that have long been available.

To be sure, there was a gap of saving over investment in the world *outside* the United States during 2002–04, which may be the source of the term *saving glut*. But the United States was saving less than it was investing during this period; it was running a current account deficit, implying that saving was less than investment. Thus, the positive saving gap outside the United States was offset by an equal-sized negative

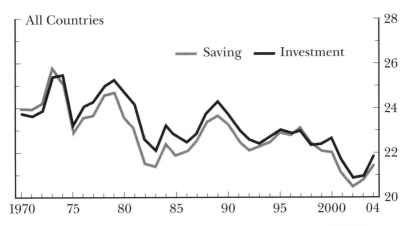

Figure 3. Global Saving and Investment as a Share of World GDP

Source: *World Economic Outlook*, IMF, Sept. 2005, chap. 2, p. 92

saving gap in the United States. No extra impact on world interest rates would be expected. As implied by simple global accounting, there is no global gap between saving and investment.

Monetary Policy in Other Countries: Central Banks Looking at Each Other?

Nevertheless there are possible global connections to keep track of when assessing the root cause of the crisis. Most important is the evidence that interest rates at several other central banks also deviated from what historical regularities, as described by the Taylor rule, would predict. Even more striking is that housing booms were largest where the deviations from the rule were largest. Three economists at the Organization for Economic Cooperation and Development (OECD), Rudiger Ahrend, Boris Cournède, and Robert Price, provide a fascinating analysis of the experiences in OECD countries during this period in their working paper "Monetary Policy, Market Excesses and Financial Turmoil" of March 2008. They show that the deviations from the Taylor rule explain a large fraction of the cross-country variation in housing booms in OECD countries. For example, within Europe the deviations from the Taylor rule vary in size because inflation and output data vary from country to country. The country with the largest deviation from the rule, Spain, had the biggest housing boom, measured by the change in housing investment as a share of GDP. The country with the smallest deviation, Austria, had the smallest change in housing investment as a share of GDP. That close correlation is shown in figure 4, which is drawn from their OECD working paper. It plots the sum of deviations from the policy rule on the horizontal axis and the change in housing investment as a share of GDP on the vertical axis.

One important question, with implications for reforming the international financial system, is whether the low interest rates at other central banks were influenced by the decisions in the United States or represented an interaction among central banks that caused global short-term interest rates to be lower than they otherwise would have been. To test this hypothesis, I examined the decisions at the European Central Bank (ECB) in a paper[2] prepared for a talk in Europe in June

---

2. "Globalization and Monetary Policy: Missions Impossible," in Mark Getler and Jordi Galí, eds., *The International Dimensions of Monetary Policy* (Chicago: University of Chicago Press for National Bureau of Economic Research, 2009).

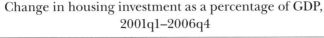

Change in housing investment as a percentage of GDP, 2001q1–2006q4

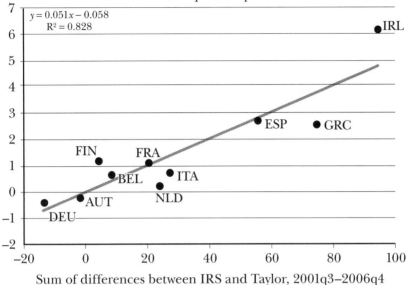

Sum of differences between IRS and Taylor, 2001q3–2006q4

Figure 4. Housing Investment versus Deviations from the Taylor Rule in Europe

2007. I studied the deviations (residuals) of the ECB interest rate decisions from the same type of policy rule as in figure 1, but using eurozone inflation and GDP data. The interest rate set by the ECB was also below the rule; in other words, there were negative residuals. To determine whether those residuals were influenced by the Federal Reserve's interest-rate decisions, I ran a regression of them during 2000–06 on the federal funds rate shown in figure 1. I found that the estimated coefficient was .21 and that it was statistically significant.

Figure 5 gives a visual sense of how much of the ECB interest rate decisions could be explained by the influence of the Fed's interest rate decisions. It appears that a good fraction can be explained in this way. The jagged line in figure 5 shows the deviations of the actual interest rates set by the ECB from the policy rule. (I have not smoothed out the high-frequency jagged movements as was done in figure 1.) By this measure, the ECB interest rate was as much as 2 percentage points too low during this period. The smoother line shows that a good fraction of the deviation can be "explained" by the federal funds rate in the United States.

Percent

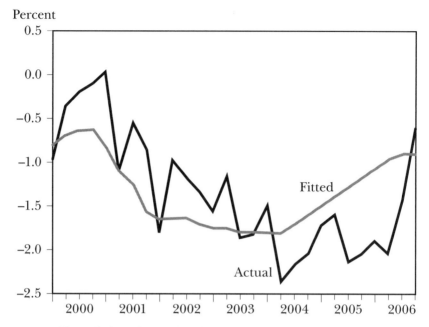

Figure 5. Actual Deviations from a Euro Policy Rule and the
Predicted Values Based on the Federal Funds Rate

The reasons for this connection are not clear from this statistical analysis, and are a fruitful subject for future research. Indeed it is difficult to distinguish statistically between the ECB following the Fed and the Fed following the ECB; similar regressions show that there is also connection the other way, from the ECB to the Fed. Concerns about the exchange rate, or the influence of the exchange rate on inflation, could generate such a relationship, as could third factors, such as changes in the global real interest rate.

Monetary Interaction with the Subprime Mortgage Problem

A sharp boom and bust in the housing markets would be expected to affect the financial markets, as falling house prices led to delinquencies and foreclosures. Those effects were amplified by several complicating factors, including the use of subprime mortgages, especially the adjustable-rate variety, which led to excessive risk-taking. In the United States such risk-taking was encouraged by government programs designed to promote home ownership, a worthwhile goal but overdone in retrospect. During 2003–05, when short-term interest rates were still unusually low, the amount of adjustable rate mortgages (ARMs) rose to about one-third of total mortgages and remained at that high level for an unusually long time. This made borrowing attractive and brought more people into the housing markets, further bidding up housing prices.

It is important to note, however, that the excessive risk-taking and the low interest monetary policy decisions are connected. Evidence for this connection is shown in figure 6, which plots housing price inflation along with foreclosure and delinquency rates on adjustable rate subprime mortgages. The figure shows the sharp increase in housing price inflation from mid-2003 to early 2006 and the subsequent decline. Observe how delinquency rates and foreclosure rates were inversely related to housing price inflation during this period. During the years of rapidly rising housing prices, delinquency and foreclosure rates declined rapidly. The benefits of holding onto a house, perhaps by working longer hours to make the payments, are higher when the price of the house is rapidly rising. When prices are falling, the incentives to make payments are much less and turn negative if the price of the house falls below the value of the mortgage. Hence, delinquencies and foreclosures rise.

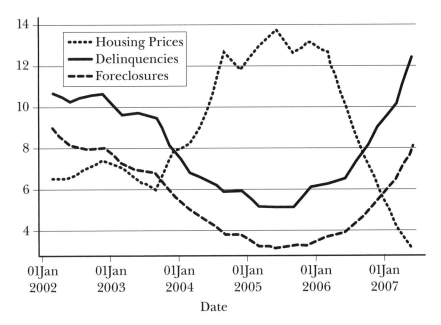

Figure 6. Housing Price Inflation, Delinquencies, and Foreclosures on Subprime Adjustable Rate Mortgages (ARM)

Mortgage underwriting procedures are supposed to take account of actual foreclosure rates and delinquency rates in cross-section data. Those procedures, however, would have been overly optimistic during the period when prices were rising unless they took into account the time series correlation in figure 6. Thus, there is an interaction between the monetary excesses and the risk-taking excesses. This illustrates how unintended things can happen when policy deviates from the norm. In this case, the rapidly rising housing prices and the resulting low delinquency rates likely threw the underwriting programs off track and misled many people.

More Complications: Complex Securitization, Fannie, and Freddie

These problems were amplified because the adjustable-rate subprime and other mortgages were packed into mortgage-backed securities of great complexity. The rating agencies underestimated the risk of these securities because of a lack of competition, poor accountability, or, most likely, an inherent difficulty in assessing risk due to the complexity. These complex mortgage-backed securities led to what might be called the "Queen of Spades problem," as in the game of Hearts. In the game of Hearts you don't know where the Queen of Spades is; you don't want to get stuck with the Queen of Spades. The Queens of Spades—and there are many of them in this game—were the securities with the bad mortgages in them and people didn't know where they were. People didn't know which banks were holding them eighteen months ago, and they still don't know where they are. That risk in the balance sheets of financial institutions has been at the heart of the financial crisis from the beginning.

In the United States other government actions were at play. The government-sponsored agencies Fannie Mae and Freddie Mac were encouraged to expand and buy mortgage-backed securities, including those formed with the risky subprime mortgages. Although legislation, such as the Federal Housing Enterprise Regulatory Reform Act of 2005, was proposed to control these excesses, it was not passed into law. The actions of these agencies should be added to the list of government interventions that were part of a great deviation from sound economic policy which led to the recent crisis.

SEVEN

IT'S NOT SO SIMPLE

Donald L. Kohn

The Role of Simple Rules in Monetary Policymaking

John Taylor has made a number of seminal contributions to the field of macroeconomics. What has distinguished John's work, in my view, is that he takes policymaking in the real world seriously.[1]

Taking policymaking seriously involves understanding the constraints imposed on our decisions by partial information and incomplete knowledge of economic relationships. It also implies the use of empirically valid models that acknowledge the efforts of households and businesses to anticipate the future and maximize their welfare over time. In the late 1980s and early 1990s, macroeconomics was focused mainly on real business cycles and endogenous growth theory. During this period, John was one of a very small number of academic economists who continued to pursue research aimed at informing the conduct of monetary policy. John's Carnegie-Rochester conference paper published in 1993 is an excellent example of this research.

Donald L. Kohn is a forty-year veteran of the Federal Reserve System. He is now a senior fellow in the Economic Studies Program at the Brookings Institution. The views expressed in this chapter are those of the author and should not be attributed to the Federal Reserve.

1. I am sure my colleagues join me in honoring John. However, my thoughts on policy rules are my own and not necessarily those of my colleagues on the Federal Open Market Committee. Jinill Kim and Andrew Levin, of the Board's staff, contributed to the preparation of these remarks.

Importantly, John's legacy to the Federal Reserve has not been confined to enhancing our understanding of monetary policy. In addition, he has turned out legions of students who have followed in his footsteps in their interest in policy. Many of them have spent time in the Federal Reserve, producing a rich array of contributions to policymaking and research.

John and I have spent countless hours discussing how the Federal Reserve arrives at decisions about monetary policy and how it *should* arrive at decisions. Those conversations began in earnest in the late 1980s, when John was on the Council of Economic Advisers, and they have continued to the present day. They have occurred not only in offices and classrooms in Washington and Stanford and at numerous conferences around the globe, but also around dinner tables in Washington and Palo Alto and on hiking trails from Vermont to Wyoming. Those conversations made me a better policy adviser and then policymaker, and they have had the added and very special bonus of allowing Gail and me to count John and Allyn among our friends. I can't think of a better way to honor John's contributions than to continue that discussion around the dinner tables of Dallas by reflecting on the role of simple rules in informing policymaking.

Three Benefits of Simple Rules in Monetary Policymaking

In his Carnegie-Rochester conference paper, John considered a simple policy rule under which the nominal federal funds rate is adjusted in response to both the gap between real and trend gross domestic product (GDP) and the gap between the inflation rate and policymakers' target. Based on data for the previous few years, John calibrated the long-run target for inflation and the two parameters that determine the responsiveness of the federal funds rate to the two gaps. The equilibrium real interest rate was based on a longer history of actual real interest rates. Figure 1A depicts the actual nominal funds rate and the Taylor rule prescriptions between 1987 and 1992, as presented in John's paper. Despite its simplicity, this policy rule fits the data remarkably well; it described a period of generally successful policymaking; and it adhered to the Taylor principle of adjusting the nominal rate more than one-for-one with changes in the inflation rate, so it provided a plausible template for future success. It is no wonder that John has been such a dedicated salesman and that his efforts have been so well received in academia and policy councils.

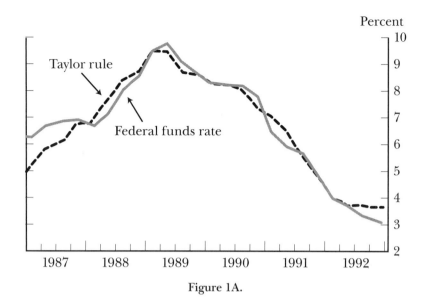

Figure 1A.

Following John's seminal contribution, many other economists have engaged in research on similar policy rules and, together with John, have identified several benefits of such rules in conducting monetary policy. I will elaborate on three of them.

The first benefit of looking at a simple rule like John's is that it can provide a useful benchmark for policymakers. It relates policy-setting systematically to the state of the economy in a way that, over time, will produce reasonably good outcomes on average. Importantly, the emphasis is on levels and gaps, not growth rates, as inputs to the policy process. This emphasis can be a problem when a level, say of potential GDP, is in question, but in many respects it is also a virtue. For the United States, the two gaps relate directly to the legislative mandate of the Federal Reserve to achieve stable prices and maximum employment. Moreover, those two gaps fit directly into most modern macroeconomic theories, which tell us something about their relationship and how that relationship can be affected by the type of shock hitting the economy.

Model uncertainties make the simplicity of the rule particularly important for the policymaker because research suggests that the prescriptions from simple rules can be more robust than optimal-control policies. Optimal-control policies can depend critically on the exact specification of the model, and clearly there is no consensus about which model best describes the U.S. economy.

Federal Reserve policymakers are shown several versions of Taylor rules in the material we receive before each meeting of the Federal Open Market Committee (FOMC). I always look at those charts and tables and ask myself whether I am comfortable with any significant deviation of my policy prescription from those of the rules.

A second benefit of simple rules is that they help financial market participants form a baseline for expectations regarding the future course of monetary policy. Even if the actual policy process is far more sophisticated than any simple rule could completely describe, the rule often provides a reasonably good approximation of what policymakers decide and a framework for thinking about policy actions. Indeed, many financial market participants have used the Taylor rule to understand U.S. monetary policy over the past fifteen years. Investors and other market participants are going to form expectations about policy and act on those expectations. The more accurate and informed those expectations are, the more likely are their actions to reinforce the intended effects of policy.

A third benefit is that simple rules can be helpful in the central bank's communication with the general public. Such an understanding is important for the transmission mechanism of monetary policy. Giving the public some sense of how the central bank sees the output and inflation gaps and how they are expected to evolve will help it understand the central bank's objectives and how policymakers are likely to respond to surprises in incoming data.

Four Limitations of Simple Rules

Simple rules have limitations, of course, as benchmarks for monetary policy. To quote from John's Carnegie-Rochester paper, "A policy rule can be implemented and operated more informally by policymakers who recognize the general instrument responses that underlie the policy rule, but who also recognize that operating the rule requires judgment and cannot be done by computer." In that context, four limitations of simple rules are important.

The first limitation is that the use of a Taylor rule requires that a single measure of inflation be used to obtain the rule prescriptions. The price index used by John in the Carnegie-Rochester paper was the GDP price deflator. Other researchers have used the inflation measure based on the consumer price index (CPI). Over the past fifteen years, the Federal Reserve has emphasized the inflation rate as measured by changes in the price index for personal consumption expenditures (PCE). Many researchers have also explored the use of core price indexes, which exclude the volatile food and energy components, as better predictors of future inflation or as more robust indicators of the sticky prices that some theories say should be the targets of policy. To be sure, over long periods, most of these measures behave very similarly. But policy is made in the here and now, and the various indexes can diverge significantly for long stretches, potentially providing different signals for the appropriate course of monetary policy.

Second, the implementation of the Taylor rule and other related rules requires determining the level of the equilibrium real interest rate and the level of potential output; neither of them are observable variables, and both must be inferred from other information. John used 2 percent as a rough guess as to the real federal funds rate that would be consistent with the economy producing at its potential. But the equilibrium level of the real federal funds rate probably varies over time because it depends on factors such as the growth rate of potential output, fiscal policy, and the willingness of savers to supply credit to households and businesses. Inaccurate estimates of this rate will mislead policymakers about the policy stance required to achieve full employment. In a similar vein, real-time estimates of potential output can be derived in a number of ways and—as shown by Athanasios Orphanides (2003) and others—they are subject to large and persistent errors. If policymakers inadvertently rely on flawed estimates, they will encounter persistent problems in achieving their inflation objectives.

The third limitation of using simple rules for monetary policymaking stems from the fact that, by their nature, simple rules involve only a small number of variables. However, the state of a complex economy like that of the United States cannot be fully captured by any small set of summary statistics. Moreover, policy is best made looking forward, that is, on the basis of projections of how inflation and economic activity may evolve. Lagged or current values of the small set of variables used in a given simple rule may not provide a sufficient guide to future economic developments, especially in periods of rapid or unusual change. For these reasons, central banks monitor a wide range of indicators in conducting monetary policy. In his Carnegie-Rochester paper, John mentioned the stock market crash of October 1987 as an example of how other variables can and should influence the course of monetary policy in some situations.

The final limitation I want to highlight is that simple policy rules may not capture risk-management considerations. In some circumstances,

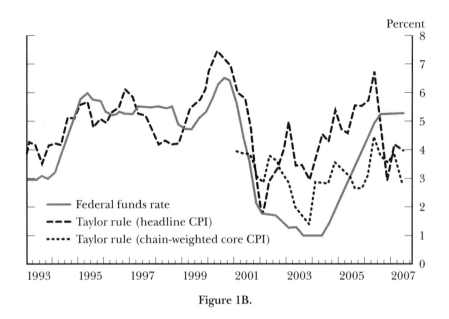

Figure 1B.

the risks to the outlook or the perceived costs of missing an objective on a particular side may be sufficiently skewed that policymakers will choose to respond by adjusting policy in a way that would not be justified solely by the current state of the economy or the modal outlook for output and inflation gaps.

Policy Rules around 2003

Some of the ambiguities and potential pitfalls in the use of simple policy rules are highlighted by considering their prescriptions for a period earlier in this decade. In figure 1B, the solid line indicates the actual federal funds rate between the first quarter of 1993 and the second quarter of 2007, and the dashed line shows the prescriptions of the Taylor rule using the same methodology that John used in his Jackson Hole remarks that year.[2] For the earlier part of the sample, the prescription from this simple rule tracks the actual funds rate relatively

---

2. Following John, the rule specification and the data used for the prescriptions closely follow the implementation of the Taylor rule in Bill Poole's speech in August 2006 (Poole 2007). The inflation measure used for this rule is the four-quarter average headline CPI inflation rate, with the benchmark value set to 2 percent. Through 2001, the gap between real GDP and its potential is the value measured in real time by the staff of the Board of Governors. Because subsequent staff estimates of the output gap are not yet publicly

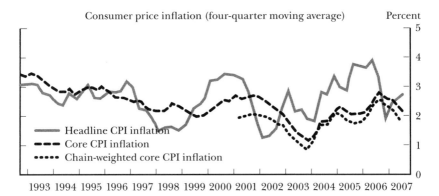

Figure 2A.

well. As John pointed out, a notable deviation happened beginning in 2002, and I would like to discuss that period to illustrate the limitations I noted earlier.

Inflation measure

The first limitation is related to the measure used for the inflation variable included in the rules. The rule prescriptions depicted by the dashed line in figure 1B are based on the headline CPI. But as you know, the FOMC often looks at core inflation, stripping out the effects of energy and food prices, as a better indicator of future price behavior. The dotted line represents the rule prescriptions based on the chain-weighted core CPI, which the Bureau of Labor Statistics has produced since 2000. Using this measure lowers the prescribed funds rate by about 2 percentage points during 2003, bringing the rule prescriptions much closer to the actual path of policy. The reason for the improvement is evident from figure 2A: even though the headline and core CPI measures were broadly similar in the mid- to late 1990s, these measures diverged substantially between 2003 and 2005.

Potential output

The second limitation relates to the challenge of judging the level of potential output in real time. To illustrate this point, figure 2B plots

---

available, the rule prescriptions for the post-2001 period are computed with the real-time output gap as constructed by the Congressional Budget Office.

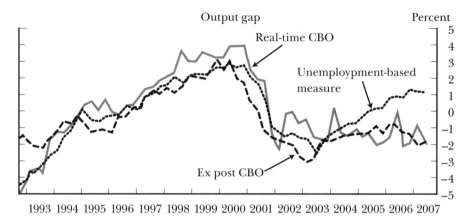

Figure 2B.

three measures of the output gap. The solid line is the real-time esti-mate by the Congressional Budget Office (CBO) that was used in the Taylor rule prescriptions in figure 1B, while the dashed line depicts the CBO's ex post estimate of the output gap as of the third quarter of 2007. Back in 2003, the CBO estimated that output at that time was below potential by only 1 percent. With the benefit of four more years of data, the CBO currently estimates that the output gap for the first half of 2003 was considerably wider—about 3 percent. In addition, the dotted line represents an alternative measure of resource utili-zation derived from the unemployment rate and an estimate of the natural rate of unemployment (NAIRU) taken from the board staff's FRB/US model. In fact, the unemployment rate was rising through the middle of 2003, so the FOMC had every reason to believe that the output gap was widening at that time. Using this unemployment-based measure rather than the real-time CBO measure would reduce the prescriptions of simple policy rules by roughly half a percentage point in early 2003.

Other variables

The third limitation in my list was that the small set of economic mea-sures included in simple rules may not fully reflect the state of the economy. Around 2003, financial market conditions may not have been adequately summarized by the assumed 2 percent equilibrium federal funds rate. Accounting scandals caused economic agents to lose con-fidence in published financial statements and in bond ratings. The

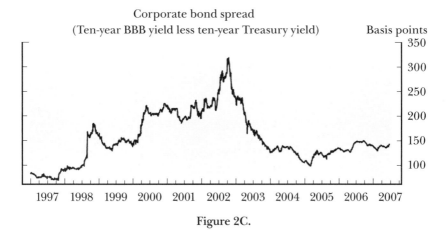

Corporate bond spread
(Ten-year BBB yield less ten-year Treasury yield)

Figure 2C.

result was higher uncertainty about the financial health of firms, and credit spreads widened substantially. Figure 2C shows that risk spreads on corporate bonds were elevated in this period. Other things equal, such spreads would reduce the federal funds rate needed to achieve full employment, perhaps explaining a portion of the gap between the actual federal funds rate and the outcome from the policy rule during this period.

Risk management

The last item on my list of limitations was that simple rules do not take account of risk-management considerations. As shown in figure 2A, the core CPI inflation rate for 2003 was falling toward 1 percent. The real-time reading of the core PCE inflation rate (not shown) was on average even lower than the comparable CPI figure. Given these rates, the possibility of deflation could not be ruled out. We had carefully analyzed the Japanese experience of the early 1990s; our conclusion was that aggressively moving against the risk of deflation would pay dividends by reducing the odds on needing to deal with the zero bound on nominal interest rates should the economy be hit with another negative shock. This factor is not captured by simple policy rules.

A Final Note

I have offered this analysis in the spirit of so many of the discussions I have had with John. His framework has been enormously important to policymaking in the Federal Reserve, and it has yielded many benefits. Nevertheless, it's important to keep in mind that some significant practical limitations also are associated with the application of such rules in real time. In other words, it's not so simple to use simple rules!

References

Orphanides, Athanasios. 2003. "The Quest for Prosperity without Inflation." *Journal of Monetary Economics* 50 (April): 633–63.

Poole, William. 2007. "Understanding the Fed." Federal Reserve Bank of St. Louis *Review* 89 (January/February): 3–14, http://research.stlouisfed.org/publications/review/past/2007.

Taylor, John B. 1993. "Discretion versus Policy Rules in Practice." *Carnegie-Rochester Conference Series on Public Policy* 39:195–214, http://econpapers.repec.org/article/eeecrcspp/default1993.htm.

———. 2007. "Housing and Monetary Policy." Speech delivered at "Housing, Housing Finance, and Monetary Policy," a symposium sponsored by the Federal Reserve Bank of Kansas City, held in Jackson Hole, Wyoming, August 30–September 1, www.kansascityfed.org/publicat/sympos/2007/pdf/2007.09.04.Taylor.pdf.

PART III

New Challenges in the Decade Ahead

EIGHT

FORECAST TARGETING AS A MONETARY POLICY STRATEGY: POLICY RULES IN PRACTICE

Michael Woodford

For several decades, John Taylor has advocated an ambitious program of research on quantitative rules that could serve as guidelines for monetary policy. While the comparative study of historical performance under alternative policies has helped to shape Taylor's views (Taylor 1999b), probably the most distinctive element of his approach to the problem has been his use of macroeconometric models for the normative analysis of alternative policy rules (Taylor 1979, 1993b, 1999c). In addition to his important contributions to the technical methods for the development, estimation, and numerical analysis of such models, Taylor has constantly been concerned with the issue of the robustness of policy proposals to model uncertainty (Taylor 1999a) and with the distillation of the results of the research literature into a form that could influence actual policy (Taylor 1993a and 1998).

These remarks were prepared for the conference "John Taylor's Contributions to Monetary Theory and Policy," Federal Reserve Bank of Dallas, October 12–13, 2007. The author would like to thank Ray Fair, Marc Giannoni, Rick Mishkin, Ed Nelson, Bruce Preston, and Lars Svensson for helpful discussions; Mehmet Pasaogullari for research assistance; the National Science Foundation for research support through a grant to the National Bureau of Economic Research; and the Kumho Visiting Professorship, Yale University, for providing the time to write this paper.

To what extent has the literature that Taylor has launched arrived at conclusions that are likely to help to improve the conduct of policy by central banks? In my view, the most important recent development with regard to the practical use of policy rules has been the development, at several central banks since the early 1990s, of methods of forecast targeting, both as a systematic approach to monetary policy deliberations and as a basis for communication with the public.[1] Forecast targeting relies heavily on the use of quantitative structural models of the effects of monetary policy, and in this respect at least the success of the approach relies heavily on the output of the research program promoted by Taylor. Moreover, forecast targeting implies a decision process focused on the achievement of specific quantitative objectives, and typically implies a greater degree of explicitness about both the goals of policy and the justification of particular policy decisions than is seen at other central banks; in these respects, it represents an important step toward the ideal of rule-based policymaking. I believe that the most likely way in which the research literature on monetary policy rules can help to improve actual policy is through contributing to the refinement of forecast-targeting procedures.

One cannot say, however, that forecast targeting, as developed at central banks in the early 1990s, represented an attempt to implement ideas from the theoretical literature on monetary policy rules. Nor has the extensive literature on monetary policy rules of the past two decades given a great deal of attention to the analysis of procedures of this kind. This paper seeks to examine the extent to which forecast targeting does represent a desirable policy rule, from the standpoint of what Taylor (2000) calls "the new normative macroeconomics," and the extent to which theoretical analyses of optimal monetary policy can provide guidelines that should improve the operation of forecast targeting regimes. In seeking to find connections between the theoretical literature and a policy framework, developed on the basis of primarily practical considerations, that is currently used at a number of central

---

1. The banks that best illustrate this approach all have inflation targets, which play a prominent role in their targeting approaches; and Svensson (1997) refers to the type of policy regime with which I am concerned as "inflation-forecast targeting." But I wish to discuss the optimal design of a forecast targeting regime without necessarily assuming that only the inflation forecast should play a role—indeed, I shall argue below that normative policy analysis indicates a role for other projections as well—and so I prefer to speak simply of "forecast targeting." Earlier discussions of forecast targeting as a general approach include Svensson (2003, 2007) and Svensson and Woodford (2005).

banks, it represents an essay in what Taylor (1998) calls "translational economics."

1. Forecast Targeting as a Policy Rule

It is first important to be clear about what I mean by forecast targeting. Lars Svensson (1997) introduced the term "inflation-forecast targeting" (IFT) to refer to a policy regime with more specific characteristics than the mere announcement of an inflation target, though the existence of a public target for some measure of inflation is an important feature of such regimes. First of all, IFT involves a commitment to a particular decision procedure for monetary policy: the central bank's operating target for the policy instrument should be adjusted in the way that is judged necessary in order to ensure that the bank's projections of the economy's future evolution satisfy certain conditions, which I shall call the target criterion, at all times. The instrument of policy is typically an overnight interest rate in an interbank market, similar to the federal funds rate in the United States, though this is not essential to the logic of forecast targeting and neither is it a feature that distinguishes this approach from the current conduct of policy at most other central banks, such as the Fed. The target criterion should be a specific quantitative property of the projections, so that (in principle at least) there should be little debate about whether a given set of projections satisfies the target criterion, even if a great deal of judgment may be involved in producing the projections themselves. As an example of what is intended, the Bank of England has often described its decision procedure as checking that the projection for a particular variable (currently, Consumer Price Index inflation) equals a particular value (the official inflation target, currently 2 percent) at a particular horizon (eight quarters in the future).[2]

---

2. See, for example, Vickers (1998) and Goodhart (2001). The justifications given for policy decisions in the Bank of England's Inflation Report more recently do not suggest quite so simple a target criterion; for example, there are frequent references to inflation projections beyond the eight-quarter horizon, as well as to the projection for output growth. However, the introduction to each Inflation Report still always includes a chart showing the projection for CPI inflation, just before the summary discussion of the most recent policy decision, and this chart always includes a horizontal line at the inflation target of 2 percent and a dashed vertical line at the horizon eight quarters in the future, allowing easy visual inspection of the degree to which the simple target criterion is satisfied.

Second, forecast targeting involves a distinctive approach to communication policy, under which the central bank regularly publishes the quantitative projections on the basis of which policy has been judged to be on track, together with extensive discussion of the reasoning underlying these projections. This is a key feature of the Inflation Reports that are published three or four times per year by the leading practitioners of IFT, such as the Reserve Bank of New Zealand, the Bank of England, Sweden's Riksbank, and the Norges Bank.[3] Forecast-targeting central banks have led the way in increasing the transparency of monetary policy deliberations, most notably through these publications, and this is not fortuitous. For the decision procedure associated with forecast targeting both lends itself more easily to such communication (because it is highly structured) and is particularly dependent on transparency for its success (because the procedure would involve little discipline if the central bank did not have to discuss its projections with anyone outside its own walls).

To what extent can a regime of this kind be considered an example of a policy rule? One might think that it is not a rule at all—or, at least, not a rule that is sufficiently well-specified to be subjected to the kind of quantitative analysis that is the hallmark of the Taylor research program—insofar as no precise recipe is given for the adjustment of a policy instrument or even a precise specification of some "intermediate target" that can be influenced relatively directly by the central bank. And it is true that forecast targeting represents a different style of specification of a policy rule—what Svensson and Woodford (2005) call a "higher-level specification" of the policy rule—than such familiar examples of policy rules as Milton Friedman's proposal of a constant target for money growth or the Taylor rule (Taylor 1993a).

Nonetheless, such a regime does serve many of the most important objectives that proponents hope to achieve through adoption of a policy rule.[4] First, it does increase the systematic character of policy decisions. Even if actual forecast targeting regimes have not made policy decisions as simple as some proposals in the academic literature would, they represent a substantial movement in this direction relative to the procedures actually followed by other central banks. This has multiple

---

3. The latter two central banks have recently changed the name of their publications to Monetary Policy Report, presumably in recognition of the fact that the inflation projection is not the sole focus of these publications.

4. Taylor (1998) provides a useful list of reasons for the growing consensus among monetary economists regarding the desirability of a policy rule.

advantages: in addition to potentially improving the reliability of policy decisions (both by structuring policy deliberations and by allowing accumulated wisdom to be more efficiently transmitted to new members of the policy committee), it helps to reduce political interference in central-bank deliberations. (It is surely no accident that the Bank of England was granted independent authority to set interest rates only after five years of experience with its IFT regime.)

And second, a forecast targeting regime serves to make policy decisions more easily forecastable by the private sector. This increases the effectiveness of policy for two somewhat different reasons.[5] On the one hand, the actual effects of monetary policy on spending decisions and ultimately on the rate of inflation occur largely as a result of the effect of central-bank actions and announcements on market expectations regarding the future path of short-term interest rates rather than through direct effects of the current level of overnight rates itself. Hence, achieving the effects of policy that are desired depends on private-sector expectations regarding agreeing with the intentions of the central bank. And on the other hand, the benefits of price stability very much depend on the degree to which economic actors remain confident of the stability of the monetary unit. Anchoring inflationary expectations is therefore important, and one of the most important arguments for commitment to a policy rule is the expectation that such a commitment should give people a better ground for expecting a particular future rate of inflation. But an IFT regime, if implemented in a credible way, is well suited to stabilize such expectations. In addition to making visible the central bank's commitment to a systematic procedure that is intended to ensure a stable rate of inflation over the medium run, the constant emphasis in public communications on the central bank's own forecast of future inflation can only help to ensure that the public understands this aspect of the policy's intended consequences.[6]

In thinking about whether a forecast-targeting procedure constrains central-bank behavior to a sufficient extent to achieve the benefits that one hopes to obtain from a policy rule, it is useful to recognize that

---

5. This issue is discussed in more detail in Woodford (2005).

6. A public commitment to a money growth rate target, by contrast, only directly helps to stabilize inflation expectations to the extent that members of the public understand the economic theory according to which a given rate of money growth should imply a particular rate of inflation, at least over long enough periods of time. Of course, any rule that succeeds in maintaining inflation at a low and stable rate over a period of time should eventually result in stable inflation expectations as a consequence of observed performance; but an IFT regime has this virtue to the same extent as other proposed rules.

the conduct of policy under such a regime can actually be described at three distinct levels. At the highest level of generality, a specification of the target criterion explains what projected outcome the central bank is seeking to achieve through its choice of its operating target for overnight interest rates, though it does not specify exactly what the interest-rate target should be. At a more specific level, one could instead describe the specific procedure that should be used to determine the appropriate interest-rate choice in each decision cycle in order to satisfy the target criterion, but without specifying exactly which repurchase operations should be conducted on any given day. And finally, at the most specific level, one could describe the way in which the central bank decides each day on the appropriate quantity of cash to supply to the money markets through its repurchase operations in order to achieve its operating target for the policy rate. At each successively lower level of the specification, one comes closer to saying precisely what the central bank ultimately must do. At each lower level, finer institutional details about the precise mechanism through which monetary policy affects the economy become relevant. And finally, at each lower level, it is appropriate for the central bank to be prepared to adjust course more frequently on the basis of more recent information. At the lowest level, a decision about the quantity of repurchases must be made daily (at most central banks), and occasionally even more frequently; at the intermediate level, the interest-rate operating target is ordinarily reconsidered only at intervals of several weeks; and at the highest level, the target criterion should remain fixed for years at a time, though here too reconsiderations will be appropriate from time to time in light of improved understanding or in response to structural change in the economy.

At which, or how many, of these levels must the nature of policy be spelled out, in order for the policy specification to count as a "rule"? I think there is wide agreement that there is no need for explicit description of the lowest-level specification of policy; the literature that compares the consequences of alternative policy rules generally takes it as given that any non-negative target for the policy rate can be implemented with a high degree of accuracy over time scales (a day or two) that are quite short compared to those that matter for the effects of interest rates on the basis of which the policy is to be judged, and that the details of the required open-market operations have little or no consequences for the objectives of policy.

It is less obvious that description of a policy solely at the highest of these three levels suffices, and the literature on the quantitative evaluation of policy rules has almost exclusively focused on rules specified as formulas to determine the value of a policy instrument that is under the relatively direct control of the central bank. Nonetheless, I think there are important advantages to considering rules that are specified by target criteria that need not involve any variable over which the central bank has direct control.

A first question is whether a mere specification of a target criterion suffices to fully determine outcomes under the policy, so that one can compare the outcomes associated with alternative policies. The answer is that it can, if one assumes that the target criterion will be satisfied at all times. One need not specify the exact actions of the central bank that result in its being satisfied in order to ask how inflation, output, and other variables would have to evolve in a rational expectations equilibrium of that kind. (In principle, the point is the same as when one proposes to analyze the consequences of a given interest-rate feedback rule, without specifying how the central bank will determine the size of repurchase operations that will be required each day in order to achieve overnight interest rates consistent with the rule—though admittedly there is greater reason to question the degree of precision with which it is feasible to satisfy the target criterion when it involves variables such as the overall rate of inflation.) One can use the target criterion itself as the "missing equation" that specifies monetary policy, allowing a solution (in the case of a suitably chosen target criterion) for a determinate rational expectations equilibrium (REE). Hence one can study the advantages of alternative target criteria, using the same methods as the literature initiated by Taylor has used to assess the advantages of alternative feedback rules.

Of course, I do not mean to claim that there should be a determinate REE associated with any target criterion whatsoever. For example, a criterion that only involves projected outcomes two or more years in the future is one that is unlikely to imply a determinate solution; there will be alternative paths by which the economy could reach a situation consistent with the criterion, and in such a case the target criterion fails to fully determine policy. In my view, it is important to adopt a target criterion that does fully determine (but not over-determine) a particular equilibrium. But this is a property that one can analyze given a specification of the target criterion alone; one need not specify the policy at a lower level in order to check this. And one should recall that there is also a question whether a given interest-rate feedback rule determines a unique equilibrium or not; one argument for the importance of choosing a rule that conforms to the Taylor principle is that in many models, rules with weaker feedback from realized inflation to the interest-rate operating target have been found to result in indeterminacy of equilibrium (e.g., Woodford 2003, chap. 4).

Nor do I wish to suggest that there are no important issues connected with the problem of implementation of target criteria. However, in the case of a target criterion that is found to satisfy the property just mentioned—that there exists a determinate REE associated with it—then there should exist a monetary policy that should satisfy the target criterion. (In fact, solution for the REE associated with the criterion should already indicate, among other things, the state-contingent evolution of the nominal interest rate that must obtain, at least under an REE, if the criterion is to be satisfied.) Thus it is possible to search for a desirable target criterion simply on the basis of a consideration of alternative policies specified at this level of generality and to turn to the problem of implementation only once one has chosen a target criterion. (Some of the subtle issues that remain with regard to implementation are taken up in section 4 below.)

A second question is whether specification of a target criterion, rather than a reaction function, is a useful way of providing a guideline for policymakers in their deliberations. Of course, a monetary policy committee has to decide on the level of overnight interest rates, so the target criterion alone does not provide the members with sufficient information to discharge their duty. Nonetheless, a target criterion relating the paths of some of the variables that the policy committee wishes to stabilize seems the appropriate level of detail for a prescription that a policy committee can agree to use to structure its discussions, that can be explained to new members of the committee, and that can ensure some degree of continuity in policy over time. Special factors are likely to be important at each meeting in deciding upon the level of interest rates consistent with fulfillment of the target criterion; hence it is difficult to impose too much structure on this kind of deliberation, without the committee members feeling that their procedures are grossly inadequate to dealing with the complexity of the situation in which they find themselves. But the considerations involved in a judgment that a particular target criterion is sensible are less likely to constantly change.

Indeed, there are good theoretical reasons (discussed further in section 3) to expect that a desirable target criterion will depend on fewer details about the current economic environment than would a desirable specification of a reaction function. Giannoni and Woodford (2002, 2005) show how to construct robustly optimal target criteria which implement an optimal response to shocks regardless of which types of shocks are more important or of the degree of persistence, forecastability, and so on of the shocks that occur. The coefficients of an optimal reaction function will instead depend on the statistical properties of the shocks.[7] Since each shock that occurs is somewhat different from any other, there will always be new information about the particular types of disturbances that have most recently occurred, making advance commitment to a particular reaction function inconvenient. The coefficients of the optimal target criterion may also change[8] in the event of a shift in the central bank's estimate of structural parameters such as elasticities of supply or demand; but information of this kind is not likely to shift as dramatically so suddenly.

Of course, the Taylor rule was not proposed as a mechanical formula that would precisely determine the federal funds rate operating target at each point in time. Instead, Taylor (1993a) describes it as a guideline that indicates how policy should be conducted under normal conditions, but from which policymakers will frequently be justified in deviating in response to special circumstances that arise. But an instrument rule subject to an open-ended escape clause of this kind deserves less to be called a policy rule than does a target criterion which is intended to be the focus of policy deliberations under virtually all circumstances, even if the considerations that should determine the policy rate consistent with the target criterion are not spelled out in advance. The target criterion approach provides a more consistent structure for policy deliberations; for example, the rule itself makes it clear when new circumstances justify a departure from standard rules of thumb for interest rate decisions: whenever the new developments cast doubt on one's normal expectations about the relation between the policy rate and the variables that enter the target criterion. The targeting approach should make the consequences of the central bank's decisions more predictable, since one should be able to count on the target variables satisfying the target criterion to a reasonable extent, even if the path of the policy rate that this involves will not always be highly predictable. And the targeting approach provides greater protection against political pressure on policy decisions, since one need not explain to the politicians why current circumstances should not provide yet another fine occasion for an exception to the usual rule of thumb; instead, the discussion can

---

7. This is illustrated by Svensson and Woodford (2005) in the context of a simple example.

8. Even this need not be so, as is illustrated by the discussion in section 3.

be kept on the plane of the relatively technical issue of which level of interest rates will lead to paths for inflation and real activity consistent with the target criterion.

Yet a third question is whether a target criterion represents a useful way of explaining the nature of a central bank's policy commitments to the public. Some might feel that a commitment to aim at satisfaction of a particular target criterion is less meaningful than a commitment to a particular instrument rule, or even than a commitment to a quantitative target for some "intermediate target" that can be fairly directly controlled by the central bank, on the ground that it is less specific about what the central bank will do, so that whether the central bank is actually complying is less directly verifiable. But there are two important counter-arguments to such a view. First, while the target criterion is less explicit about what the central bank will do with the instruments that it can most directly influence, the target criterion has more explicit implications for the evolution of "target variables" such as the inflation rate; and the main reason for wishing to establish a credible commitment to a policy rule is to anchor private-sector expectations regarding these variables. And second, while a "higher-level" description of the policy commitment might seem to reduce verifiability, this problem can be overcome, to an important extent, through a commitment to public explanation of how policy decisions have been determined by the target criterion—which is precisely the function served by the discussion of the bank's quantitative projections in a Monetary Policy Report. Moreover, accountability is increased, to the extent that the higher-level commitment represents one that can actually determine policy decisions more consistently, rather than being subject to so many "escape clauses" as will inevitably be required in the case of an explicit instrument rule.

Another important argument for policy rules does not depend on any supposition that central bankers have any difficulty determining the action that would best serve their objectives on any given occasion, or that the private sector may fail to correctly understand the systematic character of policy. Instead, Finn E. Kydland and Edward C. Prescott (1977) argue that a process of sequential optimization, with no advance commitment regarding future policy actions, is inherently flawed on the ground that a sequential optimizer will never have any reason to take into account the way in which his systematic (and hence predictable) response to current conditions has shaped prior expectations, as these expectations are already a historical fact by the time that the decision has to be made. Commitment to conduct policy in accordance with a rule, regardless of whether the required actions are those the policymaker would most prefer at the time that the actions are taken, can solve this problem. But to what extent are forecast-targeting procedures examples of systematic approaches to policy that avoid the pitfalls of discretionary policymaking identified by Kydland and Prescott?

Forecast targeting is a sequential decision procedure; rather than choosing a plan for policy over several years at one time and then sticking to it, new projections are computed and the targeting exercise is repeated afresh, several times per year. It is true that it requires a central bank to be clear about its objectives and clear about what it expects the effects of its policy actions to be; but these are also features of "discretionary" policy in the sense of Kydland and Prescott. Does forecast targeting really represent anything other than a more "scientific" way of implementing discretionary policy—one that can therefore more closely approximate the theoretical model of sequential optimization proposed by Kydland and Prescott, but that does nothing to overcome the inherent flaws of sequential optimization that they identify?

The answer to this depends on exactly how forecast targeting is implemented. It might indeed correspond precisely to discretionary policy in the sense of Kydland and Prescott, and it could also correspond to something less coherent than that, and even less successful at achieving the bank's stabilization goals. But if appropriately implemented, a forecast-targeting procedure can address the problem identified by Kydland and Prescott; in fact, under ideal circumstances, it can provide a convenient approach to implementation of the equilibrium that would result from a once-and-for-all commitment to an optimal state-contingent policy. But achieving or even approaching this ideal requires that one be careful about a number of details of what is meant by forecast targeting.

2. The Problem of Intertemporal Consistency

An important potential advantage of forecast targeting, stressed above, is the possibility that the published projections can help to clarify what the private sector should expect and thus prevent the bank's stabilization objectives from being thwarted by private actions based on mistaken forecasts. But the degree to which publication of central-bank projections can be expected to shape the expectations of private decision-makers will depend on how credible these projections are as forecasts of the economy's likely evolution. Among the possible grounds for doubt is a tension inherent in the logic of the forecast-targeting procedure itself. Production of projections of the economy's evolution several years into the future requires that the central bank make assumptions about its conduct of policy not merely in the immediate future, but over the entire forecast horizon (and even beyond, in the case of a forward-looking model). But while the projections must specify policy far into the future each time they are produced, in each decision cycle policy is only chosen for a short period of time (say, for the coming month, after which there will be another decision).

This raises a question as to whether this decision procedure should be expected to actually produce the kind of future policy that is assumed in the projections. One might imagine, for example, a central bank wishing always to choose expansionary policy at the present moment, to keep employment high, while projecting that inflation will be reduced a year or two in the future, so that the expectation of disinflation will make it possible to have high employment with only moderate inflation. But if the procedure is one in which the disinflation is always promised two years further in the future, private decision-makers have no reason ever to expect any disinflation at all.

Thus one requirement for credibility of the central bank's projections is that the forecast-targeting procedure be intertemporally consistent. This means that the future policy that is assumed in the projections should coincide with the policy that the procedure itself can be expected to recommend, as long as those aspects of future conditions that are outside the control of the central bank turn out in the way that is currently anticipated. While this may seem an obvious requirement, a number of apparently sensible approaches to forecast targeting fail to satisfy it.

2.1. Constant-interest-rate projections

A popular approach in the early years of inflation-forecast targeting—used, for example, in the Inflation Reports of the Bank of England prior to August 2004—was to construct projections conditional upon a constant interest rate over the forecast horizon (Vickers 1998; Jansson and Vredin 2003). The appropriate current interest-rate decision was then taken to be the interest rate that, if expected to be maintained over the forecast horizon, would lead to projections satisfying the target criterion (for example, 2 percent inflation eight quarters in the future). This procedure had a number of advantages. First, a bank had only to consider variations in policy over a single dimension (alternative constant interest rates), with the consequence that a one-dimensional target criterion would suffice to identify the correct policy. Hence it was enough to specify what the inflation projection should be like some years in the future, without having to take a stand on the trickier question of how one might choose among alternative nearer-term transition paths. Second, contemplated changes in the current interest-rate decision would be predicted to have non-trivial consequences, given that any change was assumed (for purposes of the projection exercise) to be a permanent change. And finally, it was possible to construct projections without the bank having to tip its hand as to the likely character of future policy.

But constant-interest-rate projections raise a number of conceptual problems (Goodhart 2001; Leitemo 2003; Honkapohja and Mitra 2005; Woodford 2005). The assumption that the nominal interest rate will remain fixed at some level, regardless of how inflation or other variables may evolve, is not a sensible one. Moreover, in forward-looking (rational-expectations) models of the kind that are now beginning to be used by central banks, the assumption of a constant nominal interest rate often implies an indeterminate price level, so that it becomes impossible to solve uniquely for an inflation forecast under any such interest-rate assumption.[9] In models with backward-looking expectations, the model can be solved, but such policies often imply explosive inflation dynamics. Such difficulties appear to have been a frequent problem with the constant-interest-rate projections of the Bank of England (Goodhart 2001), which often showed the inflation rate passing through the target rate at the eight-quarter horizon, but not converging to it. Figure 1 provides an example. In such a case, it is not obvious why anyone should believe that policy is consistent with the inflation target or expect that inflation expectations should be anchored as a result of a commitment to such a policy.

The most fundamental problem, however, is that there will often be no reason to expect interest rates to remain constant over the policy horizon. Indeed, constant-interest-rate projections themselves often imply that the people making the projections should not expect the interest rate to be maintained over the forecast horizon. Consider, for example, the inflation projection shown in figure 1, a constant-interest-rate projection on the basis of which the February 2004 Bank of England Inflation Report concluded that a 4 percent policy rate was

---

9. See Woodford (2003, chap. 4) for examples of this problem.

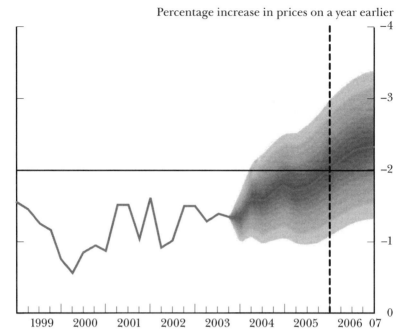

Percentage increase in prices on a year earlier

Figure 1. The February 2004 CPI projection under the
assumption of a constant 4 percent interest rate.
Source: Bank of England, Inflation Report, August 2004.

appropriate at that time.[10] The figure shows that under the assumption of a constant 4 percent policy rate, consumer price inflation was
projected (under the most likely evolution, indicated by the darkest
area) to pass through the target rate of 2 percent at the eight-quarter
horizon (indicated by the vertical dashed line) and then to continue
rising in the following year. Thus, if the policy rate were to be held at
4 percent for a year, the Bank's expectation in February 2004 should
have been that (under the most likely evolution, given what was known
then) in February 2005 a similar exercise would forecast consumer
price inflation to pass through 2 percent at the one-year horizon and
to exceed 2 percent during the second year of the projection. Hence,
the Bank has essentially forecasted that in a year's time, under the most

---

10. In the February Report, only the projection up to the eight-quarter horizon was
shown. The figure that has been extended to a horizon twelve quarters in the future is
taken from the August 2004 Inflation Report, in which the Bank explained its reasons for
abandoning the method of constant-interest-rate projections.

likely evolution, the policy committee would have reason to raise the policy rate. Thus, the February 2004 projection itself could have been taken as evidence that the Bank should not have expected the policy rate to remain at 4 percent over the following eight quarters.

As these issues have come to be understood, a number of central banks that formerly relied upon constant-interest-rate projections (such as the Bank of England, since August 2004) have switched to an alternative approach. This is the construction of projections based on market expectations of the future path of short-term interest rates, as inferred from the term structure of interest rates and/or futures markets. In the case that the projections constructed under this assumption satisfy the target criterion, the correct current interest-rate decision is taken to be the one consistent with market expectations. The use of projections based on market expectations allows a central bank to avoid assuming a constant interest rate when there are clear reasons to expect rates to change soon, while still not expressing any view of its own about the likely future path of interest rates.

But the market expectations approach does not really solve the problem of internal consistency just raised.[11] One problem is that market expectations can at most supply a single candidate forward path for policy; it is not clear what decision one is supposed to make if that path does not lead to projections consistent with the target criterion. Thus the procedure is incompletely specified; and if it is only the projections based on market expectations that are published, even though the central bank has chosen to contradict those expectations, the published projections cannot be expected to shape private decision-makers' forecasts of the economy's evolution.

Moreover, even if the forward path implied by market expectations does lead to projections that fulfill the target criterion, the exercise is not intertemporally consistent if this path does not in fact correspond to the central bank's own forecast of the likely future path of interest rates. Why should it count as a justification of a current interest-rate decision that this would be the first step along a path that would imply satisfaction of the target criterion, but that the central bank does not actually expect to be followed? And why should anyone who correctly understands the central bank's procedures base his own forecasts on published projections constructed on such an assumption?

---

11. For further discussion of problems with this approach, see Woodford (2005) and Rosenberg (2007).

2.2. Choosing an interest-rate path

In fact, there is no possibility of an intertemporally consistent forecast-targeting procedure that does not require the central bank to model its own likely future conduct as part of the projection exercise. Approaches like both of those just described—which introduce an artificial assumption about the path of interest rates in order to allow the central bank to avoid expressing any view about policy decisions that need not yet be made—necessarily result in inconsistencies. Instead, a consistent projection exercise must make assumptions that allow the evolution of the central bank's policy instrument to be projected, along with the projections for inflation and other endogenous variables. In such a case, it would be possible, but somewhat awkward, for the central bank to remain silent about the implications of its assumptions for the forward path of interest rates; and so it is natural to include an interest-rate projection among the projections that are discussed in the Monetary Policy Report.[12] This has been done for more than a decade by the Reserve Bank of New Zealand and is now done by the Norges Bank (since 2005) and the Riksbank (since 2007) as well. In the case of the latter two central banks, "fan charts" (similar to the one shown in figure 1) are presented for the policy rate; this (among other things) makes it clear that the path is simply a forecast, rather than a definite intention that has already been formulated, let alone a promise.

But how should future policy be specified in such an exercise? It is sometimes suggested that the monetary policy committee should conceive of its task as the choice of a path for interest rates, rather than a single number for the current operating target, in each decision cycle. Discussions of the feasibility of such an approach have often stressed the potential difficulty of committee voting on a decision with so many dimensions.[13] And when announcing its intention to begin publishing its own view of the path of the policy rate, the Riksbank

---

12. Since one is talking about projections for the paths of endogenous variables, rather than announcing an intention, there is no reason why there need be a projection for only one interest rate, or even for the interest rate that is most emphasized to be the policy rate. Nonetheless, there are obvious advantages in giving primary emphasis to only a small number of key variables; and it might seem disingenuous not to offer a view of the path of the policy rate, given that this is most directly under the bank's own control.

13. See, for example, Goodhart (2005) for a skeptical view; Svensson (2007) responds by proposing a voting mechanism intended to overcome potential intransitivities in majority preferences over alternative paths.

(Rosenberg 2007) indicated that it would publish "forecasts . . . based on an interest-rate path chosen by the Executive Board."[14]

However, the idea that one should simply ask the policy committee to decide which forward path for interest rates it prefers, presumably after asking its staff to produce projections for other variables conditional on each path that is considered, is problematic on several grounds that have nothing to do with the complexity of the decision or the need for committee members to agree among themselves. First of all, the specification of future policy by a simple path for a short-term nominal interest rate, independently of how endogenous variables may develop, is never a sensible choice and is unlikely to lead to well-behaved results in a sensible model. (The problems mentioned above in connection with the assumption of a constant-interest-rate path apply equally to any specification of an exogenous path; they do not result from the assumption that the interest rate does not vary with time, but from the assumption that it is independent of outcomes for inflation and other variables.) Moreover, the assumption of a specific path for interest rates, unaffected by future shocks, would seem to require one to publish a specific path for this variable, alongside the fan charts for variables such as inflation; but this would encourage the dangerous misunderstanding that the bank has already committed itself to follow a definite path long in advance.

Even supposing that these technical issues have been finessed,[15] there remains the more fundamental problem of the intertemporal consistency of the procedure. Here it is important to realize that the mere use of a consistent criterion over time to rank alternative projected paths for the endogenous variables—not just a criterion that provides a transitive ordering of outcomes within each decision cycle,

---

14. It is likely, of course, that this was only a loose way of speaking in a statement intended for a non-technical audience, and that the intention was to indicate that the Executive Board would have to endorse the assumptions about future policy involved in generating projections of an endogenous interest-rate path. The change in procedure does seem to have meant that the Executive Board is now required to approve the assumptions made in the projections in a way that was not previously true; this has made it necessary to allow for possible revisions in the projections following the meeting at which the policy decision is made (Sveriges Riksbank, Monetary Policy Report 2007/1:21).

15. For example, one might specify future policy by a policy rule, such as a Taylor rule, with some number of free parameters that are optimized, in each decision cycle, so as to result in projections that are acceptable to the monetary policy committee. If only rules are considered that imply a determinate equilibrium, the first problem is avoided. And since the rule that is chosen would make the interest rate endogenous, an assumption about the distribution of shocks in each future period would result in a probability distribution for future interest rates, just as for the future inflation rate.

but one that ranks different possible paths the same way, regardless of the date at which the decision is being made—is not enough to ensure intertemporal consistency, in the sense defined above. Thus the problems of choosing a forward path for policy are not resolved simply by asking the members of the policy committee to agree on a loss function that they will then use (for an entire sequence of meetings) to rank alternative possible outcomes, as proposed by Svensson (2007).

Even in the case of a single decision-maker who minimizes a well-defined loss function that remains the same over time, using a correct economic model that also remains the same over time, and who never makes any calculation errors, the choice of a new optimal path for policy each period will not generally lead to intertemporal consistency. For in the case of a forward-looking model of the transmission mechanism, the procedure will lead to the choice of a forward path for policy that one will not be led to by the same procedure to continue in subsequent decision cycles, even if there have been no unexpected developments in the meantime. The reason is the same as in the celebrated argument of Kydland and Prescott (1977) for the "time inconsistency of optimal plans": the forward path chosen at one time will take account of the benefits at earlier dates of certain expectations about policy at the later dates, but as the later dates approach (and the earlier expectations are now historical facts), there will no longer be a reason to take into account any effect of the policy chosen for those dates on earlier expectations. This problem does not arise solely in connection with the bias in the average rate of inflation chosen by a sequential optimizer, as in the example of Kydland and Prescott (1977). One may solve the problem of "inflationary bias" by assigning the central bank a loss function in which the target level of the output gap is not higher than the level consistent on average with its inflation target, but the optimal dynamic responses to shocks are still not generally the ones that would be chosen under sequential (or discretionary) optimization.[16]

---

16. In the literature on inflation targeting, it is sometimes supposed instead that there is no problem with allowing a central bank complete discretion in its choice of the instrument settings that will minimize its loss function, as long as the loss function involves an output-gap target that is consistent with the inflation target; hence inflation targeting is argued to differ from purely discretionary policy only in the fact that policy is made on the basis of a loss function with this property. King (1997) obtains a formal result to this effect, but in the context of a model where the aggregate-supply relation is assumed to be of the "New Classical" form assumed by Kydland and Prescott (1977). The result is in fact dependent on extremely special properties of that form of aggregate-supply relation; see Woodford (2003, chap. 7) for further discussion.

The problem can be illustrated using the familiar discussion of optimal monetary policy in Richard Clarida et al. (1999). The available trade-off between inflation and real activity is assumed to be characterized by a "New Keynesian Phillips curve,"

$$\pi_t = \kappa x_t + \beta E_t \pi_{t+1} + u_t, \tag{2.1}$$

where π_t is the rate of inflation between period $t-1$ and period t, x_t is the output gap in period t, u_t is an exogenous "cost-push shock" (a stationary process with mean zero), and $\kappa > 0$, $0 < \beta < 1$. The goal of policy is assumed to be the minimization of a quadratic loss function of the form

$$E_0 \sum_{t=0}^{\infty} \beta^t \left[\pi_t^2 + \lambda x_t^2 \right], \tag{2.2}$$

for some relative weight $\lambda > 0$. Here the specification of a target value for the output gap of zero means that the target output gap is no different from the level that is consistent with hitting the inflation target (also zero here) on average, and as a result there is no inflationary bias associated with discretionary optimization.

The optimal dynamic response to a cost-push shock is nonetheless not the one that would occur in an equilibrium[17] with sequential optimization on the part of the central bank. The difference is illustrated in figure 2, where the responses to a purely transitory positive cost-push shock in period zero are shown in the case of the two alternative policies.[18] Because the effect of the shock on the location of the inflation/output trade-off is not expected to last beyond period zero, under discretionary policy (shown by the dashed line) the central bank will choose policy that brings about zero inflation and a zero output gap from period 1 onward. (This minimizes the bank's objective from period 1 onward, and in the absence of any prior commitment it is the policy that an optimizing policy committee would choose.) In period zero, instead, it is necessary to accept either a positive inflation rate, a negative output gap, or both; the optimal policy accepts some of both

---

17. Here I mean more precisely a Markov equilibrium, in which equilibrium outcomes depend only on state variables that affect either the policymaker's objective or the set of possible outcomes from the current period onward, as is common in the literature on the suboptimality of discretionary policy.

18. This figure reproduces figure 7.3 from Woodford (2003), where the calculations are explained.

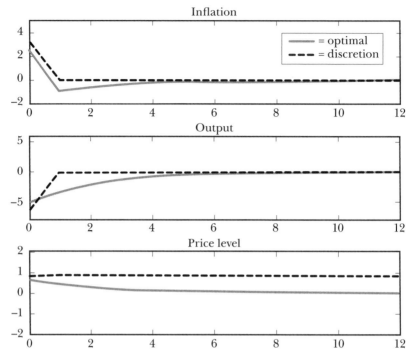

Figure 2. Impulse responses to a purely transitory cost-push
shock, under discretionary policy (dashed lines) and
under an optimal commitment (solid lines).

so as not to have losses that are too great of either kind. The equilibrium response under an optimal policy commitment (shown by the
solid line) is instead more complex: instead of allowing the output gap
to return to zero immediately following the dissipation of the shock,
it remains negative, returning to zero only gradually. The continued
tight policy results in disinflation following the dissipation of the shock,
so that the price level returns asymptotically to the level it would have
been at had the cost-push shock never occurred. The expectation of
subsequent disinflation helps to offset the shift in the inflation-output
trade-off in period zero due to the shock; as a consequence, both less
inflation and a less negative output gap are possible during the period
of the cost-push shock.

Suppose, now, that a central bank were to choose a forward path
for policy each period, given the economy's state at that time, under
the assumption that it can choose any forward path which represents a
possible rational-expectations equilibrium, though it does not commit

itself to subsequently act in accordance with the paths chosen at earlier dates. When the cost-push shock occurs, the policy committee should choose the forward path that results in responses for inflation and output shown by the solid lines in figure 2, since these responses minimize the loss function, among those paths which, if anticipated, are consistent with the structural relation (2.1). Suppose that in period zero the committee chooses the nominal interest rate associated with period zero in this equilibrium; and that the same decision process is repeated in period one. Since the effects of the shock have dissipated by period one, the policy committee now judges (correctly) that it is possible to achieve an equilibrium from then on in which $\pi_t = x_t = 0$ in all periods. This is obviously the best possible equilibrium from the standpoint of the criterion (2.2), and so this is the forward path for the policy that will be chosen in period one and later.[19] However, because the path chosen in period one does not continue the path chosen in period zero, even if nothing unexpected occurs between the two meetings, the procedure is not intertemporally consistent and the projections on the basis of which policy is chosen in period zero will not represent good forecasts of the economy's future evolution.

Moreover, if the private sector correctly understands how policy will be conducted under this procedure, the equilibrium outcome will not only fail to be optimal; it will be even worse than the equilibrium associated with discretionary policy. In response to a shock of the kind just considered, the private sector will expect no effect on inflation or the output gap in any future periods. Under these expectations (which are not the ones associated with the optimal equilibrium), the best possible outcome is the one shown by the dashed lines in figure 2. (In that equilibrium, the central bank optimally exploits the trade-off that exists in period zero, given that it recognizes that expected inflation does not shift in response to the shock.) But if the central bank instead supposes that it can choose any forward path for policy that it likes (instead of recognizing that its future behavior will predictably bring about $\pi_t = x_t = 0$ in every period), and chooses the path corresponding to the solid lines, then it will not choose the nominal interest rate in period zero associated with the equilibrium under discretionary policy; instead, it will raise the nominal interest rate much less than it would

---

19. This assumes that no further shocks occur in subsequent periods. But even if there are subsequent shocks, since they are distributed independently of the shock that occurred in period zero, they are equally likely to result in departures from the zero-inflation steady state in one direction as in the other; so the mean expected outcome from the bank's policy choices in period one and later is one in which $\pi_t = x_t = 0$ for all $t \geq 1$.

under discretionary policy.[20] As a result, the point on the inflation/output trade-off that will actually be realized will involve more inflation (though a less negative output gap) than the optimal point; and as a consequence the shock will increase the loss function (2.2) to a greater extent than it would under discretion.

2.3. Using a sequence of target criteria to determine the path of interest rates

An alternative approach that avoids this problem is to determine the forward path of policy as that path which results in projections that satisfy a sequence of quantitative target criteria, one for each of a sequence of future horizons. It is true that a single criterion—involving, say, the projections for eight quarters in the future only—can determine only a single dimension of policy, and thus can only determine an entire path if one is constrained to consider only a one-parameter family of possible paths (such as constant-interest-rate paths). But a sequence of similar criteria can independently determine the stance of policy at each of a sequence of dates, and thus can determine the entire forward path of policy. Moreover, if the sequences of target criteria for different horizons are of the same form—i.e., if the target criterion is independent of the horizon—then the forecast-targeting procedure will be intertemporally consistent.

As a practical example, consider the targeting procedure used by the Norges Bank beginning in 2005. Through the end of 2006,[21] each issue of the Bank's Inflation Report included a box labeled "Criteria for an appropriate future interest rate path."[22] According to the first of the criteria listed, "inflation should be stabilized near the target [i.e., 2.5 percent per year] within a reasonable time horizon, normally 1–3 years," and moving toward that target rate even sooner. This criterion

---

20. This follows both from the fact that it does not believe that the real interest rate needs to rise as much as in the discretionary equilibrium—it does not seek to contract current output as much, and it expects the return of output to the natural rate to be more gradual—and from the fact that it expects a given nominal interest rate to correspond to a higher real interest rate than it would in the discretionary equilibrium, because it has chosen a forward path for policy that involves disinflation in the following period.

21. Beginning with the 2007/1 issue of the Bank's Monetary Policy Report, the description of the criterion used to select the forward path of policy has been less explicit; presumably the criterion used at present is more complex than the simple one discussed in the text. (Note that the name of the report was also changed with the 2007/1 issue.)

22. The criteria are discussed in more detail in Qvigstad (2005).

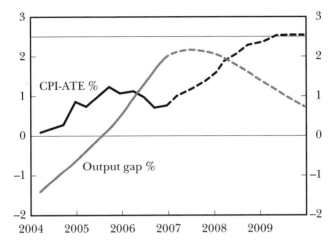

Figure 3. The inflation and output-gap projections
of the Norges Bank superimposed.
Source: Norges Bank, Inflation Report 3/2006, Chart 1.13.

alone would sound similar to the Bank of England target criterion mentioned above, except with greater vagueness about the horizon. But there is then a second criterion: that "the inflation gap [the amount by which actual inflation exceeds the medium-run target rate] and the output gap should be in reasonable proportion to each other until they close" and in particular that the two gaps "should normally not be positive or negative at the same time."[23] The second criterion indicates not only what the projections should look like in some medium run, but also what the transition path should look like: there should be an inverse relation between the inflation gap and the output gap, with the two gaps shrinking to zero together. In order to allow visual inspection of the extent to which the projections satisfy this criterion, the Norges Bank presents a figure in which the projections for its preferred measures of inflation[24] and of the output gap are superimposed, as shown in figure 3. A criterion of this kind can determine the entire forward path for policy. And with such a criterion, it is not necessary to specify independently the rate at which the inflation rate should be projected to approach the target rate; the appropriate rate is exactly

---

23. See, for example, the box on page 10 of Norges Bank, Inflation Report 3/2006.
24. The inflation measure emphasized by the Norges Bank in its targeting procedure, CPI-ATE, is a consumer price index that is adjusted for tax changes and energy prices.

the rate that allows the output gap to remain in the desired proportion to the inflation gap. (Under such a criterion, the inflation gap will be projected to close eventually, as long as it is not possible to have a non-zero permanent output gap.)

The criterion just cited applies to each of a sequence of future horizons. It can be represented formally as the requirement that

$$(\pi_{t+h,t} - \pi^*) + \phi x_{t+h,t} = 0 \tag{2.3}$$

for each horizon $h \geq \underline{h}$, for some coefficient $\phi > 0$. Here $y_{t+h,t}$ denotes the projected value at date t of some variable y, at a horizon h periods in the future; $\underline{h} \geq 0$ indicates the shortest horizon at which it is still possible for policy to affect the projections, and I suppose that a sequence of criteria (2.3) for $h \geq \underline{h}$ suffices to uniquely determine the acceptable projections (including an implied forward path for policy).[25] Suppose also that the central bank's forecast of its own forecasts in future decision cycles satisfies the principle that one should expect one's future forecasts to be the same as one's current forecasts (except, of course, as a result of developments that cannot currently be foreseen), so that

$$[y_{t+h_2,t+h_1}]_{,t} = y_{t+h_2,t}$$

for any horizons $h_2 \geq h_1 \geq 0$. Then if at date t a forward path for policy is chosen that leads to projections satisfying (2.3) for each $h \geq \underline{h}$, it should also be projected at that time that at any later date $t + h_1$, the continuation of that same path should lead to projections satisfying a corresponding sequential criterion, since at date t the bank should project that

$$[(\pi_{t+h_2,t+h_1} - \pi^*) + \phi x_{t+h_2,t+h_1}]_{,t} = 0$$

for all horizons $h_2 \geq h_1 + \underline{h}$. This makes the procedure of choosing a forward path for policy on such a basis intertemporally consistent.

I believe that this kind of targeting procedure provides the most appealing solution to the problem of intertemporal consistency. The way in which the target criterion is used to determine an appropriate

---

25. See Svensson and Woodford (2005) for algebraic analysis of a specific example. In the case considered there, prices and spending decisions are each predetermined a period in advance, so that $h = 1$.

forward path for policy is essentially the same as under the procedure used by the Bank of England prior to 2004, as discussed above, except without either the arbitrary emphasis on a single horizon or the arbitrary restriction to forward paths for policy involving a constant interest rate. Since forecast-targeting central banks already publish charts showing their projections for each of a sequence of future horizons, rather than only presenting a set of numerical forecasts for a specific horizon, discussion of a target criterion that should apply at each horizon is fairly straightforward within the existing frameworks for deliberation and communication about policy, as the example of the Norges Bank shows. Moreover, both the Norges Bank and the Riksbank now discuss quite explicitly the fact that their targeting procedures involve the choice of a forward path for policy and both publish "fan charts" for the paths of short-term nominal interest rates implicit in their projections. Hence, this aspect of the recommended approach is entirely possible within the context of existing procedures as well.

The main "practical" obstacle to such an approach, I believe, is that it would require a central bank to adopt a highly structured approach to policy deliberations and to describe that approach rather explicitly to the public. It would require the bank to be more open about its own view of the likely future evolution of policy than even some forecast-targeting central banks have been willing to be thus far. And it would require the bank to discuss explicitly the nature of the trade-offs that determine an acceptable transition path following a disturbance and not merely the nature of the "medium-run" targets that one hopes to reach some years in the future. The latter goal will almost surely require that a bank be explicit about the ways in which projections for variables other than a single measure of inflation are relevant to judgments about the appropriate stance of policy. Even though all inflation-targeting central banks appear to care about projections for real variables as well as inflation,[26] most have been quite cautious about discussing the way in which this may factor into their policy decisions. But this would have to be different if forecast targeting were to be adopted by an institution with a "dual mandate" like the U.S. Federal Reserve (at least, in the absence of a substantial modification of the Federal Reserve Act

---

26. For example, the summary justification of current policy in the introduction to each issue of the Bank of England's Inflation Report always begins by discussing the projection for real GDP growth before turning to the inflation projection, despite the apparent concern with the inflation projection alone in the simple target criterion discussed above.

by Congress). And even in the case of other central banks, I believe that it would greatly enhance the transparency of policymaking—and, ultimately, the credibility of their commitments to inflation control— by making clearer the extent to which temporary failures to return inflation immediately to its medium-run target level are nonetheless consistent with a systematic approach to policy that does indeed guarantee stability of inflation over the medium run.

3. Which Target Criterion is Appropriate?

The desirability of a forecast-targeting regime depends crucially, of course, on what kind of target criterion is used as the focus of policy deliberations. I have mentioned above one desideratum, which is that the target criterion suffice to determine a unique (or at least a unique non-explosive) rational-expectations equilibrium and hence to uniquely determine the forward path of policy that should be anticipated in each decision cycle. But of course one wants not merely to determine an equilibrium, but to determine one with desirable properties. I have suggested above that the relative flexibility of a forecast-targeting approach, by comparison with previous conceptions of policy rules, should in principle allow a greater degree of success at using monetary policy to stabilize the economy in the face of exogenous disturbances while also maintaining a reasonable degree of confidence in the future value of the currency. But what sort of target criterion should be adopted, in order to take best advantage of this flexibility?

It might be feared that a commitment to pursue a specific quantitative target criterion at each future horizon, rather than allowing the policy committee to choose the forward path associated with the most appealing projections at each point in time without any such straitjacket, means choosing a rule that will frequently involve undesirable responses to disturbances simply for the sake of making policy predictable and transparent. But a commitment to a specific target criterion need not imply any departure from an optimal stabilization policy at all; it is possible to choose a target criterion such that fulfillment of the criterion implements precisely the optimal equilibrium responses to shocks. Moreover, it is possible for this to be true not only in the case of some particular kind of stochastic disturbance, but for any member of a broad class of possible disturbances; this result makes the commitment to a target criterion a particularly useful way of specifying a central bank's policy commitment.

3.1. Example: optimal policy in the basic new Keynesian model revisited

Giannoni and Woodford (2002) show that it is possible quite generally to find a target criterion that implements optimal responses to any of a broad class of disturbances; Giannoni and Woodford (2005) illustrate the application of this method to a variety of models. Here I shall review only a very simple example that illustrates why a specification of policy in terms of a target criterion is particularly robust. Consider again the problem of optimal stabilization policy treated by Clarida et al. (1999). The problem of finding the state-contingent evolution of inflation and of the output gap that minimizes (2.2) subject to the constraint that (2.1) holds each period can be solved by minimizing a Lagrangian. This results in first-order conditions of the form

$$\pi_t + \varphi_t - \varphi_{t-1} = 0 \tag{3.1}$$

$$\lambda(x_t - x^*) - \kappa\varphi_t = 0 \tag{3.2}$$

each period, where φ_t is a Lagrange multiplier associated with the constraint (2.1) in period t.[27]

Manipulation of these constraints so as to eliminate the Lagrange multipliers then implies that, in the optimal equilibrium, a linear relation of the form

$$\pi_t + \frac{\lambda}{\kappa}(x_t - x_{t-1}) = 0 \tag{3.3}$$

should hold each period between the paths of inflation and of the output gap. Note that this can be interpreted as a target criterion. In fact, it is similar in form to the criterion of the Norges Bank discussed above and represented by equation (2.3): there is a constant long-run inflation target (here, zero), short-run departures from which are justified if they are associated with large enough projected short-run output gaps of the right sign. And the more negative the projected

---

27. These conditions must be satisfied in each period $t \geq 0$, in each possible state of the world at each date, if policy is being optimally chosen for periods $t \geq 0$. In the event that there is no additional pre-commitment of the form indicated by (3.4) below—i.e., in the conventional Ramsey policy problem—there is no constraint prior to the constraint (2.1) for $t = 0$, and so $\varphi_{-1} = 0$ in the first-order condition (3.1) for $t = 0$. If there is instead an initial pre-commitment of the kind discussed below, this multiplier can be non-zero as well, and indicates the value of relaxing that constraint.

output gap in a given period, the greater the positive inflation gap that should be accepted in the projection for that period. The crucial difference is that in (3.3) it is the change in the output gap over a given period that is relevant for determining the inflation that should be accepted over that period, rather than the absolute level of the output gap as in figure 3.

This is not only a relation that holds each period in the optimal equilibrium, but one that suffices to define the optimal equilibrium dynamics. For the system of equations consisting of (2.1) together with (3.3), if both are assumed to hold each period from some date onward, determine a unique non-explosive REE.[28] Moreover, in that equilibrium, there exists a system of Lagrange multipliers $\{\varphi_t\}$ such that the first-order conditions (3.1)–(3.2) are satisfied each period; hence, the equilibrium responses to shocks are indeed optimal, if it can be ensured that the target criterion (3.3) is satisfied each period.

More precisely, the equilibrium in which (3.3) is satisfied in each period $t \geq 0$ is the one in which the stochastic evolution of inflation and output minimize the objective (2.2), among all processes consistent with the AS relation (2.1) each period, with an initial inflation rate

$$\pi_0 = \overline{\pi}(x_{-1}; \xi_0). \tag{3.4}$$

Here ξ_t is the (exogenous) state of the world in period t, and $\overline{\pi}(x_{t-1}; \xi_t)$ is a function that indicates the equilibrium inflation rate each period in the unique non-explosive equilibrium determined by the equations (2.1) and (3.3). Thus, conformity to the target criterion each period implements a policy that is optimal subject to an initial precommitment (a constraint on what policy can bring about, but that restricts outcomes only in the initial period); this initial pre-commitment is to behave in the same way in period zero as one will in fact wish to commit oneself to behave in the subsequent periods.[29] In the absence of any such pre-commitment, an optimal commitment regarding policy from time zero onward can be characterized by fulfillment of a different target criterion in period zero only, but fulfillment of (3.3) from period 1 onward. Thus, in either case an optimal policy commitment can be implemented through a commitment to a decision procedure

---

28. For further discussion of this and other assertions made in this section, see Woodford (2003, chap. 7).

29. Policy that is optimal subject to a self-consistent initial pre-commitment of this kind is called "optimal from a timeless perspective" in Giannoni and Woodford (2002); see also Woodford (2003, chap. 7).

under which (at least in every period after the initial one) policy is chosen so as to ensure that the target criterion (3.3) is satisfied and is furthermore expected to be satisfied in all future periods.[30]

Of course, one could bring about the same equilibrium through a commitment to use policy to bring about the inflation rate $\bar{\pi}(x_{t-1}; \xi_t)$ each period. This would also be an example of an intertemporally consistent targeting procedure that results in a unique REE, which again involves responses to shocks that are optimal in the sense just discussed. However, this way of formulating an optimal target criterion is not robust to changes in the assumed character of the disturbances that make up the vector ξ_t. If one writes $\bar{\pi}$ as a function of x_{t-1} and some number of lags of u_t, for example, then the optimal dependence of the function on the various lags of u_t will depend on the autoregressive dynamics of the process $\{u_t\}$. The target criterion (3.3) instead implements the optimal responses to disturbances regardless of the assumed properties of the disturbances; note that we did not need to make any assumption about the process $\{u_t\}$ in order to derive the criterion (3.3), though we did need to make a very specific assumption (namely, that u_t is an i.i.d.—independent and identically distributed—random variable) in order to derive the dynamic response coefficients shown in figure 2. The target criterion (3.3) also has the advantage that it can be explained to the public without having to make any reference to particular types of structural disturbances; instead, the target criterion only involves "target variables," i.e., variables that are relevant to the central bank's stabilization objectives.

3.2. Robustness of the optimal target criterion

The above example relates, of course, to a single very simple model—one that is obviously too simple to provide the basis for policy deliberations in an actual central bank. Nonetheless, the possibility of implementing optimal responses to disturbances using a target criterion is not a special feature of this example. In fact, Giannoni and Woodford (2002) show that an optimal target criterion can be derived

---

30. It is of course the fact that Ramsey optimal policy involves a different target criterion in the initial period that accounts for the fact that choosing a forward path for policy in each decision cycle so as to minimize the loss function (2.2) does not lead to the same policy choices as the choice of a forward path that is expected to satisfy (3.3) at each horizon—so that the former procedure is not intertemporally consistent. Under sequential re-optimization, the current period is always treated as "the initial period," resulting in a failure to choose to continue the path of policy chosen in the previous decision cycle.

for any stabilization policy problem belonging to a fairly general family of linear-quadratic problems.[31] In any such case, the target criterion is a linear relationship among the various target variables (arguments of the quadratic loss function) such that there is a unique non-explosive REE consistent with satisfaction of the target criterion at all times; and this REE always implements the responses to disturbances associated with an optimal ex ante commitment, regardless of the statistical properties of the disturbances (as long as these are purely additive terms in the model's linear structural relations).

Hence, it is possible for any central bank that is willing to base its policy on a particular quantitative model of the transmission mechanism to derive an appropriate target criterion. (The best target criterion, of course, might be different for different economies.) Nor is there any need for the bank to reconsider its commitment to the target criterion each time a shock of some unusual type occurs. Since novel types of disturbances will occur relatively frequently (in fact, no two disturbances are ever of exactly the same type), while structural change in the economy (or a substantial change in a central bank's understanding of the structure of the economy) occurs much less often, a target criterion that is equally suitable regardless of the nature of the disturbance is one to which a central bank should be able to provisionally commit itself, even if from time to time it would still be appropriate to reconsider the target criterion in the light of new knowledge or new circumstances.[32]

But while a fully optimal target criterion of this type exists in principle, it is likely to be too complicated to be useful as the basis for communication with the public in the case of any model with even a modest claim to empirical realism.[33] The fully optimal criterion is also likely to depend on the precise parameterization of a number of

---

31. One can furthermore find a linear target criterion such that the equilibrium determined by the criterion agrees with the optimal equilibrium responses, to a linear approximation, in the case of a fairly general class of sufficiently differentiable policy problems.

32. In principle, frequent reconsideration of the target criterion is possible, without this eliminating the advantages of policy commitment, if the central bank always chooses a new policy rule that is "optimal from a timeless perspective" rather than one that seeks to exploit already existing expectations at the time of the policy change. But in practice, public understanding of the systematic character of policy, and verifiability of the bank's adherence to its alleged commitments, will be better served if reconsiderations of the target criterion do not occur every year.

33. The complexity of the optimal target criterion derived by Giannoni and Woodford (2005) for a small empirical model of the U.S. economy—a four-equation model that is still extremely simple relative to the models used for policy analysis in most central banks—

fine details of one's model of the economy—parameter values (or even model features) about which there will in fact be considerable uncertainty. As a practical matter, what one should really be interested in is a fairly simple target criterion that provides a reasonable approximation to optimal policy, even if it is not fully optimal, and one that continues to lead to an equilibrium that is not too far from optimal, even if the true model of the economy is slightly different from the one for which the rule was designed.

What we need, then, is a study of economic performance under alternative quantitative target criteria in the spirit of the Taylor program—one should study alternative target criteria in precisely the same way that alternative interest-rate feedback rules have been studied over the past fifteen years. This means that one should not only address the level of welfare associated with alternative parameterizations in the context of a single model but also investigate the degree to which a given quantitative target criterion may be robust, in the sense of achieving relatively good performance across a range of model specifications. In fact, the methods required to do this are exactly the same ones that have already been employed in the study of interest-rate rules; one simply uses the equation that states the target criterion, i.e., an equation such as (3.3) as the "missing equation" that specifies monetary policy, rather than adding an interest-rate equation (such as the Taylor rule) to one's stochastic simulation model.

Relatively little work of this kind has already been undertaken, so I cannot survey its conclusions. But there are good reasons to suppose that relatively robust target criteria can be found. A number of results that can be obtained from the study of optimal target criteria in relatively simple examples suggest that the description of desirable policy in terms of a target criterion is likely to be more robust than other ways of characterizing the same policy.

First of all, there is the fact that it is possible to state a target criterion that describes optimal policy (and that suffices to determine the optimal equilibrium—the description of optimal policy is not robust at the cost of being incomplete), regardless of the statistical properties of the disturbances to which the central bank may need to respond. This does not mean that the central bank does not need to determine the specific properties of the disturbances that have just occurred; determining

---

illustrates this point. While it is possible to give a precise statement of the optimal target criterion, I shall not attempt it here!

what adjustment of its interest-rate operating target is required in order to conform to the target criterion will require an assessment of the nature of current shocks. But the target criterion that is to be achieved can be stated more generally. A description of the optimal policy at the level of an appropriate interest-rate reaction function is not similarly robust.

Second, certain kinds of structural change will not require any change in the appropriate target criterion. In the policy problem discussed above, a change in the equations of the structural model that determine how interest rates affect spending will not have any effect on the above derivation if it does not change either the aggregate-supply relation (2.1) or the appropriate stabilization objective (2.2); and so (3.3) would continue to be the optimal target criterion. Again, this does not mean that structural change of this sort can be ignored by the central bank; it will have to be taken account of if the bank's interest-rate decisions are to have the desired effect. But it would remain possible to organize policy deliberations around the goal of satisfying an unchanged quantitative target criterion. (Again, a description of optimal policy at the level of an interest-rate reaction function would not be similarly invariant.)

But perhaps more surprisingly, even types of structural change that do change the quantitative specification of the aggregate-supply relation do not always require a change in the quantitative specification of the target criterion, in order for policy to continue to be optimal. This is because the appropriate loss function (in terms of the paths of prices and output), in order for the central bank's stabilization objective to correspond to household welfare maximization, also changes in the case of a change in those aspects of economic structure that determine the available trade-off between output and inflation, indicated by the aggregate-supply relation. In fact, there is a whole range of changes that would imply a different quantitative specification of aggregate supply, but that do not change the optimal target criterion, because the changes in the aggregate-supply relation and in the welfare-based loss function precisely cancel one another.

The aggregate-supply relation (2.1) assumed by Clarida et al. (1999) represents a log-linear approximation to the relation implied by a particular model of price-setting, namely a model in which price changes are staggered in the way proposed by Guillermo Calvo (1983). The loss function (2.2) is an appropriate objective in the case of this model, as it can be shown to be (inversely related to) a quadratic approximation to the expected utility of the representative household in the DSGE (dynamic stochastic general equilibrium) model. In the case that we assume an efficient steady-state level of output,[34] the value of λ corresponding to welfare maximization is given by

$$\lambda = \frac{\kappa}{\theta} > 0, \tag{3.5}$$

where θ is the elasticity of substitution among alternative differentiated goods (and hence the elasticity of demand faced by each monopolistically competitive producer). Hence the optimal target criterion (3.3) can alternatively be written

$$\pi_t + \theta^{-1}(x_t - x_{t-1}) = 0. \tag{3.6}$$

Note that the quantitative specification of the optimal target criterion turns out to depend on only one underlying structural parameter of the model: the value of θ. (This parameter is important because it determines the extent to which the dispersion of prices that results from variability of the inflation rate causes inefficient non-uniformity in the composition of the national product.) A variety of other parameters—parameters describing household preferences, the production technology, and the frequency of adjustment of prices—all affect the slope of the aggregate-supply curve but have no effect on the quantitative specification of the optimal target criterion (3.6). Thus the optimal target criterion is not only more robust than a representation of optimal policy in terms of a reaction function, it is also a more robust specification of the appropriate goal of policy than the loss function (2.2). This is a further reason why it is more desirable for a central bank to commit itself to a specific target criterion than for it to publicly specify its loss function.

Other, even more substantial modifications of the model are also possible without affecting the optimality of the target criterion (3.6). The basic new Keynesian model considered by Clarida et al. assumes that the utility of the representative household is additively separable over time, but empirical models often find that the data are better

---

34. This assumption simplifies the analysis of the welfare-based loss function, because it is not necessary to consider the effects of stabilization policy on the average level of output in order to obtain a welfare measure that is accurate to second order, as discussed in Woodford (2003, chap. 6). All of the results reviewed in this section are derived under that simplification. However, a welfare-based quadratic loss function can also be derived without this assumption, using the method illustrated in Benigno and Woodford (2005). For example, in the Calvo model the welfare-based loss function is of the form (2.2) even without the assumption of an efficient steady state, but the correct value of λ is in general more complicated than the simple formula (3.5).

explained by preferences that incorporate habit persistence; Giannoni and Woodford (2005) consider the consequences for optimal monetary policy of this generalization. The most important consequence of habit persistence, of course, is a change in the relation between real interest rates and the dynamics of expenditure; but this in itself is no reason for a change in the optimal target criterion, though it certainly affects the interest-rate path required by the target criterion. However, habit persistence also changes the relation between current output (or expenditure) and the marginal utility of income; as a consequence, the way that output enters both the aggregate-supply relation and the welfare-based loss function must change. Yet the two changes cancel one another in their effects on the optimal target criterion, for Giannoni and Woodford show that (3.6) continues to characterize optimal policy, regardless of the degree of habit persistence. Once again, the optimal target criterion is more robust to changes in the economic structure than is the welfare-based quadratic loss function.

All of the examples discussed thus far assume price stickiness of the form introduced by Calvo (1983). But the "new Keynesian Phillips curve" (2.1) is often criticized for its implication that inflation determination is purely forward-looking, and empirical models often incorporate some degree of structural inflation inertia. One way to motivate such inertia is to assume (contrary to the simple Calvo specification) that the probability of revision of a given firm's price is an increasing (rather than constant) function of the time since the price was set; this results in a generalization of (2.1) in which lagged inflation rates appear as determinants of current inflation, along with expectations of future inflation, as in common ("hybrid NKPC") empirical specifications. But as shown by Sheedy (2005), the appropriate welfare-based loss function changes as well, since the relation between the dynamics of aggregate inflation and the degree of cross-sectional dispersion of prices at a given point in time changes; and optimal policy continues to be characterized by the target criterion (3.6), regardless of the values of the parameters that determine the hazard rate for price changes as a function of price duration.

An alternative interpretation of apparent inflation inertia is provided by the "sticky information" model of N. Gregory Mankiw and Ricardo Reis (2002). In this model, each firm charges at all times the price that it expects at that time to maximize its current profits, but firms do not continuously update their information about market conditions; inflation inertia thus results from inertia in the average estimate of the current inflation rate. This kind of model leads to a very different kind of aggregate-supply relation, but again Ball et al. (2005) show that optimal policy is characterized by a target criterion of the form (3.6).[35] More precisely, optimal policy requires that the quantity on the left-hand side of (3.6) must be a deterministic sequence that can be perfectly forecast arbitrarily far in advance; it need not be zero (or even constant), since in this model there are no real effects of changes in the general price level that are expected by all firms, no matter how long it has been since they last updated their information. But a rule of the form (3.6) would be one example of an optimal policy rule in this model, and since this particular rule is also optimal in the case of sticky-price models, it is therefore a more robust policy choice than would result from some other deterministic sequence.

I do not mean to suggest that (3.6) should be an optimal target criterion, regardless of the structure of the economy; it is easy to give examples where the optimal target criterion is not of this form (see, e.g., Giannoni and Woodford 2005). All of the examples just reviewed have important elements in common—for example, they are all models in which only prices are sticky (not wages), and they are all models that are perfectly symmetric across sectors (different sectors have identical production technologies, the same kind and degree of nominal rigidities or informational frictions, etc.)—and I do not mean to suggest that these idealizations are adequate for practical monetary policy analysis. But these examples do indicate that even the optimal target criterion need not depend on all aspects of the model specification; this gives one reason to hope that it may be possible to find target criteria that are fairly robust across (even if not fully independent of) aspects of the model specification about which policymakers remain uncertain. In particular, they suggest that a description of desirable policy in terms of a target criterion may be more robust to model uncertainty than other descriptions that would be equally valid in the absence of such uncertainty.

4. Implementing the Target Criterion

Thus far, I have spoken about the choice of a target criterion as if one can take it for granted that there is a policy under which the target criterion will in fact be satisfied each period and that selecting a target

---

35. Note that (3.6) implies that $\log P_t + \theta^{-1}x_t$ is equal to a constant, which is how Ball et al. describe the optimal policy.

criterion means committing oneself to a decision procedure that implements that policy. (I have pointed out that one must ask whether there exists any equilibrium consistent with a given target criterion; but if there does, I have not treated the achievement of that equilibrium as problematic.) But this is hardly obvious; and a discussion of the practicality of forecast targeting as a monetary policy strategy would be incomplete without any consideration of how one should determine the actual actions to be taken by the central bank under such a strategy. Certainly one cannot compare a forecast targeting strategy to a "lower-level" specification of a policy rule, such as the Taylor rule, without also describing what forecast targeting means for the way in which the policy instrument should be adjusted over time.

I have mentioned above that in the case that the target criterion is one that implies a determinate rational-expectations equilibrium, it therefore implies a particular state-contingent evolution of the policy rate. But that does not mean that there are no further issues to address with regard to the policy actions that should be chosen in order to implement the target criterion. For even when a particular rule for setting the central bank's operating target for the policy rate is known to be consistent with the rational-expectations equilibrium that the target criterion is intended to bring about, that need not mean that this equilibrium is the only one that is consistent with that rule. Thus we again face a question about whether a particular rule determines a unique rational-expectations equilibrium, distinct from the one discussed above—and one that the theorem of Giannoni and Woodford (2002) does not address. Even if there is only one stationary REE under which the target criterion is satisfied at all times, it does not follow that a reaction function that is consistent with fulfillment of the target criterion—because it is consistent with that REE—is not also consistent with other REE; it may also be consistent with equilibria in which the target criterion is not fulfilled.

Even if this is not a problem, one has only verified that the rule for setting interest rates should have the desired consequences under the assumptions that (i) the economy will indeed reach a rational-expectations equilibrium and (ii) the central bank's structural model is correct. It remains important to ask how robust the policy is to possible departures from these ideal cases. These are issues that have been extensively addressed in the literature on simple Taylor-type rules, but they need also to be addressed for interest-rate reaction functions that are intended to implement a target criterion. Here, again, the issues are ones that can (and should) be addressed at each of two levels, in the case of a forecast-targeting strategy. One should ask first whether fulfillment of the target criterion will still lead to a fairly desirable outcome, in the case of a certain departure from rational expectations (for example); but then one should also ask whether the interest-rate rule intended to implement the target criterion still comes close to fulfilling the target criterion in the case of the departure from rational expectations. A similar question about robustness can be posed at each of the two levels for any of a variety of types of model misspecification with which one might be concerned.

Once one concedes this, it might be asked whether there is any advantage to formulations of policy commitments in terms of a target criterion at all. If one still needs to address the questions of determinacy, learnability of the rational-expectations equilibrium, and robustness to model uncertainty all over again at the level of the specification of an interest-rate reaction function, even when the target criterion (if it could be assumed to be necessarily satisfied) has been shown to be desirable on all of those grounds, why not simply search for desirable interest-rate rules without the discussion of desirable target criteria at all? The answer is that I believe that there will turn out to be advantages of a rule for the adjustment of interest rates that explicitly uses a target criterion in determining what the interest rate should be—that is, of a forecast-targeting procedure—over other interest-rate rules that might happen to support an equilibrium in which the target criterion is satisfied. (In the latter case, one would be justified in simply saying that the rule is good because it implements a desirable equilibrium, without any need to discuss the target criterion.) And the advantages that I believe such rules are likely to have are precisely the ability to exclude undesired alternative equilibria, the ability to facilitate the convergence of out-of-equilibrium expectations to the REE, and greater robustness of alternative model specifications. However, these advantages depend on a particular understanding of what it means to use the target criterion to determine the appropriate interest-rate operating target; in particular, it is necessary for the central bank to monitor private-sector expectations and to respond to them in a particular way.

4.1. The example once again

This can be illustrated using the analysis in Preston (2004) of alternative approaches to implementation of the optimal target criterion (3.3) in the basic new-Keynesian model. Preston shows that under arbitrary (subjective) private-sector expectations, the aggregate-supply relation takes the form

$$\pi_t + \kappa x_t = \hat{E}_t \sum_{T=t+1}^{\infty} (\alpha\beta)^{T-t} \left[\kappa x_T + \frac{1-\alpha}{\alpha} \pi_T + u_T \right] + u_t, \qquad (4.1)$$

where the notation is the same as in (2.1) above, but now the operator $\hat{E}_t[\cdot]$ indicates the conditional expectation under the (common) probability beliefs of private agents at date t, which may or may not correspond to the true conditional expectation (i.e., "rational expectations"). This inflation equation results from log-linearization of the optimal price-setting rule for firms in a model with monopolistic competition and Calvo staggering of price changes; $0 < \alpha < 1$ is the probability that any firm's price will not be revised in a given period. Note that under the assumption of rational expectations—so that subjective forecasts of future inflation are consistent with inflation being determined by this equation in all future periods—this equation implies the relation (2.1) used by Clarida et al. (1999); but more generally, subjective forecasts of both inflation and output for more than one period in the future affect the location of the current inflation/output trade-off.

In order to determine the interest rate required in order to implement the target criterion, one must adjoin an equilibrium relation between interest rates and private expenditure. Preston shows that under arbitrary private-sector expectations, the "intertemporal IS relation" of the standard new-Keynesian model takes the form

$$x_t = -\sigma \left(i_t - r_t^n \right) + \hat{E}_t \sum_{T=t+1}^{\infty} \beta^{T-t} \left[\left(\beta^{-1} - 1 \right) x_T - \sigma \left(i_T - \beta^{-1}\pi_T - r_T^n \right) \right], \quad (4.2)$$

where r_t^n indicates exogenous variation in the Wicksellian "natural rate of interest."[36] This is essentially a permanent-income model of expenditure by the representative household, augmented to take account of the effects of the anticipated path of real interest rates on the optimal timing of expenditure; again, under the assumption of rational expectations, it would reduce to the simpler relation (involving only

---

36. This is a function of exogenous disturbances, such as the rate of time preference and the state of technology, that indicates what the short-run real interest rate would be each period in an equilibrium where a zero output gap is maintained at all times. For further discussion of the natural rate of interest, and of the microfoundations of this model, see Woodford (2003, chap. 4).

expectations of variables one period in the future) used by Clarida et al. (1999).

We may now compare two of the approaches to implementation of the target criterion discussed by Preston. One approach would be to compute the REE implied by satisfaction of the target criterion (discussed in section 3) and determine the state-contingent path of nominal interest rates in that equilibrium. In the case of the target criterion (3.3) and structural relations (4.1)–(4.2), this leads to a solution of the form

$$i_t = \bar{\imath}(x_{t-1}; s_t) \tag{4.3}$$

for the interest rate, where s_t is the economy's (exogenous) state in period t (in general, a vector), including a full description of all information in period t about the current and future values of the disturbances $\{u_T, r_T^n\}$.[37] One approach to implementation would be to compute this solution and then use (4.3) to determine the central bank's operating target at each period, after observing the current state s_t. Note that under this approach, the target criterion would not actually be used in the routine conduct of policy; it would only be used (once) to compute the function (4.3). Moreover, the target criterion is not really needed even in that calculation; equation (4.3) is simply a (partial) description of the optimal equilibrium, and so it is really only computation of the optimal equilibrium that is required under this approach. Thus this approach would not really deserve to be called a "forecast targeting" procedure, even if it is a policy consistent with satisfaction of the target criterion.

But this approach to implementation of optimal policy has undesirable properties. For many possible values of the parameters, rational-expectations equilibrium is indeterminate under commitment to an interest-rate rule of the form (4.3).[38] The reason, essentially, is that such a policy would not conform to the Taylor principle that interest

---

37. Note that in the three relations (3.3), (4.1), and (4.2) we solve to determine the REE evolution of the endogenous variables, the only lagged endogenous variable that appears is x_{t-1}, appearing in (3.3). This ensures that if there is a determinate equilibrium, it must be described by a function of the form (4.3). Note also that the precise form of the function $\bar{\imath}(x; s)$ depends on the specification of the joint stochastic process for the exogenous disturbances, and not simply on the coefficients of the three relations just listed.

38. See the analysis in Svensson and Woodford (2005). Svensson and Woodford discuss a more elaborate version of the model, in which both pricing and spending decisions are predetermined, but the conditions on parameter values that control the determinacy of equilibrium are identical in the case discussed here.

rates should be raised in response to inflation above the target rate, and sharply enough to make the real interest rate an increasing function of inflation. While the rule (4.3) is consistent with the desired equilibrium, policy under this rule is too "passive" to ensure that this is the only possible REE.[39] Moreover, a "passive" rule of this kind is also ineffective in steering expectations closer to the REE in the case that people initially have other beliefs but update their forecasting rules on the basis of the data that they observe.[40] Preston (2004) analyzes learning dynamics in this model under the assumption that people forecast future inflation, output, and interest rates as linear functions of the exogenous state and the lagged output gap and that the coefficients of their forecasting rules are determined by OLS regressions, constantly updated as additional data are observed. He shows that often a rule of the form (4.3) implies unstable learning dynamics that will diverge from rational expectations with probability 1 even if people happen to start with forecasting rules close to rational expectations. There is also considerable reason to doubt the robustness of this kind of rule under model misspecification, even if one is not troubled by the above results (perhaps because one presumes that the economy will necessarily settle into the "minimum-state-variable" REE associated with a given policy rule, through a process that need not be explained). For example, the coefficients on the state variables in (4.3) will depend on the degree of persistence of the disturbances, so that the rule will not continue to achieve the optimal equilibrium if this has been wrongly specified, even though the target criterion (3.3) would continue to characterize the optimal equilibrium in this case.

Another approach is to use the structural relations (presumed to be correctly understood by the central bank) to determine the interest-rate operating target required in order to ensure that realized inflation and output satisfy the target criterion (3.3), given the expectations that people actually have, whether these correspond to the expectations that would be "rational" under this policy or not. This approach requires that the central bank monitor the expectations of market participants in order to adjust interest rates in a way that offsets the effects of any

---

39. On the role of the Taylor principle for the determinacy of equilibrium under certain simple families of interest-rate rules, see, e.g., Clarida et al. (2000) and Woodford (2003, chap. 4).

40. The essential intuition that a passive interest-rate policy will fail to stabilize inflation expectations if these extrapolate observed past inflation is contained in an argument of Friedman (1968).

departures of people's actual expectations from rational expectations. In order to specify concretely what this involves, Preston assumes that the private sector's period-t forecasts ($\hat{E}_t \pi_T$, etc.) are determined prior to the central bank's decision about its period-t operating target i_t,[41] though they may depend on the exogenous state s_t, and that they are observed by the central bank (along with the exogenous state) prior to its choice of i_t. Given this information, the central bank can use (4.1) together with (3.3) to determine the values of π_t and x_t that it should seek to bring about, in order for the target criterion to be satisfied in the current period. The implied current output-gap target is given by

$$\hat{x}_t \equiv \frac{\lambda}{\kappa^2 + \lambda} x_{t-1} - \frac{\kappa}{\kappa^2 + \lambda} u_t$$
$$- \frac{\kappa}{\kappa^2 + \lambda} \hat{E}_t \sum_{T=t+1}^{\infty} (\alpha\beta)^{T-t} \left[\kappa x_T + \left(\frac{1-\alpha}{\alpha} \right) \pi_T + u_T \right]. \tag{4.4}$$

It can then use (4.2) to determine the interest rate i_t that should achieve this target for the output gap. This is given by

$$i_t = r_t^n - \sigma^{-1}\hat{x}_t$$
$$+ \hat{E}_t \sum_{T=t+1}^{\infty} \beta^{T-t} \left[\sigma^{-1}\left(\beta^{-1} - 1\right)x_T - \left(i_T - \beta^{-1}\pi_T - r_T^n\right) \right], \tag{4.5}$$

where $\hat{x}_t$ is defined in (4.4). Equation (4.5) represents an alternative interest-rate rule that, like (4.3), is consistent with the REE determined by the target criterion. But it describes a policy in which the target criterion plays a crucial role in the conduct of policy; indeed, while it is possible to describe the policy using the interest-rate rule, it is much more compactly described by the prescription to use one's model of the economy, together with one's estimates of current fundamentals and the current state of private-sector expectations, to determine the interest rate needed in order to ensure that the target criterion (3.3) is satisfied.

---

41. Note that this need not be the case, though it is a property of the particular kind of learning process that Preston specifies. While the assumption is a restrictive one, it does not rule out the possibility of rational expectations, since in the REE the central bank's choice of i_t will be a perfectly predictable function of variables that have already been determined at the time that people form their period-t forecasts.

While (4.3) might seem to represent a simpler approach to policy—both one that is simpler to execute and one that makes outside verification of the central bank's compliance with the rule simpler—the rule (4.5) is a more reliable way of bringing about the desired outcome. First of all, there is necessarily a unique stationary REE consistent with rule (4.5).[42] For regardless of what the private sector may be expecting, (4.5) implies that $x_t = \hat{x}_t$ and hence that π_t and x_t satisfy (3.3). As this will be true each period, if the private sector has rational expectations, they must be expecting (and their actions will generate) the unique REE consistent with the target criterion. Moreover, Preston (2004) shows that if instead private-sector expectations evolve through least-squares learning, in the case of rule (4.5) the learning dynamics converge to the REE.[43] This is because this rule involves responses to variations in private-sector expectations that neutralize the effects of the errant expectations on aggregate outcomes, thus short-circuiting the process through which out-of-equilibrium expectations might become self-fulfilling. Finally, while this has been less thoroughly studied, it is likely that performance under rule (4.5) is more robust to variations in the model specification. For example, rule (4.5) implements the optimal dynamic responses to disturbances regardless of the degree of persistence of the disturbances, unlike the rule (4.3). Note that no assumptions about the disturbance processes have been used in deriving (4.5). It would be desirable to study the robustness of a rule like this to other forms of model misspecification, as has often been done in the case of simple Taylor rules. As discussed in section 3, it is known that for a variety of alternative models of price adjustment, (3.3) continues to be an optimal target criterion. Hence the prescription "act so as to ensure that (3.3) holds" is a robust policy, within this set of alternative models, even if the more specific formula (4.5), which depends on the structural relations (4.1)–(4.2), will not be equally robust.

---

42. Thus, there is a value to a commitment to respond to potential departures from rational expectations, even if one is confident that the economy must end up in a REE, for responding in this way ensures that there are not other REEs besides the one in which the target criterion is always satisfied.

43. More precisely, Preston shows that the REE is "E-stable" in the sense of Evans and Honkapohja (2001). This implies convergence to the REE in expectation, and convergence with probability 1 in the case that certain bounds are imposed on how far peoples' forecasting rules can depart from the REE rules.

4.2. *Comparison with the Taylor rule*

To what extent is an analysis of the kind proposed here—the search for a robust approach to implementation of a robust target criterion— likely to lead to recommendations for policy that differ from those obtained from the Taylor research program, namely, the search for a simple interest-rate reaction function with robust properties? I suspect that many of the most important conclusions from Taylor's research will also be supported by an inquiry of this kind. That is to say, a desirable forecast-targeting framework will involve a conduct of policy that conforms to many of the broad guidelines for sound policy emphasized by Taylor.[44]

This is illustrated by the presentation above of an optimal targeting procedure in the context of the basic new-Keynesian model. The interest-rate reaction function (4.5) that implements the optimal target criterion shares a number of features with the simple rule advocated by Taylor (1993). In fact, it could be called a sort of "forward-looking Taylor rule," insofar as the prescribed short-term interest rate i_t is an increasing function of expected future inflation, expected future output gaps, and the current and expected future levels of the natural rate of interest. One respect in which (4.5) differs from more familiar examples of forward-looking Taylor rules is that it also involves forecasts of future interest rates. Because it is the expected path of interest rates that determines aggregate demand, rather than the current short rate alone, higher future short rates can substitute for a higher short rate now; so the required current short rate is a decreasing function of expected future short rates, given expectations regarding inflation, the output gap, and the natural rate of interest.

Moreover, this reaction function conforms to the Taylor principle insofar as an average of current and expected future nominal interest rates is specified to be an increasing function of an average of expected future inflation rates (for given expectations regarding the output gap and the natural rate), with a response coefficient that is greater than one. We can alternatively write (4.5) in the form

$$\hat{E}_t \bar{i}_t = \phi_\pi \hat{E}_t \bar{i}_{t+1} \ldots,$$

44. The observed conduct of actual forecast-targeting central banks has often been found to look fairly similar to the policy that would follow from a Taylor rule. For example, Nelson (2003) finds that U.K. policy has been much more similar to the kind prescribed by Taylor (1993) after the introduction of inflation-forecast targeting in 1992 than was true in earlier periods.

where $\bar{\imath}_t$ is a weighted average of the interest rates i_T in periods $T \geq t$, $\bar{\pi}_t$ is a weighted average of the inflation rates π_T in periods $T \geq t$, and the omitted terms involve (both actual and expected values of) the output gap and the exogenous disturbances. When the rule is expressed in this way,

$$\phi_\pi = 1 + \frac{\kappa\sigma^{-1}}{\kappa^2 + \lambda} \frac{\beta(1-\beta)(1-\alpha)}{1-\alpha\beta} > 1,$$

in accordance with the Taylor principle. This aspect of the reaction function is probably not unrelated to its success in eliminating instability due to self-fulfilling expectations.

Nonetheless, while this policy is similar to the policy prescribed by the Taylor rule in certain important respects, it does not follow that a central bank would therefore be best advised to simply try to follow the Taylor rule or to explain its decisions to the public in those terms. There is an alternative, fairly simple description of the policy prescription represented by (4.5) that is also more precise: it is a prescription to set interest rates as required in order for inflation and output to satisfy the target criterion (3.3).

Moreover, this alternative prescription is more sophisticated in important respects. If the basic new-Keynesian model were correct, and the economy were to follow the REE associated with the policy, it would lead to optimal dynamic responses to all disturbances. Even more generally, some of the ways in which it differs from the simple Taylor rule are likely to be desirable. For example, (4.5) prescribes that the interest rate should be an increasing function of expectations of the future output gap relative to its recent past level, rather than the absolute level of the gap as in the simple Taylor rule. A rule of this kind will be less vulnerable to the possibility that a persistent error in estimating the natural rate of output can lead to persistent inflation above the central bank's long-run target.[45] Because it is much easier to imagine a substantial, persistent error in a central bank's estimate of the level of the natural rate than in its estimate of the growth rate, a rule that

---

45. Orphanides (2003) warns that this may be a serious risk under a Taylor rule that involves the absolute level of the output gap. He shows that U.S. policy in the 1970s was fairly consistent with a forward-looking Taylor rule of the same kind as also describes U.S. policy in the Greenspan period, if one assumes that the FOMC responded to estimates of the output gap that were available at the time; in this interpretation, the policy led to a decade of inflation as a result of a failure to recognize the slowdown in trend productivity growth.

depends only on the projected change in the output gap is likely to be much more robust to possible errors of this kind.[46]

The targeting procedure also differs from the simple Taylor rule in the way that it requires the central bank to respond to measures of private-sector expectations. Under the simple Taylor rule, private-sector expectations can be ignored; one trusts that a rule with desirable stabilization properties will stabilize expectations as well. The targeting procedure instead directs the central bank to respond to variations in private-sector expectations so as to offset their projected effects on the particular combination of inflation and output growth that constitutes the target criterion. To the extent that sufficient information about expectations exists to allow such a response, such a response should tend to stabilize the economy regardless of the vagaries of expectations—and should therefore stabilize expectations themselves more reliably as well.

5. Conclusion

I have argued that forecast-targeting procedures provide a useful way of implementing a rule-based approach to the conduct of monetary policy and that the normative study of monetary policy rules would do well to pay more attention to proposed rules of this type. This would involve analysis of two distinct, though obviously complementary, issues: on the one hand, the desirability of satisfying a given target criterion (specified as a relation among endogenous "target variables"), on the assumption that this can be arranged; and on the other hand, the efficacy of alternative procedures for adjusting the instrument of policy as ways of ensuring that the target criterion should be satisfied. In the case of each of these issues, it is important not only to analyze the question for a given model specification that is assumed to be precisely correct, and under the assumption that the state variables referred to in the model are precisely observable by the central bank, but also to consider the robustness of a given prescription to possible errors in either the model specification or in the evaluation of current conditions.

Forecast-targeting procedures are especially desirable classes of policy rules for two reasons. On the one hand, this way of specifying a rule

---

46. Orphanides (2003) shows that real-time errors in estimates of the quarter-to-quarter change in the output gap were quite modest during the 1970s, if one assumes that the Fed's estimates by the 1990s were roughly correct.

of conduct seems especially likely to provide a useful basis for explaining the systematic character of policy to the public, while at the same time allowing policy to respond in a flexible way to unexpected developments, including changes in the central bank's understanding of the character of disturbances and of the structure of the economy. And at the same time, it is a form of rule-based policy that is fairly close to the kind of procedures already being adopted by a number of central banks; hence, it is a kind of policy rule that, if found to have desirable properties in theory, is particularly plausible for central banks to consider. Further study of forecast-targeting procedures would thus serve the laudable goal that has animated much of the research program of John Taylor: providing a "translation" of the conclusions of normative economic theory into terms that can guide actual policy decisions.

While more work on rules of this class is needed, some provisional conclusions are already possible that may allow improvement upon the current practices of forecast-targeting central banks. The projections that are central to forecast targeting should be based on intertemporally consistent assumptions about future monetary policy. The most practical way to do this is to seek to determine an endogenous path for future policy that ensures the satisfaction of a particular target criterion at each of an entire sequence of future horizons, rather than some single horizon. Furthermore, the target criterion must apply to relatively near horizons and not only to outcomes several years in the future. It is important to specify not merely the inflation rate that should be expected in the "medium run" (though it is crucial that a central bank be clear about that particular implication of the targeting procedure), but also the nature of an acceptable transition path by which an economy currently away from the medium-run target inflation rate is expected to approach it. This in turn will inevitably require that a central bank be more explicit than most forecast-targeting central banks have thus far been about the way in which projections for variables other than a single overall measure of inflation are taken into account in the policy decision. Finally, a robust approach to the implementation of the target criterion requires that the central bank monitor private-sector expectations (through the variety of direct and indirect sources of information about expectations that is available to it) with a view to correcting the effects on the macroeconomy of departures from the beliefs that the bank itself would regard as correct.

No central bank currently conforms very fully to all of these precepts, so I believe that there is ample room for further productive dialogue between students of the theory of monetary policy and its practitioners.

But forecast targeting as it has developed over the past fifteen years already represents an important step toward more systematic and more transparent policy. This is highly desirable, for reasons that monetary theory has made clear, and the further refinement of forecast targeting procedures represents the best hope at present for putting the insights provided by that theory into practice.

REFERENCES

Ball, Laurence, N. Gregory Mankiw, and Ricardo Reis. 2005. "Monetary Policy for Inattentive Economies." *Journal of Monetary Economics* 52:703–725.

Benigno, Pierpaolo, and Michael Woodford. 2005. "Inflation Stabilization and Welfare: The Case of a Distorted Steady State." *Journal of the European Economics Association* 3:1185–1236.

Calvo, Guillermo. 1983. "Staggered Prices in a Utility-Maximizing Framework." *Journal of Monetary Economics* 12:383–98.

Clarida, Richard, Jordi Galí, and Mark Gertler. 1999. "The Science of Monetary Policy: A New Keynesian Perspective." *Journal of Economic Literature* 37: 1661–1707.

———. 2000 "Monetary Policy Rules and Macroeconomic Stability: Evidence and Some Theory." *Quarterly Journal of Economics* 115:147–180.

Evans, George W., and Seppo Honkapohja. 2001. *Learning and Expectations in Macroeconomics*. Princeton, NJ: Princeton University Press.

Giannoni, Marc P., and Michael Woodford. 2002. "Optimal Interest-Rate Rules: I. General Theory." National Bureau of Economic Research (NBER) working paper no. 9419, December 2002.

———. 2005. "Optimal Inflation Targeting Rules." In *The Inflation-Targeting Debate,* eds. Ben S. Bernanke and Michael Woodford. Chicago: University of Chicago Press.

Goodhart, Charles A. E. 2001. "Monetary Transmission Lags and the Formulation of the Policy Decision on Interest Rates." Federal Reserve Bank of St. Louis *Review,* July/August: 165–181.

———. 2005. "The Interest Rate Conditioning Assumption." Financial Markets Group discussion paper no. 547, London School of Economics, October 2005.

Honkapohja, Seppo, and Kaushik Mitra. 2005. "Performance of Inflation Targeting Based on Constant Interest Rate Projections." *Journal of Economic Dynamics and Control* 29:1867–1892.

Jansson, Per, and Anders Vredin. 2003. "Forecast-Based Monetary Policy: The Case of Sweden." *International Finance* 6:349–380.

King, Mervyn A. 1997. "Changes in UK Monetary Policy: Rules and Discretion in Practice." *Journal of Monetary Economics* 39:81–97.

Kydland, Finn E., and Edward C. Prescott. 1977. "Rules Rather than Discretion: The Inconsistency of Optimal Plans." *Journal of Political Economy* 85:473–491.

Leitemo, Kai. 2003. "Targeting Inflation by Constant-Interest-Rate Forecasts." *Journal of Money, Credit and Banking* 35:609–26.

Mankiw, N. Gregory, and Ricardo Reis. 2002. "Sticky Information versus Sticky Prices: A Proposal to Replace the New Keynesian Phillips Curve." *Quarterly Journal of Economics* 117:1295–1328.

Nelson, Edward. 2003. "UK Monetary Policy 197297: A Guide Using Taylor Rules." In *Central Banking, Monetary Theory and Practice: Essays in Honour of Charles Goodhart, vol. 1,* ed. Paul Mizen. Cheltenham, UK: Edward Elgar.

Orphanides, Athanasios. 2003. "The Quest for Prosperity without Inflation." *Journal of Monetary Economics* 50:633–663.

Preston, Bruce. 2004. "Adaptive Learning and the Use of Forecasts in Monetary Policy." Princeton University, unpublished.

Qvigstad, Jan F. 2006. "When Does an Interest Rate Path 'Look Good'? Criteria for an Appropriate Future Interest Rate Path: A Practitioner's Approach." Norges Bank staff memo 2005/6, April 2006.

Rosenberg, Irma. 2007. "Riksbank to Introduce Own Path for the Repo Rate." Speech at Danske Bank, Stockholm, January 17, 2007. [Text available at www.riksbank.com.]

Sheedy, Kevin D. 2005. "Resistance to Persistence: Optimal Monetary Policy Commitment." Cambridge University, unpublished.

Svensson, Lars E. O. 1997. "Inflation Forecast Targeting: Implementing and Monitoring Inflation Targets." *European Economic Review* 41:1111–46.

———. 2003. "What is Wrong with Taylor Rules? Using Judgment in Monetary Policy through Targeting Rules." *Journal of Economic Literature* 41:426–77.

———. 2007. "Optimal Inflation Targeting: Further Developments of Inflation Targeting." In *Monetary Policy under Inflation Targeting,* eds. Frederic Mishkin and Klaus Schmidt-Hebbel. Santiago: Central Bank of Chile.

———. and Michael Woodford. 2005. "Implementing Optimal Policy through Inflation-Forecast Targeting." In *The Inflation-Targeting Debate,* eds. Ben S. Bernanke and Michael Woodford. Chicago: University of Chicago Press.

Taylor, John B. 1979. "Estimation and Control of a Macroeconometric Model with Rational Expectations." *Econometrica* 47:1267–86.

———. 1993a. "Discretion Versus Policy Rules in Practice." *Carnegie-Rochester Conference Series on Public Policy* 39:195–214.

———. 1993b. "The Use of the New Macroeconometrics for Policy Formulation." *American Economic Review: Papers and Proceedings* 83(2):300–05.

———. 1998. "Applying Academic Research on Monetary Policy Rules: An Exercise in Translational Economics." Harry G. Johnson Lecture, *The Manchester School* 66 Suppl.:1–16.

———. 1999a. "Introduction." In *Monetary Policy Rules*, ed. John B. Taylor. Chicago: University of Chicago Press.

———. 1999b. "A Historical Analysis of Monetary Policy Rules." In *Monetary Policy Rules*, ed. John B. Taylor. Chicago: University of Chicago Press.

———. 2000. "How the Rational Expectations Revolution Has Changed Macroeconomic Policy Research." In *Advances in Macroeconomics*, ed. Jacques Drèze. London: Palgrave.

Vickers, John. 1998. "Inflation Targeting in Practice: The U.K. Experience." Bank of England *Quarterly Bulletin*, November.

Woodford, Michael. 2003. *Interest and Prices: Foundations of a Theory of Monetary Policy*. Princeton, NJ: Princeton University Press.

———. 2005. "Central-Bank Communication and Policy Effectiveness." In *The Greenspan Era: Lessons for the Future*. Kansas City: Federal Reserve Bank of Kansas City.

NINE

THE DUAL NATURE OF FORECAST TARGETING AND INSTRUMENT RULES

John B. Taylor

Michael Woodford's chapter is filled with fascinating ideas and insights, each carefully explained. Most importantly, he proposes an ambitious future research program with the specific practical purpose of implementing "forecast targeting" by central banks.

By forecast targeting Woodford means a policy framework in which monetary policymakers set their policy instruments so that the expected future values of certain target variables follow optimal paths. For example, policymakers would set the interest rate so that the forecast of a linear combination of the inflation rate and the GDP gap follow a certain path.[1]

Why do we need a research program on forecast targeting? While some central banks follow procedures similar to forecast targeting, none do it the way Woodford proposes here. Hence, as with early work on "instrument rules"—in which the interest rate is related to inflation

---

John B. Taylor is the George P. Shultz Senior Fellow in Economics at the Hoover Institution and the Mary and Robert Raymond Professor of Economics at Stanford University.

1. In the models Woodford considers, the GDP gap is the percentage difference between actual GDP and its potential level. The GDP gap appears in the case of the "discretionary" solution to the optimization problem while the change in the GDP gap appears in the case of the "optimal" solution.

and the GDP gap—he suggests that the focus now should be on "translational economics" or translating the theoretical ideas on forecast targeting into "the actual actions of the central bank."

He draws a useful analogy between this proposed research program and my research program of the 1980s and 1990s which endeavored to translate theoretical work on instrument rules into practice by focusing on workable suggestions—for example, that central bank staff should present simulations of policy rules at monetary policy committee meetings—and by examining robustness and learning issues. Similarly, with forecast targeting, policymakers still must decide on settings for the instruments and need procedures to do so. As Woodford puts it: "Certainly one cannot compare a forecast targeting strategy to [an instrument] rule, without also describing what forecast targeting means for the way in which the policy instrument should be adjusted over time."

Forecast Targeting Versus Instrument Rules?

I have no doubt that the proposed research program will be very useful, probably in more ways than we can imagine now. However, in giving a rationale for the proposed research, Woodford suggests that forecast targeting rules are better than instrument rules. For example, he argues that forecast targeting "provides greater protection against political pressure," is "more predictable," and is more deserving of being called a policy rule because, in practice, instrument rules are used as guidelines rather than as mechanical formulas.

As I see it, forecast targeting and instrument rules are complementary, rather than alternatives. I think it is important that researchers pursue both approaches. Forecast targeting and instrument rules are duals to the same policy optimization problem. One is a condition for optimality and the other is a decision rule. There are many examples in economics where optimality conditions and decisions rules are used together. Economists do not need to choose, for example, between the condition that a firm sets marginal cost equal to price versus the supply curve showing the quantity the firm supplies at each price. They can and do use both. Indeed, as I will try to show below in the case of monetary policy, this duality has been a significant help in the design of instrument rules.

The illuminating exchange between Lars E. O. Svensson (2005) and Bennett T. McCallum and Edward Nelson (2005) brings out many of the important differences between instrument (mostly interest rate) rules and forecast targeting, but viewing forecast targeting and interest rate rules as mutually exclusive misses important aspects of policy in practice. For example, in the countries where central banks have operating procedures similar to Woodford's proposed forecast targeting—the United Kingdom, Norway, and Sweden—instrument rules serve as a cross-check on policy decisions. Moreover, outside analysts—including those in the private sector, in other branches of government, and even at other central banks—use instrument rules to help assess the policies of these central banks.

One reason why research on monetary policy rules should continue even as the research program Woodford proposes proceeds is that the currently popular interest rate rules, which were derived from monetary models developed in the 1970s and 1980s, embed key principles of monetary policy that have led to significant improvements in the macro economy. The Great Moderation of the 1980s and 1990s was closely associated in time with a monetary policy shift toward monetary policy rules. Even if we were sure about a causal connection between this rule-like behavior of central banks and the improved economic performance, we should not be complacent. As the world economy changes and our ability to model the monetary aspects of the economy gets better—exemplified by Michael Woodford's own contributions—policy rules will likely have to adapt in order to preserve this improved economic performance.

The Road to Instrument Rules Went through the Land of Forecast Targeting

To illustrate the close link between forecast targeting and instrument rules, let me consider several "case studies" and try to draw some lessons. The first two come from my own research and the third from observing Federal Reserve policy during the past two decades.

An international comparison of output and price stability in the bad old days

The first example is drawn from Taylor (1980b), where I used an equation to investigate the nature of optimal monetary policy using data from a number of countries. Here is the equation:

$$y_t + \beta p_t = v_t \tag{1}$$

where p_t is the price level, y_t is the GDP gap, and v_t is a random shock. The left-hand side of this equation is a linear combination of two target variables much in the spirit of Woodford's equation (2.3) with the policy lag due to the moving average disturbance. The policy objective is to maximize stability of y and p. Higher β means more weight on price stability; lower β means more weight on output stability. Under the assumption that some temporary price rigidities exist, one can derive a variability trade-off curve between these two stability goals, with output stability on one axis and price stability on the other axis. Note that this was price level targeting rather than inflation targeting.

The temporary price rigidities were described with a forward-looking staggered price setting model of the form I had recently proposed (Taylor 1980a). This was still a few years before Calvo (1983) proposed a geometric weighting in the staggered price setting model, but the properties are very similar to equation (2.1) in Woodford's chapter, as is clear from John Roberts' (1995) work.

I estimated β for ten countries including Norway, Sweden, the United Kingdom, Germany, and the United States. The sample period was from the bad old days of high and rising price and output volatility (1956–1976). The estimates are shown in the following table with the asterisks indicating statistical significance at the 5 percent level.

	β
Austria	0.0114
Canada	0.0901*
Denmark	0.0373
Gemany	0.3727*
Italy	0.2967*
Netherlands	0.0008
Norway	0.1255*
Sweden	0.1317*
United Kingdom	0.1165*
United States	0.2936*

Note that Germany had the highest value of β at .37. The United States had a value of .29. Norway and Sweden were close together at

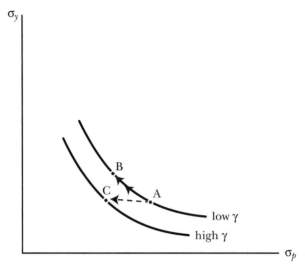

Figure 1. Effect of a policy induced shift in the output-price stability tradeoff.

.13. Canada and the United Kingdom were somewhat lower. In my view all these values of β implied too little weight on price stability. I speculated—thinking about the Lucas critique—about the possibility that the trade-off between output and price stability might shift in a favorable direction if β were higher. If so, we could get more output stability and more price stability with a higher β. Such a shift would occur if the speed of price adjustment increased. The speed was determined by a parameter in the staggered pricing model.

I illustrated this possibility with the following trade-off curve (which is figure 1 from the 1980 paper). If shifting policy to increase β had the effect of increasing the speed of price adjustment, then economic performance would not have to move from A to B; it could move from A to C or to any other point on the improved trade-off curve.

The history since the early 1980s shows that a shift in monetary policy did lead to improvements in both price and output stability, which can be explained by a shift in the trade-off curve, as shown above and as discussed by Ben Bernanke elsewhere in this book.

The question I was addressing in the late 1970s and early 1980s was: how could the rule for setting the instruments of monetary policy be changed in order to increase β? Using the terminology of Woodford, the challenge was to get a larger coefficient in the "high level" targeting rule with a new "low level" instrument rule.

Nominal GDP targeting and the business cycle

My second example is from a paper prepared for a conference several years later (Taylor 1985). In this paper I considered what would now be defined as forecast targeting in which the growth rate of nominal GDP would be held constant.[2] The targeting equation in that paper was written as follows:

$$y_t - y_{t-1} + p_t - p_{t-1} = 0. \tag{2}$$

Though not fully optimal, this nominal GDP rule was widely discussed at the time; I simulated it with a very simple macro model estimated with annual data in the United States. This is the kind of simulation exercise that Woodford is proposing in order to evaluate the robustness of forecast targeting rules in different models.

By studying the dynamic properties of output and inflation with this rule inserted in a model, I found that the rule actually made the business cycle worse. The rule amplified the boom-bust cycle by slowing down the economy when it was far from potential and speeding up the economy when it was nearing potential.

So instead of this targeting rule, I proposed another targeting rule, a modified nominal GDP rule of the form:

$$y_t + (p_t - p_{t-1}) = 0. \tag{3}$$

This is also a forecast targeting rule according to Woodford's definition, but one where the growth rate of real GDP is replaced by the level of GDP relative to potential. I found that this modified version of the rule significantly outperformed the nominal GDP rule.

Finally, I considered a slight generalization of equation (3):

$$y_t + \beta(p_t - p_{t-1}) = 0 \tag{4}$$

in which the slope β could be chosen optimally to yield better performance than (3). Despite the similarity between equation (4) and the proposed forecast targeting rule in Woodford, the underlying models

---

2. Analogously, Svensson (2005) calls a constant growth rate rule for the money supply a forecast targeting rule because the central bank would likely achieve this target by using a money demand equation to determine the appropriate level of the interest rate.

are quite different. Equation (4) does not work as well as equation (2) in the model that Woodford studies, but it works better than (2) in the model I was using. I believe this is because there is more inertia in the model I used (Taylor 1985) than in Woodford's model, but the difference illustrates the importance of looking at different models in robustness studies.

The finding that targeting rule (3) or (4) worked better than targeting rule (2) suggested that any good instrument rule should have the interest rate reacting to the *level* of the GDP gap rather than to the *rate of change* in GDP, even though this had the disadvantage of making policy more sensitive to uncertain estimates of potential GDP. The obvious lesson from this experience is that research on forecast targeting rules helps us understand, find, and improve on interest rate rules.

Interest rate decisions at the Federal Reserve

A third connection between forecast targeting and instrument rules may help explain why the decisions of some central banks have come close to simple monetary policy rules and to the so-called Taylor "greater than one" principle, even if they do not literally follow such rules or principles. Of course, the fact that they use monetary policy rules as a cross-check is one explanation, but another is that a decision-making process with some of the features of forecast targeting will tend to lead to such policy rule behavior.

In my commentary (Taylor 2005) at the Jackson Hole conference celebrating the service of Alan Greenspan as Fed chairman, I provided an explanation based on the idea that the Fed practiced an informal type of forecast targeting, though not nearly as formal as Woodford suggests in his chapter. I wrote in this commentary that "I believe the literal description by which the FOMC has achieved the 'greater than one' principle is close to the following. The Fed staff uses models, such as their FRB/US model. When there is an increase in inflation, or a forecast of an increase, the Fed staff, by simulating the model, will show the FOMC that an increase in the funds rate will be needed to reverse it, or prevent it. Now according to any good model that treats expectations and price adjustment sensibly (and FRB/US certainly is in this category), this will require an increase in the *real* interest rate, and will therefore require increasing the federal funds rate by more than one-for-one with the increase in inflation. So, if the Fed is using its model this way, as I believe it is, then the 'greater than one' principle would be implemented by this procedure. To the extent that this process is regularized at FOMC meetings, then the Fed is effectively following the principles imbedded in the policy rule."

Of course, the caveat that the model "treats expectations and price adjustment sensibly" is essential. There is no guarantee that such a decision-making process will lead to good monetary policy if the policymakers do not have a good model or do not use it properly.

Conclusion

In sum, while I have no criticisms of Woodford's research proposal on the practical application of forecast targeting rules, the case for such research, in my view, does not rest on defects with instrument rules, which have helped—and are continuing to help—guide policy.

Though monetary policy rules have accomplished a lot already, they can and must be improved and reassessed as theory and the world change. We also need better principles for "off the rule" behavior as in the case of liquidity shortages, frozen markets, or risk-management priorities. In my view new research shows that closer adherence to policy rules would be advisable. If past experience is any guide, and I have argued it is with some simple historical examples in this chapter, then research on forecast targeting will improve the performance and design of monetary policy rules for the instruments in the future.

References

Calvo, Guillermo. 1983. "Staggered Contracts in a Utility-Maximizing Framework." *Journal of Monetary Economics* 12:282–398.

McCallum, Bennett T., and Edward Nelson. 2005. "Targeting Versus Instrument Rules for Monetary Policy." Federal Reserve Bank of St. Louis *Review* 87(5) (September/October): 597–612.

Roberts, John M. 1995. "New Keynesian Economics and the Phillips Curve." *Journal of Money, Credit and Banking* 27(4) (November): 975–84.

Svensson, Lars E. O. 2005. "Targeting Versus Instrument Rules for Monetary Policy: What Is Wrong With McCallum and Nelson?" Federal Reserve Bank of St. Louis *Review* 87(5) (September/October): 613–26.

Taylor, John B. 1980a. "Aggregate Dynamics and Staggered Contracts." *Journal of Political Economy* 88(1) (February): 1–23.

————. 1980b. "Output and Price Stability: An International Comparison." *Journal of Economic Dynamics and Control* 2(1) (February): 109–32

————. 1985. "What Would Nominal GNP Targeting Do To the Business Cycle?" *Carnegie-Rochester Series on Public Policy* 22 (Spring): 61–84.

————. 2005. "Commentary: Understanding the Greenspan Standard." In *The Greenspan Era: Lessons for the Future.* Proceedings of Jackson Hole Symposium, Federal Reserve Bank of Kansas City.

TEN

EVALUATING
MONETARY POLICY

Lars E. O. Svensson

Introduction

In January 1999, a number of legislative changes came into force in Sweden that made the Riksbank more independent. As a result, the monetary policy decisions since then have been made by an Executive Board consisting of six members who are not permitted to seek or take instructions in the course of their work. These legislative changes can be seen as part of an international trend that has now been under way for a couple of decades—a trend toward an institutional framework for monetary policy with the aim of making monetary policy more effective and more able to promote both monetary stability and stability in the real economy.

This institutional framework for monetary policy rests on three pillars:

This chapter is taken from remarks prepared for Sveriges Riksbank, Stockholm University, CEPR, and NBER, revised August 2011.

I am grateful to Björn Andersson, Mikael Apel, Carl-Andreas Claussen, Paolo Giordani, Gabriela Guibourg, Tora Hammar, Neil Howe, Eric Leeper, Lina Majtorp, Mattias Villani, Staffan Viotti, and Anders Vredin for assistance and helpful comments. The views presented here are my own and not necessarily those of other members of the Riksbank's executive board or staff or of the Federal Reserve System.

1. A mandate for monetary policy from the government or parliament, normally to maintain price stability
2. Independence for the central bank to conduct monetary policy and fulfill the mandate
3. Accountability of the central bank for its policy and decisions

The central bank's independence gives its governors a lot of power. In a democratic society, it is natural that the activities of the central bank are monitored and evaluated and that its independent management can be called to account. This contributes to maintaining the democratic legitimacy of the central bank. Accountability and regular evaluations of monetary policy also give the central bank stronger incentives to fulfill its mandate and motivate the central bank to develop its monetary policy analysis in the best possible way.

It also appears that detailed evaluations of monetary policy are becoming increasingly common. In Sweden, an annual evaluation is conducted by the Parliament's Committee on Finance, based on detailed material supplied and published by the Riksbank. An external and more comprehensive evaluation of ten years of Swedish monetary policy between 1995 and 2005 was carried out on behalf of the Committee on Finance by Francesco Giavazzi and Frederic Mishkin (Giavazzi and Mishkin 2006). The Committee on Finance then decided that Swedish monetary policy should be evaluated by external experts every fourth year. Goodhart and Rochet (2011) is the next evaluation in this series. On behalf of the Norwegian Ministry of Finance, an annual evaluation of monetary policy in Norway is carried out by Norges Bank Watch, a group of independent experts. I have taken part in two evaluations of monetary policy myself—an evaluation of ten years of monetary policy in New Zealand on behalf of the New Zealand Minister of Finance in 2001 (Svensson 2001) and an evaluation of monetary policy in Norway as chairman of Norges Bank Watch in 2002 (Svensson, Houg, Solheim, and Steigum 2002).

Evaluations of monetary policy are important and appear to be becoming common practice. One must therefore ensure that reasonable principles and appropriate methods for evaluations are developed and applied. This is what I intend to discuss here. What should we consider when we evaluate monetary policy? What are the principles for a good evaluation of monetary policy, and what is practically possible? How can principles and practice be developed compared with how evaluations are carried out today? Here I present a few suggestions for such development.

Why Not Just Examine whether Inflation Equals the Target?

An increasing number of central banks focus their monetary policy on achieving an explicit published inflation target. My discussion today will therefore be about evaluations of monetary policy with an explicit inflation target, what is known as inflation targeting. Given an announced inflation target, you may ask why an evaluation of monetary policy should be so complicated. When there is an inflation target, is it not simply enough to compare the actual outcome for inflation with the inflation target? There are at least two circumstances that make such an evaluation inadequate.

Unanticipated shocks affect outcomes

First, monetary policy does not provide complete control over inflation. A central bank is therefore unable to ensure that inflation will be exactly on target at every point in time. In fact, monetary policy is normally conducted under conditions of considerable uncertainty. The knowledge of the economic situation is not complete and neither is the knowledge of how monetary policy affects inflation and the real economy, the so-called transmission mechanism of monetary policy. There is a considerable time lag before monetary policy measures have an impact on inflation, and the duration of this time lag also varies depending on the circumstances. The impact is normally gradual and becomes apparent over the course of a few years.

As monetary policy works with a time lag, it is most effective if it is based on forecasts. In order to achieve a given inflation target rate, it is therefore best to set the policy rate so that the inflation forecast a couple of years ahead equals the inflation target. However, during the time it takes for changes in the policy rate to have a full impact on inflation the economy will be affected by new and unexpected shocks. The inflation outcome a couple of years ahead will therefore have been affected by events that could not be predicted when the monetary policy decisions were made.

A direct comparison of outcomes and targets for inflation may therefore lead to the wrong conclusions. The inflation outcome may be in line with the target even if the monetary policy decisions were incorrect because the central bank was lucky and unexpected shocks nevertheless resulted in the right inflation outcome. Alternatively, the inflation outcome may deviate from the target even if the monetary policy decisions were correct because the central bank was unlucky and unexpected disruptions resulted in the wrong inflation outcome.

Inflation targeting is flexible

A second circumstance that implies that a simple comparison of outcomes and targets for inflation is inadequate is that the Riksbank and all the other inflation-targeting central banks conduct *flexible* inflation targeting rather than *strict* inflation targeting. Flexible inflation targeting means that monetary policy aims at stabilizing *both* inflation around the inflation target and the real economy, whereas strict inflation targeting aims at stabilizing inflation *only*, without regard to the stability of the real economy, what Mervyn King (1997) has described like being an "inflation nutter."[1]

In many situations, a conflict may arise between stabilizing inflation and stabilizing the real economy. Let us assume that a shock, such as a sharp rise in the oil price, has driven up inflation at the same time as output has slackened significantly. If, in such a case, the aim of monetary policy is to quickly bring inflation back to the target, a significant policy-rate increase may be required which will dampen output even further. By quickly stabilizing inflation—which would be the case with strict inflation targeting—the central bank would destabilize the real economy. By not aiming to bring inflation back to the target as quickly as possible, the central bank would help to stabilize the real economy. How long it should take to return inflation to the target depends, among other things, on the type, magnitude, and duration of

---

1. The terms "strict" and "flexible" inflation targeting were to my knowledge first introduced and defined in a paper of mine presented at a conference at the Bank of Portugal in 1996, later published as Svensson (1999). The term "inflation nutter" for a central bank that is only concerned about stabilizing inflation was introduced in a paper by Mervyn King at a conference in Gerzensee, Switzerland, in 1995, later published as King (1997). Heikensten and Vredin (2002) state that "[s]ince the mid 1990s, however, the Riksbank has explicitly declared that it is not a 'strict' but a 'flexible' inflation targeter (like most other central banks today)." They also clarify that this is consistent with the Riksbank's mandate: "This policy also has legal support. In the preparatory documents on [the law on] the Riksbank's independence it is said that the 'Riksbank, as an agency under the Riksdag, should accordingly have an obligation to support the general economic policy objectives to the extent that these do not conflict with the price stability objective.' The task of the Executive Board is thus to implement this notion of 'flexible' inflation targeting." Sveriges Riksbank (2010) is even more explicit: "[I]n addition to stabilising inflation around the inflation target, [the Riksbank is] also striving to stabilise production and employment around long-term sustainable paths. The Riksbank therefore conducts what is generally referred to as flexible inflation targeting."

the shock that has occurred and the importance that the central bank attaches to stability of the real economy.

A difference between the outcome and the target for inflation may thus be deliberate. It may be part of an appropriate compromise between stabilizing inflation and stabilizing the real economy. It is, therefore, simply not good enough to just compare outcomes and targets for inflation in an evaluation of monetary policy.

What Does Flexible Inflation Targeting Entail?

Before I begin to discuss what evaluations of monetary policy should focus on, let me go into a little more detail about what characterizes flexible inflation targeting.

As I have already said, flexible inflation targeting entails the central bank striving to stabilize inflation around the inflation target and at the same time to stabilize the real economy. Stabilizing the real economy may be more precisely described as stabilizing resource utilization at a normal level.

There is an asymmetry between the impact of monetary policy on inflation and its impact on the real economy that it is very important to understand. Monetary policy can affect both the average level and the variability of inflation. Monetary policy cannot, on the other hand, affect the average level of real quantities such as output, employment, and resource utilization. Historically, attempts to use monetary policy to affect the average level of real variables such as employment and unemployment have led to serious mistakes and high inflation. In the case of the real economy, monetary policy can only affect, and to a certain extent dampen, fluctuations in real variables around their average levels. For monetary policy, it is thus meaningful to select a certain target for average inflation, but it is not meaningful and in fact is counterproductive to select a certain target for average output or employment, other than the normal level that is determined by the workings of the economy and factors other than monetary policy.

Because of the lags between monetary-policy actions and the effect on inflation and the real economy, effective flexible inflation targeting has to rely on forecasts of inflation and the real economy. Flexible inflation targeting can be described as "forecast targeting." The central bank chooses an instrument-rate path so that the forecast of inflation and resource utilization "looks good." By a forecast that looks good I mean a forecast in which either inflation is already on target and resource utilization is already normal, or in which inflation is approaching the target and resource utilization is approaching a normal level at an appropriate pace. To be more precise, it means a forecast for inflation and resource utilization that as effectively as possible stabilizes inflation around the inflation target and resource utilization around its normal level and, in the event of conflicting objectives, achieves a reasonable compromise between inflation stability and resource utilization. Different central banks express this in slightly different words. The Riksbank has often used the term "a well-balanced monetary policy."[2]

We can formalize and specify this reasoning somewhat by saying that it is a case of selecting a policy-rate path that minimizes an intertemporal forecast loss function, written as the following standard quadratic form:

$$\sum_{\tau=0}^{\infty} \delta^{\tau} \left(\pi_{t+\tau,t} - \pi^* \right)^2 + \lambda \sum_{\tau=0}^{\infty} \delta^{\tau} \left(y_{t+\tau,t} - \bar{y}_{t+\tau,t} \right)^2.$$

Here, δ is a discount factor satisfying $0 < \delta \le 1$, $\pi_{t+\tau,t}$ denotes the mean forecast in quarter t for inflation in quarter $t + \tau$, π^* denotes the inflation target, λ is a constant weight placed on the stabilization of resource utilization relative to the stabilization of inflation, $y_{t+\tau,t}$ denotes the mean forecast for (the logarithm of) output, and $\bar{y}_{t+\tau,t}$ denotes the mean forecast for (the logarithm of) potential output. The output gap $y_{t+\tau,t} - \bar{y}_{t+\tau,t}$ is thus used as a measure of resource utilization here. Let us call the difference between inflation and the inflation target the inflation gap. The sums of squares of the mean forecast gaps normally converge also for a discount factor equal to one. Let me for simplicity assume through the rest of the paper that the discount factor is equal to one. It is then a case of minimizing the sum of squares of the inflation-gap forecast, $\Sigma_{\tau=0}^{\infty}(\pi_{t+\tau,t} - \pi^*)^2$, plus the weight λ times the sum of squares of the output-gap forecast, $\Sigma_{\tau=0}^{\infty}(y_{t+\tau,t} - \bar{y}_{t+\tau,t})^2$.[3]

---

2. The idea that inflation targeting implies that the inflation forecast can be seen as an intermediate target was introduced in King (1994). The term "inflation-forecast targeting" was introduced in Svensson (1997) and the term "forecast targeting" in Svensson (2005). See Svensson and Woodford (2005) and especially Woodford (2007a, b) for more discussion and analysis of forecast targeting.

3. The loss function should ideally be minimized under commitment in a timeless perspective in order to ensure consistency over time of policy. The former deputy governor of Norges Bank, Jarle Bergo, has discussed this in a pedagogical manner in Bergo (2007). For a more technical approach see, for example, Woodford (2003), Svensson and Woodford (2005), and Adolfson, Laséen, Lindé, and Svensson (2011), or Svensson (2011b).

Evaluation Ex Ante—Given the Information
Available at the Time of the Decision

So, given that a central bank conducts flexible inflation targeting, how should we evaluate the monetary policy the bank conducts? When evaluating monetary policy, as when evaluating decisions in general, we may adopt one of two different starting points. The first option is to base our evaluation on the information that is currently at hand; that is also including the information that has become available since the decision was made. This is, in other words, an evaluation after the fact. We can call this ex post evaluation. The second option is to put ourselves in the position of the decision-makers at the time the decision was made and to try to evaluate the decision given the information that was then available. We can call this ex ante evaluation.

When evaluating monetary policy, the most interesting question is not whether the decision could have been better after the fact. As I said earlier, monetary policy is conducted under conditions of considerable uncertainty—there is a time lag before monetary policy has an impact on inflation and the real economy and the economy is constantly subject to new shocks. It is almost self-evident that monetary policy could have been better if the decision-makers had been aware when they made their decision that these shocks would happen. It is often equally self-evident that it was not possible to foresee the shocks at the time the decision was made. The relevant question is therefore primarily whether monetary policy could have been better given the information on the state of the economy and other factors that the central bank had access to when the decisions were made.

How then should an ex ante evaluation of monetary policy be carried out? I believe that we must take flexible inflation targeting seriously. For a central bank that conducts flexible inflation targeting it is important, as I mentioned earlier, to choose a policy-rate path so that the forecast for inflation and resource utilization "looks good" in terms of stabilizing both inflation and the real economy and, in the event of conflicting objectives, entails a reasonable balance between stabilizing inflation and stabilizing the real economy. An ex ante evaluation should then aim to assess whether the central bank has succeeded in doing this.

Before making such an assessment of whether the central bank's forecasts look good, it is natural to first examine the general quality of the forecasts. Any assessment of the quality of the forecasts obviously entails an ex post analysis with the help of historical forecast errors. If the assessment is that the forecasts are of a reasonable quality, it then becomes a question of assessing the monetary policy deliberations held on the basis of the forecasts the central bank makes. This primarily entails an ex ante analysis.

Obviously, the publication of central-bank forecasts of inflation and the real economy is a prerequisite for assessing whether the forecasts are accurate and whether they look good.

Were the Forecasts Good Enough?

The first question we should ask is whether the central bank's forecasts are normally good enough. It would of course be going too far to demand that the central bank's forecasts should be perfect. As I have said, the economy is constantly subject to unexpected shocks, which means that the forecasts are always likely to be incorrect to some extent. Analyzing the accuracy of a forecast in an individual year thus provides limited information. A significant forecasting error may indicate that the forecast was poor, but it may also be due to the fact that a shock occurred that could not have been predicted.[4]

Do the forecasts systematically over- or underestimate the actual outcomes?

A reasonable requirement is that the forecasts for inflation, resource utilization, and so on do not systematically over- or underestimate the actual outcomes. In other words, the forecasts should not have any bias. If, for example, the forecasts for inflation over a long period of time on average over- or underestimate the actual inflation outcome, then this is a sign that there is information that the central bank is missing and that could be used to improve the forecasts. It is, however difficult to determine whether the forecasts are unbiased on the basis of a small number of outcomes.

How do the central bank's forecasts compare with other forecasts?

Another reasonable requirement is that the central bank's forecasts are on average not poorer than those of other forecasters. If the central

---

4. Uncertainty about, and the revisions of, GDP and other data make forecasting more difficult and also make it more difficult to evaluate the forecasts.

bank's forecasts are systemically poorer than those of other forecasters, then this is obviously an indication that it would have been possible to make better assessments than those made by the central bank. This also means that better information was available which the central bank would have been able to use as a basis for its decision-making.

It is important to remember, however, that there are special conditions governing forecasting for a central bank that differ somewhat from those for many other forecasters. For the central bank it is not enough that the forecasts are accurate. This is *one* very important quality, but there are others. It must be possible, for example, to understand the driving forces behind the forecasts: Why does the forecast look the way it does? How is the forecast affected by changes in assumptions regarding, for instance, demand abroad or the oil price? The central bank also needs a forecasting apparatus that can effectively investigate the consequences of alternative monetary policies. For the Riksbank, which publishes its own interest-rate path, this is very important. To put it more technically, the central bank must use so-called structural models to assess the consequences of various policy-rate paths, while other forecasts can mainly be produced with the help of statistical models alone. Normally, there are good reasons for believing that structural models provide poorer forecasts than statistical models. However, the Riksbank's main structural model, Ramses, has very good forecasting properties (Adolfson, Laséen, Lindé, and Villani 2008).

When making historical comparisons between the forecasts of central banks and those of other forecasters, we also face a number of other difficulties. The first is that it is not certain that the central bank's forecasts are based on what the bank really believes is the best forecast of the policy rate and other variables. For a long time, the Riksbank, for example, based its forecasts on the assumption that the policy rate, the repo rate, would remain unchanged during the forecast period. Some central banks base their forecasts on both a constant policy rate and a constant exchange rate, which are often completely unrealistic assumptions. In such cases, the forecasts for inflation and the real economy are of course not the best forecasts. For a while, the Riksbank instead used the assumption that the repo-rate path would be given by the market's expectations of future repo rates. Although this is a more realistic assumption, it is not necessarily the same as the Riksbank's best forecast. These difficulties no longer apply to the Riksbank's forecasts as, since February 2007, the forecasts for inflation and the real economy are based on the Riksbank's best forecast for the future repo rate.

In order to arrive at a fair comparison of the forecasts of various forecasters, we should also take into account the fact that the forecasts are made at different times and are therefore based on different quantities of information. A forecaster that, for example, always publishes its forecasts later than other forecasters has generally more information on the economic situation when the forecasts are made. A comparison of the accuracy of the forecasts should therefore make adjustments for the forecasts being made at different times. Such an adjustment was included for the first time in a more systematic way in the material for the evaluation of monetary policy in the period 2006–08 that the Riksbank published in February 2009 (Sveriges Riksbank 2009a). The Riksbank now annually publishes such material for the evaluation of monetary policy in the previous two years.

Figures 1 and 2 show a comparison of the accuracy of the forecasts in the period 1999–2008 for CPI inflation and GDP growth for a number of forecasters. The darker bars on the left of each column show the absolute mean error adjusted for differences in publication dates. The lighter bars show the mean error with positive or negative signs. The

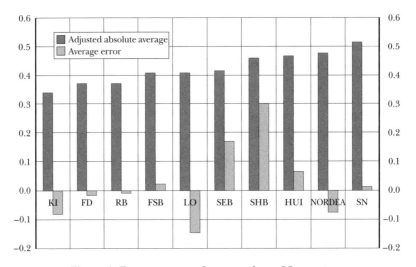

Figure 1. Forecast errors for a number of forecasters
1999–2008, CPI inflation, percent

Sources: National Institute of Economic Research and the Riksbank.
KI denotes the National Institute of Economic Research, FD the Ministry of Finance,
RB the Riksbank, FSB Swedbank, LO the Swedish Trade Union Confederation,
SHB the Svenska Handelsbanken, HUI the Swedish Retail Institute, and
SN the Confederation of Swedish Enterprise.

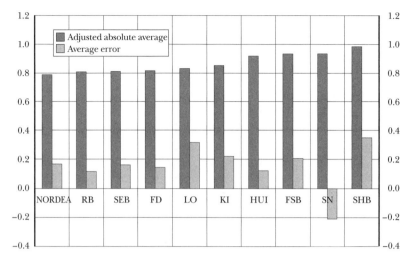

Figure 2. Forecast errors for a number of forecasters
1999–2008, GDP growth, percent
Sources: National Institute of Economic Research and the Riksbank.

shorter the lighter bars, the smaller the systematic over- or underestimation has been and the less bias the forecasts have had. If the bar is above the zero line, the mean error has been positive and the forecasts have on average been too low, and vice versa. In the case of both inflation and GDP growth, the Riksbank's accuracy has been relatively good and its bias relatively small compared to other forecasters.

Was Monetary Policy Well-Balanced Ex Ante?

Given that it has been determined that the central bank's forecasts are normally satisfactory, the next step is to analyze, ex ante, the monetary policy deliberations the central bank has conducted on the basis of the forecasts.

Was monetary policy efficient?

The first question to answer is whether the monetary policy conducted has been *efficient*. Given the information available at the time the decision was made, would it have been possible, by selecting a different policy-rate path, to have stabilized inflation or the real economy better

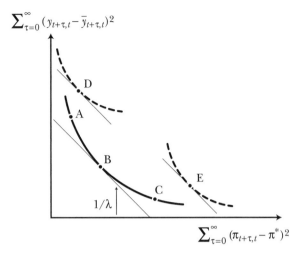

Figure 3. The forecast Taylor curve

without stabilizing the other less well? Would it even have been possible to achieve a better stabilization of both?[5]

The idea behind an efficient monetary policy can be illustrated using a modified Taylor curve. The original Taylor curve illustrates the efficient trade-off between the unconditional variances of inflation and output (Taylor 1979). The modified Taylor curve, what I call the forecast Taylor curve, illustrates the efficient trade-off between the conditional variability of the inflation- and output-gap forecasts.[6]

As I have said above, under flexible inflation targeting the central bank aims to stabilize inflation and resource utilization; that is, to minimize the deviations from the inflation target and the normal level for resource utilization. In figure 3, the sum of squares of the inflation-gap forecast is measured along the horizontal axis and the sum of squares of the output-gap forecast along the vertical axis. The curve through points A, B, and C is the forecast Taylor curve, that is, all the efficient combinations of forecasts for inflation and resource utilization, respectively,

5. Norges Bank has specified a few criteria for an appropriate interest-rate path that are reported in each issue of its *Monetary Policy Report* and were developed by Qvigstad (2005).

6. The original figure in Taylor (1979) plotted the unconditional standard deviation of the output deviation from trend against the unconditional standard deviation of inflation. Svensson (2011b) provides more details on the forecast Taylor curve and shows how evaluation with the help of the forecast Taylor curves can be adjusted to take into account commitment in a timeless perspective, following Svensson and Woodford (2005).

that it is possible to achieve in a certain decision-making situation with the help of different policy-rate paths. Points to the left and below the curve cannot be reached due to the initial state of the economy and the transmission mechanism between inflation, resource utilization, and the policy rate. Points to the right and above the curve are inefficient in the sense that it is possible for monetary policy to achieve a smaller sum of squares of the inflation-gap forecast for a given sum of squares of the output-gap forecasts, or vice versa.

In its *Monetary Policy Reports,* the Riksbank usually presents alternative scenarios with a different repo-rate path in addition to the main scenario. These generate other paths for inflation and the output gap. Figures 4, 5, and 6 show examples from February 2008, February 2009, and July 2009. Panel "a" in each figure shows the alternative repo-rate paths (with "Main" denoting the majority decision and what is called the main scenario in the corresponding *Monetary Policy Report* or *Update*), panel "b" shows the corresponding inflation forecasts (the underlying CPI inflation measure CPIX is shown for February 2008 whereas CPIF, the CPI with housing costs calculated for a constant interest rate, is shown for February and July 2009), and panel "d" shows

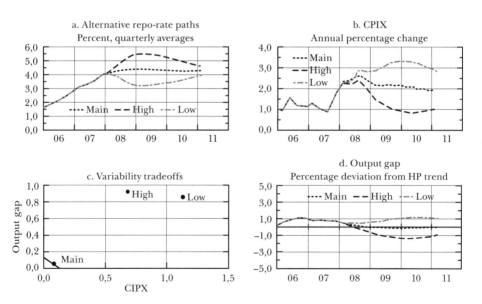

Figure 4. Forecasts for the repo rate, inflation, and output gap and variability trade-off, February 2008

Sources: Statistics Sweden and the Riksbank

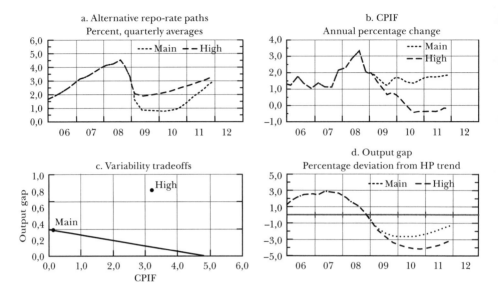

Figure 5. Forecasts for the repo rate, inflation, and output
gap and variability trade-off, February 2009

Sources: Statistics Sweden and the Rijksbank

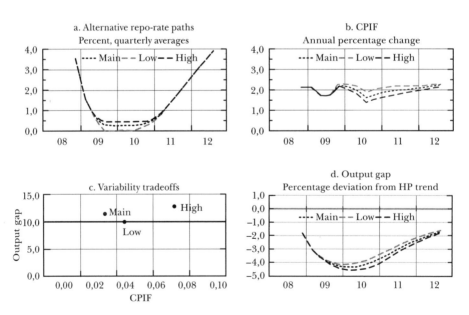

Figure 6. Forecasts for the repo rate, inflation, and
output gap and variability trade-off, July 2009

Sources: Statistics Sweden and the Riksbank

the corresponding output-gap forecasts (with the output gap measured as deviation from an HP trend).[7]

Panel "c," labeled Variability trade-offs, in figures 4–6 shows the corresponding mean squared gaps, the average sums of squares of the inflation-gap and output-gap forecasts (calculated over the forecast horizon of normally twelve quarters). These mean squared gaps then illustrated the variability of the inflation-gap and output-gap forecasts and the trade-off between them for different repo-rate paths, as for the forecast Taylor curve in figure 3.[8]

Figure 7 shows the variability trade-offs from these examples in the same figure. Several observations can be made here.

First, for February 2008 and 2009, the mean squared gaps for the main scenario are smaller than in the alternative scenarios; the main scenario is closer to the origin of the axes. The main scenario is thus more successful in terms of stabilizing both inflation and resource utilization.[9] The alternative repo-rate paths are clearly inefficient compared with the main scenario. This does not necessarily mean, however, that monetary policy is efficient in the sense that the main scenario lies on the forecast Taylor curve. There may be a repo-rate path that would stabilize inflation and resource utilization even better. Excluding this possibility requires a comparison with many more alternative scenarios.

Second, for July 2009, the main and alternative repo-rate paths are very similar with regard to the degree of inflation-gap stabilization, although the main repo-rate path results in a slightly smaller mean squared gap for the inflation gap, as can be seen in panel "c" of figure 6. However, the repo-rate paths result in different degrees of output-gap stabilization, where the low repo-rate path stabilizes the output-gap better and the high repo-rate path worse than the main scenario. The

---

7. The CPIX is a core inflation price index that excludes mortgage costs and effects of indirect taxes and subsidies. After June 2008, the Riksbank has downgraded the role of the CPIX and increased the emphasis on CPI. During 2009, when the policy rate has been adjusted in large steps, the interest-rate effects on the CPI have been large and the Riksbank has therefore increased the emphasis on the CPIF, the CPI adjusted for a constant interest rate (see Wickman-Parak 2008).

8. The mean squared gaps for the inflation-gap and output-gap forecasts are calculated as $\Sigma_{t=0}^{T} (\pi_{t+\tau,t} - \pi^*)^2 / (T+1)$ and $\Sigma_{t=0}^{T} (y_{t+\tau,t} - \bar{y}_{t+\tau,t})^2 / (T+1)$, where T is the forecast horizon (normally twelve quarters).

9. I use expressions such as "stabilizing the inflation gap" and "stabilizing the inflation-gap forecast" interchangeably. The conditional variance of the future inflation gap equals the squared inflation-gap forecast plus the variance of the forecast errors, and the variance of the forecast errors is here considered exogenous.

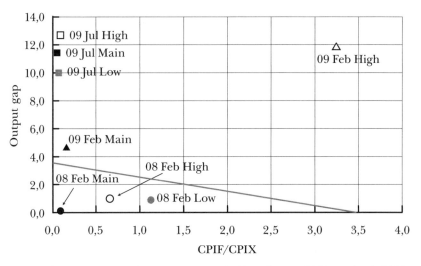

Figure 7. Variability trade-offs: February 2008, February 2009, and July 2009

Sources: Statistics Sweden and the Riksbank

high repo-rate path results in an inefficient outcome with higher mean squared gaps for the inflation- and output-gap forecasts.

Third, the position of the forecast Taylor curve may vary considerably depending on the initial state of the economy. The situation in July 2009 was worse than that in February 2009, which was worse than that in February 2008. The point in figure 7 that corresponds to February 2008 is not far from the origin, while the points that correspond to February 2009 and July 2009 are much farther away from the origin.

Assessing whether monetary policy has been efficient thus entails attempting to determine whether monetary policy has been on the forecast Taylor curve or not. The analysis is therefore ex ante, which means that the starting point is the central bank's forecast for inflation and resource utilization rather than the actual outcomes. In practice it is of course difficult to perform a more precise analysis; it becomes rather a question of determining to what extent monetary policy has been clearly inefficient in the sense that it is easy to find another policy-rate path that would stabilize inflation more without stabilizing resource utilization less, or that would even stabilize both more. A factor that can make the analysis even more complicated is if the central bank, apart from inflation and a measure of resource utilization, also includes other targets or limitations in its monetary policy deliberations. One such conceivable factor is so-called interest-rate smoothing, in which the central bank also chooses to even out the changes in the policy rate and ensure that they are made in relatively small and regular steps, for example by 0.25 percentage points at a time. With such a restriction, monetary policy will be located at a point above and to the right of the forecast Taylor curve. Alternatively, one can say that an additional axis and thus an additional dimension are required that correspond to the sum of squared changes in the policy rate, so that the forecast Taylor curve becomes a three-dimensional, bowl-shaped surface. A separate issue is whether there is any good reason for such implicit or explicit interest-rate smoothing. During last year's dramatic events, several central banks adjusted their policy rates in larger steps than usual, and it remains to be seen whether there will be less interest-rate smoothing during more normal times in the future.

A major difficulty in this analysis is that it may be unclear what is meant by stabilizing resource utilization around a normal level. The problem is that resource utilization can be measured in several ways. A reasonable and commonly used measure of resource utilization is the so-called output gap, that is, the difference between actual output and potential output. However, potential output is not a magnitude that can be observed directly—it must be estimated. There is considerable uncertainty, both theoretically and empirically, about the best way to define, estimate, and forecast potential output. The output gap shown in the figures are output deviations from an HP trend, which has significant weaknesses. It is important and desirable from several points of view that the Riksbank and other central banks develop better measures of resource utilization and potential output and that they publish their measurements and forecasts. Such work is under way at the Riksbank.

More recently, observing the difficulties with the Riksbank's estimates and forecasts of potential output, I have come to the conclusion that a better, more transparent, and more robust indicator of resource utilization is the unemployment gap between the unemployment rate and the long-run sustainable unemployment rate (the steady-state equilibrium unemployment rate), see Svensson (2011a, c).

Was monetary policy well-balanced?

Assuming, however, that we nevertheless conclude that monetary policy has not been clearly inefficient in the sense that I described earlier, the next step is to focus on what combination of the stabilization of inflation and the real economy the central bank actually selected or, in other words, which of all the possible points on the Taylor curve the central bank selected. There are many different efficient monetary policy alternatives to choose between every time a monetary policy decision is made. But did the central bank make a good choice? In the event of a conflict between stabilizing inflation and stabilizing the real economy, did the combination chosen by the central bank represent a reasonable balance between the two? Did the central bank attach reasonable importance to the stabilization of the real economy in relation to the stabilization of inflation?

In the literature, as in the case of the forecast loss function I presented earlier, the constant that is the relative weight that the central bank gives to the stabilization of the real economy in relation to the stabilization of inflation is often denoted by the Greek letter lambda, λ. In figure 3, we can show the intertemporal forecast loss function with the help of isoloss curves for combinations of sums of squared inflation-gap and output-gap forecasts that generate equally large losses. Such isoloss curves are in this case downward-sloping, straight lines with a slope of $1/\lambda$, the reciprocal of lambda. Isoloss lines closer to the origin correspond to lower losses. The ideal, but normally unattainable, situation would be an isoloss line at the origin, which represents a loss of zero and means that the forecast for inflation is exactly on target and that the forecast for resource utilization is exactly equal to the normal level. However, the forecast Taylor curve shows the minimum sums of squares that are possible on each decision-making occasion. The best monetary policy therefore entails selecting a point on the Taylor curve so that the isoloss line for the loss function is as close to the origin as possible. This is the point at which the isoloss line is a tangent to the Taylor curve. Figure 3 shows an isoloss line that is a tangent to the Taylor curve at point B. For the given lambda, which determines the slope of the isoloss lines, this point thus represents a well-balanced monetary policy.

As I have emphasized, the position of the Taylor curve depends on the initial state of the economy at the time the decision is made. In a situation in which it is more difficult to stabilize resource utilization, the Taylor curve will be closer to the vertical axis than to the horizontal axis, for example like the dashed curve above point A. The point of tangency for an isoloss line with the same slope, which represents a well-balanced monetary policy, will then be at D. In a situation in which it is more difficult to stabilize inflation, the Taylor curve will instead be closer to the horizontal axis than to the vertical axis, for example like the dashed curve to the right of point C. The point of tangency for an isoloss line with the same slope will then be at E.

A central bank that has a low numerical value for lambda—that is, a lower weight placed on the stability of the real economy—has steeper isoloss lines. For a central bank with such a lambda, the point of contact with a given Taylor curve for a given decision-making situation will be higher up to the left in the figure—for example, at point A—where the Taylor curve is steeper. The inflation forecast will then be closer to the target but the forecast for resource utilization will deviate more from the normal level. A central bank with a high numerical value for lambda—that is, a high weight placed on the stability of the real economy—has isoloss lines that are flatter. In the case of such a lambda, the point of contact will be lower down to the left—for example, at point C—where the Taylor curve is flatter. The inflation forecast will then be further from the target while the forecast for resource utilization will be closer to a normal level.

Neither the Riksbank nor other central banks, except Norges Bank, have yet announced whether they apply a specific lambda and if so what this lambda is.[10] In those cases where the decisions are made by a committee made up of several members, as at the Riksbank, it is possible that different members attach different degrees of importance to the stability of the real economy.

If the central bank's forecasts are only based on a known model, like the Riksbank's main model Ramses, it is possible to determine the position of the forecast Taylor curve and which point the Riksbank's main scenario in each *Monetary Policy Report* corresponds to.[11] In practice, the Riksbank's forecasts and those of other central banks are based on several different models and a great deal of judgment. This means that it is not quite as easy to determine the position of the forecast Taylor curve. It is still possible, however, to enter the position of various forecast alternatives on the graph and at least assess whether the forecast is extreme in any respect with regard to the deviation of inflation from the target and the deviation of resource utilization from the normal level. As yet, it is in practice mainly a question of whether the choice of policy-rate path was extreme in either direction in the sense that the central bank gave considerable or very little relative weight to the stability of the real economy. Another interesting aspect to investigate is whether the

---

10. Bergo (2007) and Holmsen, Qvigstad, and Røisland (2007) report that optimal policy with $\lambda = 0.3$ has replicated policy projections published by Norges Bank (with a discount factor of 0.99 and a weight on interest-rate smoothing of 0.2).

11. This can be done using the methods developed in Adolfson, Laséen, Lindé, and Svensson (2011).

weight attached to the stability of the real economy actually has been constant over time. If it has not been constant then the central bank's loss function has not been consistent over time, or it is more complicated than the quadratic loss function that I have discussed here and that is regarded as normal and reasonable in the literature on monetary policy.

As a reference point, I here use an equal weight on stability of the inflation and output gaps, that is, a λ equal to one. The solid negatively sloped lines in panel "c" of figures 4, 5, and 6 and in figure 7 hence show an isoloss line for a forecast loss function with equal weight on inflation- and output-gap stabilization.

As an example of the use of an equal weight, in the Bluebook for the Federal Reserve's FOMC meeting in May 2002 (Federal Reserve Board 2002) there is a description of a method involving what is (arguably somewhat misleadingly) called a "Perfect Foresight Policy" that minimizes an intertemporal forecast loss function with equal weight on inflation-gap and output-gap stabilization (and with a small weight on interest-rate smoothing). This method was used in the Bluebooks at the time to present policy alternatives for the FOMC. Svensson and Tetlow (2005) provide a detailed description of this method, which calculates optimal policy in the Federal Reserve's FRB/US model using information from the Greenbook forecast. They argue that "Optimal Policy Projections" is a better name, since perfect foresight need not be assumed.[12]

Figures 6 and 7 and the situation in July 2009 can be studied more closely in the light of this discussion. For July 2009, the main and alternative repo-rate paths are very similar with regard to the degree of inflation-gap stabilization, although the main repo-rate path results in a slightly smaller mean squared gap for the inflation gap, as can be seen in panel "c" of figure 6. However, the repo-rate paths result in different degrees of output-gap stabilization, where the low repo-rate path stabilizes the output-gap better and the high repo-rate path worse than the main scenario.

For an equal weight on inflation- and output-gap stabilization the low repo-rate path results in lower intertemporal forecast loss. This is apparent from the isoloss line for λ equal to one that is shown in both figures 6 and 7 (in figure 6 the isoloss line looks horizontal because the scales for the horizontal and vertical axes are so different). For the

---

12. Bluebooks and other material from the FOMC meetings are published with a five-year lag and are available at www.federalreserve.gov.

main repo-rate path to give a lower loss than the low repo-rate path, one needs a value of λ lower than 0.08.

At the policy meeting of July 2009, the main repo-rate path entailed lowering the repo rate from 50 basis points (from the April 2009 decision) to 25 basis points and keeping it there through 2010. The low repo-rate path entailed lowering the repo rate to zero. I dissented in favor of the low repo-rate path, on the grounds that it would entail a better-balanced monetary policy, with higher resource utilization and without inflation deviating too far from the target. The detailed discussion at the meeting is published in Sveriges Riksbank (2009b), including arguments about the lower bound for the repo rate.[13]

Finally, before I move on to discuss the evaluation of monetary policy after the event, I would like to emphasize that ex ante evaluations have the major advantage that they can be carried out on an ongoing basis in real time and that you do not need to wait several years to see the outcomes for inflation and the real economy. It is hence possible to evaluate whether monetary policy *is* well-balanced currently, not only whether it *was* well-balanced in the past. If competent ex ante evaluations become a lasting feature of the ongoing public debate on monetary policy, they could constantly encourage the central banks to improve their policy and analysis.

Evaluation Ex Post—after the Fact

The most relevant starting point for an evaluation of monetary policy is, as I said earlier, the information and data that were available when the monetary policy decisions were made. That is an ex ante evaluation. However, an ex post analysis may also be relevant. The forecast evaluation that I discussed earlier was, for example, ex post. But an evaluation of monetary policy after the event can also provide valuable insights regarding the monetary policy conducted.

The question we should then ask is: given what we know today, what form would a better monetary policy have taken? Would it have been possible with a different monetary policy to achieve a better stabilization of resource utilization without undermining the stabilization of inflation, or vice versa? As this is an analysis in which we know what

---

13. As discussed in Goodhart and Rochet (2011), the Riksbank has chosen inefficient policies for a long period since October 2008. I have dissented, as discussed in Svensson (2011a).

actually happened and what the results were, it is rather likely that we will discover that this would in fact have been possible. We would then have to get to the bottom of why such a monetary policy was not chosen. Could any of the outcomes have been predicted ex ante? Anyone may of course have luck with a single forecast. But was there another forecaster who in a convincing way actually predicted the shocks to the economy that occurred and that the central bank missed?

A large part of this analysis will thus concern evaluating and explaining forecast errors—even individual errors—and deviations from the central bank's targets. It is actually fairer to focus on forecast errors than deviations from targets, as deviations from targets under flexible inflation targeting may be deliberate on the part of the central bank.

Evaluating the central bank's forecasts is thus important: that is, investigating whether the forecasts systematically overestimate or underestimate outcomes and so on. It is also interesting to compare forecast errors for inflation, for the real economy—irrespective of the measure of resource utilization used—and for the policy rate if the central bank publishes such a forecast. Which forecast errors are most relevant for explaining why monetary policy, with the benefit of hindsight, could have been better? What caused these forecast errors?

A disadvantage of an ex post evaluation is that we have to wait at least a couple of years to see the full impact of the monetary policy measures on inflation and the real economy. As I emphasized earlier, an ex ante evaluation can on the other hand be performed in real time as a part of the ongoing public debate on monetary policy.

Was Monetary Policy Credible?

The credibility of monetary policy is always an important factor. The credibility of an inflation-targeting regime is usually measured by the proximity of private-sector inflation expectations for different time horizons to the inflation target. The closer the expectations are to the target, the higher the degree of credibility. This provides a direct indication of the private sector's level of confidence in the ability of the central bank to meet the inflation target.

Figure 8 shows how inflation expectations among money-market agents developed in 2008 and early 2009. It is evident that expectations for both one and two years ahead have been revised significantly downward recently, which is hardly surprising given the development

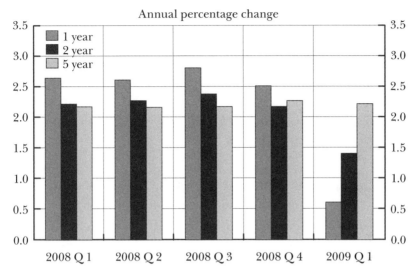

Figure 8. Inflation expectations among money-market
agents 1, 2, and 5 years ahead, 2008:Q1 to 2009:Q1
Sources: Prospera Research AB

of the economy. For the five-year horizon, however, the expectations
are well anchored around the target.

How well inflation expectations are anchored around the target also
has a direct impact on how well the central bank succeeds in meeting
the target and on the possibilities the central bank has to also stabilize
the real economy. This is because inflation expectations directly affect
price- and wage-setting in the economy. Stable inflation expectations
eliminate a potential source of shocks and make it easier for the central
bank to stabilize both inflation and the real economy. More stable inflation expectations affect the transformation mechanism of monetary
policy and shift the forecast Taylor curve in figure 3 closer to the origin
and make the trade-off between the stability of inflation and the stability of the real economy more favorable.

As the central bank's inflation forecasts in the short and medium
terms may deliberately deviate from the target, it is also interesting to
compare inflation expectations with the central bank's inflation forecasts. If the economic agents share the central bank's view of how inflation will approach the target, inflation expectations at different time
horizons should be close to the central bank's forecasts. The degree of
correspondence between inflation expectations and the central bank's

inflation forecasts then becomes a measure of how credible the central bank's inflation forecasts and analyses are. Such a correspondence between expectations and forecasts is of course also desirable for forecasts for the real economy and, not least, for forecasts for the policy rate, which I will now discuss.

Was the Implementation of Monetary Policy Effective?

I have spoken earlier about what characterizes efficient monetary policy decisions. This was in relation to the trade-off between stabilizing inflation and stabilizing the real economy given the information available at the time of the decision. Another important aspect is to investigate how effective the *implementation* of monetary policy has been, in the sense of affecting the economy in the desired direction and to the right amount. An effective implementation of monetary policy presupposes that there is a high level of private-sector confidence in the central bank with regard to both the inflation target and the monetary policy analysis. It also requires that the central bank is successful in communicating its analysis and intentions. In other words, a likely precondition for an effective monetary policy implementation is that the central bank is open and transparent.

Most central banks use a short-term interest rate as the policy rate to implement monetary policy. However, the actual policy rate in the few months prior to the next monetary policy decision plays a very minor role in the economy. Expectations regarding future policy rates, on the other hand, do play an important role. They affect interest rates with longer maturities which in turn are the interest rates that have an impact on the economic decisions of households and companies. The Riksbank and a few other central banks have taken this seriously and publish their own policy-rate paths to facilitate the formation of expectations regarding future policy rates and to influence these expectations more effectively.[14]

If the central bank is successful in its communication, the market participants should be able to predict rather well how new information or new shocks will affect the central bank's forecast for the policy rate. If the central bank's analysis is credible, the market's expectations regarding the future policy rate should also change in line with the

---

14. Blinder (1998) and Woodford (2005) emphasize the role of expectations in monetary policy and that monetary policy is largely the management of expectations.

Percent

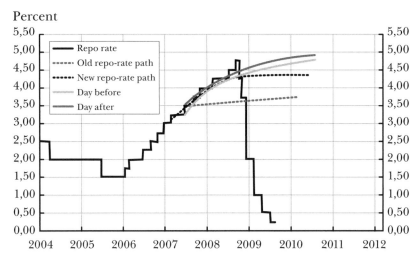

Figure 9. The Riksbank's repo-rate path and
market expectations, June 20, 2007
Source: The Riksbank

revised policy-rate path of the central bank. One way of evaluating how
effectively the central bank implements monetary policy is therefore
to simply investigate how well the market participants have predicted
the changes in the central bank's policy-rate path. We can also analyze
how well the expectations regarding the future policy rate adapt to the
central bank's new policy-rate path after the announcement.[15] Figures
9 through 11 are examples of the type of figures that can be studied
in this case. They relate to the policy decisions in June 2007, February
2009, and July 2009. The solid black line shows the actual repo-rate
path, the dark dotted line shows the new repo-rate path, the light dotted line shows the previous repo-rate path, the light solid line shows
market repo-rate expectations on the day before the announcement of
the policy decision, and the medium solid line shows the market expectations after the announcement.[16] June 2007 and February 2009 show
instances when the market anticipated the repo-rate path reasonably

---

15. A preliminary analysis of the policy implementation from February 2007 through
December 2008 is carried out in Svensson (2009b).

16. Market expectations are implied forward-rate curves that have been adjusted by the
staff for possible risk premiums, so as to be the staff's best estimate of market expectations
of future repo rates. Depending on the maturity, the forward-rate curve is derived from the
rates for STINA (Tomorrow-Next Stibor interest-rate swaps) contracts, FRAs (Forward Rate
Agreements), or interest-rate swaps.

Percent

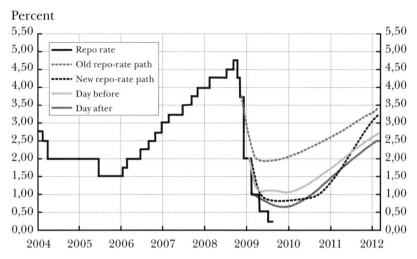

Figure 10. The Riksbank's repo-rate path and
market expectations, February 11, 2009
Source: The Riksbank

well and when expectations after the announcements were reasonably well in line with the new path. As discussed in Svensson (2009b), this has mostly been the case since the Riksbank introduced its own repo-rate path in February 2007. However, July 2009 (and also April 2009, not shown here) are instances when market expectations before and after the announcement differed considerably from the announced path and expected higher future repo rates. On those instances, the Riksbank's implementation of monetary policy has hence been less effective. The reasons for and consequences of such differences between market expectations and the published repo-rate path are discussed in the July 2009 minutes (Sveriges Riksbank 2009b) and in Svensson (2009a).[17]

Conclusions

Let me conclude by first returning to the question I raised at the start: when evaluating monetary policy with an inflation target, why is it not enough to simply compare outcomes and targets for inflation? One

---

17. From February 2010, market expectations have fallen much below the published repo-rate path. Aspects of this are discussed in Svensson (2011c).

Percent

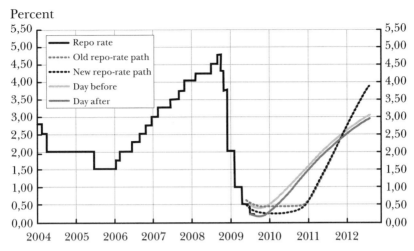

Figure 11. The Riksbank's repo rate path and
market expectations, July 2, 2009

Source: The Riksbank

reason is that inflation reacts with varying time lags and to different de-grees to monetary policy measures. Inflation is also affected by shocks that are difficult to identify or that occur at a later date. The central bank does not therefore have complete control over inflation. Inflation can be on target even if the central bank has acted wrongly but been lucky, or deviate from the target even if the central bank has acted cor-rectly but been unlucky. Another reason is that the Riksbank and other central banks with inflation targets conduct flexible inflation targeting, which means that they strive to both stabilize inflation around the infla-tion target and stabilize the real economy. Inflation may then deliber-ately deviate from the target if this provides a better balance between stable inflation and a stable real economy.

As there is a significant time lag before monetary policy measures have an impact on inflation and the real economy, monetary policy is most effective when it is based on forecasts. With flexible inflation targeting, it is thus a question of choosing a policy-rate path so that the forecast for inflation and the real economy stabilizes inflation and the real economy as effectively as possible. It is thus possible and desir-able to evaluate monetary policy ex ante and in real time by assessing to what extent the central bank's forecasts optimally stabilize both in-flation and the real economy. However, before we do this it is neces-sary to assess whether the central bank's previous forecasts have been reasonably accurate and of good quality, for example, in comparison with those of other forecasters.

With the help of a modified Taylor curve—a forecast Taylor curve that illustrates the efficient trade-off between stabilizing the inflation forecast around the inflation target and stabilizing the resource-utilization forecast around a normal level—it is possible to evaluate (ex ante and even in real time) more precisely whether monetary policy is efficient and well-balanced. Forecast variability trade-offs can be illustrated by plotting mean-square gaps of inflation and output-gap forecasts for alternative policy-rate paths.

It is also of interest to evaluate monetary policy ex post—that is, after the event. As target deviations and forecast deviations are unavoidable due to the considerable degree of uncertainty about the future development of the economy and the delayed impact of monetary policy measures, an ex post evaluation is mainly a question of whether it would have been possible to predict the shocks and deviations that occurred, particularly if other forecasters have systematically been able to predict them.

It is also relevant to assess the credibility of monetary policy in terms of how well inflation expectations correspond to the inflation target. The degree of correspondence between expectations and the central bank's forecasts for inflation and the real economy is also a measure of the credibility of the central bank's analyses and forecasts.

As monetary policy is mainly about managing expectations, particularly expectations concerning future policy rates, it is of great interest to see to what extent a published policy-rate path has been predicted by the market and other forecasters. It is also interesting to know to what extent market expectations are adapted to the new policy-rate path. This can be seen as a measure of how effectively the central bank implements monetary policy.

REFERENCES

Adolfson, Malin, Stefan Laséen, Jesper Lindé, and Lars E. O. Svensson. 2011. "Optimal Monetary Policy in an Operational Medium-Sized DSGE Model." *Journal of Money, Credit and Banking* 43:1287–1331.

Adolfson, Malin, Stefan Laséen, Jesper Lindé, and Mattias Villani. 2008. "Evaluating an Estimated New Keynesian Small Open Economy Model." *Journal of Economic Dynamics and Control* 32:2690–2721.

Bergo, Jarle. 2007. "Interest Rate Projections in Theory and Practice." Speech on January 26, 2007, www.norges-bank.no.

Blinder, Alan. 1998. *Central Banking in Theory and Practice.* Cambridge, MA: MIT Press.

Federal Reserve Board. 2002. "Monetary Policy Alternatives." Prepared for the Federal Open Market Committee meeting May 2, 2002, www.federalreserve.gov.

Giavazzi, Francesco, and Frederic S. Mishkin. 2006. "An Evaluation of Swedish Monetary Policy Between 1995 and 2005." Reports from the Riksdag 2006/07: RFR1, www.riksdagen.se.

Goodhart, Charles, and Jean-Charles Rochet. 2011. "An Evaluation of the Riksbank's Monetary Policy and Work with Financial Stability 2005–2010." Reports from the Riksdag 2010/11:RFR5, www.riksdagen.se.

Heikensten, Lars, and Anders Vredin. 2002. "The Art of Targeting Inflation." Sveriges Riksbank Economic Review 4/2002: 5–34.

Holmsen, Amund, Jan F. Qvigstad, and Øistein Røisland. 2007. "Implementing and Communicating Optimal Monetary Policy." Norges Bank Staff Memo No. 2007/3, www.norges-bank.no.

King, Mervyn. 1994. "Monetary Policy in the UK." *Fiscal Studies* 15(3):109–28.

———. 1997. "Changes in UK Monetary Policy: Rules and Discretion in Practice." *Journal of Monetary Economics* 39:81–97.

Qvigstad, Jan F. 2005. "When Does an Interest Rate Path 'Look Good'? Criteria for an Appropriate Future Interest Rate Path." Norges Bank Working Paper 2005/6.

Svensson, Lars E. O. 1997. "Inflation Forecast Targeting: Implementing and Monitoring Inflation Targets." *European Economic Review* 41:1111–46.

———. 1999. "Inflation Targeting: Some Extensions." *Scandinavian Journal of Economics* 101:337–361.

———. 2001. "Independent Review of the Operation of Monetary Policy in New Zealand." Report to the Minister of Finance, www.larseosvensson.net.

———, Kjetil Houg, Haakon O. Aa. Solheim, and Erling Steigum. 2002. "An Independent Review of Monetary Policy and Institutions in Norway." Norges Bank Watch 2002, www.larseosvensson.net.

———. 2005. "Monetary Policy with Judgment: Forecast Targeting." *International Journal of Central Banking* 1(1):1–54.

———, and Robert J. Tetlow. 2005. "Optimal Policy Projections." *International Journal of Central Banking* 1(3): 177–207.

———, and Michael Woodford. 2005. "Implementing Optimal Policy through Inflation-Forecast Targeting." In *The Inflation-Targeting Debate,* eds. Ben S. Bernanke and Michael Woodford, 19–83. Chicago: University of Chicago Press.

————. 2009a. "Policy Expectations and Policy Evaluations: The Role of Transparency and Communication." *Sveriges Riksbank Economic Review,* forthcoming, www.larseosvensson.net.

————. 2009b. "Transparency under Flexible Inflation Targeting: Experiences and Challenges." *Sveriges Riksbank Economic Review* 1/2009:5–44, www.riks bank.com.

————. 2011a. "For a Better Monetary Policy: Focus on Inflation and Unemployment." Speech at Luleå University of Technology, March 8, 2011, www.lars eosvensson.net.

————. 2011b. "Inflation Targeting." In *Handbook of Monetary Economics, Volume 3a and 3b,* eds. Benjamin M. Friedman and Michael Woodford. Amsterdam: North-Holland.

————. 2011c. "Practical Monetary Policy: Experiences from Sweden and the U.S." Prepared for the Fall 2011 issue of *Brookings Papers on Economic Activity.* Brookings Institution.

Sveriges Riksbank. 2009a. "Material for Assessing Monetary Policy 2006–2008." February 2009, www.riksbank.com.

————. 2009b. "Minutes of the Executive Board's Monetary Policy Meeting on 1 July 2009," www.riksbank.com.

————. 2010. "Monetary Policy in Sweden 2010," www.riksbank.se.

Taylor, John B. 1979. "Estimation and Control of a Macroeconomic Model with Rational Expectations." *Econometrica* 47:1267–86.

Wickman-Parak, Barbro. 2008. "The Riksbank's Inflation Target." Speech on June 9, 2008, www.riksbank.com.

Woodford, Michael. 2003. *Interest and Prices: Foundations of a Theory of Monetary Policy.* Princeton, NJ: Princeton University Press.

————. 2005. "Central-Bank Communication and Policy Effectiveness." In *The Greenspan Era: Lessons for the Future,* Federal Reserve Bank of Kansas City.

Woodford, Michael. 2007a. "The Case for Forecast Targeting as a Monetary Policy Strategy." *Journal of Economic Perspectives,* Fall 2007.

————. 2007b. "Forecast Targeting as a Monetary Policy Strategy: Policy Rules in Practice." In *From the Great Moderation to the Great Deviation: A Round-Trip Journey Based on the Work of John B. Taylor,* eds. Evan Koenig and Robert Leeson, forthcoming.

PART IV

Taylor's Influence on Policymaking: Firsthand Accounts

ELEVEN

OVERVIEW

Ben S. Bernanke

It is a privilege for me to open this conference dedicated to our colleague and friend, John Taylor. John's influence on monetary theory and policy has been profound indeed. That influence has been manifest in undergraduate lecture halls and graduate seminar rooms, in the best research journals, and in the highest ranks of government. His ability to crystallize important analytical insights and apply them to policy issues is unsurpassed. Indeed, in a speech a few years ago, I noted three concepts named after John that are central to understanding our macroeconomic experience of the past three decades—the Taylor curve, the Taylor rule, and the Taylor principle (Bernanke, 2004). I'd like to take a few minutes to review John's career and impressive body of work.

After receiving his PhD from Stanford nearly thirty-five years ago, John began his career as an assistant professor at Columbia University. Even in those early years, John revealed his interest in applying the analytical tools of economics to practical policy issues. He took a leave of absence from academia in 1976–77 to serve on the staff of the Council of Economic Advisers. I suspect that the circumstances of the mid-1970s intensified John's motivation to help improve economic performance through sound policymaking.

Ben S. Bernanke is chairman of the Federal Reserve Board. This chapter is based on his opening remarks to the Conference on John Taylor's Contributions to Monetary Theory and Policy, Federal Reserve Bank of Dallas, October 12, 2007.

During the late 1970s and early 1980s, John published a number of highly influential papers, including: "Conditions for Unique Solutions in Stochastic Macroeconomic Models with Rational Expectations," "Estimation and Control of a Macroeconomic Model with Rational Expectations," "Aggregate Dynamics and Staggered Contracts," and "Solution and Maximum Likelihood Estimation of Dynamic Nonlinear Rational Expectations Models." (As you can tell, John has always had a penchant for catchy titles.) Beyond its important technical contributions, this work showed that the insights and methods of the rational expectations revolution could be applied to models with sticky wages and prices. That observation has proved enormously influential in subsequent policy research.

The rational expectations revolution helped to kill the idea of a long-run trade-off between the *levels* of inflation and unemployment. However, John's analysis showed that, in the presence of aggregate supply shocks, attempts by monetary policymakers to reduce the *volatility* of inflation over time could be associated with higher volatility in unemployment, and vice versa. John's visual depiction of this policy trade-off has come to be known as the Taylor curve. Interestingly, John's work anticipated the possibility that improvements in the conduct of monetary policy or changes in the structure of the economy could result in a shift of the Taylor curve—that is, a change in the ability of policy to smooth both inflation and employment. And indeed, what economists have dubbed the Great Moderation—a simultaneous reduction in the volatility of inflation and the volatility of real economic activity—has occurred in the United States and in many other economies over the past quarter-century.

Over the course of the 1980s, John continued his work on rational expectations issues and monetary policy and macroeconomics more generally. He also began to broaden his focus to matters of international economics. He developed a multi-country rational expectations econometric model—a truly ambitious undertaking, especially in light of the limited computing capabilities of the era. By this point in his career, John had firmly established his reputation as a leader in the profession.

In 1989, John became a member of the first President Bush's Council of Economic Advisers. During the next four years, he played a key role in shaping the administration's positions on macroeconomic, fiscal, international finance, and trade issues. The U.S. economy was entering a difficult period at that point. Among other problems, significant pressures on bank balance sheets were beginning to emerge that would damp economic growth for the next several years. While dealing with the serious economic issues of the time, John and the other members of the Council simultaneously produced an impressive manifesto for policymaking. They developed a rules-based approach to the conduct of monetary and fiscal policy and published it in 1990 in the *Economic Report of the President.*

That essay laid the foundation for what is perhaps John's most well-known contribution to economics—the simple description of the determinants of monetary policy that eventually became known as the Taylor rule.[1] John's analysis triggered an avalanche of studies examining the stabilization properties of Taylor rules in the context of macroeconomic models. Other work investigated the ability of variants of the Taylor rule to describe empirically the actual course of monetary policy in the United States and in other economies.

The Taylor rule also embeds a basic principle of sound monetary policy that has subsequently been referred to as the Taylor principle.[2] According to this principle, when a shock causes a shift in the inflation rate, the central bank must adjust the nominal interest rate by more than one-for-one. This ensures that the real interest rate moves in the right direction to restore price stability. The Taylor principle provides essential guidance for central banks on how to anchor long-run inflation expectations and foster stable growth and low inflation.

Ever since its inception, John has emphasized that the Taylor rule should not be applied mechanistically. The world is far too complicated for that. But he has argued that such rules can serve as useful benchmarks for the practical conduct of monetary policy. In fact, policymakers at the Federal Reserve and many other central banks do routinely consult various policy rules as they make judgments on the appropriate stance of monetary policy.

After a decade back at Stanford, Taylor was called again to Washington by President Bush—this time the current President Bush. He served as under-secretary for international affairs at the U.S. Treasury from 2001 through 2005. Our economy faced severe challenges during that

---

1. The number "two" and its inverse, one-half, played a key role in this rule: The benchmark setting for the federal funds rate would be 2 percent, plus the current rate of inflation, plus one-half times the gap between current inflation and 2 percent, plus one-half times the output gap.

2. This principle originally became apparent through numerical simulations of macroeconomic models with rational expectations (including Taylor's multi-country model); refer also to Bryant, Hooper, and Mann (1993). The phrase "Taylor Principle" was introduced by Woodford (2001), who demonstrated this principle analytically in a stylized New Keynesian model.

period—the terrorist attacks of September 11, a recession and the threat of deflation, corporate governance scandals, and economic issues posed by the conflicts in Afghanistan and Iraq. Suffice it to say, John earned his stripes as the leader of the "Global Financial Warriors." As detailed in his book of the same title, John worked extensively on the financial reconstruction of Iraq and on the development of financial tools for fighting terrorism. The Treasury Department recognized his efforts in 2004 with its Distinguished Service Award and in 2005 with the Alexander Hamilton Award for leadership in international finance.

After his stint at Treasury, John returned once again to the less tumultuous life of a professor, ensconced in his offices at Stanford University and the Hoover Institution. I'm sure that, in between teaching and guiding the work of graduate students, he will continue to offer insightful commentary on monetary policy and other economic issues. And doubtless he will also continue to do path-breaking research. Indeed, with our appetites whetted by the Taylor rule, principle, and curve, we now look forward to the Taylor dictum, the Taylor hyperbola, and maybe even the Taylor conundrum.

REFERENCES

Bernanke, Ben S. 2004. "The Great Moderation." Remarks at the meetings of the Eastern Economic Association, February 20, Washington, D.C. http://www .federalreserve.gov/boarddocs/speeches/2004/20040220/default.htm

Bryant, Ralph C., Peter Hooper, and Catherine L. Mann. 1993. *Evaluating Policy Regimes: New Research in Empirical Macroeconomics.* Washington, DC: Brookings Institution.

Taylor, John B. 2007. *Global Financial Warriors: The Untold Story of International Finance in the Post 9/11 World.* New York: W.W. Norton & Co.

Woodford, Michael. 2001. "The Taylor Rule and Optimal Monetary Policy." *American Economic Review* 91(2):232–237.

TWELVE

THE VIEW FROM INSIDE THE FED

Janet Yellen

In looking back at John Taylor's work, I am struck by how thoroughly his research has affected the way policymakers and economists analyze the economy and approach monetary policy. His influence and, indeed, his name are heard whenever people talk about monetary policy, whether it's the Taylor curve, the Taylor principle, or, of course, the Taylor rule. I'm told that an unwary indexer once even credited him with the Taylor expansion that we all learned in our calculus classes— something that surely made Brook Taylor spin in his grave.

I'll focus my comments today on the aspects of Taylor's research that have shaped the discussion of monetary policy issues at the Federal Reserve and at central banks around the world. I have divided Taylor's contributions to monetary policy into three branches: analyzing nominal rigidities, modeling the global economy, and developing principles of monetary policy.

To start with, it's useful to go back to the debates raging in macroeconomic theory in the 1970s when Taylor began his research. Recall that at that time, and through the 1980s, many models incorporating

I am deeply grateful to John Williams for outstanding assistance in the preparation of these remarks. Janet Yellen is vice chair of the Board of Governors of the Federal Reserve System. The views expressed in this chapter are those of the author and should not be attributed to the Federal Reserve.

rational expectations had the feature that predictable monetary policy actions would have no effect on the real economy. This result led many economists to criticize the Fed's dual mandate of price stability and maximum growth on the grounds that efforts at macroeconomic stabilization using monetary policy were at best ineffective and potentially destabilizing if "surprise" inflations were used to boost the economy. Accordingly, the policy recommendation was that central banks should focus exclusively on maintaining price stability and abandon all efforts at taming the business cycle.

Much of this literature assumed that prices and wages were completely flexible, adjusting day by day to changing economic conditions. Taylor and several others challenged this assumption and the corresponding conclusion that rational expectations implied monetary policy irrelevance and the need to ignore output stabilization. His paper with Ned Phelps (1977) showed that even under rational expectations, if prices or wages are sticky, systematic monetary policy had real effects and could be used to stabilize fluctuations in real output.[1]

In a later paper, Taylor (1979) showed that central banks face a trade-off in terms of the magnitude of fluctuations in inflation and output. This result became enshrined in what is now commonly known as the Taylor curve, which plots out the frontier of the feasible set of outcomes in terms of the variances of inflation and the output gap. Importantly, the Taylor curve is entirely consistent with the Fed's dual mandate—the twin goals of stabilizing inflation and output—in the face of a short-run trade-off in achieving them. Nowadays, discussions of monetary policy strategy are often boiled down to "picking a point on the Taylor curve."

Taylor's research showed that nominal rigidities were not merely a theoretical possibility, but were a feature of the actual economy. He developed and estimated his now-famous model of staggered nominal wage-setting (Taylor 1980). This paper made two important breakthroughs. First, his model was an early example of what is now commonly referred to as a "New Keynesian Phillips Curve," in which prices depend on expectations of future prices as well as past prices. Second, he provided strong empirical evidence of nominal wage rigidities in the United States, supporting the case for a stabilization role for monetary policy even in models with deep micro foundations and rational expectations.

---

1. See also Fischer (1977).

Moreover, the insight into the key role played by rigidities in wage-setting continues to influence the development of macro models and our understanding of the effects of monetary policy on the economy. Although many simple macro models used in teaching and research assume sticky prices and abstract from sticky wages, in larger models used in central banks, such as the Federal Reserve Board/United States (FRB/US) model used at the Board of Governors, wage rigidities play a central role. In addition, recent research using micro-founded Dynamic Stochastic General Equilibrium (DSGE) models as well as the papers at this conference have confirmed that wage rigidities are important empirically and have also improved our understanding of the role of sticky wages as a source of the trade-off policymakers face and of the welfare costs of business cycles.[2]

The second branch of Taylor's research that has had a lasting influence on our policy discussions is his work on developing empirical macro-econometric models with rational expectations. This work also led him to collaborate with Ray Fair in the early 1980s to develop a method to simulate nonlinear large-scale rational expectations models that is still used at central banks twenty-five years later (Fair and Taylor 1983). During the 1980s, he single-handedly developed an estimated model of the G7 economies that incorporated rational expectations, forward-looking behavior by households and firms, sticky prices and wages, and international linkages in a large-scale macro-econometric model (Taylor 1993a). This project demonstrated conclusively that it was possible to construct, estimate, and simulate such a model for real-world policy analysis. At the time, he was one of just a few academics working on such large-scale models. If it were not for Taylor's success at keeping the flame alive during that period, I fear that the ongoing development of new generations of macro models that incorporate better micro foundations and explicit treatment of expectations at the Board of Governors and other central banks would never have occurred.

Finally, let me turn to what I think of as the most important of Taylor's contributions to policymaking: the development of a set of principles of good monetary policy. Perhaps not surprisingly, these principles are each exemplified by the Taylor rule.

The first principle is that policy should be systematic and predictable. Remember that his famous paper was titled "Discretion versus

---

2. See, for example, Erceg, Henderson, and Levin (2000) and Christiano, Eichenbaum, and Evans (2005).

Policy Rules in Practice" (Taylor, 1993b). This principle permeates the analysis and discussions at the Fed today. The board staff regularly reports the policy prescriptions from estimated monetary policy rules, and the model simulations that are used to illustrate risks assume policy will respond according to an estimated policy rule. Of course, extraordinary or novel circumstances can arise where policy needs to deviate from its standard approach, but that should be the exception, not—so to speak—the rule.

I should mention at this point how influential Taylor's call for systematic policy has been at the Fed. When I became a governor back in 1994, I was privy to little analysis that used monetary policy rules. At the time, I argued that the Federal Open Market Committee (FOMC) should, at a minimum, routinely monitor the recommendations of Taylor-type policy rules as a check on its judgmental decisions. In particular, I felt that the internal use of such Taylor-type rules might prove helpful in preventing the FOMC from overreacting to shocks—falling into the so-called "thermostat trap." Nowadays, I am pleased to say, such analysis is routinely provided and discussed.

The second principle is the Taylor principle, namely, that the nominal interest rate must rise or fall by more than one-for-one with a corresponding movement in the inflation rate.[3] In a variety of models where spending depends on real interest rates, the Taylor principle is a necessary condition to avoid potentially catastrophic outcomes. In forward-looking models it is needed to assure a unique rational expectations equilibrium; in backward-looking models it is needed to avoid explosive behavior. This principle seems obvious now, but Clarida, Galí, and Gertler (2000), among others, have argued that the Federal Reserve did not satisfy it during the 1970s, contributing to the poor economic performance during this period. Although there is an ongoing debate about how the Fed went wrong in the 1970s, we all agree that we need to satisfy the Taylor principle today.

The third principle, and one that is embedded in the Taylor rule, is that policy should "lean against the wind" in response to deviations from the desired levels of inflation and output. In response to a demand shock that lowers output and inflation, the funds rate is cut, restoring output and inflation back to their desired levels. In response to a supply shock that lowers output but raises inflation, the Taylor rule implicitly embeds the trade-offs of the objectives in the dual mandate

---

3. This principle is discussed in Taylor (1999a). Woodford (2001) is one source for referring to this as the Taylor principle.

by producing a path for policy that ultimately restores inflation to its long-run values but does so only gradually, avoiding sharp swings in output. Of course, the specification of the monetary policy rule that best achieves the central bank's goals is the subject of ongoing research, but the basic principle is widely accepted.

Finally, the fourth principle is that any monetary policy rule should be robust to uncertainty.[4] Indeed, the specification of the original Taylor rule was not chosen to be optimal in any one particular model, but was based on its "good" performance in monetary-policy-rule evaluation exercises using a variety of macroeconomic models.[5] This approach places greatest weight on getting the "basics" right; that is, it emphasizes policy prescriptions in which we have the most confidence. This approach is purposefully modest in that it does not attempt to take advantage of all the potential benefits of the optimal policy in a given model. In fact, subsequent research has shown that the cost of insuring against model misspecification is relatively small because fully optimal rules yield typically only small stabilization benefits over simple rules like the Taylor rule.[6]

Unlike the other principles which are uncontroversial, this last principle is still the subject of research and debate. But, based on my experience, Taylor's position on the benefits of robustness seems the right one to me. As a policymaker who relies on models and forecasts myself, I recognize the great degree of uncertainty about all aspects of our models and our limited ability to predict the future. Indeed, one of the strengths of the FOMC is that it brings together nineteen different views of how the economy behaves and nineteen different forecasts of the future. It would be a mistake to ignore these differences and rely too much on one particular model to guide our decision-making.

Looking ahead, the biggest challenge for macroeconomists and monetary policymakers in creating more realistic models will be how to incorporate some forms of deviations from perfect rationality and knowledge in macro models used for policy analysis. This may take the form of near-rational behavior as in behavioral economics or bounded rationality as in models of learning. I should note that one of Taylor's (1975) earliest papers was concerned with the behavior of the economy while people learned. The asset price movements over the past decade

---

4. See Taylor (1993 and 1999b) and McCallum (1988) for further discussion of this principle.

5. See the volume edited by Bryant, Hooper, and Mann (1993).

6. See, for example, Levin, Wieland, and Williams (1999).

amply illustrate that the economy does not always behave the way our standard models predict. More generally, small deviations from full rationality in consumer or firm behavior can have large consequences on the behavior of the macroeconomy. This is a big challenge, but I am confident the payoffs will be large.

References

Bryant, Ralph C., Peter Hooper, and Catherine L. Mann. 1993. *Evaluating Policy Regimes: New Research in Empirical Macroeconomics.* Washington, DC: Brookings Institution.

Calvo, Guillermo. 1983. "Staggered Prices in a Utility Maximizing Framework." *Journal of Monetary Economics* 12(3) (September): 383–98.

Christiano, Lawrence J., Martin Eichenbaum, and Charles L. Evans. 2005. "Nominal Rigidities and the Dynamic Effects of a Shock to Monetary Policy." *Journal of Political Economy* 113(1) (February): 1–45.

Clarida, Richard, Jordi Galí, and Mark Gertler. 2000. "Monetary Policy Rules and Macroeconomic Stability: Evidence and Some Theory." *Quarterly Journal of Economics* 115(1) (February): 147–180.

Erceg, Christopher J., Dale W. Henderson, and Andrew T. Levin. 2000. "Optimal Monetary Policy with Staggered Wage and Price Contracts." *Journal of Monetary Economics* 46(2) (October): 281–313.

Fair, Ray C., and John B. Taylor. "Solution and Maximum Likelihood Estimation of Dynamic Nonlinear Rational Expectations Models." *Econometrica* 51(4) (July): 1169–85.

Fischer, Stanley. 1977. "Long-term Contracts, Rational Expectations, and the Optimal Money Supply Rule." *Journal of Political Economy* 85(1) (February): 191–205.

Levin, Andrew, Volker Wieland, and John Williams. 1999. "Robustness of Simple Monetary Policy Rules under Model Uncertainty." In *Monetary Policy Rules,* ed. John Taylor, 263–99. Chicago: University of Chicago Press.

McCallum, Bennett T. 1988. "Robustness Properties of a Rule for Monetary Policy." *Carnegie-Rochester Conference Series on Public Policy* 29 (Autumn): 173–203.

Phelps, Edmund S., and John B. Taylor. 1977. "Stabilizing Powers of Monetary Policy under Rational Expectations." *Journal of Political Economy* 85(1): 163–90.

Rotemberg, Julio J. 1982. "Sticky Prices in the United States." *Journal of Political Economy* 90(6) (December): 1187–1211.

Taylor, John B. 1975. "Monetary Policy during a Transition to Rational Expectations." *Journal of Political Economy* 83(5) (October): 1009–21.

————. 1979. "Estimation and Control of a Macroeconomic Model with Rational Expectations." *Econometrica* 47(5) (September): 1267–86.

————. 1980. "Aggregate Dynamics and Staggered Contracts." *Journal of Political Economy* 88(1) (February): 1–23.

————. 1993a. *Macroeconomic Policy in a World Economy.* New York: W.W. Norton & Co.

————. 1993b. "Discretion versus Policy Rules in Practice." *Carnegie-Rochester Conference Series on Public Policy* 39:195–214.

————. 1999a. "An Historical Analysis of Monetary Policy Rules." In *Monetary Policy Rules,* ed. John Taylor. Chicago: University of Chicago Press.

————. 1999b. "The Robustness and Efficiency of Monetary Policy Rules as Guidelines for Interest Rate Setting by the European Central Bank." *Journal of Monetary Economics* 43(3) (June): 655–79.

Woodford, Michael. 2001. "The Taylor Rule and Optimal Monetary Policy." *American Economic Association Papers and Proceedings* 91(2) (May): 232–37.

THIRTEEN

THE VIEW FROM INSIDE THE EUROPEAN CENTRAL BANK

Otmar Issing

Before I had the privilege to meet John Taylor personally—being still at the university—I was deeply impressed by his monumental contributions to modern macroeconomics. In short it is a vast array of concepts and models that have become common currency in monetary economics. Quoting from Taylor's (1977) list of the five key components of modern macroeconomics, at least two of them—the *third:* the existence of a short-run trade-off between inflation and unemployment; and the *fifth:* monetary policy decisions are best thought of as rules or reaction functions—rest on Taylor's own lifetime contributions to economic thinking.

Taylor contracts—together with Stanley Fischer's (1977) alternative specification of sticky wages—have been the technical device through which the newly discovered rational expectations paradigm could start a long transition from abstract theory to applied macro-analysis. I surmise that without Taylor's model of staggered wage formation, that transition would have taken longer. True, Bob Lucas's information-based way to explain monetary policy non-neutralities in the short run

I would like to thank Massimo Rostagno for his valuable contribution.

Otmar Issing is president of the Center of Financial Studies at Frankfurt Goethe University. From 1998–2006, he was a member of the executive board of the European Central Bank.

under rational expectations provides a beautiful alternative theory to sticky contracts. But that beautiful theory still awaits to this very day a convincing empirical validation. Taylor wage contracts, instead, spawned a great blossoming of empirical models of price and wage rigidities that proved critical to the building of the new macroeconomic consensus. That consensus could solidify, in my view, only because: "[it] is practical in the sense that it is having a beneficial effect on macroeconomic policy, especially monetary policy, and has resulted in improvements in policy in the last 15 years" (Taylor 1997). I suspect that without those practical implications—without a demonstration that rational expectations models can generate reasonable econometrics and fit the data satisfactorily—the rational expectations revolution, and all that it meant for central bankers like myself, could hardly have born all the fruits that it did in retrospect.

"Practicality" is a characteristic which I learned to fully appreciate when I had become a central banker. Taylor is for me an outstanding—and rare—example combining research at the frontier and demonstrating always a sense for the needs of practical policymakers. My gratitude on that is not just abstract; Taylor's visit to the European Central Bank (ECB) when we were in the midst of preparation for the start of our monetary policy was of great importance for us, including the opportunity to discuss so many issues in an open and at the same time confidential way with him.

He did not just present wonderful ideas or models but had an understanding for the extreme uncertainty we were in before the start of monetary union—uncertainty on data and models, plus uncertainties related to the interactions of a new central bank with the markets and the public at large.

Let me now come to Taylor's eponymous creature, the most famous of all—and, I guess, the most beloved by its father—the Taylor rule.

Once, the headline of a *U.S. News & World Report* article about his monetary policy rule was "Amaze Your Friends! Predict the Fed's Next Move!" Having spent part of my time as a central banker objecting to statements such as that one—and having argued time and again against oversimplifications of the monetary policy problem—let me pay tribute to Taylor's last and perhaps most important invention.

The models we use are nowhere near the point where it is possible to obtain a tightly specified policy rule that could be recommended for practical use with great confidence. Nonetheless, the Taylor rule embodies one fundamental finding of modern economics. At first thought, a discretionary response to shocks might seem exactly what one would expect of a professional central banker. After all, each economic contingency is a unique combination of circumstances that is in its way unprecedented, and will likely never repeat itself again in that precise form. So, each new contingency would seem to command a different, tailor-made—and I apologize for the inadvertent quotation—response on the part of monetary authorities.

There is some grain of truth to this. But forty years of reflections on the role of expectations in macroeconomics and Taylor in 1993 have taught us that monetary policy is not a sequence of isolated policy actions. When forming their expectations, agents seek to capture the general pattern of monetary policies, and it is that pattern that matters in shaping their economic behavior. Therefore, the relevant problem to solve for central banks is not so much, say, about the size and the timing of a given interest-rate move in response to a particular contingency. It is about the strategy for repeatedly adjusting the policy instrument in response to the state of the economy, whatever this might be.

The risk of discretionary decisions creating time inconsistency and causing moral hazard is prevalent in so many fields of policymaking. Taylor never lost sight of these problems. Therefore, one should not be surprised to find a chapter subtitle "Rules versus Discretion" in his recent book *Global Financial Warriors* (2007) when analyzing the practice of International Monetary Fund lending.

The Taylor rule has become a benchmark for monetary policy in many respects. At the ECB we were confronted with extreme uncertainty on data for the output gap and the equilibrium interest rate (Issing, Gaspar, Angeloni, and Tristani 2001). Notwithstanding this difficulty, it was important always to monitor estimates of the Taylor rule using a variety of data. In macroeconomics the Taylor rule also serves as a starting point for many approaches like models on learning (Walsh 2007).

This is what I take away from his revered 1993 paper: a formal, rigorous, and memorable illustration that monetary policy is about commitment and strategic design. Present-day monetary theory and best central banking practice are founded on this bedrock principle, which Taylor—as only the greatest thinkers can do—has made straightforward and tangible.

References

Taylor, John B. 1997. "A Core of Practical Macroeconomics." *American Economic Review Papers and Proceedings* 87(2):233–35.

Fischer, Stanley. 1977. "Long-Term Contracts, Rational Expectations, and the Optimal Money Supply Rule." *Journal of Political Economy* 85.

Issing, Otmar, Vitor Gaspar, Ignazio Angeloni, and Oreste Tristani. 2001. *Monetary Policy in the Euro Area*. Cambridge: Cambridge University Press.

Walsh, Carl E. 2007. "The Contribution of Theory to Practice in Monetary Policy: Recent Developments." In *Monetary Policy, A Journey from Theory to Practice*, ed. European Central Bank, Frankfurt.

ʝ

FOURTEEN

THE VIEW FROM CENTRAL BANKS IN EMERGING MARKETS

Guillermo Ortiz

As a central banker, it's hard for me to envision monetary policy today without the framework developed by John Taylor. His contributions, not only to monetary theory but to economics in general, have been of great relevance and have been widely put into practice, particularly in central banks.

In this short presentation, I discuss two related issues. Firstly, the recent Mexican experience in the conduct of monetary policy. By providing this overview, the relevance of John's work for countries like Mexico becomes evident. And secondly, I discuss some of John's main contributions and the way they have paved a new path in monetary economics.

I. Monetary Policy: The Mexican Experience

During the eighties, as a result of academic progress and the experience of many countries, significant changes in central banking started to take place. In particular, priority was given to inflation control and

Guillermo Ortiz is chairman of Grupo Financiero Banorte-IXE. He was governor of the Bank of Mexico from January 1998 to December 2009.

a trend toward granting autonomy to central banks began throughout the world. In the case of Mexico, in 1993, autonomy was granted to *Banco de México*. In addition, preserving the stability of the currency's purchasing power was set at the constitutional level as monetary policy's main objective.

With the adoption of a floating exchange rate regime at the end of 1994, monetary policy became the nominal anchor of the Mexican economy. This was a difficult step because we had no prior experience with floating exchange rates, nor did any other emerging market. After the financial crisis of 1995, monetary policy focused on both reestablishing orderly conditions in financial markets and containing inflationary pressures. These actions were accompanied by significant fiscal restraint, financial and credit-support programs, and the liquidity provided by the international financial community.

In order to consolidate the central bank's commitment to price stability, an inflation targeting framework for the implementation of monetary policy was formally adopted in 2001 (certain elements of this framework had already been introduced in previous years). The results of inflation targeting have been encouraging. Inflation is currently converging to the 3 percent target and macroeconomic stability has led to lower interest rates, which has in turn favored financial intermediation and fostered economic growth. In this regard, the framework of a floating exchange rate regime plus inflation targeting and the public perception that *Banco de México* was committed to achieving its inflation target have played a key role in building credibility for the monetary authority.

In Mexico, monetary policy gears around the following four elements:

1. **The announcement of an explicit inflation target.** *Banco de México* implements monetary policy to maintain inflation permanently around a 3 percent target with an interval of plus/minus 1 percentage point.
2. **Analysis of economic conditions, inflationary pressures and the determination of the monetary policy stance.** The central bank's monetary policy actions have a lagged effect on the economy, especially on the price level. To attain the inflation target, the monetary authority must therefore base its decisions on a careful assessment of both current and prospective economic conditions and the outlook for inflation. An accurate identification of the origin of inflationary pressures (supply versus demand) and its possible effects on economic agents' expectations is therefore crucial for monetary policy decisions. *Banco de México* carries out a systematic analysis of

economic conditions and of the inflationary pressures derived from these conditions, using a wide range of variables and indicators and different economic and statistical models. Among these, the monetary rules proposed by John Taylor deserve special attention. Specifically, both Taylor and optimal rules are routinely used by *Banco de México* to evaluate the monetary policy stance. On the basis of this information, a number of exercises are carried out in which alternative policy scenarios are evaluated. This analysis allows identification of the factors that affect the behavior of inflation and its impact on inflation expectations.

3. **Definition of the instruments used by the Central Bank to attain its objectives.** In recent years, *Banco de México* has phased out the use of the *corto* (a non-borrowed reserves target such as the one the Fed used for many years back in the 1980s and early '90s) in favor of more direct views about the overnight interbank interest rate.

4. **A communication policy that fosters monetary policy's transparency and accountability.** In order to attain price stability through an inflation targeting framework, the central bank must communicate clearly to the public its objectives, strategy, and instruments. Greater transparency, together with a broad communication policy, has contributed to strengthen the accountability of *Banco de México*.

*   *   *

Initially, the global financial crisis and all its ramifications barely touched emerging markets. If you think about it, this is quite a remarkable fact. Many other episodes of financial crisis and volatility were initiated by emerging market problems, or the first cycle of contagion was precisely in emerging markets. However, by the end of 2007 in Latin America, and certainly in Mexico, we barely felt any disruptions in our financial system. Of course we had corrections in asset markets but the spread for emerging market debts and other indicators moved very little in relation with other markets in more developed countries and with previous experiences.[1]

---

1. The U.S. financial crisis subsequently turned into a full global crisis. As is by now well known, the latter had its origins in a prolonged period of excess liquidity and credit expansion coupled with financial innovations leading to growing global imbalances (facilitated by the ample availability of financing of current account deficits and the willingness to accumulate large foreign exchange reserves in surplus countries) and the mispricing of risk. This crisis has reflected a major institutional failure including financial institutions, regulators, rating agencies, and international financial institutions, as well as other more informal mechanisms of international cooperation.

The challenges emerging markets are facing now are of a different nature and have to do with the surge in inflation. Emerging markets are coping with inflation along with a rapid strengthening of their currencies as a result of increased liquidity coming from stimulus applied in advanced economies. In accommodating this, the authorities of developing markets have to be very careful about second-round effects and contagion to the wage and price formation mechanisms, making sure that expectations remain well anchored.

In Mexico, with inflation levels under control along with inflation expectations well anchored, the Mexican central bank is not facing such monetary policy dilemmas and it is likely to remain on hold during an extended period of time, further supporting economic recovery. The point, which is related to John Taylor's framework, is that in the case of Mexico and in the case of all the central banks of emerging markets I'm familiar with, we all use more or less the same kinds of models, which are based on Taylor rules and optimal rules. Then we test all kinds of scenarios, calibrate the results, and hope we get it right.

II. Some of John Taylor's Contributions to Monetary Economics

Let me now talk very briefly about three topics related to John's work, which are closely related to a central bank's operation: the question of nominal rigidities, the Taylor rule, and monetary policy implementation under uncertainty.

Taylor's staggered contracts

A crucial issue for central banks is to understand the nature of nominal rigidities prevalent in an economy, its consequences and its implications for monetary policymaking. On that respect, John has enhanced our understanding not only about the microeconomic foundations behind these rigidities, but on the effects that they may have on the prices' behavior as well. His pioneering on staggered contracts has been of utmost relevance for modeling and characterizing inflation inertia.

John's models continue to be very important due to their inherent intuition, the inclusion of rational expectations, and their ability to provide an explanation of the inertia observed in inflation and unemployment. The starting point of John's models is that annual wage revisions are a common event for most workers; however, not all of these revisions are made at the same time. In fact, recent related models and surveys have corroborated his basic idea: wages and prices are not changed very often and not always in a synchronized fashion. John formalized that, in an economic context characterized by nominal rigidities and rational expectations, inertia in inflation and a negative correlation between the change in the price level and unemployment rate are likely to arise. Thus, monetary policy may have important short-run effects.[2]

Taylor concludes that inflation inertia comes from two sources:

a) the influence of current contracts since, as I said earlier, some of them are established in previous periods, causing shocks to be passed on from one contract to another.

b) the change in expectations about the future developments of aggregate demand originating from changes in monetary policy.

The above leads to an important point: to stabilize prices, monetary policy can affect the expectations component of inertia only through the second source. This implies a trade-off between stabilizing inflation and output, given that monetary policy can be more accommodative in inflation only by increasing output's variability, or vice versa.[3]

The Mexican experience in the eighties may serve as a good example to illustrate the relevance of John's work on this topic. Up to 1987, the economy experienced high inflation, and staggered contracts for wages and prices were common. Under these conditions, policymakers put into place the so-called "Economic Stabilization Pact" (*Pacto de Solidaridad Económica*) at the end of 1987, which included income policies and, in particular, an agreement to set wage contracts and prices in a synchronized way. This allowed us to break the inertia of the high inflation equilibrium. Thus, an understanding of the effects of staggered contracts on inflation dynamics was crucial in order to design the elements needed to lead the economy toward a low inflation equilibrium in the late eighties.

---

2. See Taylor, John. (1980). "Aggregate Dynamics and Staggered Contracts." *Journal of Political Economy* 88(1): 1–23, and Taylor, John. (1979). "Staggered Wage Setting in a Macro Model." *American Economic Review* 69(2): 108–113.

3. Fiscal policy is not incorporated into the model.

Taylor's monetary policy rule

We all know that Taylor rules have become a very important area of research in both academia and the central banks. This rule instructs that interest rates should rise if inflation is above its target and output is above its long-run potential. Such a rule leads to what is known as the Taylor principle—increases in nominal interest rates need to be greater than the rise in inflation (in order to stabilize inflation)—which suggests how much tightening has to take place in response to deviations of inflation from its target.

As I have suggested earlier, and I believe most of my colleagues coincide, rules *à la* Taylor are very useful benchmarks. However, following the prescriptions from a predetermined or mechanical rule could restrict the flexibility needed for implementing monetary policy. Still, the use of these types of rules is, to some extent, a simple way to connect the central bank's policy instrument to a very few variables. This simplifies some of the communication challenges faced by central banks.

It should be also stressed that, as is well known, the calculation of the equilibrium interest rate and potential output is subject to serious estimation problems, discussion, and analysis. Hence, more research and scrutiny on these issues may provide further insights to the Taylor rule and improve the way in which monetary policy is conducted. In fact, a large part of the research done at *Banco de México* is aimed at understanding these types of rules and their ability to characterize *Banco de México*'s monetary policy.

At *Banco de México,* we also consider fully optimal rules, which are obtained from the first-order conditions of the central bank's welfare maximization subject to the particular model of the economy. Hence, such rules seek to minimize the welfare loss function given the characteristics of the economy and the nature of the shocks affecting it. As has been formalized, fully optimal rules imply a contingent plan for the future path of interest rates. This allows private sector expectations to stabilize and, as a result, inflation is controlled at a lower cost in terms of output volatility.

Monetary policy implementation under uncertainty

The systematic evaluation of the risks faced by the monetary authorities has been a key element of the disinflation process in Mexico. From a theoretical point of view, in the last years the literature has attached a great deal of importance on how to incorporate uncertainty to monetary policy implementation. The literature emphasizes that monetary policy decisions should not be made based only on the expected (base) scenario, but on the distribution of all possible results. In practice, this framework suggests central banks should adopt measures to supply the economy with a hedging mechanism against scenarios that can be particularly costly for the population. Given that only a limited number of risks can be quantified, this approach must incorporate the judgment of decision-makers.

The "risk management" framework has special relevance for the implementation of monetary policy in emerging market economies. First, since these economies are relatively more vulnerable to different shocks, uncertainty regarding the magnitude and persistence of these shocks can be greater. Second, the measurement of the economy's performance is subject to larger margins of error. Third, most of the time, these economies experience structural changes of greater magnitude and with a higher frequency. Therefore, a relatively broader range of models should be considered to evaluate economic policy decisions. Fourth, the costs associated with certain adverse scenarios for the economy may be higher.

It is worth mentioning that, in general, *Banco de México* considers Taylor rules as a useful tool in its constant evaluation of the stance of policy for a wide range of scenarios (i.e., stress tests and simulations). Certainly, at *Banco de México* this simple but quite informative rule is used in our battery of models for monetary economic analysis. In any case, the way we should use these rules, as Taylor has argued, is as "guideposts" to help central banks. This is crucial because a central bank needs flexibility.

* * *

To conclude, I would like to thank John for his excellent work and passion toward economics and for sharing his ideas with us. Through his ideas and models, we have improved our understanding of some of the complex issues surrounding monetary economics and the different obstacles and limitations we face. I cannot conceive modern central banking without John's contributions. He made our work and our life much more manageable.

FIFTEEN

A VIEW FROM THE FINANCIAL MARKETS

John P. Lipsky

John Taylor's[1] important contributions to understanding the interactions between financial markets and economic policy have been highly relevant to financial market participants; John personally has sought to model these interactions in a way that few others have. He has been a frequent visitor to financial institutions in order to test his views against actual practice. Thus, the practical relevance of John's work has not been accidental.

In fact, the importance of John's work was recognized by financial market participants at least as rapidly as by academic colleagues. Consider the paper that introduced what is known everywhere today as the Taylor rule for monetary policy. It was presented first at a November 1992 Carnegie-Rochester conference in Pittsburgh and was subsequently published as a Working Paper of the Center for Economic

---

John Lipsky is Special Advisor to the Managing Director of the International Monetary Fund.

1. I believe that I have known John and his wife, Allyn, longer than most. So I can vouch personally for something that I'm sure those who know them have long realized: John's many accomplishments owe much to Allyn's support. As a Stanford classmate of John's and on behalf of John's classmates—incidentally, he was the first of us to finish his degree and to head off to at least the academic version of the real world—I can state that we're proud of what he has accomplished, but not surprised.

Policy Research at Stanford (now SIEPR) with the title "Discretion versus Policy Rules in Practice."

Please think back to mid-1993. At that time, the funds rate was 3 percent, where it had been lodged since 1992. The economic recovery from the 1990–91 recession had been more sluggish than had been generally anticipated. Fed Chairman Alan Greenspan blamed the headwinds that seemed to be holding the economy back. However, it's easy to forget that the Consumer Price Index inflation was 3 percent and ten-year Treasury bond yields were about 6 percent.

At that time, I was working on Wall Street as the chief economist of Salomon Brothers. My Salomon Brothers colleagues and I became convinced that Fed policy was becoming too accommodating and that tightening was needed. This view was not shared at all by most financial market participants, and it was not reflected in market prices. We were searching for a clear and systematic argument in favor of our view that policy tightening was needed. And that's how we came to incorporate into our own work the analysis in John Taylor's Carnegie-Rochester paper only a few months after its initial presentation.

We had been struck by how well Taylor's formulation matched the Fed's record from 1987 onward. But if you look at figures 1A and 1B in Don Kohn's paper in this volume, you'll see that the Taylor rule in late 1993 provided a clear indication that Fed policy was overdue for tightening.

I'm going to read to you a few quotes from the December 1993 edition of Salomon Brothers' annual *Prospects for Financial Markets*. The specific title of the 1993 edition was "Keeping Inflation Low in the 1990s." I believe that this quote reflects the first practical use of what came to be known as the Taylor rule. At the same time, the quotes will remind you how far we have come in thinking about monetary policy goals and operations from the then-prevailing conventional wisdom. You will also recognize the impact of the analysis that underpinned the development of the Taylor rule.

In a section of the 1993 *Prospects* entitled "The Fed's Inflation Test," we claimed that the key element in the United States' historic post-1970s disinflation was the Federal Reserve's three waves of monetary restraint implemented during the 1980s. In that vein, we stated, "Fed policy largely will determine whether the trend of declining inflation cycles will be sustained." We warned, "The lack of a clear-cut monetary policy guide still creates cyclical inflation risks. Forward-looking indicators signal that current Fed policy will have to be tightened soon if any eventual inflation revival was to be kept modest and short-lived.

"Nonetheless, the prospect of timely Fed action—together with cyclical and structural forces—justifies optimism that long-term inflation expectations will continue to trend downward, eventually pulling long-term interest rates to new lows." We continued, "If the Fed meets its inflation goals—namely, if monetary policy's success would become a reality rather than an abstract mantra—further significant declines in U.S. long-term bond yields would be likely. For example, if inflation retreats to an average of 2 percent or less, long-term Treasury bond yields above 6 percent would offer substantial value. If the prospect of sustained low inflation eventually gains credibility, not impossible considering that consumer price inflation has been 2 percent or lower through six of the past ten decades, even long-term bond yields below 5 percent would be possible in the coming years."

That sounds archaic, doesn't it? We continued, "At present, however, market participants increasingly are skeptical of the Fed's prospective success. Despite the drop in inflation, the Fed's primary task for more than four years has been accommodation. To many observers, therefore, the recent progress in reducing inflation does not reflect new Fed initiatives as much as other factors.

"Some analysts argue that the Fed's policy was tighter than indicated using traditional measures and probably was tighter than the Fed had intended. Such [a view] has been encouraged among other things by a recent study indicating that until last year, the Fed's policy actions were consistent with an implicit 2 percent inflation target, but its failure to hike rates during the past year has called into question the stringency of the Fed's policy goals."

Of course, the "recent study" we footnoted was "Discretion versus Policy Rules . . ." This may not have been the first citation anywhere of John's seminal paper, but for sure it was the first practical use of the analysis—and well before the Taylor rule had been christened with its now universally recognized name.

These quotes date from mid-December 1993. Chairman Greenspan testified in Congress on January 28, 1994. Although journalists seemed to hear an unclear message that day, my Salomon Brothers colleagues understood him to be warning that a rate hike was imminent. In response, we went around our trading floor warning, "The Fed is coming! The Fed is coming!" And on February 3 came the market-shocking twenty-five basis point rate hike.

To our chagrin and frustration, Salomon Brothers suffered massive losses, principally on the mortgage-trading desk. It was a searing moment. Not only had it been demonstrated vividly how unconvincing we had been with our trading colleagues, it also underscored how counterintuitive our Taylor-rule-encouraged conclusions had seemed at the time.

I don't say this as a sort of bitter self-congratulation—after all, we had failed, in that we hadn't been convincing enough to allow our firm to benefit from our non-consensus but accurate forecast—but to highlight how Taylor rule-type reasoning at the time was anything but conventional wisdom. Today, in contrast, such an approach strikes most market participants as nothing more than codifying the obvious. And virtually all central banks today—like the economic research groups of virtually all major financial institutions—maintain their own Taylor rule calculations to provide perspective on their policy decisions. Surely, this is the mark of a powerful insight.

Parenthetically, residential mortgage-backed securities at the time were still a relatively new asset class. The early versions of these securities mainly were designed to translate changes in mortgage interest rates into securities prices. When the Fed raised rates in early 1994, it became clear that many financial market participants had a very imperfect understanding of how changes in Treasury bond yields would alter prices for mortgage-backed securities.

Despite the massive losses absorbed in 1994 by Salomon Brothers and others, lessons were learned. Today, conventional mortgage-backed securities form an important part of modern financial markets. The current bout of difficulties with mortgage-backed securities deals primarily with a newer family of instruments (that include so-called "non-conforming" mortgages, among other elements) that also map changes in credit quality into market prices. At present, we can see that practitioners have had difficulty in understanding that mapping. That doesn't mean that securities like collateralized debt obligations (CDOs) have no useful role, but rather that market participants have serious lessons to learn from the latest difficulties.

Returning to the situation in 1993, it is easy to see how significantly thinking about monetary policy has developed under the influence of John Taylor and others. Following John's and others' research, my Salomon Brothers colleagues and I argued that earlier reliance on M1 was outdated. We claimed that the Fed also had lost an anchor in M2, at a time when the Fed was still relying on something called P-Star analysis. That analysis was based on the notion that there was a predictable long-term relationship between M2 and the price level. But that analysis had substantially over-predicted the inflation decline that had occurred at that time. Thus, we concluded—based in part on John's work—the evidence indicated that policy was overly accommodating.

To demonstrate this conclusion, we used John's formula (duly footnoted) to show graphically that if the economy were at full capacity, growing at trend, and if the Fed were aiming at price stability, the nominal funds rate should lie between 2 percent and 4 percent. Given the circumstances at the time, this analysis indicated clearly that a 3 percent funds rate was too low to be consistent with a presumed 2 percent long-term inflation goal. In fact, we claimed that the deviation between the actual funds rate and that indicated by John's formula was approaching a magnitude that in the past had been associated with accelerating inflation.

It's worth noting the obvious: the Fed responded by a notable policy tightening during 1994 and beyond; financial market participants altered their views about monetary policy decisions and they altered their expectations of Fed actions. Most importantly, the economy subsequently outperformed consensus expectations in terms of stronger growth and lower inflation.

In sum, while the early 1980s effort to lower U.S. inflation had strong monetarist overtones, anti-inflation logic subsequently has rested much more on Taylor rule logic regarding the practical combination of formal inflation targeting (or the setting of medium-term inflation goals) plus output gap considerations. Moreover, the rapid securitization of capital markets has reduced sharply the potential temptation of governments to use inflation as a policy tool, as the negative financial market reaction to heightened inflation risks has become more powerful. With the benefits of low and stable inflation more clearly acknowledged, the case for central bank independence has become recognized more widely. This occurred not just in advanced economies, but in emerging market economies, as well.

I also would like to highlight a June 1995 Salomon Brothers publication entitled "Policy Rules Shed New Light on Fed Stance" authored by my then-colleague Robert DiClemente. As far as I can ascertain, this publication represented the first time that we referred to the Taylor rule in print using this name (although we had referred to it frequently in generic terms, always footnoting the original Taylor paper). My modest claim is that we at Salomon Brothers were the first anywhere to apply the name Taylor rule to John's seminal monetary policy formula.

In that 1995 publication, we examined the prospect that policy rules could improve monetary policy performance. The publication focused on three rules that we defined by the authors' names: the Taylor rule, the McCallum rule—which uses monetary base growth as the instrument—and the Judd rule that calculates the needed change in short-term interest rates as a function of the difference between actual and targeted nominal income growth.

This publication stated, "The historical perspective of the Taylor rule underpins the general usefulness of this approach to assessing policy. Funds rates calculated with the Taylor formula dating back in time indicate the sharp change in monetary policy that occurred with the strong anti-inflation commitment introduced in October 1979. Virtually throughout the periods since 1980 the actual funds rates has been at or above the level prescribed by the Taylor rule. All of the rules that we have considered indicate that Fed policy may have become too accommodating during the latter stages of easing in 1992."

The publication illustrated that the funds rate in the fifteen years leading up to the 1979 policy shift was continuously below that prescribed by the Taylor rule, even when the funds rates moved above 10 percent late in the decade. Thus, it stated, "The illusion that interest rates were high at that time is not borne out by the rule. The mirror of this illusion may have been at work recently when many market participants judged that a 6 percent funds rate was unlikely to yield much slowing in economic momentum, while the rule characterized policy as appropriately positioned to head off serious inflation."

My concluding points are consistent with John's work on the international aspects of monetary policy encompassing both the globalization of policy approaches and the effect of globalization itself on policy choices. It's clear that John's work has had a substantial effect on the way monetary policy is conducted around the world.

At Salomon Brothers in 1993, we thought that it was novel and noteworthy to assert that the Fed was likely to take its anti-inflation goals seriously. At the time, only a few other central banks would have been characterized as serious about inflation goals. Yet what has been referred to as the Great Moderation has been associated with the spread of inflation-focused central banks operating with much greater independence than was the case previously.

Economies and financial markets also have changed importantly since 1990. After all, it's only since 1990 that we have operated in what can reasonably be called a truly global trading system and a global financial market. This is very new by historic standards, but already it is having an effect on economic performance.

In Chairman Greenspan's 2007 book and in some of his recent quotes, he's called into question whether the current favorable environment can be sustained. Contrary to consensus expectations following the 2000–01 slowdown, this has become the most rapid and best-balanced period of global growth in many decades, while core inflation has remained low.

It's clear that we can't take this exceptional performance for granted going forward. In fact, it seems to me that we are now at the initial moment of a new policy debate and the conduct of monetary policy very much will be involved.

Rapid productivity growth and the international conditions of opening markets and improving policies that helped catalyze the Great Moderation have made it much easier for policymakers to initiate an economic and financial virtuous circle, featuring smoothed output fluctuations and reduced inflationary expectations. However, we simply can't assume conditions will remain this favorable indefinitely.

What is the future of the Great Moderation?

If conditions become less favorable, we should anticipate some major challenges.

First, it can't be taken for granted that the prevailing view will be retained that low and anchored inflation produces the best economic results. On several levels, it is possible that the support for anti-inflationary policies could erode. We are at a point at which potential challenges should be taken seriously.

The key economic and policy challenges facing us are going to be global, and not just domestic. Among other things, the role of policy coordination will need to be rethought. Somewhat neglected issues such as exchange rates and international payments imbalances will need to be dealt with effectively. Simply put, we can't take for granted a continuation of the environment that has benefited the global economy so dramatically in the past several years despite recurring challenges.

We at the International Monetary Fund are hard at work trying to help establish and sustain a favorable global environment. The nature of the challenges that lie ahead is relatively clear, but their parameters are not. There are difficult but crucial aspects that will require support and cooperation from policymakers around the world. And there are aspects that will require insights from the academic community to help provide guidance. Among other things, I know that we will be looking to John for innovative views and wisdom and from all of you here as well.

APPENDIX

The Pursuit of Policy Rules:
A Conversation between
Robert Leeson and John B. Taylor

RL: Let's begin with your college years, 1964–68. You majored in economics at Princeton. Who (and what) influenced you most there? What sparked your interest in policy rules?

JT: I decided to major in economics after realizing that I enjoyed it much more than math, physics, or engineering, which are what I first thought about doing. The "new economics" was getting a lot of play in the media at the time; it was introduced with great fanfare by the Kennedy administration and the Council of Economic Advisers, especially under Walter Heller and Arthur Okun. I liked how you could use mathematics to study and understand these current events. I was very fortunate to have had many good teachers and advisers at Princeton. Dick Quandt gave me good advice about using mathematics in economics. He told me not to bother taking the undergraduate econometrics course, but rather the more advanced probability and statistical inference course in the Statistics Department. Burt Malkiel gave a great lecture course on finance, which was kind of a precursor to his famous book, *A Random Walk Down Wall Street*.

But looking back I would say that Phil Howrey had the most influence on me, at least in areas that turned out to be closely related to my career as an economist. Phil had a great deal of interest in time series

Excerpts from an interview conducted in October 2007.

analysis as it applied to macroeconomics. For example, he had written an important paper on the "Long Swing" hypothesis with Michio Hatanaka. Hatanaka had published a book in 1964 with Clive Granger on *Spectral Analysis of Time Series*. Granger visited Princeton at the invitation of Oskar Morgenstern, who had an interest in applying frequency domain techniques to economic data. While I met Morgenstern then, I did not meet Granger until many years later.

I think my initial interest in policy rules goes back to a course I took from Howrey; except for Economics 101, it was probably my first introduction to macroeconomics. But we didn't study the IS-LM macroeconomic model or the other textbook models of the time; instead we studied dynamic models of the economy, with equations that included lags and shocks defining the stochastic processes. In retrospect, it was quite unusual that I had the opportunity to learn about these methods as an undergraduate, but at the time I had no idea that it was unusual. The methods forced me to think of the economy as a moving dynamic structure. So the only way one could think about policy was with some kind of policy rule. You couldn't say, let's shift the LM curve by increasing the money supply by one unit or do whatever people would be doing at the time. Instead you had to have some kind of policy rule. So to me it was natural. I couldn't think of how else you would do it in those models.

When it came time to choose a topic for a senior thesis, I approached Phil Howrey, saying that I was interested in macroeconomic policy issues and wanted to work with the types of models we studied in his course. He suggested that I look into stabilization policy in a model that combined economic growth and the cycle, which we called "endogenous cyclical growth" at the time; he said that no one had done this before, and so it sounded like a great topic and that is what I did. In the preface to my senior thesis I thanked Phil "for suggesting the topic and indicating how I might proceed." In the end the thesis was about simulating different types of monetary policy rules of the kind that engineers had used to stabilize mechanical processes. It combined two strands of A. W. Phillips' work: evaluation of policy rules (*Economic Journal*, June 1954) and his model of cyclical growth (*Economica*, November 1961). The monetary policy rules I examined had the money supply on the left-hand side, rather than the interest rate. I assumed that the central bank could control the money supply by buying and selling bonds in the open market. I considered different types of feedback rules—what engineers called proportional, derivative, and integral policy. I also considered fiscal feedback rules.

I really loved working on this project, and I spent long hours in a carrel in the basement of the library reading and deriving equations in the winter and spring of 1968. I did the simulations of the differential equations both on a digital computer (an IBM 7094) and on an electro-analog computer—essentially a circuit that combined capacitors, resistors, and amplifiers which I hooked up to an oscilloscope. The professors in the Economics Department must have liked the thesis, because much to my surprise (and all my friends) I won the prize for "the outstanding thesis by a senior in the field of economics." After the experience of writing this thesis, I decided that I would like to get a PhD in economics, rather than an MBA, which is where I was headed. I had already been accepted to Stanford's Graduate School of Business and I somehow convinced the Stanford Economics Department to let me in even though I had not taken the Graduate Record Examination in economics.

RL: The period from the breakdown of the Phillips curve to the construction of the Taylor rule was a turbulent time for macroeconomics. Your introduction to economics coincided with the onset of this turbulence: do you recall some of this turmoil infiltrating classrooms at Princeton?

JT: Milton Friedman's 1968 American Economic Association presidential address was given during the middle of my senior year. Since I had a Phillips curve in the model used in my thesis, I am sure I discussed the issue with my advisers. In the thesis I did not exploit the long-run trade-off implicit in the Phillips curve by increasing the money growth rate and the inflation rate permanently to get a permanently higher utilization rate. This could have reflected a judgment that one could not in practice exploit the curve this way, despite what the algebra said. More likely it was simply that I was interested in stabilization policy rules, and such rules, very sensibly, did not even consider such a possibility.

RL: Like A. W. Phillips, your father applied mathematical analysis for practical purposes. Your first publication (whilst a senior at Princeton) was "Fiscal and Monetary Stabilization Policies in a Model of Endogenous Cyclical Growth" (October 1968), which builds on A. W. Phillips' curve and cyclical growth model.

JT: Most of the applied math work of my father was related to the nuclear submarine program, which was classified at the time, so I did not know the details. I do recall his general appreciation of applied math as distinct from pure theory. And A. W. Phillips focused on applying math to dynamic economic problems. The October 1968 paper, which was in the Princeton Econometric Research Program series, was actually an abridged version of my senior thesis at Princeton. It was quite a boost to learn that my paper would be included in that series, which had published papers by such luminaries as Morgenstern, Granger, Howrey, Hatanaka, Bob Aumann, Steve Goldfeld, and Quandt.

RL: Your purpose, as stated in your 1968 paper, was to "describe the product and money markets as developed by Phillips, and derive the government policies which will regulate the model." Your money market had the interest rate as a function of the price level, actual income, and the money supply. If monetary policy simply keeps the money supply fixed, the authorities effectively set an interest rate which depends on the prices and income, which is not unlike the Taylor rule. Without exaggerating the similarities, do you see any continuity from the twenty-one-year-old to the forty-five-year-old?

JT: The equation for the interest rate in that model was simply an inverted money demand equation in which the interest rate was solved; it is true that for some fixed money supply rules, that equation looks like an interest rate rule, but I did not explicitly have an interest rate rule in mind. Rather, I was examining feedback rules for the money supply. I did not think about interest rate rules until much later, perhaps for the first time in my paper with Nick Carlozzi at the Philadelphia Fed. I think there is quite a big difference between money supply rules and interest rate rules. But I do see continuity: I was still searching at age forty-five for good monetary policy rules to stabilize the macro economy, just as I was at age twenty-one. I guess you could say that the search took over twenty years, or even more since research on policy rules is still quite active. My PhD dissertation was part of that search, as were my papers on learning, non-uniqueness in rational expectation models, staggered wage/price setting, trade-off curves, non-linear solution techniques, and multi-country models in the 1970s and 1980s.

RL: You obtained your PhD from Stanford in 1973. Who (or what) influenced you most at that time?

JT: My main field of study was econometrics and I was fortunate to have had two of the most accomplished econometricians/statisticians in the world as my teachers: Takeshi Amemiya and T. W. (Ted) Anderson. In addition to taking their field courses, I participated in their seminars where we read and presented chapters from recent time series books, including George Box's and Gwilym Jenkins' book on ARIMA models, Masanao Aoki's *Optimization of Stochastic Systems* (1967), and Peter Whittle's *Prediction and Regulation* (1963). Ted Anderson had also recently finished his own book on time series, which added to his classic book on multivariate statistics. I also maintained my interest in monetary economics—benefiting from Ron McKinnon's seminar, where I recall we plowed through Bob Mundell's recent book, *Monetary Theory*—and I developed an interest in monetary history in Paul David's seminar, where I wrote a paper on the greenback period in the United States.

My PhD thesis adviser was T. W. Anderson, and I think he was the most important influence. I learned an enormous amount of time series analysis from him, and about how to prove formal theorems in mathematics. As I mentioned, like my undergraduate thesis, my PhD thesis was on policy rules. The problem was to find a good policy rule in a model where one does not know the parameters and therefore has to estimate and control the dynamic system simultaneously. An unresolved issue was how much "experimentation" should be built into the policy rule through which the instrument settings would move around in order to provide more information about the parameters, which would pay off in the future. I proved theorems and did simulations, which showed various convergence properties of the least squares or Bayesian learning rules. My main conclusion from that research, however, was that in many models simply following a rule without special experimentation features was a good approximation. That made future work much simpler, of course, because it eliminated a great deal of complexity.

I had two extended periods away from Stanford before I finished my PhD there. First, I left Stanford in December 1968 to join the U.S. Navy. After completing Officer Candidate School in Newport, Rhode Island, I was assigned to the Anti-Submarine Systems Project Office outside of Washington, D.C. My job was to help determine optimal formations for U.S. anti-submarine warfare forces to maximize the probability of their detecting and intercepting Soviet submarines with sonar. We used a computer simulation model; it was calibrated with actual data collected from sonar readings as U.S. surface ships cruised over our own submarines. When this job was finished I was given the opportunity to leave the Navy, and decided to return to Stanford in January 1970 to complete the PhD.

Another time away was during the summer of 1971 when I was invited to participate in a time series seminar for graduate students and young faculty at Princeton organized by Gregory Chow. Gregory was finishing a book on optimal stochastic control and I learned a great deal from his lectures on that subject.

RL: In 1946 (the year of your birth) two competing intellectual leaders died: Henry Simons (the leader of the Chicago "rules party") and John Maynard Keynes (whose name is associated with "sticky" wages and prices). In 1946, Milton Friedman returned to Chicago (by 1951 he had rediscovered the quantity theory as a tool for challenging his Keynesian opponents) and the 1946 Employment Act created the CEA and initiated the Economic Report of the President. The Act also sought to "promote maximum employment, production, and purchasing power." By the 1960s most economists saw an irreconcilable conflict between promoting "maximum employment, production" and promoting stable prices (maximum purchasing power). At what stage did you first encounter the Chicago rules party? Sticky wages and prices? Monetary targeting?

JT: I was of course familiar with the Friedman constant growth rate rule—the main example of monetary targeting—as an undergraduate at Princeton. And I studied Keynes' idea of fixed money wages in graduate school. I first started working on a new dynamic model of sticky (staggered) wages as part of an effort to construct an empirically accurate model of aggregate wage and price dynamics with rational expectations.

RL: Law and economics is part of the anti-discretion movement, stable money and the rule of law being seen as central to the preservation of civilization. Did you have much interaction with Aaron Director at Stanford at this time or later?

JT: No. I viewed policy rules as a natural way to evaluate policy in the kinds of macroeconomic models which I learned and worked on at Princeton and Stanford. It was more practical than philosophical or political.

RL: You started your academic career at Columbia as an assistant professor (1973–1976).

JT: It was a very productive time for me. Joining me as assistant professors in January 1973 were Guillermo Calvo and Carlos Rodriguez, and we talked economics morning, noon, and night. Our senior colleagues included Ned Phelps, Phil Cagan, and Bob Mundell. My research continued to be on policy rules, though now within the context of econometrically estimated models which had rational expectations. I got interested in how learning issues could affect monetary policy and wrote a paper on that subject in the *Journal of Political Economy* in 1975; after that paper (and my PhD thesis) I decided I could more productively concentrate on finding optimal policies under the approximation that the parameters of the model were known. I also worried about non-uniqueness problems and what they might imply for monetary policy issues and published a paper in *Econometrica* in 1977 on that subject. I also wrote a paper with Ned Phelps in which we added sticky prices on to rational expectations models, which we published in the *Journal of Political Economy* in 1977. I then moved on to staggered wage setting models and estimation.

RL: You took a year of absence to work as senior staff economist at the president's Council of Economic Advisers (CEA) in Washington in 1976–77. Your job description states that you were responsible for monetary policy, capital markets, interest rates, and housing. Did you actively seek an opportunity to work in Washington? Who organized this for you?

JT: Yes. I was interested in applying economic policy in practice. I mentioned my interest to Phil Cagan, who offered to put my name in the hopper. Eventually I was hired by Alan Greenspan and Burt Malkiel.

RL: You served under both Ford and Carter. Were you identifiably a Republican at that time? If so, was it unusual to work for a Democratic president? What were you working on at the CEA?

JT: No, I was not active in any political campaigns at that time. I joined the staff of the CEA in September 1976 when Ford was president and Alan Greenspan was still chair of the CEA. When Ford lost the election to Carter, Alan was replaced by Charlie Schultze, who asked me to stay on and I agreed to finish the academic year there. While Alan was chair I worked on current economic analysis and (along with Peter Clark) on a new measure of potential GDP and the full employment/

unemployment rate. I recall doing a project for Alan on the usefulness of housing permits as a way to forecast housing starts, and report-
ing that there was surprisingly little value at the time. It was because
of this forecasting-related work that I went on to work with Alan at
Townsend-Greenspan when I returned to New York in 1977 until I
moved to Princeton. Working with Alan in New York was a great learning experience as we built models of the coffee market, the copper
market, and the whole flow of funds market of the United States.

The 1977 *Economic Report of the President* also took a lot of my time
(during the period when Greenspan was there). It contained the revised estimates of potential GDP. After the election I worked on tax
reform proposals, including a proposal to integrate the corporate income tax with the personal income tax. We all worried about inflation
and why it could be costly to reduce. So while I had written a very
early draft of my 1979 *Econometrica* paper before going to the CEA, it
was there that I think I realized that we needed to do a better job at
explaining the persistence of inflation with rational expectations. That
is where the staggered contract model came from.

RL: After the CEA you returned to Columbia as associate professor
(1977–79) and then full professor (1979–80), with a year at Yale (1980).
After leaving the CEA you began to think systematically about the administrative dynamics of policy making at this time?

JT: Yes, I think experience in a policy job is very useful for being able to
judge which of many potential research topics in economics are worth
working on. It also got me thinking about how economic research was
used in a democracy and how the research could be designed to be
more useful.

RL: You published the "Taylor curve" paper in *Econometrica* in 1979
after you returned from Washington.

JT: Yes, I wrote the first draft of that in 1976 before I went to Washington,
but after I returned I revised it in ways that made it more practical and
more useful in practice. That paper had the first empirically realistic
monetary policy rule that was calculated with new rational expectations methods; in a sense it showed me that this "rules agenda" was
worth pursuing. Looking back on this period in his 1999 Homer Jones
lecture in St. Louis, Ben McCallum also makes this assessment. His lecture also describes how research work on monetary policy rules waned

considerably in the 1980s, except for the work of small groups "toiling in the vineyards." I call it the "dark ages" in another paper; it seemed like nearly everyone interested in the new rational expectations methods in the 1980s was working on real business cycle models without a role for monetary policy; it was a tough time for monetary policy rules research.

In any case that 1979 paper was reviewed favorably at the time by people on both sides of the spectrum. The favorable review from Robert Lucas was certainly a big boost for me. And because it showed that this approach to monetary policy could work in practice, it was a very big development on the road to the Taylor rule. The monetary policy rule in that paper had exactly the same variables on the right-hand side as the eventual Taylor rule. The rule had the objective of minimizing the weighted sum of the variance of output and variance of inflation; it also presented and estimated the first variance trade-off (Taylor curve) with inflation and output and contained a simple staggered price setting model (laid out in an appendix and covered in much more detail in my 1980 *Journal of Political Economy* paper). The big difference from what would come later, of course, was that the money supply was on the left-hand side. The transition from the money supply to the interest rate on the left-hand side of the rule occurred a few years later.

RL: The Taylor curve paper was rejected by the *American Economic Review?*

JT: Yes. So I submitted it to *Econometrica,* and it was published there. It may have been too technical for the *AER* anyway.

RL: How and when did you begin to move from money to the interest rate on the left-hand side—from a money rule to an activist interest rate rule?

JT: I think the first published work was done with Nick Carlozzi at the Philadelphia Fed. We were interested in international issues and the easiest best way to model the interest-rate—exchange-rate interaction was with interest rate rules. Our paper was published in 1985 under the title "International Capital Mobility and the Coordination of Monetary Rules." A little later I wrote a paper on fixed versus flexible exchange rates using my large multi-country model; the first version had money supply rules, the final published version had interest rate rules.

RL: You once said you saw an interest rate rule as complementing the framework provided by the quantity equation of money so usefully employed by Milton Friedman and Anna Schwartz in their *Monetary History of the United States.*

JT: Yes, this actually goes back to the inverted money demand equation in my 1968 paper. Such an inverted equation can generate interest rate behavior with similar characteristics to interest rate rules. When GDP rises, the interest rate also rises, for example. But the coefficients are not usually the same as interest rate rules like the Taylor rule.

RL: Jim Tobin invited you to Yale's Department of Economics and Cowles Foundation in 1980 to discuss and to work on "New Keynesian" rational expectations models. Were you influenced strongly by Tobin or vice versa?

JT: Jim asked me to team-teach a course with him where I would lecture on new rational expectations modeling and policy techniques. I have never liked the phrase "New Keynesian" because it is used to mean so many different things. But I learned a lot during that course, and during the whole visit, about Jim's approach to finance and monetary theory, which emphasized the wide range of assets that people can hold. I also worked on a solution method for rational expectations models with Ray Fair while I was at Yale. That method turned out to be very useful and is still used today. I thought it was important to find faster and more accurate solution techniques, and a few years later I organized several conferences on solution methods and published a solution technique comparison paper with Harold Uhlig. After my visit, Yale asked me to stay on in a permanent position, and it was hard to say no, but that is when I moved to Princeton.

RL: Do you recall Tobin suggesting to Paul Volcker that he cut interest rates to mitigate the rise in unemployment? What was Volcker's response?

JT: Yes, but that was a few years later, in 1982 in Washington. Volcker responded that he doesn't set the interest rate. He sets the money supply, and the market sets the interest rate.

RL: Do you think that monetary targeting for Volcker was a "stealth tactic"?

JT: I would put it this way: confidence was slipping fast when Volcker was appointed Fed chairman. He had to put together a coalition of people with many different views on the Federal Open Market Committee to get support for the disinflation and re-establish confidence in the principle that the Fed would let interest rates rise by enough to bring inflation down. Focusing on the money supply was part of his strategy. That way he could answer questions like the one Tobin asked by saying that the market pushed the interest rate up. It helped him carry out this very difficult political task, which he did successfully.

RL: In your 1980 *JPE* paper you concluded that "aggregate-demand policy makes a substantial difference for the behavior of output, wages, and prices. The choice of a target rule for aggregate-demand policy is therefore no less important than the choice of a target unemployment rate or a target inflation rate. It should therefore be considered as carefully in the political process as the other two targets typically are."

JT: By this I meant that the rule for setting the instruments of policy, which is aimed to achieve your goals, is as important as the goals themselves, and should be discussed in a democracy as much as the goals are. This issue re-emerged years later in discussions of inflation targeting where I urged that setting this inflation goal is not enough. You need to specify as much as possible how you get to the goals.

RL: Together with Stanley Fischer, your 1977 paper with Ned Phelps rescued from the clutches of Tom Sargent and Neil Wallace's Policy Ineffectiveness Proposition the "old doctrine" that "systematic monetary policy matters for fluctuation of output and employment," as you put it in that paper, adding that you "bottle[d]" the "old wine" in a rational expectations model.

JT: My main objective in this work was not to rescue a doctrine but rather to build a better model to evaluate monetary policy rules. For this purpose it made sense to incorporate rational expectations into the models that I had been using for several years. One reason was that the rational expectations assumption made much more sense for this purpose than static or adaptive expectations. Another reason was that rational expectations provided a way to deal with the Lucas critique. If you simply added rational expectations to a model with perfectly flexible prices, as Sargent and Wallace showed, there was no reason to evaluate monetary policy rules, since they did not matter. So combining price and wage rigidities with rational expectations seemed like the way to go, but it was not easy to do this correctly.

RL: Are there unacknowledged risks associated with attaching adjectives such as "perfect," "natural," and "rational" to scientific hypotheses?

JT: Yes, you have to think about communication and not use words that get in the way of understanding. When we wrote about policy "rules" in the 1990 *Economic Report of the President,* for example, we said "systematic" policies instead of rules so as not to confuse people who might think that a rule meant a fixed setting for the policy instrument.

RL: In your paper presented in August 1982 at the first Jackson Hole conference on monetary policy, you almost appear to be suggesting a Keynesian New Classical Synthesis to tackle the low inflation stabilization problem.

JT: I recall that this paper was mainly about the ongoing disinflation, but I may have begun to think about the post-disinflation period of low inflation. I thought, and still think, that models that combined rational expectations and staggered wage and price setting were essential to understand both disinflation and low inflation policy issues.

RL: In referring to your 1979 *Econometrica* paper, Robert Lucas (in a 1981 *Journal of Economic Literature* review of a book by Tobin) noted that "the best policies under Taylor criterion are not fixed money growth rules but rules which direct monetary policy to lean against the wind in a pre-announced fashion. Is this what Tobin and others mean by a Keynesian model? If so, we have come a very long way towards restoring seriousness to our discussions of macroeconomic policy . . ." You were making both Tobin and Lucas happy.

JT: Yes, but maybe a little unhappy too as the models had features that Tobin (rational expectations) and Lucas (price rigidities) were not particularly comfortable with at the time.

RL: You then returned to Princeton and you also had four more years (1981–84) as a research adviser at the Philadelphia Fed. Did Edward G. Boehne, the president at Philadelphia from 1981–2000, recruit you?

JT: Yes, but Ed was director of research when I started working there. He later was promoted to president. I appreciated how he was very open about my participation in policy conference calls, especially those about what was going on in the money markets.

I usually went there one day a week, driving or taking the train, and I worked with people there on several projects.

RL: During your time at the Philadelphia Fed, you assessed monetarist rules and nominal GNP targeting. With respect to nominal GNP targeting, you detected merits and explanatory power but also a fundamental flaw: that it contributed to the cycle by causing overshooting and "boom-bust" behavior. As an alternative you proposed a modified nominal GNP rule that keeps constant the sum of the inflation rate and the proportional deviations of real output from trend.

JT: Yes, this modified rule was similar to the Taylor rule, but I was still not discussing the interest rate as the instrument. In any case I was worried about nominal GDP rules adding to economic fluctuations because they did not take sufficient account of the dynamics of the business cycle.

RL: You returned to Stanford in 1984.

JT: Yes, at Stanford I worked along with a group of terrific graduate students on a large econometrically estimated multi-country model, and gradually started shifting from money supply rules to interest rate rules. The multi-country model turned out to be an excellent way for students to learn about monetary policy evaluation techniques with rational expectations, and many of the students from this period are still involved in monetary policy work, including Ellen McGrattan, Joe Gagnon, Andy Levin, John Williams, Pete Klenow, Volker Wieland, and many others.

RL: In your August 1988 inaugural Phillips Lecture on "Monetary Policy and the Stability of Macroeconomic Relationships," which stressed continuity with Phillips, you wrote: "My research today can be viewed as a stochastic, rational expectations, empirical generalization of Phillips's work, but this research has yet to go as far in synthesizing growth and fluctuations as Phillips did in his 1961 article," and you outlined some "recently developed theoretical underpinnings of the Phillips curve." Do you see a similarity between the theoretical Phillips curve—a relationship between price inflation and levels of production—and the (implicit) Phillips curve which underpins the Taylor rule?

JT: Yes, there are similarities. But combining rational expectation with the Phillips structure was very difficult to do, and in the end the effort resulted in a whole new class of sticky wage and price models. If you just added an expectations augmentation term to the Phillips curve, then when that expectations term became rational you got the Sargent/Wallace policy ineffectiveness result. The staggered contract model was the only way to avoid that outcome, explain the facts, and still be consistent with the rational expectations theory. It naturally generated persistence even though expectations were rational. I think that the continued use of this model in one form or another, including the geometric version of Guillermo Calvo, the inflation persistence version of Jeff Fuhrer and George Moore, and most recently empirical work by Pete Klenow, is evidence in support of this view. To be sure, the stylized version of that model, where everyone sets contracts to last four quarters, is not rich enough to be empirically accurate, so I used more general models in empirical work, including in my 1979 and 1980 working papers on an econometric business cycle model.

RL: You were a member of President Bush's CEA (June 1989–August 1991); Richard Schmalensee (MIT) was also a member and Michael Boskin (Stanford) was the chair. One of your roles on the CEA was to liaise with the Fed. What else were you working on?

JT: Yes, I worked closely with Fed people at the time, including with the chair, Alan Greenspan, whom I knew from my previous stint at the CEA and at Townsend-Greenspan in New York. I also did a lot of work relating to the first Gulf War, the global recession, and the debt crisis in Latin America. But the two things most memorable were the fall of the Soviet Union and the Structural Impediments Initiative, which took me to Japan many times. I went to Poland a couple of times in 1990 and worked with Condi Rice to persuade the Treasury of the benefits of a billion-dollar stabilization fund for Poland. Condi frequently refers to this collaboration between the National Security Council, where she worked at the time, and the CEA. We did persuade the Treasury, and the stabilization fund was a great success.

RL: Allan Meltzer, who had organized the Carnegie-Rochester Conference on Public Policy for many years, asked you to present a paper in November 1992 in Pittsburgh, which would become the Taylor rule paper. Was the February 1990 *Economic Report of the President* a "translational" play toward that paper? Was chapter 3 of the *Report* a "rules party" manifesto? You got a letter of support from Robert Lucas, but you intentionally eschewed the use of the word "rule" in that *Report*.

JT: Yes, chapter 3 of the 1990 *Economic Report of the President* was a precursor of the mathematical version of the rule I presented at the Carnegie-Rochester conference and the rule in that paper would eventually be called the Taylor rule. As I discussed earlier, we used the word "systematic" rather than "rule" at the CEA. We wanted to persuade people about the benefits of rules without scaring them off. Our work on policy rules in that 1990 *Report* was featured in the *Wall Street Journal* and they even put my picture on the front page. Bob Lucas wrote a letter to me congratulating us for the effort. I wrote about this episode in my 1993 book on policy in an international economy.

RL: The 1990 *Economic Report of the President* noted that the "simple" (Friedman-style) monetary growth rule had become "unworkable"; it was "inappropriate" to follow "rigid monetary targeting," but that the Fed had "not regressed to an undisciplined, ad hoc approach to policy . . . a purely discretionary approach." Rather it had "attempted to develop a more systematic, longer-run approach." Policies should be designed to "work well with a minimum of discretion . . . the alternative to discretionary policies might be called systematic policies . . . Unpredictable changes in economic and financial relationships imply that appropriate policy rules in some circumstances are rather general." You wrote that section?

JT: Yes, along with the very helpful assistance of Brian Madigan (who was on leave from the Monetary Affairs Division of the Fed) and others on the staff and with the complete support from Mike [Boskin] and Dick [Schmalensee]. The language of the CEA reports must be vetted throughout the administration and the Fed; so effectively this language was approved by the Fed and represented administration policy.

That experience strongly influenced my decision to accept Allan Meltzer's invitation to go to Pittsburgh in 1992 and to present something about policy rules in practice, which is what led to the Taylor rule paper, "Discretion Versus Policy Rules in Practice." It was successful beyond my dreams in bringing my long academic interest in research on policy rules into the real world of policymaking.

About the Contributing Authors

PIER FRANCESCO ASSO is Professor of History of Economics at the Department of European Studies and International Integration, University of Palermo. His research interests lie in the areas of banking and monetary history and in the history of American economic thought. Recently his research has focused on regional innovation systems and development. His works have been published in leading international journals and in a series of volumes on the history of the Italian banking system. He was the editor of the *Complete Works of Francesco Ferrara.* He is serving as scientific director of Fondazione Res and is co-editor of *History of Economic Thought and Policy.*

BEN S. BERNANKE was chairman of the president's Council of Economic Advisers before his appointment as Fed chairman. He has served the Federal Reserve in several roles. He was a member of the Federal Reserve Board of Governors; a visiting scholar at the Federal Reserve Banks of Philadelphia, Boston, and New York; and a member of the academic advisory panel at the Federal Reserve Bank of New York. Bernanke has held numerous teaching positions at Princeton, Stanford, and New York universities and the Massachusetts Institute of Technology. He has published articles on a wide variety of economic issues, including monetary policy and macroeconomics, and is the author of several scholarly books and two textbooks. He has held a Guggenheim Fellowship and a Sloan Fellowship, and he is a fellow of the Econometric Society and the American Academy of Arts and Sciences. Bernanke served as director of the Monetary Economics Program of the National Bureau of Economic Research and as a member of the NBER's Business Cycle Dating Committee. He is former editor of the *American Economic Review.* Bernanke received a bachelor's degree in economics from Harvard

University and a PhD in economics from the Massachusetts Institute of Technology.

RICHARD W. FISHER is the president and CEO of the Federal Reserve Bank of Dallas. Fisher began his career in 1975 at the private bank of Brown Brothers Harriman & Co. In 1987, he created Fisher Capital Management and served as deputy U.S. trade representative with the rank of ambassador from 1997 to 2001. He is former vice chairman of Kissinger McLarty Associates. A fellow of the American Academy of Arts and Sciences and an honorary fellow of the Hertford College at Oxford University, Fisher serves on Harvard University's Board of Overseers.

OTMAR ISSING is president of the Center of Financial Studies at Frankfurt Goethe University. From 1998–2006 he was a member of the Executive Board of the European Central Bank, responsible for the General Directorates Economics and Research. He was a member of the Executive Board of the Deutsche Bundesbank from 1990–1998. Before that, he was Professor for Economics at the Universities of Erlangen-Nueremberg and Wuerzburg.

GEORGE A. KAHN is a vice president and economist at the Federal Reserve Bank of Kansas City. In this capacity, he serves as an adviser to the Bank's president and board of directors on monetary policy issues and conducts basic and applied research on issues of relevance to the Federal Reserve System. Kahn received a bachelor's degree from the University of North Carolina at Chapel Hill and a PhD in economics from Northwestern University. He serves on the Board of Directors of the National Association for Business Economics.

EVAN F. KOENIG is a vice president and senior policy adviser at the Federal Reserve Bank of Dallas and adjunct professor at Southern Methodist University. He oversees macroeconomic research and policy analysis in the Dallas Fed's Research Department, briefs senior Bank officials on national economic conditions, and writes articles for Bank publications and scholarly journals. In his research, Koenig seeks to predict and explain movements in prices, output, and employment, particularly as these movements are affected by monetary policy. Koenig holds bachelor's degrees in mathematics and economics from the University of Wisconsin and a PhD in economics from Harvard University. He joined the Dallas Fed in 1988 after several years teaching at the University of Washington.

DONALD L. KOHN is a senior fellow in the Economic Studies Program at the Brookings Institution. He also serves as an external member on the Financial Policy Committee at the Bank of England. He is an expert on monetary policy, financial regulation, and macroeconomics. He was a forty-year veteran of the Federal Reserve System and served as vice chairman of the Board of Governors of the Federal Reserve from 2006 to 2010. Before becoming a member of the Board of Governors, he served on its staff as an adviser to the Board for monetary policy, secretary of the Federal Open Market Committee, director of the division of monetary affairs, and deputy staff director for monetary and financial policy. Kohn has written extensively on issues related to monetary policy and its implementation by the Federal Reserve. He received a Distinguished Achievement Award from the Money Marketeers of New York University and a Distinguished Alumni Award and honorary doctor of laws from the College of Wooster. He received a bachelor's degree in economics from the College of Wooster and a PhD in economics from the University of Michigan.

ROBERT LEESON is a Visiting Professor of Economics at Stanford University, Visiting Professor of Economics at the University of Trento, Visiting Fellow at the Hoover Institution, and Adjunct Professor of Economics at the University of Notre Dame Australia. He was previously Bradley Fellow at the University of Western Ontario and National Fellow at the Hoover Institution. For the last quarter of a century he has been investigating the dynamics of macroeconomic policy formation. He has published in numerous top-class journals, including the *Economic Journal, Economica, the Cambridge Journal of Economics,* and the *History of Political Economy.* He is currently editing (with Charles Palm) *The Collected Writings of Milton Friedman.*

JOHN LIPSKY was appointed Special Advisor to the Managing Director of the International Monetary Fund in September 2011, following a five-year term as the IMF's first deputy managing director. Previously, he was vice chairman and chief economist of JPMorgan Investment Bank. Earlier, Lipsky had been a managing director of Chase Manhattan Bank and of Salomon Brothers. Before joining Salomon Brothers in 1984, he spent a decade at the IMF, where he helped manage the Fund's exchange rate surveillance procedure and analyzed developments in international capital markets. He also participated in negotiations with several member countries and served as the Fund's resident representative in Chile. He currently is a Director of the National Bureau of Economic Research and is a Trustee of the Stanford Institute for Economic Policy Research (SIEPR). Lipsky holds a PhD in economics from Stanford University.

ROBERT E. LUCAS JR. is the John Dewey Distinguished Service Professor of Economics at the University of Chicago. He is a fellow of the Econometric Society, American Academy of Arts and Sciences, and American Philosophical Society and is a member of the National Academy of Sciences. He has served as president of the Econometric Society and the American Economic Association. In 1995, he received the Nobel Memorial Prize in Economic Sciences. He was a member of the faculty of the Graduate School of Industrial Administration at Carnegie Mellon University from 1963 to 1974. Among his books are *Studies in Business-Cycle Theory* (1981); *Rational Expectations and Econometric Practice* (1981, co-edited with Thomas Sargent); *Models of Business Cycles* (1985); and *Recursive Methods in Economic Dynamics* (1989, with Nancy Stokey and Edward Prescott). His *Lectures on Economic Growth* was published in 2002. Lucas received a bachelor's degree in history and a PhD in economics from the University of Chicago.

EDWARD NELSON is the chief of the Monetary Studies section in the Division of Monetary Affairs at the Federal Reserve Board. Prior to joining the Board in 2009, Nelson served at the Bank of England from 1998 to 2003, as an economist in the Bank's Monetary Assessment and Strategy Division and later as a research advisor to the Monetary Policy Committee. He then worked from 2003 to 2009 at the Federal Reserve Bank of St. Louis, becoming an assistant vice president in 2006. Nelson's research area is monetary economics, and he has published numerous articles in this area. He received his undergraduate degree in economics from the University of Sydney and his PhD in economics from Carnegie Mellon University.

GUILLERMO ORTIZ is chairman of Grupo Financiero Banorte-IXE. He was Governor of the Bank of Mexico from January 1998 to December 2009, serving two consecutive six-year terms. From December 1994 to December 1997, Ortiz served as Secretary of Finance and Public Credit in the Mexican Federal Government. Prior to heading the Finance Ministry, he served briefly as Secretary of Communications and Transportation. In 2006, he was appointed to the Board of the Bank of International Settlements (BIS) and was elected Chairman of the Board in

2009. From 1984 to 1988 he was executive director of the International Monetary Fund. In addition, Ortiz is a member of the Group of Thirty and serves as a director on several corporate and nonprofit boards. He has taught at universities in both the United States and Mexico and is the author of two books and numerous papers on economics and finance. Ortiz holds a bachelor's degree from the Universidad Nacional Autónoma de México and a PhD from Stanford University.

LARS SVENSSON is Deputy Governor of Sveriges Riksbank (the central bank of Sweden) since May 2007 and Affiliated Professor at the Institute for International Economic Studies, Stockholm University, since June 2009. He was Professor of Economics at Princeton University during 2001–2009 and Professor of International Economics at the Institute for International Economic Studies, Stockholm University, from 1984–2003. He received his PhD in economics from Stockholm University. He was active as adviser to Sveriges Riksbank from 1990–2007 and was a member of the Monetary Policy Advisory Board and the Economic Advisory Panel of the Federal Reserve Bank of New York until his appointment as Deputy Governor of the Riksbank. He has regularly consulted for international, U.S., and Swedish agencies and organizations. In 2000–2001 he undertook a review of monetary policy in New Zealand, commissioned by the New Zealand government, and in 2002 he chaired a committee reviewing monetary policy in Norway.

JOHN B. TAYLOR is the George P. Shultz Senior Fellow in Economics at the Hoover Institution and the Mary and Robert Raymond Professor of Economics at Stanford University. He is an award-winning teacher and researcher, specializing in macroeconomics, international economics, and monetary policy. Among other roles in public service, he served as a senior economist (1976–77) and as a member (1989–91) of the President's Council of Economic Advisers and as undersecretary of the Treasury for international affairs (2001–2005). His book, *Getting Off Track: How Government Actions and Interventions Caused, Prolonged, and Worsened the Financial Crisis,* was one of the first on the financial crisis. He has since followed up with two books on preventing future crises, co-editing *The Road ahead for the Fed* and *Ending Government Bailouts As We Know Them* in which leading experts examine and debate proposals for financial reform and exit strategies. Before joining the Stanford faculty in 1984, Taylor held positions as a professor of economics at Princeton University and Columbia University. He received a bachelor's degree in economics summa cum laude from Princeton and a PhD in economics from Stanford University in 1973.

MICHAEL WOODFORD is the John Bates Clark Professor of Political Economy at Columbia University. His treatise, *Interest and Prices: Foundations of a Theory of Monetary Policy,* received the 2003 Association of American Publishers Award for Best Professional/Scholarly Book in Economics; in 2007 he was awarded the Deutsche Bank Prize in Financial Economics. He is also co-author or co-editor of several other volumes, including a three-volume *Handbook of Macroeconomics,* with John B. Taylor (1999); *The Inflation-Targeting Debate,* with Ben S. Bernanke (2006); and a two-volume *Handbook of Monetary Economics,* with Benjamin M. Friedman (2010).

JANET L. YELLEN took office as vice chair of the Board of Governors of the Federal Reserve System on October 4, 2010, for a four-year term and simultaneously began a 14-year term as a member of the Board of Governors. Prior to her appointment as vice chair, she served as president and CEO of the Federal Reserve Bank of San Francisco. From 1997 to 1999, Yellen served as chair of the Council of Economic Advisers. Yellen is a professor emeritus at the University of California-Berkeley, where she was the Eugene E. and Catherine M. Trefethen Professor of Business and Professor of Economics and has been a faculty member since 1980.

About the Hoover Institution's

WORKING GROUP ON ECONOMIC POLICY

THE WORKING GROUP ON ECONOMIC POLICY brings together experts on economic and financial policy at the Hoover Institution to study key developments in the U.S. and global economies, examine their interactions, and develop specific policy proposals.

For twenty-five years starting in the early 1980s, the United States economy experienced an unprecedented economic boom. Economic expansions were stronger and longer than in the past. Recessions were shorter, shallower, and less frequent. GDP doubled and household net worth increased by 250 percent in real terms. Forty-seven million jobs were created.

This quarter-century boom strengthened as its length increased. Productivity growth surged by one full percentage point per year in the United States, creating an additional $9 trillion of goods and services that would never have existed. And the long boom went global with emerging market countries from Asia to Latin America to Africa experiencing the enormous improvements in both economic growth and economic stability.

Economic policies that place greater reliance on the principles of free markets, price stability, and flexibility have been the key to these successes. Recently, however, several powerful new economic forces have begun to change the economic landscape, and these principles are being challenged with far reaching implications for U.S. economic policy, both domestic and international. A financial crisis flared up in 2007 and turned into a severe panic in 2008 leading to the Great Recession. How we interpret and react to these forces—and in particular whether proven policy principles prevail going forward—will determine whether strong economic growth and stability returns and again continues to spread and improve more people's lives or whether the economy stalls and stagnates.

Our Working Group organizes seminars and conferences, prepares policy papers and other publications, and serves as a resource for policymakers and interested members of the public.

Current members of the working group include John B. Taylor (chair), Gary S. Becker, Michael J. Boskin, John D. Ciorciari, John F. Cogan, Andrew Crockett, Darrell Duffie, John A. Grundfest, John A. Gunn, Charles B. Johnson, Monika Piazzesi, John F. Powers, Martin Schneider, Kenneth E. Scott, John Shoven, and George P. Shultz.

INDEX

accountability
  of central banks, 246
  communication policy and, 295
  target criteria and, 194
  Taylor rule and, 91
accounting scandals, 180–81
activism, 113
activist feedback rules, 46
adaptive inflationary expectations formula,
  27, 29–32
adjustable rate mortgages (ARMs), 170–71,
  171f
AEA. *See* American Economic Association
aggregate supply shock, 148
aggregate-demand policy, 319
aggregate-supply relation, 222
  changes in, 216
  New Classical, 202n16
Ahmed, Shaghil, 155
Ahrend, Rudiger, 168
Amemiya, Takeshi, 313
America Faces the Future (Beard), 26
American Economic Association (AEA),
  xii–xiii, 31
American Economic Review, 317
Anderson, T. W., 140, 313
Ando, Albert, 5–6
Aoki, Masanao, 313
applied math, 311–12
area-wide model (AWM), 86
ARIMA models, 313
ARMs. *See* adjustable rate mortgages
Arrow, Kenneth, 30, 139
Asso, Francesco, x, 64
Aumann, Bob, 312
AWM. *See* area-wide model

Bagehot, Walter, 7, 10, 18–19
Bagehot rule, 18–19
balance of risk, 66
balance sheets, 172
Ball, Laurence, 51
Banco de México, xviii, 294
bank notes, regulation of, 16
Bank of Canada, 67
Bank of England, 8, 10–11, 91–93
  Inflation Report, 187n2, 196–97
  Issue department of, 17
  Palmer rule and, 15
Bank of International Settlements (BIS), 85
Bank of Japan, 44, 83, 88–91
Bank of Korea, 95
Banking School, x, 8–9, 15
Barsky, Robert, 157
Bayesian learning rules, 40
Beard, Charles, 26
Bernanke, Ben, xiv, xvii–xviii, 44, 44n12, 65
  forward-looking Taylor rules and, 76
  output fluctuations and, 128
BIS. *See* Bank of International Settlements
Blanchard, Olivier, 145
Blinder, Alan, 44n12, 73
Bluebook, 77n10, 264
Boehne, Edward G., 320–21
Boskin, Michael, 322
Box, George, 313
Bretton Woods system, 66
Broaddus, Alfred, 77, 80
Brookings Institution, 6, 43
Brown, Henry Phelps, 29, 34
Bryant, Ralph, 44
Bullion Report, 8, 16
Bullionists, 13–14

Bundesbank, 67n3
Bureau of Labor Statistics, 179
Burns, Arthur F., 48
Bush, George H. W., 278–79, 322
business cycle behavior, 127, 128n38,
    240–41, 322
Business Week, 68

Cagan, Phillip, 30, 315
Calvo, Guillermo, 119–20, 216, 315
Calvo contracts, 120
capital investment, 156
Carlozzi, Nick, 312, 317
Carnegie-Rochester Conference on Public
    Policy of 1992, 3, 44, 64, 301–2,
    322–23
Carter, Jimmy, 315
Cassel, Gustav, 12, 20
CBO. *See* Congressional Budget Office
CDOs. *See* collateralized debt obligations
CEA. *See* Council of Economic Advisors
Center for Economic Policy Research, 6,
    301–2
"Central Bank Behavior and the Strategy
    of Monetary Policy" (Bernanke & Mish-
    kin), 44
Central Bank of Chile, 95
central banks, xii
  accountability of, 246
  communication by, 176
  forecast targeting and, 186, 253
  forecasts, xvii, 252–55
  impact of Taylor rule on, 84–85
  independence of, 246
  international, 168–70
  issuing, 10–11
  judgment of, 25
  nationalization of, 14
  performance, xvii
  private-sector expectations and, 189
Chari, V. V., 123
Chicago Harris Foundation, 24–25
Chicago "rules party," 4, 314
Chow, Gregory, 313
Christiano, Lawrence J., 122
City factor, 20
Clarida, Richard, 48, 203
coefficient of expectation, 28n4
Cogley, Timothy, 155
collateralized debt obligations (CDOs),
    304
Columbia University, 277, 314–15
Committee on Finance (Sweden), 246

commodity standard, 21
communication policy
  central bank, 176
  forecast targeting and, 188
  transparency and, 295
compensated dollar, 21
Congressional Budget Office (CBO), xv,
    48, 180
constant-money-growth rule, 108–11,
    240n2, 314, 322
Consumer Price Index (CPI), 73
  chain-weighted, 179
  forecasts, 254, 254f
  inflation, 52, 166, 176, 179f, 302
  projection, 198f
consumption
  expected income and, 30
  functions, 28
  increased, 77
  inflation stability and, 156
  See also personal consumption
    expenditures
contracts
  Calvo, 120
  price, 119
  rational expectations and, 40–43
  shocks, 125
  staggered nominal, xi, 104–5, 121,
    296–97
  Taylor, 289–90
  wage, 118, 289–90, 296–97
  wage and price, 118
control theory, 112
convertibility rule, 13–15
  expansion of, 16–17
  See also gold convertibility
corporate bond spread, 181f
cost-push shocks, xiv, 125–26, 203
  impulse responses to, 204f
  inflation and, 204–5
Council of Economic Advisors (CEA), 4,
    40–41, 115, 139, 277, 278, 315, 322
Cournède, Boris, 168
Court, Robin, 38, 40
CPI. *See* consumer price index
CPIF, 257, 259n7
CPIX, 257, 259n7
credibility, 266–68
credit crunch of 1992–93, 82
credit market interventions, 84
Croushore, Dean, 81n13
Currency School, x, 8, 15–16
Currie, Lauchlin, 23

David, Paul, 313
deflation, xiv
delinquencies, 171, 171f
demand shocks, 284
Department of Defense, 139
deregulation, 146
determinacy, 221
DiClemente, Robert, 305
direction of bias, 66
Director, Aaron, 314
"Discretion Versus Policy Rules in Practice" (Taylor), 283–84, 301–2, 323
discretionary macroeconomic management, 24–25
disinflation, 204, 206n20
  deliberate *versus* opportunistic, 74–75
  expectation of, 196
  Volcker, 107
DSGE. *See* dynamic stochastic general equilibrium
dynamic analysis, 39
dynamic general equilibrium, 131
Dynamic Process Analysis Project, 39
dynamic stochastic general equilibrium (DSGE), 216, 283

ECB. *See* European Central Bank
"Econometric Policy Evaluation" (Lucas), 37–38
Econometrica, 124–25, 315–16
econometrics, 312–13
  See also macroeconometric models
economic analysis
  ECB and, 86
  Friedman-Phelps formula and, 30
  in Mexican monetary policy, 294–95
economic growth, price stability and, 69, 282
Economic Journal, 30, 32
economic policy, professionalization of, 139
Economic Report of the President, 5, 42–43, 115, 279, 314, 323
economic shocks
  effects of, 247–48
  inflation expectations *versus*, 157
  inflation targeting and, 92
  monetary policy and, 156–57
  responding to, 87–88
  simple rules for, 115–16
  sources of, 127–31
  targeting criteria and, 192–93
  variance of, 155

economic slack, xiii, 83n15
Economic Stabilization Pact, 297
economies
  initial state of, 262
  small open, 51–52
  stability of, 263
The Economist, ix–x, 163–64
economists
  divisions among, 5
  early, 103
  quantitative, 141
Edie, Lionel D., 22
Eichenbaum, Martin, 122
emerging markets, 94–95, 295, 307
Employment Act of 1946, 5, 314
EMU. *See* European Monetary Union
endogenous variables, 123, 200n12
equilibrating forces, 36
Erceg, Christopher, 123
ESCB. *See* European System of Central Banks
"Estimation and Control of a Macroeconomic Model with Rational Expectations" (Taylor), 112
European Central Bank (ECB), 85–88, 168–70, 170f, 290
European Exchange Rate Mechanism, 67
European Monetary Union (EMU), 92
European System of Central Banks (ESCB), 46
Evaluating Policy Regimes (Taylor), 5
Evans, Charles, 122
ex ante analysis, 251–52, 265
ex post evaluations, 180f, 265–66
exchange rates
  flexible, xviii
  floating, 294
  nineteenth century, 10
  in small open economies, 51–52
  stability, 19
expected income, 30
external equilibrium, 17

Fair, Ray, xviii, 283, 318
fan charts, 200, 209
Fannie Mae, 172
federal funds rate, 3
  actual *versus* counterfactual, 164f
  ECB policy rule *versus*, 170f
  equilibrium real, 64, 74, 77–78
  forward-looking Taylor rule and, 83–84
  gradual adjustment of, 47–48
  Greenbook and, 71

federal funds rate (*continued*)
  importance of, 69
  nominal real, 175f
  output gap and, 48
  policy shifts in, 306
  targets, 74
  Taylor rule *versus*, 178f
  zero interest rate bound and, 79
Federal Housing Enterprise Regulatory
  Reform Act of 2005, 172
Federal Open Market Committee
  (FOMC), xi–xii, 3–4, 66, 176, 284
  equilibrium real federal funds rate and,
    77–78
  interest rate smoothing and, 80–83
  policy rules and, 70–71
  Taylor rule and, 70–71
  zero interest rate bound and, 78–79
Federal Reserve, 47–48
  in 1970s, 83
  interest rates and, 241–42
  policy, xiv
  policy decisions, 163–65, 174
  price stability and, 12–13, 22
  quantitative easing and, 84
  since 2003, 83–84
  staffing of, 139
Federal Reserve Act, 22
Federal Reserve Bank of Dallas, x, 3
Federal Reserve Bank of Philadelphia,
  320–21
Federal Reserve Board/United States
  (FRB/US) model, 78, 81, 180, 241,
  264, 283
Federal Reserve System Committee on Financial Analysis, 45
"Federal Reserve's Reaction Function"
  (Bernanke & Blinder), 44n12–45n12
feedback rules, 111, 312
financial markets
  equilibrium real federal funds rate
    and, 74
  frozen, 242
  macroeconomic volatility declines and,
    146
  sensitivity of, xix
  simple rules and, 176
  Yellen and, 71
Financial Times, 68
"Fiscal and Monetary Stabilization Policies
  in a Model of Endogenous Cyclical
  Growth" (Taylor), 26
fiscalists, 5

Fischer, Stanley, xii, 289, 319
Fisher, Irving, 12–13, 20–22
FOMC. *See* Federal Open Market
  Committee
Ford, Gerald, 315
Ford Foundation, 33
forecast targeting, xv–xvii, 186, 186n1
  business cycle and, 240–41
  central banks and, 186, 253
  communication policy and, 188
  criteria, 191–93
  flexible inflation targeting and, 249
  instrument rules *versus*, 236–37
  market expectations and, 189
  as policy rule, 187–95
  research programs on, 235–36
  rules-based monetary policy and, 229
  sequential process of, 195
  short-term interest rates and, 227
  structural models and, 186
  Taylor rule and, 227–29
  transparency and, 231
  See also inflation targeting; target
    criteria
forecasts
  of central banks, xvii, 252–55
  CPI, 254, 254f
  errors, 254f, 255f, 266
  GDP, 254, 255f
  inflation, 252–555, 257f, 258f
  inflation expectations and, 267–68
  loss function, 262
  of macroeconomic variables, 85
  output gap, 257f, 258f
  repo-rate, 257f, 258f
  Taylor curve, 256, 256f, 260–61
  variability trade-offs, 272
  See also projections
foreclosures, 171, 171f
foresight simulations, 77–78
forward-looking behavior, 76, 118–19
FRB/US model. *See* Federal Reserve
  Board/United States model
Freddie Mac, 172
Friedman, Milton, 4–5, 311, 318
  constant-money-growth rule and, 108–11
  cost-push shocks and, 125–26
  early, 103–4
  expansionary effects of reduction in un-
    employment and, 36
  forward-looking behavior and, 118–19
  framework of, 108–11
  growth rule of, 140–41

inflation and, 108–9
instrument rules and, 114–15
Lange and, 29–30
later views of, 116–17
money growth rate target and, 188
natural rate model and, 31
nominal rigidity and, 117–18
output fluctuations and, 130–31
output gaps and, 109–11
Phillips, A. W. H., and, 26–27
policymaker objectives and, 106–7
price stickiness and, 124
reference date for expectations and, 120–21
Taylor and, 37
Friedman-Phelps formula, 30
Fuhrer, Jeffrey, 45, 122
Fullarton, James, 9
full-employment objective, 107

Gagnon, Joe, 321
Galí, Jordi, 48
GDP. *See* gross domestic product
General Theory (Keynes), 24
Gertler, Mark, 48
Giannoni, Marc, 120
Giavazzi, Francesco, 246
Global Economic Model, 51
global financial crisis, 295, 295n1
    mortgage-backed securities and, 172
Global Financial Warriors (Taylor), 140, 280, 291
global investment, 167f
global savings, 167–68, 167f
globalization, 306
GNP targeting. *See* gross national product targeting
gold convertibility
    compensated dollar and, 21
    resumption rule and, 19–20
gold standard
    Bagehot rule and, 18–19
    British suspension of, 8
    Fisher and, 12
    Keynes and, 20
    World War I and, 19
Goldfeld, Steve, 312
Goldsborough, T. Alan, 22
Goodfriend, Marvin, 79, 157
Goodhart, Charles, 46
Gordon, Robert, 141
gradualism, 9, 19–20
Gramlich, Edward, 72, 80

Granger, Clive, 310, 312
Great Disinflation, 5
Great Inflation, 5, 106
Great Moderation, xiv, 127, 145, 278
    explanations of, 147–48
    future of, 307
    policy rules and, 128–30
    shift towards policy rules in, 237
    systematic monetary policy in, 166
    Taylor curve and, 149–50
Great Recession of 2008–09, 83
'greater than one' principle, 241–42
Greenbook, 71, 264
Greenspan, Alan, 47–48, 64–65, 302, 315–16
    modeling concerns of, 82n14
Greider, William, 66
gross domestic product (GDP)
    deflator, 73, 176
    forecasts, 254, 255f
    measuring potential, 115
    monetary policy and, 42
    output gap *versus*, 48
    real growth of, 49n16
    targeting, 240–41
    uncertainty, 252n4
    See also output gap
gross national product (GNP) targeting, 42, 321
growth rules, 140–41

Hall, Robert, 49
Hansen, Alvin, 24–25, 31
Harberger, Arnold, 139
Harland Ltd., 33
Hatanaka, Michio, 310, 312
Hawtrey, Ralph, 12, 20
Heller, Walter, 139, 309
Henderson, Dale, 43–44, 123
Hooper, Peter, 44
Hoover Institution, 280
house-price boom, 165–66, 166f, 171f
    subprime mortgage problem and, 170–71
housing investment, 169f
housing permits, 316
Howrey, Phil, 309–10
Hume, David, 17

IFT. *See* inflation-forecast targeting
IMF. *See* International Monetary Fund
impulse responses, 204f
independence, 52, 246

indexing schemes, 21
inflation
  bias, 202
  coefficients, 50
  cost of, 119n28
  cost-push shocks and, 204–5
  CPI, 52, 166, 176, 179f, 302
  expected, 132
  forecasts, 252–555, 257f, 258f
  Friedman and, 108–9
  gap stabilization, 259, 264–65
  gaps, 174
  inertia, 81–82, 218, 297
  measures, 73, 176–77, 179
  monetary policy and, 42
  nutter, 248n1
  outcomes, 247–48
  output gap and, 68–69
  pessimism, 152–53
  Phillips, A. W. H., and, 34
  pressures, 294–95
  price shocks and, 132
  projections, 207f
  reducing policy, 74
  response to, 154
  scares, 157
  shocks, 45n12
  stability, 37, 156, 262–64
  state-contingent evolution of, 211
  time lags and, 271
  trade-off with output gap, 107
  trade-offs between unemployment and,
    278
  variance, 124–27, 150f
  volatility, xiv, 145–47, 278
  wage, 35, 123n35
  weighting, 73–74
  Wicksell and, 23
inflation expectations
  adjustments, 131–32
  anchoring, 189, 267, 296
  destabilizing effects of, 32–33
  development of, 266–67, 267f
  deviations from, 284
  economic shocks versus, 157
  forecasts and, 267–68
  forward-looking behavior and, 119
  money growth rate target and, 189n6
  predicting, 30
  reference date for, 120–21
  as source of volatility, 158
Inflation Reports, 67, 187n2, 188, 196–97

inflation targeting, xviii, 64, 66–67
  Bank of England and, 91–92
  economic shocks and, 92
  evaluating, 247–49
  explicit, 294
  flexible, 94, 248–50, 248n1, 271
  Friedman and, 108–9
  minimizing loss function in, 202n16
  strict, 248, 248n1
  uncertainty, 80
  See also forecast targeting
inflation-forecast targeting (IFT), 187
instrument rules, xv, 93, 114–15
  business cycle and, 240–41
  case studies, 237–42
  defining, 295
  forecast targeting versus, 236–37
interest rates
  constant, 196–99
  determination, 190, 206–10
  ECB, 169
  endogenous, 94
  equilibrium real, 116, 174, 177, 298
  Federal Reserve and, 241–42
  Keynes and, 24
  market expectations and, 199
  monetary policy and, 24, 46
  natural, 222n36
  passive policy of, 224
  paths, 200–206
  pegging, 114
  policy, 7n1, 268–69
  projections, 200n12
  reaction function, 6, 227
  real time estimates of, 87
  rules, 44n11, 111, 312, 317–18
  saving glut and, 167
  sequence of target criteria and, 206–10
  smoothing, 80–83
  voting mechanisms, 200n13
  Wicksell and, 22–23
  zero bound, xv, 78–79, 88–89
  See also short-term interest rates
"International Capital Mobility and the Coordination of Monetary Rules" (Taylor
  & Carlozzi), 317
International Monetary Fund (IMF), xix,
  167, 307
intertemporal consistency, 195–96, 202,
  208–9
inventory investment, 156
inventory management, 146n3

Iraq, 280
isoloss curves, 262
Issing, Otmar, xviii, 86–87
issuing banks, 10–11, 18

Japan
    deflation in, xiv
    monetary policy in, 90–91
    zero interest rate bound and, 79
    See also Bank of Japan
Jenkins, Gwilym, 313
Johnson, Harry, 31
Jordan, Jerry, 78
Journal of Political Economy, 315
JP Morgan Chase, xix
Judd, John P., 47
Judd rule, 306
jump variables, 119

Kahn, George, xi, 63
Kalecki, Michel, 28
Kehoe, Patrick, 123
Keynes, John Maynard, 5, 12, 314
    discretionary macroeconomic manage-
        ment and, 24–25
    gold standard and, 20
    interest rates and, 24
Keynesian New Classical Synthesis, 320
Kilian, Lutz, 157
King, Mervyn, 66, 105, 247
Klau, Marc, 95
Klein, Lawrence, 141
Klenow, Pete, 321
Kohn, Donald, xv, 68, 73, 76n9–77n9, 302
k-percent money growth rule, 4–5, 29
Kydland, Finn E., 194

labor costs, 25
Lagrange multipliers, 211
Laidler, David, 9, 44
Lange, Oskar, 29–30
Laubach, Thomas, 128
Laxton, Douglas, 51
learning dynamics, 224
least-squares learning, 226
Leeson, Robert, x, 64
legislative rules, 12
Lehfeldt, R. A., 20
Levin, Andrew, 123, 155, 321
Lindsey, Lawrence, 74–75
Lipsey, Richard, 31
Lipsky, John, xix

liquidity shortages, 242
London School of Economics (LSE), 4,
    27, 39
Long Swing hypothesis, 310
loss function, 49–50
    forecast, 262
    minimizing, 202n16, 250n3
    optimal target criterion *versus,* 217
    welfare-based, 217n34, 218
lower real shock variance, 129n39
Loyd, Samuel Jones. *See* Overstone, Lord
LSE. *See* London School of Economics
Lucas, Robert, 37–38, 131, 289, 317, 320,
    323
Lucas critique, 5, 37–40

M2 model, 110, 304–5
M3 model, 94
Maastricht Treaty, 67n3
macroeconometric models, xviii, 140, 241
    global, 281
    for normative analysis, 185
    with rational expectations, 283
Macroeconomic Policies in an Interdepen-
    dent World, 6
*Macroeconomic Policy in a World Economy:
    From Econometric Design to Practical Op-
    eration* (Taylor), 43
Macroeconomic Theory (Sargent), 6
macroeconomic volatility declines, 145–46,
    159
Madigan, Brian, 323
Malkiel, Burt, 309, 315
Mankiw, N. Gregory, 218
Mann, Catherine, 44
market expectations, 17, 269f, 269n16,
    270f, 271f
    forecast targeting and, 189
    interest rates and, 199
    monetary easing and, 89
Markov equilibrium, 203n17
maxi/min analysis, 76
McCallum, Bennett T., 47, 105, 141, 236,
    316
McCallum rule, 90, 306
McGrattan, Ellen, 123, 321
MCI. *See* monetary conditions index
McKibbin, Warwick, 43–44
McKinnon, Ron, 313
McNamara, Robert, 139
Meade, James, 39
Meiselman, David, 5–6

Meltzer, Allan, 322–23
metal standards, 8
Metzler, Lloyd, 28n4
Mexico, xviii–xix, 293–96
Meyer, Laurence, 72, 75–76, 79
Mill, James, 14
Mill, John Stuart, 9
Mishkin, Frederic, 44, 65, 128, 246
model identification, 38
Modigliani, Franco, 5–6
Mohanty, M. S., 95
monetarists, 5
monetary aggregates, xi, xix, 69–70,
    86, 95
monetary analysis, 85–86
monetary base expansion, 79
monetary conditions index (MCI), 51
monetary easing, 89
Monetary History of the United States (Fried-
    man & Schwartz), 318
monetary policy
  Bagehot rule and, 18–19
  certainty of, 130
  conduct of, 69
  as contingency plan, 95
  credibility, 266–68
  deficiencies in, 159
  deliberations, 65
  discretionary, 195
  discretionary *versus* optimal commit-
    ment, 204f
  domestic price stability and, 20–21
  duty of, 131–32
  economic shocks and, 156–57
  effectiveness, 151–55
  errors, 82–83
  evaluations, 246, 251–52
  flexible inflation targeting and, 249–50
  GDP and, 42
  globalized, 306
  guide for, 71–72
  implementation of, 268–70
  improved, 155–58
  inflation and, 42
  inflation reducing, 74
  inflation volatility and, 147
  interest rates and, 24, 46
  international, 168–70
  Japanese, 90–91
  legislative rules and, 12
  loose fitting, 163–65
  in Mexico, 293–96
  more efficient, 131

  new framework for, 65–70
  optimal, 203, 214–15, 237–38
  power of, 131–32
  price stability in, 246
  principles, 281
  REE and, 191–92
  resumption rule and, 19–20
  rules *versus* discretion in, 23–25
  rules-based, 186, 229
  shocks, 127
  short run effects of, 297
  simple rules in, 173–74
  stabilization role of, 113, 151
  subprime mortgage problem and,
    170–72
  systematic, 84, 95, 166
  uncertainty and, 298–99
  variability of output and inflation and,
    150f
  well-balanced, 250, 261–65
"Monetary Policy, Market Excesses and Fi-
    nancial Turmoil" (Ahrend, Cournède
    & Price), 168
"Monetary Policy Alternatives," 77n10
Monetary Policy Committee (MPC), 92
Monetary Policy Report, 188n3, 194, 200,
    257
monetary restraint, 302
monetary targeting, 106–7
monetary theory, xi
Monetary Theory (Mundell), 313
money demand shocks, 113–15
money growth targeting, 188, 189n6
  ECB and, 87
  k-percent, 4–5, 29
  rules, 116–17
money neutrality, 17
money rules
  post-World War I, 11–12
  usefulness of, 9–11
Moore, George, 45, 122
Morgenstern, Oskar, 310, 312
mortgage underwriting procedures, 172
mortgage-backed securities, 172, 304
MPC. *See* Monetary Policy Committee
Mundell, Bob, 313, 315
mystique, 66

NAIRU. *See* non-accelerating inflation rate
    of unemployment
Nakahara, Noboyuki, 90
Napoleonic Wars, 7
National Physical Laboratory (NPL), 33

natural rate model, 31, 105, 107
  errors, 153–54
  restriction, 133
"The Nature and Stability of Inventory
  Cycles" (Metzler), 28n4
Nelson, Edward, xiii, 48n14, 103, 153, 236
Nerlove, Marc, 30
New Keynesian Phillips curve, 121, 203,
  218, 282
New Keynesians, 25, 131
New Zealand, 66–67
Newsweek, 31
nominal income, 141
nominal rigidities, xiv, xviii, 103, 282, 296
  Friedman and, 117–18
  output fluctuations and, 128
  Taylor and, 121–22
non-accelerating inflation rate of unem-
  ployment (NAIRU), 79, 180
Norges Bank, xvi, 188, 200, 206, 209,
  256n5
Norges Bank Watch, 246
NPL. *See* National Physical Laboratory
Nyquist stability criterion, 33

objective function, 104–7
  robustness and, 51
  Rotemberg-Woodford, 105n2
  weighting of, 91
OECD. *See* Organization for Economic Cooperation and Development
oil price shocks, 156–57
Okun, Arthur, 309
OLS regressions, 224
optimal control, 112
Optimization of Stochastic Systems (Aoki),
  313
Organization for Economic Cooperation
  and Development (OECD), 168
Orphanides, Athanasios, 4, 48, 110,
  153n10, 158, 177
Ortiz, Guillermo, xviii
output
  estimates, 177
  fluctuations, 127–28, 130–31
  natural level of, 51
  nominal rigidities and, 128
  optimism, 152–53
  potential, 179–80, 261, 298
  price stability *versus,* 237–39, 239f
  stability, 51
  variability, 150f
  volatility, 145–47

output gap, 174
  absolute level of, 228n45
  coefficients, 50
  deviations, 284
  economic slack and, 83n15
  estimating, 115–16, 153n10
  ex post estimates, 180f
  federal funds rate and, 48
  forecasts, 257f, 258f
  Friedman and, 109–11
  GDP *versus,* 48
  inflation and, 68–69
  level *versus* rate of change, 241
  policy rule robustness and, 51
  projections, 207f
  real time estimates of, 48, 87, 110
  resource utilization and, 261
  stabilization, 109–10, 264
  state-contingent evolution of, 211
  trade-off with inflation, 107
  uncertainty, 47–49, 79–80
  variance, 124–27
  weighting, 73–74
  zero target, 105, 110
Overstone, Lord, 7, 11, 16–18

Palmer, John Horsley, 15
Palmer rule, 15
paper money, 8, 14
Parry, Robert, 72, 75
Patinkin, Don, 25
PCE. *See* personal consumption
  expenditures
Peel Act of 1844, 8, 15–17
period-by-period optimization, 63, 84
personal consumption expenditures
  (PCE), 177
Pesenti, Paolo, 51
Phelps, Edmund, xii, 140, 282, 315, 319
Philadelphia Federal Reserve, 42
Phillips, A. W. H., xi, 4, 26–27, 310
  adaptive inflationary expectations for-
    mula, 29–32
  applied math and, 311–12
  empirical Phillips curve and, 33–37
  Lucas-style critique of, 37–40
  Phillips machine and, 27–29
  theoretical Phillips curve and, 32–33
Phillips, Peter, 38, 40
Phillips curve
  breakdown of, 311
  empirical, 33–37
  equation, 26–27

Phillips curve (*continued*)
expectations in, 131
forward-looking, 190
inflation expectations adjustments and, 131–32
linearized, 121n32
natural-rate restriction and, 133
New Keynesian, 121, 203, 218, 282
price rigidity and, 133
shocks, 126n36, 127, 129
theoretical, 32–33
theoretical underpinnings of, 321–22
trade-off, 45
wages and, 31
Phillips machine, 27–29
policy control, 38
Policy Ineffectiveness Proposition, 41, 319
policy rules, 40
around 2003, 178–81
commitment to, 194–95
constant-money-growth, 108–11, 240n2, 314, 322
desirability of, 188n4
ECB *versus* federal funds rate, 170f
econometric modeling for analysis of, 185
evaluation of, 310
feedback-based, 191–92
FOMC and, 70–71
forecast targeting as, 187–95
general theory of, 40–43
Great Moderation and, 128–30
improving, 242
inertia in, 81–82
levels of, 190
optimal, 49–50, 298
optimal-control-based, 112
origins of, 140–41
robustness, 50–51
shift towards, 237
simple, 112–16
specification of, 188
structural models and, 115
in Taylor framework, 111–12
transitioning between, 75
unforeseen circumstances and, 65
See also simple rules
"Policy Rules Shed New Light on Fed Stance" (DiClemente), 305
Policy Targets Agreement (PTA), 67
policymaker objectives, 104–7
Poole, William, 82, 164
Posen, Adam, 128

"Positive Proposal for Laissez Faire" (Simons), 25–26
practicality, 290
Prediction and Regulation (Whittle), 313
Prescott, Edward C., 194
Price, Robert, 168
price stability, 12–13
domestic, 20–21
ECB and, 86
economic growth and, 69, 282
exchange rate stability and, 19
Federal Reserve and, 12–13, 22
inflation inertia and, 297
in monetary policy, 246
monetary targeting and, 106–7
output *versus*, 237–39, 239f
Stable Money Association and, 22
Wicksell and, 22
"Price Stabilization in the 1990s" (Laidler), 44
price stickiness, xvi, 218
output fluctuations and, 128
wage stickiness *versus*, 122–24
prices
adjustment equation, 124–25
contracts, 118–19
expectation effect, 37
jump *versus* predetermined, 119
level rule, 4
rigidity, 133, 238
shocks, 126, 132, 148–49, 156–57
Princeton University, 309–10
private-sector expectations, xvi, 222
anchoring, 194
central banks and, 189
least-squares learning and, 226
monitoring, 221, 230
stabilizing, 298
"Project on Dynamic Process Analysis" (Phillips, A. W. H.), 33
projections
constant-interest-rate, 196–99
CPI, 198f
inflation, 207f
interest rate, 200n12
market expectations-based, 199
output gap, 207f
See also forecasts
Prospects for Financial Markets, 302
P-Star analysis, 304–5
PTA. *See* Policy Targets Agreement
Purchasing Power of Money (Fisher), 13

QMA. *See Quarterly Monetary Assessment*
Quandt, Dick, 309, 312
quantitative easing, ix
  Bank of Japan and, 89
  Federal Reserve and, 84
quantity theory of money, 12–13, 22
Quarterly Monetary Assessment (QMA), 86

Ramses forecast model, 253, 263
Ramsey optimal policy, 213n30
A Random Walk Down Wall Street (Malkiel), 309
Rapping, Leonard, 37
rational expectations, 278, 322
  contracts and, 40–43
  departure from, 226n42
  forward-looking behavior and, 118–19
  models, 282–83
  with staggered nominal contracts, 104–5
rational expectations equilibrium (REE), 191–92, 204, 213–14
  determinate, 220
  E-stable, 226n43
  learnability of, 221
rational inattention, 156
RBNZ. *See* Reserve Bank of New Zealand
reaction functions, 130
  coefficients, 193
  estimates, 76
  interest rate, 6, 227
  policy, 85, 95n26, 192
  target criteria *versus*, 192
real bills doctrine, 9
recessions, 146n2
REE. *See* rational expectations equilibrium
Rees, Albert, 31
reference date for expectations, 120–21
Reifschneider, David, 78
Reinhart, Vincent, 77–78
Reis, Ricardo, 218
repo-rate, 253, 265
  forecasts, 257f, 258f
  market expectations and, 269f, 269n16, 270f, 271f
  paths, 257, 269–70
repurchases, 190
Reserve Bank of Australia, 45, 94
Reserve Bank of New Zealand (RBNZ), 67, 94, 188, 200
resource utilization, 180, 249, 252, 256, 261
resumption rule, 19–20
Ricardo, David, 7–8, 14

Riksbank, 188, 200, 209, 245
risk management, 177–78, 181, 242, 299
Roberts, John, 120–21, 238
Robertson, Dennis, 27
robustness, 285
  policy rule, 50–51
  target criteria, 213–19
Rodriguez, Carlos, 315
Rostow, W. W., 139
Rotemberg, Julio, 105
Rotemberg-Woodford objective function, 105n2
Rudebusch, Glenn, 47, 68, 81
Rules Party, 23–25
"Rules Versus Authorities in Monetary Policy" (Simons), 23–24
Russian debt default of 1998-99, 82

Sack, Brian, 81n13
Salomon Brothers, xix, 68, 302–5
Samuelson, Paul, 31
Sargent, Thomas, 6, 140, 155, 319
saving glut, 167–68
savings, global, 167–68, 167f
Schmalensee, Richard, 322
Schultze, Charlie, 315
Schwartz, Anna, 318
Secrets of the Temple (Greider), 66
Selden, Richard, 23
Short Brothers, 33
short-term interest rates
  ARMs and, 170–71
  ECB and, 86
  forecast targeting and, 227
  monetary policy implementation and, 268
Simon, John, 145
Simons, Henry, 4, 23–26, 124, 140, 314
"A Simple Model of Employment, Money and Prices in a Growing Economy" (Phillips, A. W. H.), 34
simple rules, 173–74
  benefits of, 174–76
  for economic shocks, 115–16
  limitations of, 176–78
Sims, Christopher, 50, 140
small open economies, 51–52
Smith, Adam, 8
Snyder, Carl, 22
Solow, Robert, 6, 31, 139
Spectral Analysis of Time Series (Hatanaka & Granger), 310

"Stability of 'Self-Correcting' Systems"
    (Phillips, A. W. H.), 36
stabilization models
    simulations, 33
    theoretical Phillips curve and, 32
    for zero output gap, 110
Stable Money Association, 22
Stanford University, 43, 277, 301–2,
    312–13, 321
Stark, Jürgen, 87
statistical fit, 50
sterilization policies, 18n3
Stern, Gary, 74–75
sticky information models, 46
sticky-price models, 25–26, 46
Stigler, George, 29
stochastic control, 313
Stock, James, 155
stock market crash of October 1987,
    177
Stone, Richard, 39
Strong, James A., 22
structural models, xiii, 70, 133
    forecast targeting and, 186
    policy rules and, 115
structural relations, 115, 223–24
subprime mortgage problem, 170–72
Suda, Miyako, 91
supply shocks, 69, 125, 284–85
Svensson, Lars, xvii, 105, 187, 236
Swiss National Bank, 67n3, 94

target criteria, 191–93
    accountability and, 194
    appropriate, 210–19
    determinate REE and, 220
    in determining interest rates, 206–10
    implementing, 219–21
    intertemporal consistency and, 196
    linear, 214n31
    optimal, 214–15, 217
    quantitative specification of, 217
    reconsideration of, 214n32
    robustness of, 213–19
    sequence of, 206–10
targeting rules, 93
Taylor, John, 3, 140, 277–80, 301–2
    CEA and, 40–41
    contributions of, 283–84
    early economists and, 103
    Economic Report of the President and,
        42–43

forecast targeting and, xvi–xvii
framework of, 111–12
Friedman and, 37
interest rate rules and, 317–18
nominal rigidity and, 121–22
Phillips, A. W. H., and, 26
policy rules and, 40
policymaker objectives and, 104–6
pre-Taylor rule, 43–46
price contract scheme and, 119
publications of, 5–6
simple rules and, 112–16, 173
staggered nominal contracts and, 296–97
Taylor contracts, 289–90
Taylor curve, 41, 150f, 278
    forecast, 256, 256f, 260–61
    Great Moderation and, 149–50
    initial state of economy and, 262
    monetary policy effectiveness and,
        151–55
    publication of, 316–17
    shifting, 155–58
    variability trade-off and, 148–51
Taylor expansion, 281
Taylor principle, 43, 228, 279, 284
Taylor rule, ix–x, 3–4, 154, 283–84, 290–91,
    298, 306
    accountability and, 91
    accuracy of, 302
    analysis using, 73
    appeal of, 68–70
    as benchmark, 279
    caveats, 73–74
    ECB skepticism of, 86–88
    equation, 64
    equilibrium real interest rate and, 177
    federal funds rate versus, 178f
    FOMC and, 70–71
    forecast targeting and, 227–29
    forward- versus backward-looking, 75–77
    forward-looking, 83–84, 227
    historical analysis of, 47–49
    impact on central banks of, 84–85
    macroeconomic research on, 46–52
    nominal real federal funds rate versus,
        175f
    since 2003, 83–84
    in small open economies, 51–52
terrorism, 280
Tetlow, Robert, 81n13
Theory of Economic Dynamics (Kalecki), 28
Thornton, Henry, 7, 9, 14

time lags, xiii, 247, 271
time-consistency, 52
Tizard, Richard, 33
Tobin, James, 31–32, 139, 318
Tooke, Thomas, 8–9
Torrens, Robert, 8, 13
trade unions, 25
trade-offs, 107, 124–27, 282
  between inflation and unemployment, 278
  New Keynesian Phillips curve and, 203
  output-price stability, 239f
  permanent, 152n9
  Phillips curve, 45
  variability, 148–51, 257f, 258f, 260f, 272
Traditional Liberal Principles, 24
translational economics, 187
transparency, 52
  communication policy and, 295
  forecast targeting and, 231
  of issuing banks, 18
Treasury bonds, 302
Treasury Department, 279–80
Treasury-Federal Reserve Accord of
  1951, 69

uncertainty, 285
  GDP, 252n4
  inflation targeting, 80
  modeling, 185
  monetary policy and, 298–99
  output gap, 47–49, 79–80
unemployment
  expansionary effects of reduction in, 36
  output optimism and, 152
  trade-offs between inflation and, 278
  See also non-accelerating inflation rate of unemployment
"Unemployment as a World Problem" (Keynes), 24–25
unforeseen circumstances, 65
University of Chicago, 31
usury laws, 11n2

VAR model, 94
variability trade-offs, 148–51, 257f, 258f, 260f, 272
velocity movements, 114
Vines, David, 29
volatility
  in emerging markets, 295
  inflation, xiv, 145–47, 278
  inflation expectations as source of, 158
  macroeconomic, 145–46, 158
  output, xiv, 145–47
Volcker, Paul, 48, 66, 318–19
  disinflation and, 107

wages
  adjustment models, 46
  contracts, 118, 289–90, 296–97
  expectations, 25
  inflation, 35, 123n35
  nominal *versus* real, 31
  setting, 282
  staggering, 124, 282
  stickiness, 25, 122–24
Wallace, Neil, 319
Watson, Mark, 155
The Wealth of Nations (Smith), 8
welfare function, 45, 105–7, 217n34, 218
  discounting and, 105n2
  social, 117
  wage inflation and, 123
Whittle, Peter, 313
Wicksell, Knut, 22–23
Wieland, Volker, 321
Williams, John, 78, 158, 321
Wilson, Beth Anne, 155
Woodford, Michael, xv, 105, 120, 235
World War I, 10, 11, 19

Yamaguchi, Hirohide, 91
Yellen, Janet, xviii, 4, 68, 71–72
Yrjo Jahnsson Lectures, 141

zero interest rate bound, xv, 78–79, 88–89

BOOKS OF RELATED INTEREST
FROM HOOVER INSTITUTION PRESS

Getting Off Track:
How Government Actions and Interventions Caused,
Prolonged, and Worsened the Financial Crisis

by John B. Taylor

The Road Ahead for the Fed

edited by John D. Ciorciari and John B. Taylor

Ending Government Bailouts as We Know Them

edited by Kenneth E. Scott, George P. Shultz,
and John B. Taylor